THE STORY
of the
BRITISH
ISLES
in
100
PLACES

www.penguin.co.uk

Neil Oliver was born in Renfrewshire in Scotland. He studied archaeology at the University of Glasgow and worked as an archaeologist before training as a journalist. In 2002 he made his television debut presenting BBC2's *Two Men in a Trench*, in which he and Tony Pollard visited historic British battlefields. Since then he has been a regular on TV, presenting *A History of Scotland*, *Vikings* and *Coast*. He was appointed President of the National Trust in Scotland in 2017. He travels all the time, but his home is in Stirling, with his wife, three children and an Irish wolfhound.

For more information on Neil Oliver and his books, see his website at www.neiloliver.com

THE STORY
of the
BRITISH
ISLES
in
100
PLACES

NEIL OLIVER

BLACK SWAN

TRANSWORLD PUBLISHERS
Penguin Random House, One Embassy Gardens,
8 Viaduct Gardens, London SW11 7BW
www.penguin.co.uk

Transworld is part of the Penguin Random House group of companies
whose addresses can be found at global.penguinrandomhouse.com

Penguin
Random House
UK

First published in Great Britain in 2018 by Bantam Press
an imprint of Transworld Publishers
Bantam Press edition reissued 2019
Black Swan edition published 2020

A CIP catalogue record for this book
is available from the British Library.

ISBN
9781784165352

Typeset in 9.9/13.47pt Minion Pro by Jouve (UK), Milton Keynes.
Printed and bound in Great Britain by Clays Ltd, Elcograf S.p.A.

The authorized representative in the EEA is Penguin Random House Ireland,
Morrison Chambers, 32 Nassau Street, Dublin D02 YH68.

Penguin Random House is committed to a sustainable future
for our business, our readers and our planet. This book is made
from Forest Stewardship Council® certified paper.

MIX
Paper from
responsible sources
FSC® C018179

5 7 9 10 8 6 4

To my mum and dad,
Norma and Pat

Contents

List of Illustrations

SCOTLAND
(See page xviii)

IRELAND
(See page xx)

WALES
(See page xix)

ENGLAND
(See pages xvi/xvii)

0   120 miles

0   195 km

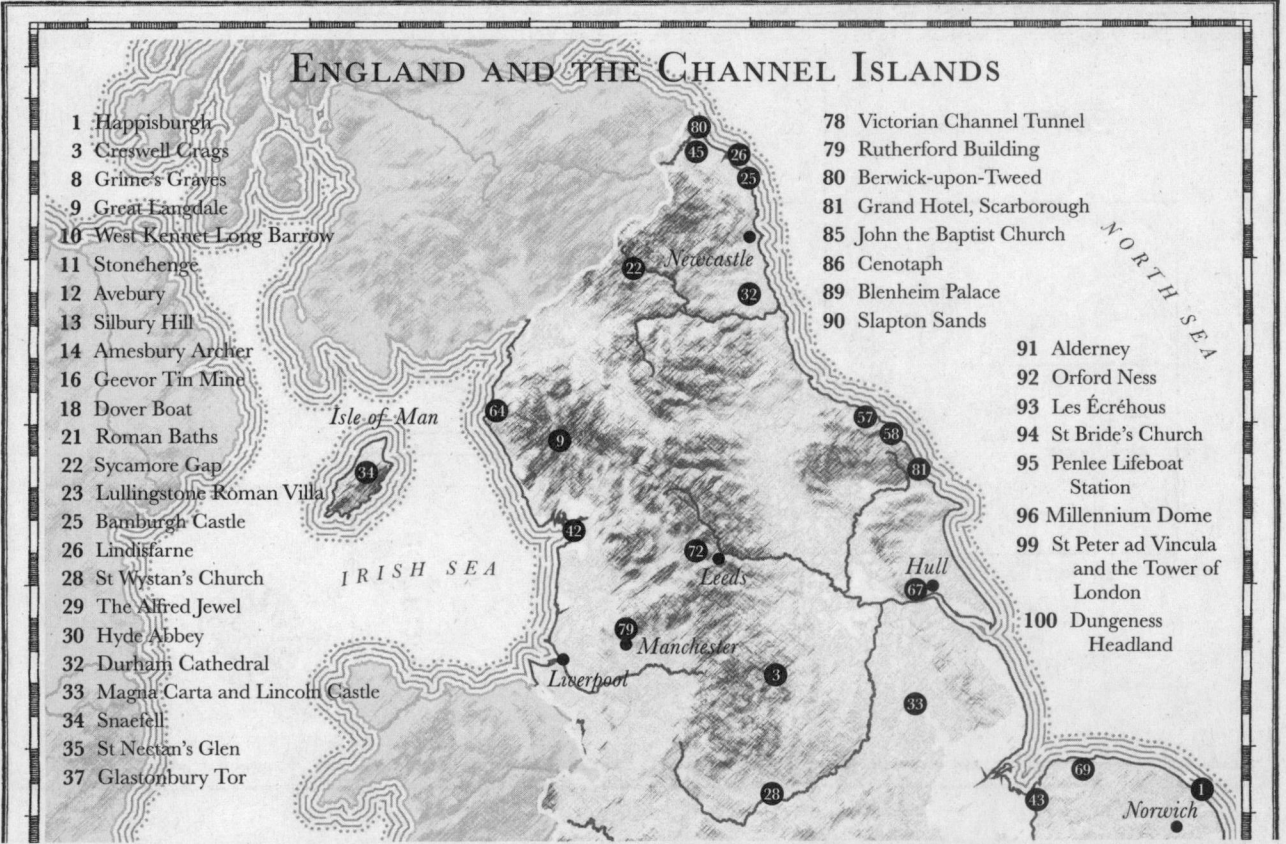

ENGLAND AND THE CHANNEL ISLANDS

1 Happisburgh
3 Creswell Crags
8 Grime's Graves
9 Great Langdale
10 West Kennet Long Barrow
11 Stonehenge
12 Avebury
13 Silbury Hill
14 Amesbury Archer
16 Geevor Tin Mine
18 Dover Boat
21 Roman Baths
22 Sycamore Gap
23 Lullingstone Roman Villa
25 Bamburgh Castle
26 Lindisfarne
28 St Wystan's Church
29 The Alfred Jewel
30 Hyde Abbey
32 Durham Cathedral
33 Magna Carta and Lincoln Castle
34 Snaefell
35 St Nectan's Glen
37 Glastonbury Tor

78 Victorian Channel Tunnel
79 Rutherford Building
80 Berwick-upon-Tweed
81 Grand Hotel, Scarborough
85 John the Baptist Church
86 Cenotaph
89 Blenheim Palace
90 Slapton Sands

91 Alderney
92 Orford Ness
93 Les Écréhous
94 St Bride's Church
95 Penlee Lifeboat
   Station
96 Millennium Dome
99 St Peter ad Vincula
   and the Tower of
   London
100 Dungeness
   Headland

Newcastle
Isle of Man
IRISH SEA
Leeds
Hull
Manchester
Liverpool
Norwich
NORTH SEA

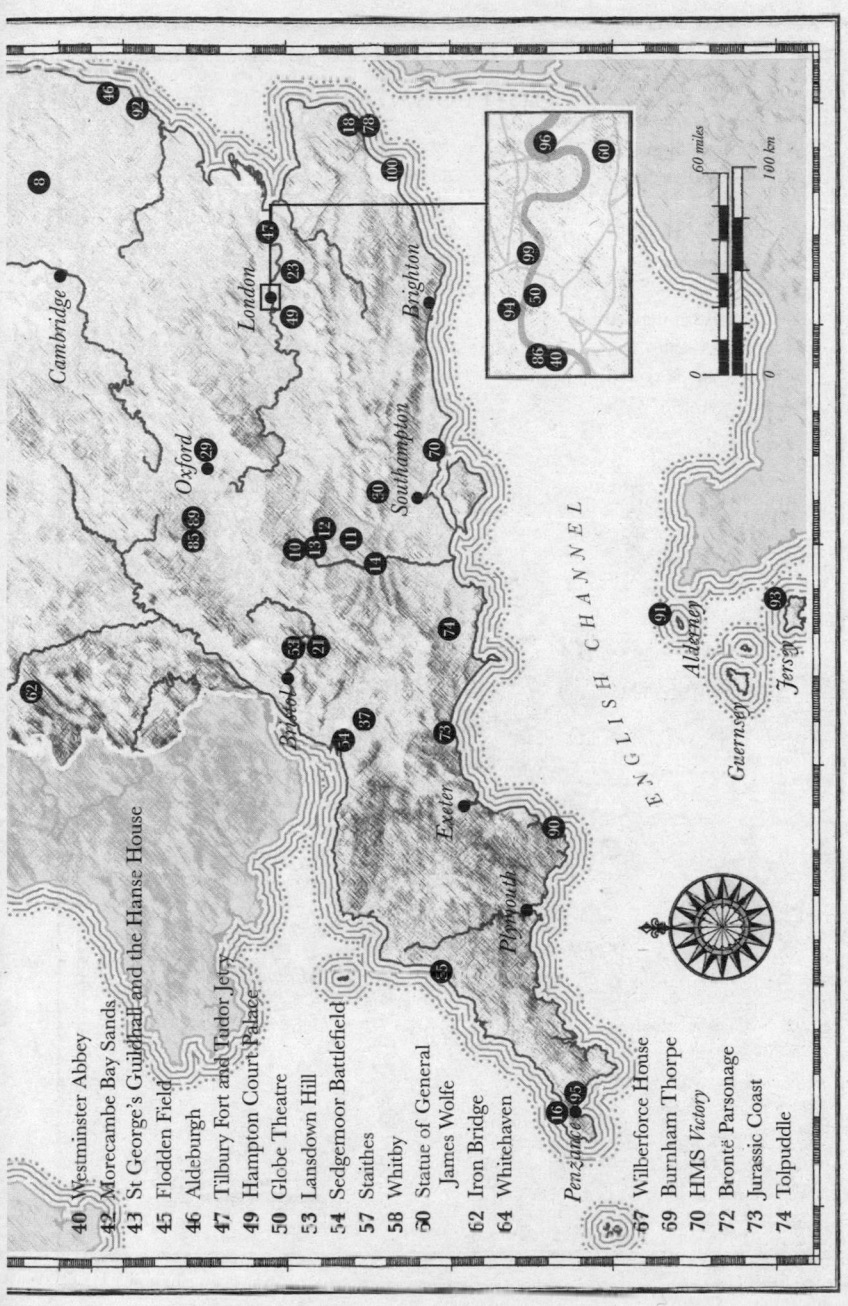

SCOTLAND

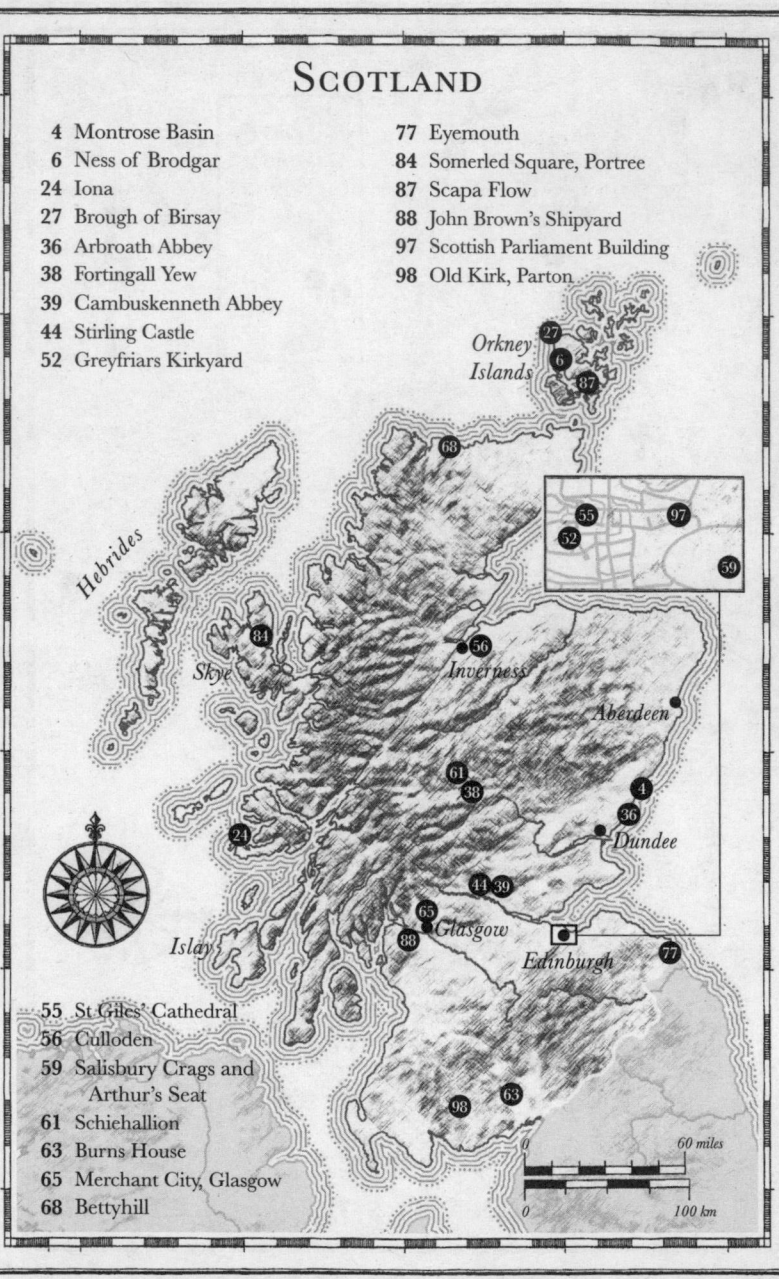

WALES

IRISH SEA

ST GEORGE'S CHANNEL

Swansea

BRISTOL CHANNEL

Cardiff

0   50 miles

0   80 km

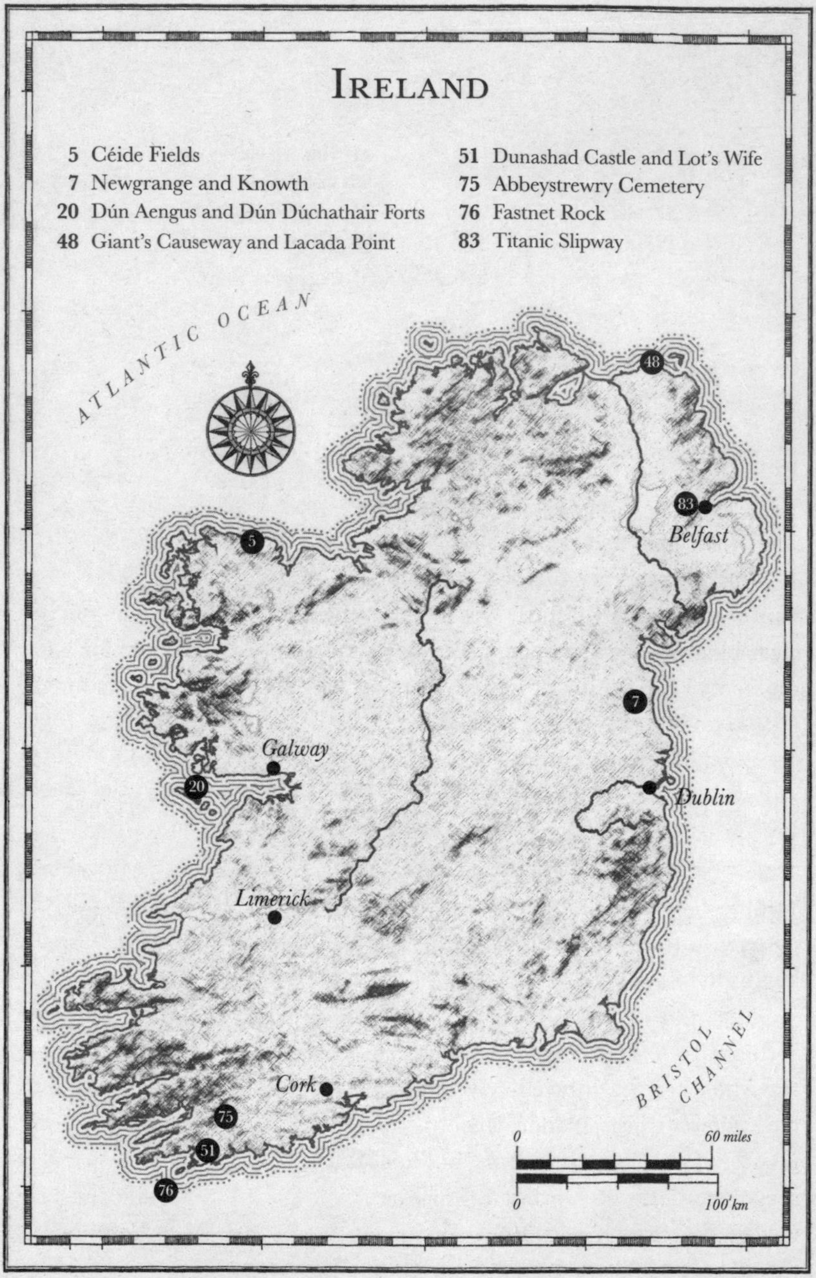
IRELAND
5 Céide Fields
7 Newgrange and Knowth
20 Dún Aengus and Dún Dúchathair Forts
48 Giant's Causeway and Lacada Point
51 Dunashad Castle and Lot's Wife
75 Abbeystrewry Cemetery
76 Fastnet Rock
83 Titanic Slipway
ATLANTIC OCEAN
48
83
Belfast
5
7
Galway
20
Dublin
Limerick
Cork
75
51
76
BRISTOL CHANNEL
0
60 miles
0
100 km

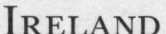

Introduction

PEOPLE STOP ME in the street and say, 'You've been everywhere ... which are the places I should visit?'

I usually stall for time, saying there's so much, so many places that I hardly know where to start. This is true. When the question comes out of a clear blue sky, it's like being asked to name my favourite book: for a few moments I can't think of any books at all, far less any contenders for the number-one spot.

But after careful consideration of that places question, this book is the answer I have to give.

The stories and places relevant to telling the story of these British Isles are like stars in the night sky, too numerous to count. At first sight their volume is overwhelming. But if you have someone to point out the patterns – the constellations, planets and galaxies – then the mass of it begins to make sense.

I have seen a great deal of the British Isles. I have circumnavigated the archipelago several times. The coast is like the hem of a garment – fixing the whole against unravelling – but I have explored the interior as well. I have viewed these islands on foot, from microlights, helicopters, stunt planes, vintage aircraft, trains and automobiles, and from every kind of seagoing craft a person might imagine, from kayaks to warships. I have looked out from the summits of lofty peaks, the tops of lighthouses, through castle battlements, from church roofs and city tower blocks.

I have even been under the sea in scuba gear and on board a nuclear sub-marine. Now and again I have considered the possibility that I have seen more of these islands, in a shorter time, than anyone else.

Why do we remember the places we remember? The particular places in the landscape that we commit to collective memory – that we write about and photograph and thereby make monuments of – are a skeleton's bones poking through skin. We, the people, are the flesh – thin, fragile and soon to decay. The skeleton lasts longer, perhaps for ever. We are continually drawn, in wonder, fascination, fear, sadness, joy, to where the white of bone has been revealed by great and terrible moments. The attention paid to certain places and times – and, where appropriate, to unforgettable human characters who helped make those places and events significant – is part of how we seek to remember who we think we are as a people and as a nation.

After all my travelling around the islands, some sites and stories have stayed with me. I have also made destinations of a handful of objects – artefacts, even the written word – since these too are worthy of a visit, time spent. *The Story of the British Isles in 100 Places* is a personal sketch rather than a full-blown painting. I have chosen what I consider to be the most characteristic features of the face I have grown to know and love. What they have to say seems to me fundamental to an understanding of the long, slow shaping of the British Isles we live in today. In this present climate of public fear, disagreement and uncertainty about the future, I think it is timely to look again at the past, the story of this place from its earliest times.

How did all this happen? Why did a tiny group of islands off the coast of north-west Europe come to exert such influence over a whole planet? During the past fifteen years I have seen enough of the wider world to realize that the answer lies in the nature of the place. It is a place, a landscape, built of the fragments of ancient continents – Gondwana, Pangea . . .

Some of the rock here is not much younger than Planet Earth itself. The gneiss of Lewis and parts of Scotland's north-west are perhaps three and a half billion years old. Here and there upon rocks elsewhere in the isles are the footprints of dinosaurs that walked across those land rafts long ago, leaving their marks in silts and sands that were themselves transformed into rock by pressure and heat and time. The ragged slivers that finally came together as an archipelago, hundreds of millions of years ago, have the world's back-story ribboned through them like brightly coloured writing through a stick of Blackpool rock.

It is this that has made these islands a place apart. They in turn have made the people who have come to live here different, and they are still doing it.

People have been drawn here to these British Isles since a time beyond the reach of memory. Our ancient cousins were first – *Homo antecessor*, *Homo heidelbergensis*, the Neanderthals, all of them in pursuit of great beasts that roamed. Our own kind, *Homo sapiens*, were next and last – walking dry-shod like all those that went before into the west, on to the peninsula that pointed towards the setting sun. Maybe they heard about the place not from others of our own kind but from spokesmen for other species entirely – human like ourselves in some ways, but also fundamentally other. However they learned about this destination, they came in their turn and lived and hunted, cared for their dead. Some of them cared enough or understood enough about the workings of the universe that they were moved to make works of art in the hidden dark of caves and in other nooks that seemed sacred to them.

The world wobbled drunkenly on its axis and set itself upon an orbit that took it further from the sun. For long then, this fragile promontory was made empty, grown too cold for any life at all. After an aeon, and even as the glaciers of the last ice age were withdrawing, relinquishing their hold, them-like-us came back – were eager to return in search of a place only their ancestors remembered. They stalked the wild horse and the red deer. After them it was the tenancy of the first farmers, the builders of monuments in stone, the metalworkers – a long slow procession of shadows and ghosts. Phoenicians came for Cornish tin, then Romans for more of the same, and gold and copper too, and fair-skinned, blue-eyed, black-haired Celts for slaves, and their noble wolfhounds as well.

Everyone who settles here is changed by the place. Even those all-conquering Romans found it necessary to adapt, to alter their ways, in order to thrive. The kind of Roman culture that evolved here – known as Romano-British – was unlike any they practised anywhere else in the known world. They learned to behave differently here. They became – or allowed themselves to become, British Romans.

In the shadow of the legions, Christian wanderers made a home. Their faith would survive its darkest hour here in the farthest west, maintaining a toehold. Then Angles, Saxons, Vikings, Norman French – the list of invaders goes on and on. Pilgrims came seeking saints – Wystan at Repton, Thomas at Canterbury. Others bent the knee before King Arthur and his Guinevere at Glastonbury where the Holy Grail was buried and a thorn tree flowered in midwinter.

Inhabitants of any and every other country might claim that their homeland is special and unique, but there has always been something remarkable about these islands. This place grew in time to change the whole world. Laws and a system of governance were established. Later the kingdoms were united and then parliaments. There was enlightenment. Our Industrial Revolution empowered the building of the greatest empire the world has yet seen. The language that evolved here – English – is the language of the world.

People have always come here, coveted life here, and likely always will. Most recently the newcomers have arrived in hope of the freedom made sacred by our democracy, the protection promised and enshrined by our laws. Our light attracts as strongly as ever, perhaps more strongly.

What now for us, the people who call these islands home? It seems to me that for a long time we have been preoccupied with our rights, with what we believe we are entitled to do and to have – even living as we do in a society that grants us so many freedoms and privileges while keeping us safe and secure for a lifetime. I have been around a bit and know that most of the world is not like this, not even close. This way we live here, have lived, is not in the natural order of things. Natural is a damned mess. Instead of focusing so much on what more we would like, we should humbly be looking at what we have and trying to repay some fraction of the debt we owe for all that we have been gifted by the past. Rather than demanding someone or something else to make our lives easier still, we would do better each to shoulder some responsibility for the well-being of this astonishing place in which we live. It starts with having a look around – a proper look. It might even begin with picking some litter off a beach or tending a garden.

These islands have a story to tell, a story as long as it is grand. It is woven right through the fabric of the place and might yet reveal to us all we need to know about how we got here, why things are the way they are. It is important to get out there, see each place in turn, or even just some of them, and pay attention to the wonder of it all. We are the youngest children of this place. It is time for us to grow up and show that we appreciate and deserve our inheritance, and that we know we are a lucky, blessed people.

1

Happisburgh, Norfolk

In the footsteps of pioneer man

THE VILLAGE OF Happisburgh is being preyed upon by the relentless sea. Year upon year the coastline here is eroded. Soft sands and silts, of which much of the coastline of East Anglia is made, offer little resistance to the waves and so they are consumed, yard by yard, mile by mile. For years the locals sought help to shore up their patch of green and pleasant land, but in their hearts they knew – and know – what King Cnut demonstrated in the eleventh century when he issued his command to the waves: the sea does what the sea does and will not be defied.

And so the waves gnaw their way through the soft mud and soil – and homes, roads and gardens are surrendered one by one. If ever a person needed a lesson in humility in the face of the forces of nature, it is to be had at Happisburgh.

In 2013, archaeologists examined an area of compacted, ancient sediment that had recently been exposed by the sea. Sealed for many centuries beneath a cliff of compacted muds and silts, the long-lost level surface had been returned to daylight by the eroding waves. There in the mud, revealed for the first time in almost a million years, were human footprints. A total of fifty were recorded in a patch measuring 40 square metres. Of those, a dozen were complete, showing heel, foot arch and toes. Analysis suggested they were left behind by five people – adults and children – who walked over the soft mud on some lost day perhaps 950,000 years ago. Given the location, archaeologists believe those folk were foraging for food – seaweed, crabs, shellfish and the like.

Nothing remains of the footprints now. So ephemeral were they – just prints in mud – that successive tides in the days following their discovery saw to their final vanishing. All we have are the photographs and casts taken by the archaeologists, who worked against the clock and in pouring rain to record this precious glimpse of a distant moment.

I've seen such footprints with my own eyes, at a place called Goldcliff, near Newport in Wales. They were made around 8,000 years ago by hunters in the Mesolithic period, or the middle Stone Age. More than anything, I was struck by the feeling of glimpsing something I was never meant to see – some fleeting, private moment in the lives of people who left no other traces, and did not mean to do so. As well as the prints of adults and children – some walking, some running – there were also the delicate fleur-de-lis hoof marks left behind by startled deer. But although I saw those for myself, still I struggle to hold on to the thought of footprints preserved, like shrimps in aspic, for *a million* years. A million years sounds more like the time frame for the levelling of a mountain, the raising up of a valley. And yet we were there then – if not us exactly, then our likenesses, those approximations of men that walk behind us in the famous image of the ascent of our species from stooped ape to upright man.

The mud that cradled and preserved the Happisburgh footprints for so long was laid down in an estuary of the River Thames at a time in the past when that river followed a quite different course, joining the sea much further north than now. Britain then was part of the European continent, and would be for hundreds of thousands of years to come. Where there is now the North Sea, there was then dry land and the morphology dictated an alternative meandering, nudging the river towards the north and what is now East Anglia.

By the time of the discovery and recording of the footprints, Happisburgh was already well known to archaeologists seeking traces of our earliest ancestors. In 2010, a research team from the Ancient Human Occupation of Britain Project, led jointly by the Natural History Museum and the British Museum, had found seventy-eight stone tools buried within ancient sediments. The humans who made those stone tools were not us – not quite. Given that archaeologists know the Thames last followed that particular course to the sea sometime between 840,000 and 950,000 years ago, the tools must have been dropped on to the soft riverbank at some point during that period. It was the time of an ancestor known as *Homo antecessor* – pioneer man – a cousin of our species but from another twig on the same branch of the same tree of life.

The interior of the British peninsula was heavily wooded then – much of it difficult, if not impossible, terrain for people on foot. Those pioneer men and women would therefore have followed the coast, or routes cleared by rivers like the Thames, taking advantage of the resources of wide, marshy floodplains. Perhaps the tools were made somewhere inland and then, during the centuries and millennia until the present, were moved, by the river, out to the coast near what is now Happisburgh.

For the last three million years of Earth's history, the planet has been victim to one ice age after another. (The next one is long overdue, perhaps held in check by global warming.) When those cousins of ours were eking out their living beside that ancient Thames, the temperatures may well have been dipping down towards another period of unbearable cold. The climate might have been similar to that of modern Scandinavia, with short, hot summers and long, cold winters. They may have been being forced steadily southwards, before abandoning the whole peninsula to the inevitable glaciers.

The only proof we have of the existence of that population, likely no more than a few hundred strong at any one time, is those footprints and those few handfuls of simple tools. Nothing whatever has been found of the people themselves – not one scrap of bone. We have no evidence of whether or not they wore clothes against the cold, or whether they made a fire. All we have as proof of their lives are those seventy-eight flint tools, cutting edges fashioned by people separated from us by an unimaginable gulf of time and ice – those and some photographs of the marks a family made during the course of a single stroll.

Faint though the human traces are, the landscape around Happisburgh is none the less of huge importance to our picture of the way our land was colonized by successive waves of our kind. It was long assumed that the

British peninsula would have been too cold, too inhospitable for those early peoples. *Homo antecessor* left Africa nearly two million years ago. In 2008, archaeologists working in the Atapuerca mountains of northern Spain were lucky enough to unearth the holy grail of palaeontology: human bones. Analysis showed they were of *Homo antecessor* and as much as 1.3 million years old. Given the cold climate further north, it might have been assumed those early hunters would have given the most northerly extremes of Europe a wide berth. Over the past few decades, however, archaeologists working in Britain have found more of the tell-tale shadows. In 2005, an assemblage of stone tools unearthed at Pakefield, near Lowestoft in Suffolk, was found to be perhaps 700,000 years old.

The earliest find of actual human bones in Britain was at Boxgrove, in West Sussex, and dates from 500,000 years ago. Modest though his (or her) traces are, still they paint a picture of a life. Just two pieces of a shinbone and two teeth are all that have survived of so-called Boxgrove Man, who was possibly a member of a more recent antecedent of ours known as *Homo heidelbergensis* (and is possibly a woman; there is no way to tell from such slight remains). The bone is extremely robust, suggesting a powerfully built, heavily muscled individual weighing perhaps 90 kg (14 stone). The teeth are scored with fine lines and archaeologists have concluded he or she was in the habit of gripping meat or other food between tightly clenched jaws and then sawing off portions with a sharp-edged stone tool that left faint scores in the enamel. As well as tools of stone and antler, archaeologists found remains of rhinoceros and bears that Boxgrove Man had hunted and butchered.

We live in a Britain so cluttered with our own creations, so littered with our own mess, it can be hard to make room in our imaginations for the lives of earlier tenants of the place. On the East Anglian coast at Happisburgh, the relentlessly transformative power of nature is plain to see for anyone who walks the coastline there, or follows roads and paths from the village to the point where they are abruptly truncated by vertical drops to unexpected beaches. Even our modern world is being removed and redesigned there – the page wiped clean for a fresh beginning.

Happisburgh is a reminder that Britain is not finished – rather a work in progress.

2

Goat's Hole Cave, Gower Peninsula, West Glamorgan

The Red Lady of Paviland

Already more than 900,000 years have passed in a blur, no man-raised stones or lived-in bones to mark them each in turn. We are falling feet-first through time, fingers scraping down the face of it, flailing after any purchase to slow our descent towards today. This is the great edifice of the past, the nine-tenths of the iceberg no one ever sees, the empty dark. These are the years made of landscapes shattered and bulldozed by ice. For great swathes of time, these islands were devoid of them-like-us, and so its passing mattered not a jot. It was about rock and ice; agonized, storm-lashed tundra; the dappled shade of forests known only to animals that did not remember and did not care. None of that time without us mattered. Without us to breathe existence into them, to awaken them with the exhalation of our consciousness, years and aeons passed uncounted and unmourned.

There are places in Britain where the world feels old, where she shows her age. Yellow Top headland, in Paviland on the Gower Peninsula of south Wales, is one of those. Viewed from the sea, the blunt end of the headland has the look of a giant, ground-down molar set in an ancient jawbone, gaps either side left by other teeth gone altogether. There are caves everywhere on this part of the Gower.

The whole coastline hereabouts feels wearied from the endless, enervating attention of the sea. With the passing of years, and then millennia, the land gets old and tired, but the sea feels new-born every day and filled with an energy that takes a relentless toll on everything it touches. The trees that cling to life here are small. Twisted and humbled by the constant wind and old before their time, they keep their heads down to concentrate all their effort on the business of holding on. The soil and grasses are stretched thin at best, or worn right through until the limestone beneath is exposed like bone. Here and there are stubborn clumps of broom and gorse, their roots clenched to the contours. Coaxing life from hollows where the wind cannot quite reach, their flowers are brighter than the lichen of Yellow Top itself, fragile little silken slippers. For the most part only toughened, tussocky grass prevails, pale and stubborn but comforting enough, like a well-worn shawl. There is no place for vanity here. At Paviland the face of the world is stripped bare, scrubbed clean so that you see her for who she really is. But don't get me wrong – Paviland is also as bonnie as the world ever gets.

To reach the famous caves, you leave the South Gower road at Pilton Green and follow the footpath out towards the sounding sea. The tides mean the cave itself is accessible from the beach for only a couple of hours a day – unless you plan on allowing yourself to be cut off by dangerous deeps and spending the night in splendid isolation. If you're lucky, you will go there on a day when the wind is blowing hard, the sea booming in reply. I am sure the place looks lovely with the sun on it, but when the sky is low and the mist rolls in, the modern world feels far away from Paviland and almost irrelevant. It is easy on such a day to imagine the Reverend William Buckland, clad as always in his academic gown, making his way out to the edge of Yellow Top in the third week of January 1823.

A man of God, and therefore a creationist convinced of the Bible's literal truth, Buckland was also a scientist of sorts, and would become a better one in the years to come. In addition to studying divinity at Oxford University he had attended lectures in geology and mineralogy, and was determined the new disciplines would prove the truth of Genesis. For his own part, he was researching a book he would call *Relics of the Flood*. When word reached him that elephant bones, of all things, had been found in a sea cave at the foot of a cliff at Paviland, he felt duty-bound to see for himself whether the discovery might be evidence of creatures that had perished in the biblical flood.

(Buckland was a bona fide eccentric. As well as keeping a hyena as a pet, he also set himself the challenge of tasting every animal, bird and insect in existence. He would later report that, while only bluebottles had nothing at all to recommend them, he was not over fond of moles either.)

By his own account, he was so excited when he arrived at Yellow Top that he immediately secured a rope and climbed down the vertical cliff to the cave in question. Known as Goat's Hole, its mouth has the shape of a pear toppled to one side. Inside he found the pitted, uneven floor littered with animal bones. As well as elephant, he confidently identified the remains of rhinoceros, bear, hyena, wolf, horse, ox, deer and many more species besides. (It is fascinating to consider how much untouched archaeological evidence survived undisturbed as late as the early decades of the nineteenth century. It seems that, in the main, our forebears walked past and ignored all manner of relics that had lain wherever they fell when our ancient ancestors cast them aside hundreds or even thousands of years before. Inaccessible cave sites like Goat's Hole were uniquely precious places where time had all but stood still, cradling every last lost crumb.)

Not content with surface finds, Buckland opened a trench close by what he thought was the skull of an elephant. Just a few inches down, he found a human skeleton, or most of one at least. The bones and the surrounding soil were darkly stained with red ochre. Also in the mix were numerous periwinkle shells, each pierced with a neat little hole, as well as rods of ivory, whittled from tusks and each as thick as a man's finger.

Because of what he took to be feminine jewellery – and also the presence of so much red powder – Buckland assumed he had found the remains of a woman, and a scarlet woman at that. On the cliff above he had spotted what he took to be the remains of a Roman camp (actually an earlier Iron Age fort) and so drew the conclusion that she was a prostitute who had chosen the cave in order to be close to her soldier clients. It followed that, when she eventually died, she had been laid to rest as she had lived, beyond the reach of decent society.

He was wildly wrong on every count. Although the remains are still known as the Red *Lady* of Paviland, they are the bones of a young man who died in his mid-twenties. As a creationist, Buckland could not conceive of a world older than 6,000-odd years. In any case, he had no way of knowing what only modern radiocarbon testing would reveal much later – that the man had lived and died some 34,000 years ago. The skull and other bones the Reverend had identified as having belonged to an elephant were in fact those of a mammoth.

Goat's Hole Cave at Paviland is a place of pilgrimage for anyone following the trail of early human life in Britain. The Red Lady – or, as I prefer, the Red Laddie – is the oldest anatomically modern skeleton found in Britain so far. Perhaps he was a mammoth-hunter who came to grief nearby, felled by his quarry, and whose fellows saw fit to bury him in the cave along with all the finery they could muster – a necklace of little seashells and carefully made ivory rods for some ritual or other, a coating of red ochre to mimic the colour of life. Maybe they marked his grave with a mammoth skull in honour of his bravery. In any event, his is the oldest ceremonial burial of a modern human being in western Europe.

This young man knew a place unimaginably different from our Britain. He lived and died during an interstadial, a warm break during an ice age, on what was then still a peninsula of north-west Europe. From the mouth of Goat's Hole his grieving companions would have looked out over an open plain that was home to mammoths, rhinos, oryx, sabretooth cats and deer. Since sea levels then were much lower, the coastline would have been as much as 70 miles away to the west. The Bristol Channel might have been visible as a river, a silvered thread cast across the green below.

Excavations in the years after Buckland's discoveries recovered thousands of pieces of worked flint and other tools. The cave was clearly used by human beings of one sort or another for thousands of years, even long before that ill-fated hunter's time. In the millennia that followed the Red Laddie's interment, global temperatures dropped and all life was driven away to the south, leaving him utterly alone.

His bones are stored now in the Oxford University Museum of Natural History and are regarded as too fragile, or perhaps too precious, to display.

Stained red as rhubarb stalks, they are a strange sight – but suggestive of a man who was gracile and strong, made trim and fit by running and walking over great distances. In some ways his form appears more African than European. His skull is long gone – perhaps scoured out of his grave by an especially powerful storm. What has survived are the long bones of his right side and also his vertebrae. It is as though Buckland caught him in the very act of leaving the cave, after all that time.

People come and sleep in Goat's Hole Cave from time to time, some lying as close as possible to the Red Laddie's grave as though seeking some kind of communion. There are those who believe his remains ought never to have been removed, as his presence endowed the space with a holiness of sorts. But in the end, his bones are just bones. For me it is the cave itself that matters – as it mattered to his fellows. Even without the Red Laddie, something yet survives at Goat's Hole of the Britain of before.

3

Creswell Crags, Derbyshire– Nottinghamshire Border

The horse head of Robin Hood's Cave

QUASIMODO MEANS 'as if' or 'in a way'. In the context of the character in Victor Hugo's novel *Notre-Dame de Paris*, it means the rough approximation of a man. As a human being, Quasimodo the hunchback was only halfway there, a clumsy attempt. Humans exactly like us are the ideal and anything else must fall short. The famous 'Ascent of Man' image has a tall, straight-backed hunter striding confidently at the front of a line of lesser beings. The closer they are to him, the more evolved they appear. Those towards the rear are, each in turn, more stooped in their posture, more primitive, more animal. At the back of the line is a knuckle-dragging ape. The message is clear: we are the best and all others fell away, round-shouldered and lumpen, in our wake.

Planet Earth has brought forth and let live many different kinds of mankind. By four million years ago there were upright, walking figures on the African savannah. Palaeontologists use the word *Australopithecus* – southern ape – to describe them. After those came other marques, other variations on the theme of *Homo* – human . . .

Homo habilis, the handy man . . . *Homo ergaster*, the working man . . . *Homo antecessor*, the pioneer man . . . *Homo erectus* (guaranteed to raise a snorted laugh from every schoolboy), the upright man . . . *Homo heidelbergensis*, from near the German town of the same name . . . *Homo soloensis*, from the Solo valley in Java . . . *Homo floresiensis*, from the island of Flores in Indonesia . . . *Homo denisova*, from the Denisova Cave in Siberia . . . *Homo neanderthalensis*, from the Neander Valley in Germany . . . *Homo sapiens*, the wise man, us. And those are only the ones we know about. Since you could fit all the physical evidence of our predecessors in a few packing crates, chances are there are more of our cousins still waiting to be unearthed.

It is easy to forget we were not the first tenants of this Earth. We were not even the first tenants of these islands, as testified by *Homo antecessor*'s footprints in the silty mud at Happisburgh and the remains of Boxgrove Man, *Homo heidelbergensis*, in West Sussex. The first inhabitants of Creswell Crags, a set of caves eroded into both sides of a limestone gorge on the Derbyshire–Nottinghamshire border, were Neanderthals who took advantage of the shelter to be had there around 50,000 years ago, when the sea level was lower and we were still part of the European mainland. Those Neanderthals would have come on foot, following herds of bison, mammoths and horses. At Creswell Crags they found ready-made homes, places to sleep, butcher their prey, make tools. They left behind hand axes made of flint and other cutting tools, proof of life.

Our species, *Homo sapiens*, evolved in Africa at least 200,000 years ago – maybe more; the number keeps changing, getting bigger. We were prolific, good at breeding. After many tens of thousands of years, some of our kind ventured out of that continent. It is not necessarily the case that any of them had wanderlust and so set off to explore beyond the horizon. More likely the peopling of the land further and further away was just the result of successive generations moving to find space in which to hunt. Gradually then, very gradually, there was a spreading into the north and east towards Asia and then eventually south again towards Australia. The hardiest of all walked across dry land between what we know as Siberia and the continent of North America, and then the push southwards began again, all the way to Tierra del Fuego and the end of the world. Others spread north and west into Europe. For several thousand years our ancestors shared the world with some of the relatives. We do not yet know just how many other cousins were alive at the same time as us, but we must have kept company with a few along the way. In Europe we certainly met the Neanderthal people – and we retained souvenirs of these encounters in our DNA, keepsakes of ancient couplings. The bones of the so-called Red Lady of Paviland, from that cave in south Wales, are thirty-odd thousand years old and it is possible he and his kind mingled with the Neanderthals, the last of them in this part of the world; but if so, proof is yet to be found.

Whatever happened next, we are alone now – the last of the humans. Maybe our ancestors took exception to the competition for resources and wiped the others out with weapons and cunning: unprecedented violence. Perhaps our sort was just too successful, too overbearing, and forced those others out to the fringes, and then all the way into extinction. We do not know yet, and perhaps we never will.

The last ice age, which drove our forebears south towards the Mediterranean, peaked around 20,000 years ago. The land that would one day be these islands was crushed beneath ice two thirds of a mile thick. By perhaps 16,000 years ago temperatures had begun to rise again. As the ice melted and withdrew slowly northwards once more, bands of *Homo sapiens*, hunters, began to return to the newly exposed landscapes, following the great herds of migratory animals, and some of them occupied the caves that had been used thousands of years before by the Neanderthals.

The climate was still harsh and cold. Life would have been hard and those hunters would have had to draw upon all their skills and imagination in order to survive. For some of them it was important to create what today we regard as works of art. In cave systems elsewhere – Lascaux in France, Altamira in Spain – they conjured into being whole herds of bison, deer and other animals. Working by the light of torches and taking advantage of the contours of the rock walls, they made images as affecting as anything achieved since. 'After Altamira,' said Picasso, 'all is decadence.'

For a long time it was assumed by archaeologists that life in the British Isles at that period was too hard to allow for anything so fanciful as producing works of art. But perhaps those people made images for other than aesthetic reasons. If it seemed to them that they might influence the behaviour of the animals they depended upon for food and clothes by making paintings of them in which the creatures did what was wanted, then in a landscape as unforgiving as these Islands at the tail end of an ice age, the making of that magic may have seemed all the more essential. In any event, it turns out that artists were at work in Britain too.

In 1876 a horse bone was found in Robin Hood's Cave at Creswell Crags. It bears a heartbreakingly evocative depiction of a horse's head. Given that the bone, a piece of rib, is only a few inches long, and the image realized with just a few confident strokes of the point of a blade, it hints tantalizingly at the skill of its maker. Early commentators insisted it was a fake, but in time it was accepted as real, made around 13,000 years ago. Even then it was assumed it was the only fragment of Palaeolithic art in Britain. The thinking was it had been dropped by an artist used to working in warmer climes who had brought the piece along with him from somewhere further south where the living was easier.

In 2003, however, a team of specialists paid proper attention to the walls of the Creswell caves for the first time and so revealed a lost gallery of marvels. Almost invisible to the naked eye, the shapes of all manner of animals and birds were found etched into the limestone. Maybe they were originally coloured with pigments long since faded; or perhaps they were always faint – intended for the sharper eyes of gods and spirits rather than fellow human beings. One of the caves, Church Hole, was found to contain as many as a hundred separate artworks.

The caves on either side of the gorge have the look of a film set. Were a director of a mind to make a Stone Age drama – an Upper Palaeolithic *Coronation Street*, if you will – he would be hard-pushed to find a more perfect setting. Walk among them and it is easy to imagine lives lived there in an altogether different England. Creswell Crags is another reminder of how old our story is, how long – and that before the advent of our kind some of the starring roles were taken by earlier experiments with the notion of what it is to be human and alive.

4

Montrose Basin, Angus

Separated by the Storegga Slide

THE BIRTH OF these British Isles was a bloody affair. We were torn from our mother in a single day, our umbilical cord cut through by a cold blade that parted flesh and cast us away from her for ever.

Perhaps there was time to run before the axe, but no refuge. The world had shrugged, like a bull throwing off a fly with a twitch of its shoulder. A hundred miles to the west of Norway, deep beneath the waves of the Norwegian Sea, an earthquake had dislodged 700 cubic miles of rock and mud – a volume of material almost impossible to imagine. It would have been enough slurry to bury the whole of Scotland 25 feet deep, and it had slumped into deeper water. If that image is hard to conjure, then think of a fat man slipping under the surface of his bath and pushing a sloshing wall of water towards his feet. A wave was on its way, travelling south and east at awful, terrible speed.

That ancient seismic event occurred more than 8,000 years ago. Names like Britain, Scotland and Montrose lay in a future too distant and strange to have been imagined then. Think only of a land mass – bare rock in the highlands, forests on the slopes, open woodland on the valley floors, brackish marshland and dune fields on the coast. Red deer in the dappled shadows of the woods, wild boar, wolves. Sharing this unspoiled demesne were a few bands of hunters. That human population, accustomed to ranging widely over the land in pursuit of game and wild foods, may have numbered only in the hundreds or perhaps a few thousands. They were

Homo sapiens, just the same as us. Only their circumstances were different, but unimaginably so.

Anyone down on the beach that day at what is now the Montrose Basin may have witnessed the tell-tale withdrawal of the sea, exposing more and more sand and rock, beaching crabs and fish. Claws clacked in the air and scales glinted in the unexpected light. Countless startled cries then – not of people at first, but of seabirds denied their resting place upon the waves and rising into the sky in annoyance and confusion. Would that in itself, that sudden cacophony, have been a warning of what was to come? Even if it was, it could and would have made no difference.

It is easy to imagine people there on what had, moments before, been the water's edge. Parents hand in hand with children, lone walkers in search of mussels, cockles and other foodstuffs. It all happened much too quickly for anyone properly to raise the alarm, so that only the roar of millions of tons of water, building like fear and travelling at the speed of sound, came on faster than the approaching apocalypse.

The wave that followed the first wall of sound would have reared up at the last moment like a monster, some great, grey beast rising from the deep. There in the north-east of the land that would one day be called Scotland was a tsunami 50 feet high and moving at hundreds of miles per hour. Any and every living thing in its path would have been utterly destroyed, smashed and torn to pieces by the impact. Obliterated.

The water swept south along the coast of the long island, and inland for a distance of perhaps 25 miles, scouring away the surface and everything upon it – people, animals, forests, grass, soil. The withdrawal of the water would have taken longer – hours if not days – and, when at last it was gone, it had left behind a shroud of sand and sediment that covered the land. The most violent natural disaster anywhere in the world during the last 8,000 years was over, but its consequences would last for ever.

This then was the event known to geologists and archaeologists as the Storegga Slide. *Storegga* is Norwegian for 'great edge' and refers to the subsea terrain, 100 miles west of the mainland of that country, where the descent into deep water begins.

Before the great wave rolled, the southern part of the eastern coast of

Britain was still connected to the European mainland. The great ice sheets were melting, what we know as the North Sea gradually spreading and encroaching, but a bridge of land remained. It was a low-lying landscape, a mix of dry land and marsh. Nowadays it lies a few tens of feet beneath the North Sea. Dutch fishermen were among many who would, much, much later, take advantage of rich fishing in the shallow waters there. They would call their boats 'doggers' – we have all heard of Dogger Bank in the weather forecast for shipping. Before the fishing grounds and before the Storegga Slide, it was a happy hunting ground, a vast terrain known to archaeologists as 'Doggerland'. We imagine it teeming with life – deer, wild cattle, birds and the rest of the riches upon which depended the lives of tribes of hunters and gatherers.

When it came, the tsunami completed in an instant a much more subtle work of nature that had been going on for thousands of years. Since the ending of the last ice age – a slow thawing punctuated by spells of renewed cold – the sea had been encroaching upon Doggerland day by day, week by week, gnawing at its edges, insinuating its way between plant roots and seeping into brackish lakes from below. The water's advance from above as well as below, the deepening and linking together of ponds and lakes, was inexorable, insidious. It may have been just fast enough to perplex the people who knew that landscape as part of their territory and who had to withdraw in the face of the water year by year.

Maybe some of the roots of the story of the Flood, a web of threads that links folk myths and legends from one end of the world to the other, took hold in places like Doggerland, as the sea snuck in like a thief. In any event, the water level was rising and this low-lying land was most likely doomed to eventual drowning with or without a great wave.

As well as flooding Doggerland once and for all, drowning animals and people (who knows how many score . . . or hundreds . . . a thousand?), the tsunami cut the land bridge linking the south-eastern corner of England to France. The English Channel (or La Manche, if you prefer) was created in that instant too.

'If a clod be washed away by the sea, Europe is the less,' wrote the poet John Donne in 1624. And so it was, and so the archipelago of the British

Isles was born. Drowned and dead around the newly sketched coastline lay her miscarried children – those hunters who had known her only as a misshapen nose of land thrust out from the main and into the great sea beyond, the limit of their wanderings, the end of the world . . . *ultima Thule*.

The bones of the dead are gone now, and long since. But those seeking evidence of it all, a glimpse of the severing of our islands from the body of continental Europe, may find it at many points along the coast of eastern Scotland.

The Montrose Basin is a shallow estuary at the point where the South Esk river meets the North Sea – the largest inland saltwater basin in Britain. Excavations here have revealed a thick layer of sand that has no business being where it is. Spread like pale cream over the dark sponge that is an old land surface, it can only have got there by being left behind in the aftermath of that mighty wave. Radiocarbon dates from organic material recovered from the long-buried turf make plain that a slathering of sand was washed ashore just over 8,000 years ago.

The basin is not large, a rock pool if you like, left behind by time as well as tide. A walk around its rim and along the beach is a journey back to that ancient cataclysm, the time-accident that made all the difference to this part of the world, and which showed that nothing is for ever upon this ribbon where the land meets the sea.

5

Céide Fields, County Mayo

The introduction of farming and the daily grind

EVERYONE KNOWS WHAT is meant by the daily grind: the everyday round of chores, the endlessly returning cycle of duties that must be performed. There is a hopelessness about the term, that sense of a person having no choice but to submit to being worn down, ground down by the inevitable boredom of thankless, mind-numbing tasks that will never be finished. Nowadays it is used to describe the day job, the captivity of the wage slave, but here in the British Isles the daily grind began around 6,000 years ago with the adoption of farming.

Before that, we hunted and gathered our food from the wild wood and from the rivers and the sea. For many or most of us in those days there was little concept of a permanent, settled home. Instead it was better to move with the seasons, going wherever the food was likely to be at a given time of year. Sometimes it would have been about where and when the wild foods were available for collection; at other times movement would have been dictated by the whereabouts of prey animals and their young. For those who found themselves in rich terrain, a semi-settled life may have been possible, or at least the chance of extended stays in a given location while the living was good. Winters had only to be endured, maybe on the coast where the worst weather might be softened.

Sometimes it sounds like a lost idyll, a carefree existence of wandering from place to place. We tend to think of women and children collecting nuts, berries and other fruits, while their menfolk were off in pursuit of deer, wild pigs, mammoths. But no doubt the truth of the hunter-gatherer lifestyle was often different from what we imagine, desperately different. During good times the life may well have offered a healthy diet – lots of green stuff supplemented by the occasional helping of cooked meat – not to mention all the cardiovascular exercise demanded by its acquisition; but there would have been lean times as well, when the wild fruits did not ripen due to drought, or too much rain, or late frost. There would have been weeks, months when the animals remained elusive or when luck was not with the hunters or fishers. Hunters would also have faced the constant threat of injury or death beneath pounding hooves or goring horns. Endlessly moving from place to place would have been physically and emotionally demanding too. Only limited numbers of infants could have been coped with by a clan perpetually on the move – perhaps one or two per couple – raising the spectre of infanticide or some other means of limiting and controlling reproduction. Good or bad, our ancestors lived like that for the longest time – for by far the majority of our time on this Earth, in fact.

Homo sapiens has been abroad in the world for 200 millennia, give or take. Farming, the domestication of plants and animals, was learned by some of the species just 10,000 years ago in the eastern Mediterranean and beyond – in that swathe of territory that used to be called the Levant, the land where the sun rises. This is what we know as Egypt and the area of Mesopotamia – literally 'between two rivers', the Tigris and the Euphrates, which equates to today's Iraq, with parts of Iran, Syria and Turkey. That fruitful zone has had many names – the Cradle of Civilization, the Fertile Crescent – and it was here that the first farmers developed their new science.

Wild, long-stemmed grasses, the ancestors of our wheat and barley, were naturally plentiful, and it is there and then that we come to a biological, evolutionary conundrum. At the ends of the stems of some species of grass, the seeds had evolved to be loosely fixed, easily detached and scattered by the wind or, when brushed against, by passing animals. This would have amounted to an advantage, you would think – in that such a species would have spread easily, colonizing new areas with abandon until the whole Earth was carpeted by them. On other stems, on other species, the edible grains were more firmly attached, stubbornly holding on. These would have been less effective, less efficient in the wild world, and therefore such plants should have been at an evolutionary disadvantage. Ruthless, mindless Darwinism ought to have seen to it that the 'easy' grasses grew to conquer the Earth, while the stubborn ones dwindled.

But for humans going about the business of collecting wild provender, the stems with the well-fixed seeds would have made the more attractive prospect. The gatherers could cut away those heads with their stone-edged sickles and knives without fear of losing too many of the seeds in the process. Thus our ancestors forged a relationship, symbiotic in its way, with the plants that would in time come to dominate the fields, spreading from horizon to horizon under the careful care of humankind.

Over time, rather than merely waiting for the wild crop and gathering it in its season, some industrious and imaginative souls took matters into their own hands and began keeping back some of the seeds and planting them. From then on, instead of having to look for wild stands of the edible grasses they liked, they could have fields wherever they chose to set them. They were gatherers no longer, but farmers. Writers like Jared Diamond and others have suggested we might think of those stubborn-headed grasses domesticating the hunters, rather than the other way round.

Once they got the knack of it, the first arable farmers were more or less guaranteed a food supply. So long as the rain fell at the right time, and the sun shone, their crops would grow. There was no need to move around any more – in fact, it was necessary to stay close by and tend the plants, chase off would-be thieves. Homes became permanent. A person might have to look out at the same neighbours for the whole of a lifetime. Guaranteed, plentiful food made it possible to have more children than before. More to the point, plenty of children were almost a necessity, since they could do the donkey work of clearing more fields, planting and harvesting more crops.

In no time at all, large families were fixed in place – tethered to their fields. By then, you couldn't have gone back to hunting and gathering even if you had wanted to. There were too many children to make it possible to keep everyone on the move and fed. Like it or lump it, you had made your bed and you would jolly well have to lie in it.

There were, too, those who farmed not crops but livestock. From around 11,000 years ago, also in the Near East, people began domesticating animals. Rather than having always to hunt for meat, it made sense to capture some beasts, keep them and breed them. It seems likely that sheep and goats were early candidates. Those animals, in the wild, were relatively small and incapable of inflicting much harm on humans determined to take hold of them. Altogether more daunting was the aurochs, the wild ancestor of all domesticated cattle. Taller than a man, with mighty horns and pounding hooves backed by an aggressive nature, it must have been brave folk indeed that set themselves the task of catching some alive and then keeping them in captivity as a reliable source of meat and milk, as well as of leather, bone and horn. Daunting or not, the job was done. Archaeologists are presently of the opinion that the first captive herd was formed within that territory we call Iran between perhaps 10,000 and 11,000 years ago. Such activity must have necessitated the construction of places to contain the animals – at least at first – corrals and the like. It would have occasioned too the need for access to grasslands where the herd might be fed, and also plentiful water.

No other domestication has mattered so much to the dinner table as that of the bull and the cow. There are now more than a billion head of cattle on the planet. Whole swathes of landscape have been cleared of forest to provide the necessary grass. From 'cattle' we get 'chattel' – the very essence of personal property. The Sanskrit word for war translates as something like 'the hunger for cattle' – meaning early conflict between groups of farming people was inspired as often as not by the desire to increase the herd by raiding and acquiring someone else's livestock.

Even given the hunters' uncertainty, the constant threat of hunger, I always think of farming as a hard sell. Instead of roaming free – following the herds, catching the fish, gathering the wild foods – farming meant staying put, rising with the sun and working in the fields until evening came. Each day the same and for ever. Worse, surrounded by your own waste, cheek by jowl with the neighbours, disease became more of a problem. The food might be guaranteed but the diet would have been monotonous – bread and porridge most of the time.

It was the bread that set in train the cycle of chores. Every day someone had to spend hours bent over, rocking back and forth with a heavy grinding stone, or quern, in both hands, working hard to provide enough flour for the family. Analysis of the vertebrae of early farmers shows the toll such repetitive labour took on their bodies, wearing them out before their time. Welcome to the daily grind.

Once farming was learned and adopted – arable or animal – its spread was inexorable. Archaeologists are still debating how it travelled, how long it took for the necessary thinking and technologies to cover all the miles from Mesopotamia to the rest of the old world. From time to time it has been fashionable to imagine great folk movements – whole populations migrating in search of pasture for their animals, fertile soil for their crops. In this way the hunters would therefore have been displaced – steadily pushed aside and out to the fringes of the world as more populous groups of farmers colonized the land valley by valley, clearing by clearing. Others insist it was not people that moved, but only the relevant ideas – spreading by word of mouth, a kind of osmosis, or like a virus, until all of humankind was infected. Having taken root first of all in that fertile crescent, the farmers themselves, or just the necessary technology, had certainly reached the shores of these islands by around 6,000 years BC.

The west coast of Ireland is dominated, like perhaps no other in the British Isles, by the presence of the Atlantic Ocean. People there live off the land, but it is the sea that sets the tone of every day. County Mayo – which means 'the Plain of the Yew Tree' – has one tired shoulder turned always towards the ocean. It is an oceanic climate, with salt in the air, and the sky often close enough to touch. Life on that coast is akin to a life at sea, subject to the wind and the weather born of endlessly moving clouds.

Now and for thousands of years County Mayo has provided the perfect conditions for the growth of blanket peat bog. Peat is a strange and fascinating beast and begins to form where rainfall is so heavy that it accumulates faster than it can be evaporated by the available wind and sunlight. Plants suited to wet ground grow, live and die between the puddles – but on account of the prevailing acidic, anaerobic conditions, the dead stuff does not properly decay. Instead it accumulates, layer by layer, like a bed heaped with more and more covers. First it's just a sheet . . . then a blanket . . . then lots of blankets – until finally the original ground surface is piled high, muffled and buried. Blanket bog has been growing in this way, in some places, since around the end of the last ice age 10,000–15,000 years ago. By now it can be 15 feet deep or more.

The aforementioned conditions – relatively low pH, absence of the bacteria that would normally set about the business of rotting down organic material – mean blanket bog effectively stops time for everything beneath or within it.

Here is the sort of place where human corpses are preserved for millennia – so-called 'bog bodies', tanned dark brown or black but in every other way as perfect as the day they were immersed in mush as dark as stewed tea. Sadly, their long slumber disturbed at last, they are often revealed by the peat-cutting machines that make mincemeat of them. Usually it is only parts that are spotted – just a torso perhaps, or a head and an arm.

Blanket bogs are also 'carbon sinks' – in that the green plants growing on their surfaces effectively absorb the carbon dioxide that naturally oozes from the peat below, silent but deadly. In this way, those bogs maintain a healthy equilibrium – healthy for us humans at least. The bogs have also been – and continue to be – an important source of fuel for people's homes. In Mayo, as in the rest of Ireland, they call it turf – and turf burns with a pleasing smell and a rosy glow.

It was while cutting peat back in the 1930s that schoolteacher Patrick Caulfield, from Belderrig near Ballycastle in north Mayo, discovered not bodies but big stones. He noticed two things: first, the stones were put there not by the random hand of nature but carefully placed, one course on top of another and stretching off in all directions; second, they were so deep down they were actually *beneath* the blanket, on a land surface that pre-dated the formation of the peat itself. They had therefore been set down on open ground a very long time ago.

Patrick did no more about it – just gathered his turf and stacked it for drying as usual. It was his son, Seamus, who set about the business of unravelling the mystery of the stones in the place they called Céide Fields – 'the fields on the flat-topped hills'.

Seamus Caulfield studied archaeology and then dedicated decades of his life to investigating the buried walls his father had found. Rather than damage the peat over-much by digging trenches, he opted instead for probing its depths with a long metal rod. It was an ancient technique in that part of the world – used by farmers to locate buried prehistoric timber (in a landscape largely devoid of trees, ancient timber was better than none). With this simple, non-invasive technique, Seamus has located and mapped more than 70 miles of buried walls. It is nothing less than the largest Neolithic field system anywhere in the world. They were planned and built around 5,500 years ago, when the climate was quite different in that part of the world – drier and warmer – and long before the peat began to form.

Since the Céide Fields are still as they have been for five and a half millennia, still a vast bog stretching as far as the eye can see, the best place for newcomers to start is at the visitor centre 5 miles or so west of Ballycastle. Sitting near a 370-foot drop to the ocean, it is a spectacular pyramid topped with glass and affording panoramic views over the whole area. The interior is dominated by a perfectly preserved 4,000-year-old pine tree that gives a sense of what must still remain sealed beneath and within the soggy blanket.

Inside the visitor centre, or out on a guided tour of the fields, you get that vital sense of what is otherwise still invisible, still sleeping undisturbed. Five and a half thousand years ago, the walls were built to enable farmers to look after and manage their cattle – separate enclosures for milking cows, cows with calves, bull calves, bulls, whatever. It is on a mind-boggling scale and would have been the daily preoccupation of an entire community. It provides a glimpse of an organized, sophisticated way of life. The biology and botany of the fields is explained too – heathers, lichens and mosses. In summer the bog is carpeted with all the colours of bog cotton, milkwort, orchids, tormentil and a host of other plants.

Best of all, though, is the chance to wield one of the rods, twice the height of a man and still the best tool for interrogating the silence. With a little effort, they can be made to penetrate the peat and then it is the distant sound that gets you – the sound of metal striking a stone that was set in place by a farmer five millennia before. When the tip of the rod hits one, and you feel it and hear it, the intervening years fall away.

By now the peat too has been well studied. It has kept a record of all that ever grew on the fields before the climate turned from drier to wetter. Before the farmers came, it was a place of pine trees – the pollen grains say so. When the farmers arrived, they set about clearing the trees, and grasses grew – food for the herds of cattle. There is cereal pollen too, from wheat and barley. Folded within the depths of that thick, thick blanket, then, is the evidence of the agreeable plants and the domesticated animals that transformed the landscape and human society for ever.

6

The Ness of Brodgar, Orkney

The heart of power

THE BRITISH ISLES are often made to feel like a place where importance and significance dwindle the further north you travel. So much of the economy – the much-vaunted and revered financial sector, the headquarters of big business – is centred around London and the south-east. The so-called 'mother of parliaments' is there too, in hallowed halls where so many world-shaping decisions have been made, along with the principal residences of the monarch. All this imbues that nub closest to the European mainland with a gravitational pull that attracts and then holds the mass of the population.

To journey north, breaking free of that force and all the noise and hubbub of the horde, must surely be to leave behind everything that seems to matter, that has ever mattered. By the time a traveller arrives at the northeast coast of Scotland and looks out over the Pentland Firth, one of the most challenging and unpredictable stretches of water anywhere in these islands, the overwhelming feeling is of having reached the edge not just of Britain but of the world. Turn around there, put your back to the sea and face south, and you sense the great mass of the long island stretching away. It is enough to give a person vertigo.

Cross the Pentland Firth by ferry or by plane, make landfall in the archipelago of Orkney, and you discover another world entirely. There are around seventy islands in Orkney (don't ever say 'the Orkneys' – just don't), of which perhaps twenty are actually inhabited by humankind. Just over

21,000 people make their homes there, the bulk of them on the largest of the islands, known as Mainland.

Orkney feels like nowhere else – not Scotland, not Britain, not Shetland, not even Scandinavia. It has a look and, more than that, an atmosphere and a personality that means Orkney is just . . . Orkney. It stands alone. It can be disorientating. Only 18 miles from mainland Scotland, from mainland Britain, and yet in many ways it might as well be another planet. It certainly feels remote. When the sky is low enough to wrap around the shoulders and the wind is blowing until you must stand and walk like a half-shut knife, Orkney can seem like a green raft that has slipped its mooring to float adrift on the open sea. When the clouds break and light rains down out of the blue, it is more like the arrivals lounge for Heaven itself.

This sense of Orkney being the very epitome of *peripheral* is an illusion born of our present tenancy of Britain – indeed of north-west Europe. The centre of gravity may be in the south-east of England now, but there was a time when the reality was quite different, and for reasons that confront a person with a whole new sense of what it meant to be abroad in a younger world.

Like the rest of the British Isles, Orkney has been inhabited by our species since around the end of the last ice age. When the first hunters arrived 10,000 years ago a great deal of seawater was still locked up in the ice sheets further north and the sea level was the best part of 150 feet lower than now. The land was also rising up – a process called isostatic or crustal rebound – after millennia of being crushed beneath the unimaginable weight of ice two thirds of a mile thick. Like a cushion freed from the weight of a fat bottom, it began steadily to recover. This combined and complicated process of rising land competing with rising sea has slowed, but it continues to this day. Suffice to say there is less Orkney and more sea than there was ten millennia ago and land that was known to and used by those hunters is now submerged.

The hunters, maybe a few hundred of them at any one time, had the place to themselves for 3,000 years or so, but their dominion could not and did not last. Farmers had made their way to the islands by 5,000 or 6,000 years ago, bringing seed crops and domesticated animals across the

Pentland Firth in simple boats. The hunters had probably known a landscape of scrubby woodland – birch and hazel, perhaps some stands of pines. If they began the process of clearing the land, then the farmers almost certainly completed it. They needed open spaces for their plants and animals, and also wood for building and equipping themselves with tools and furnishings and the rest of the detritus of settled life.

Soon enough Orkney was mostly treeless, but that absence did not deter those Neolithic farmers from building – far from it. By 5,000 years ago, the people there were in the grip of a veritable mania for building, using the abundant local sandstone. The rock of which Orkney is made turned out to be ideal construction material. The sandstone split easily into great long sheets and flagstones. Soon those giant splinters were being employed in all manner of projects – homes, tombs for the dead, as well as great circles of towering standing stones.

It was at this point that Orkney had its own gravitational pull and may, for as many as a thousand years, have exerted its influence over the whole length of Britain. There is fun to be had simply in taking a map of the British Isles and northern Europe and rotating it through 180 degrees. All at once there is a different sense of place to be had. For one thing, Orkney – and Shetland – are revealed as the hub of the wheel. For people on the move around northern Britain, north-western Europe and Scandinavia, those archipelagos appear like roundabouts, way stations en route from somewhere to everywhere else.

Orkney has been a treasure house for archaeologists for the best part of a century. The sheer volume of spectacular upstanding and visible monuments – like the Stones of Stenness, the Ring of Brodgar, the chambered burial tomb of Maeshowe and the village of Skara Brae – brought UNESCO World Heritage Status to Mainland in 1999. So clearly defined was the best of it, a set of world-class monuments within walking distance of one another, the central cluster is now known collectively as the Heart of Orkney. It was a chance discovery in 2003, however, that raised the international significance of Neolithic Orkney by what feels like a whole order of magnitude. Just to make the story even more perfect, the discovery in question was made at the literal heart of the Heart of Orkney.

Near the geographical centre of Mainland, an elegant finger of land separates the fresh water of the Loch of Harray from the seawater of the Loch of Stenness. At one end of the isthmus sits the Ring of Brodgar, at the other the Stones of Stenness. The nearby softly rounded green hump of Maeshowe is visible from both. At the centre of the isthmus is a whale-backed rise, a knuckle joint in the finger, called the Ness of Brodgar. The word 'ness' is descriptive and has some of the same roots as nose. Sometime in the 1920s, a farmer working the land there unearthed a stone bearing a beautifully incised design. It can be hard to stick a spade in the ground on Mainland without striking some archaeological remnant, so he merely put it to one side and thought no more about it. But in 2003, a farmer using a modern plough in the same place uncovered what appeared to be a large lump of dressed masonry, a carefully prepared stone from a building. It was this that finally attracted the attention of archaeologists.

The Ness was such a big lump that folk thereabouts had always assumed it was just a natural land form. Given its location right at the heart of the Heart of Orkney, however, it was deemed prudent to investigate the vicinity of that dressed stone. Now, fifteen years later, the exploration is still going on and has long since altered our understanding of the entire Neolithic period in north-western Europe. What has been revealed at the Ness of Brodgar so far is a vast complex of prehistoric buildings.

Rather than being a natural feature, the Ness is the product of a thousand years – at least – of building, demolition and then more building. During the Neolithic, two colossal walls defined the Ness, carefully cutting it off from the rest of the landscape. With access restricted, the space within made special, those farmer architects got on with the business of designing and constructing a whole series of buildings, numerous as mushrooms in a field.

Revealing them is one thing, interpreting and understanding them quite another. For the archaeologists it is a flowing, evolving process. Every season, even every day, the story changes. The buildings had either domestic or ritual functions, or perhaps both. Some of the building stones were engraved, incised or pecked with geometric patterns and cup marks. Others were coloured with pigments. Sometimes the artistic designs were hidden within the fabric of structures – their maker knowing in advance his work would never be seen. Some of it is about the importance of the act of creation. Perhaps it was enough to know the patterns were there, woven through the whole, understood and appreciated by the gods or the ancestors.

Stone tools were incorporated into the buildings as well. Axes of flint, mace heads fashioned from glacial pebbles harvested from beaches. Craftsmen of consummate skill and limitless patience took advantage of natural grains and patterns in the pebbles to create finished pieces of heart-stopping beauty. Many are broken, but whether the damage was accidental or deliberate, part of a bigger process that may have demanded things be put beyond use before they could be incorporated into a building, is anybody's guess. All of it adds to the allure of a site that has been drawing archaeologists and visitors to the Ness from all around the world for the past decade and more.

Having begun developing the site, the farmers and their descendants kept going for at least a millennium. Towards the end of the life of the Ness, one especially large building was created. It was on such a scale – as big as a modern barn – that it has been dubbed 'the Temple of Orkney'. It seems to have been in use for a generation, or perhaps longer, and was built at a point when many of the other structures appear to have been demolished and levelled. When the time came to put the Temple – and the Ness – beyond use as well, a great feast was held and 400 head of cattle were slaughtered for the occasion. Their shinbones were then piled around the outside of the building and the whole edifice demolished on top of them.

There is simply nothing else, nowhere else, quite like the Ness of Brodgar. For an unimaginably long time that complex hidden behind its towering walls would have been a focal point not just for the people of Orkney but possibly also for others from much further afield. Whatever it was called by the people who knew it as a living place, that name may have been known the length and breadth of the British Isles, even elsewhere in Europe.

There is a special, distinctive style of Neolithic pottery called Grooved Ware that is found all over these islands. The oldest of it is found on

Orkney. The architecture at the Ness and at domestic sites like Skara Brae and Barnhouse, where buildings feature distinctive rounded corners and internal features like dressers made of stone, is also older than elsewhere. Whoever they were, the people expressing in stone their thinking and their philosophy at the Ness of Brodgar and elsewhere on Orkney were innovators. Their ideas spread south, throughout the British Isles, eventually reaching places like Avebury and Stonehenge and shaping the thinking of people there.

That special strangeness of the Neolithic, that still mostly impenetrable, private world of 5,000 years ago, was profoundly affected by what was happening in Orkney. Once upon a time that archipelago was not peripheral, not on the edge of anything. It was the heart then – not just of Orkney but perhaps of the whole of the *British* archipelago.

7

Newgrange and Knowth, County Meath

Monumental Megalithic art

W E HAD BEEN hunters for the longest time, but the discovery of farming changed everything. Not just the way we lived but also how we understood the world and the cosmos.

The first farmers built stone homes for the dead long before they thought about anything remotely similar for the living. It was all about the new way of life, rooted among a few fields. They had laboured to clear them – felling any trees, digging up the roots, gathering all the stones and boulders the crops or animals did not like. Once the seeds were scattered, there was more work to be done. The crops were disinclined to thrive among other species and so anything but the wheat or oats or barley had to be removed, insects and bugs crushed between fingers and thumbs. The fields were places of labour, of bent backs and sweat, of endless repetition of the same few tasks, and they had to be watched over ceaselessly. Instead of feeling, as the hunters had, owned by the wider landscape of rolling hills, woodland, rivers and streams, the farmers felt they owned the fields over which they toiled, into whose soil they sweated.

If and when strangers arrived, it mattered to show them – to prove to them – that this land was already taken. Before any newcomers could even think of settling down, they had to be made to see that these fields were the work not just of the families labouring in them now but also the fruit of toil by those who had gone before. With that in mind, each living generation kept and treasured the mortal remains of some of their dead. Notable figures – strong men, perhaps, who had kept the wolves at bay, women who had borne many children and so were fertile like the soil – were to be remembered and revered, and stored for all time.

It was not enough to have the bones tucked beneath the beds of home or displayed upon a shelf. Far better to build special homes for them where they would be safe, where the ancestors would be together, a well of wisdom that might be visited and drawn from. Those ancestors were the trunk and branches of the great tree from which the present living had come. The special homes of the dead had to be permanent, fixed in the landscape so that any visitor would see the proof, the right of ownership.

County Meath lies in the east of Ireland, with just a meagre portion of its mass touching the Irish Sea. The River Boyne has some of its path through Meath, and its valley there is home to an ancient landscape they call Brú na Bóinne – 'the Palace of the Boyne'. The name fits well enough, for the Neolithic monuments constructed there around 5,000 years ago – circles of standing stones, tombs and those creations known as henges, circular ditches surrounded by banks made of the resultant spoil – are among the finest, the most affecting, in all of these islands.

Newgrange is the most famous ancient monument in Ireland. It appears now as a large circular mound, grass-topped and 250 feet across, surrounded by a façade of white quartz pebbles. This exterior is a modern reconstruction that followed extensive excavation of the site in the 1960s and 1970s. The facelift was and remains controversial, but whether or not it is to your taste should not detract from the ancient masterpiece preserved within. A long, narrow passage reaches 60 feet towards the centre of the mound and terminates in a chamber with a corbelled roof – a structure achieved by placing the roofing slabs in ever-decreasing circles, until the final gap can be covered by a single capstone. On three sides of the chamber are shallow recesses.

Most impressive of all the architectural wonders of Newgrange is the special effect achieved by a 'roof box' built above the entrance to the passage. Having carefully aligned the passage with the spot on the horizon where the sun rises each midwinter's morning, the builders made an opening above the lintel to allow those first rays to penetrate the darkness within. Since the chamber sits 6 feet higher than the entrance, the passage slopes steadily upwards. Such was the skill of the Neolithic architects and builders they were able to angle the light box to ensure the sunlight would reach all the way to the back wall of the chamber. Even on the clearest midwinter morning the effect lasts only seventeen minutes, but when the sky is clear the pale finger of light reaches out and touches a carefully positioned work of art. Briefly illuminated then, or plucked like a string until it resonates with ancient life, is a triskelion – a triple spiral symbolizing life itself, the ceaseless unspooling of time.

Nearby Knowth is less famous than its glamorous neighbour, but as always it would be a shame to be fooled by outward appearances. There is much more in the way of so-called Megalithic art there. Another great mound, and within sight of Newgrange, it is surrounded by seventeen smaller tombs.

In the context of creations like Knowth and Newgrange – and West Kennet and all the rest of the places in which the first farmers sometimes placed the bones of their dead – the word 'tomb' seems not quite right. None of them was found to contain the remains of more than a handful of people. Whatever function or functions they served, the storage of the dead was only part of the lifetime's use of such buildings. Just as churches and temples are about more than mourning, so the burial chambers the Neolithic farmers raised were surely more than tombs.

Places like Knowth have something of the feel of wombs. If people brought the bones of their loved ones here, or to Stonehenge and Avebury (and we know they did), then perhaps it was in the hope of finding new life. If they went to Stonehenge in the deepest dark of winter, then maybe it was because they knew the light of spring must follow.

Within the pregnant body of Knowth there lie not one but two wombs. They are back to back – with one entered via the east and the other from the west. The western chamber is small and poor, but that in the east is a triumph of ancient engineering. As at Newgrange, the chamber is made by corbelling so that the final form is shaped like a beehive, rounded and narrowing towards the top. Archaeologists found the cremated remains of 121 people – a tiny proportion of the population that must have lived and died in the mound's shadow during the centuries it was open and in use.

Also discovered within Knowth, and on display in the Museum of Dublin, is a mace head made of flint. In all likelihood the raw material came from Orkney, suggesting long-distance links between farmers in Ireland, Scotland and no doubt Wales and the England of Stonehenge and Avebury as well.

The product of hundreds or even thousands of hours of effort by an artist of humbling skill, the mace head is heartbreakingly lovely, and perfect. The flint from which it has been fashioned is a mix of white and rusty red, the colours swirling together like liquids incompletely stirred. Hold your hand up as though preparing to deliver the Yorick lines from *Hamlet* and unconsciously your fingers will have made the perfect cradle to hold it. A round hole has been painstakingly drilled through it, as though for the shaft of a handle. Even that must have taken countless hours with a wood drill tipped with abrasive powders obtained by grinding down hard stone like quartz. Above the hole the artist has carved two swirls, coiling in opposite directions and side by side like eyes, so that the whole effect is of a face with a mouth opened wide in surprise or alarm. It is a work of genius.

Artistry abounds at Knowth. Around the outside of the mound, as part of the kerb or incorporated into the fabric of the interior, are something in the region of 400 carved stones – half of all the Megalithic art discovered so far in western Europe.

There is a seeming simplicity about Newgrange and Knowth. They are monumental in every sense, loaded with mystery. They belong to another world entirely. What is most striking is their primitive nature – blocks roughly hewn, darkness, cramped spaces. But long before any plans were drawn up for the building of the Great Pyramid at Giza, the great mounds by the River Boyne were already old, centuries old. It is another, older, valley of the kings, and to walk there is to spend time in the shadow of ancient understanding and intent.

8

Grime's Graves, Norfolk

Mining for flint in the Neolithic

FOR AT LEAST two million years our ancestors depended on flint for making tools with sharp, cutting edges. It is lovely stuff, as appealing to look at and touch as any semi-precious stone. In many areas of England nodules of flint have been used, for hundreds of years, as building material. Its incorporation into a wall adds a distinctive touch and colour, and the sight of it lets a person know what part of the world they must be in. Flint was used to ignite black powder in muskets and flintlocks, and even now it is used as a fire-starter, struck against steel. But for all that flint has been part of the toolkit of humankind since a time beyond the reach of memory, we still do not properly understand exactly what it is.

Flint certainly formed long ago, in the world's oceans, from the silica that had made up parts of the bodies of simple animals such as sponges and plankton. Other tiny swimming, floating beasties had bodies formed in part of calcium. When all those creatures died, the silica and calcium dissolved back into the seawater and hung suspended there, like infinitesimal flecks and specks of dust. After millions upon millions of years, all the calcium collected upon the seabed in unimaginably vast quantities, forming a layer hundreds of feet deep. Pressure saw it compacted into solid chalk. Molluscs and other animals burrowed into the increasingly thick beds of chalk, leaving hollows, tunnels and chambers. By some process still not properly understood, the accumulated silica seems to have existed for a while as a sort of thick gel. That gel, with a texture like cough syrup, found its way into the hollows and tunnels and, by some other barely understood process, solidified there. It is for these reasons that nodules – irregular, globular lumps of flint – occur within much more massive layers of chalk.

In the intervening aeons and ages, what was once seabed became dry land – thrust up by geological events of apocalyptic violence or gently exposed by the retreat and diminution of the ocean. Our ancestors would have first encountered flint on the land surface as beach pebbles or seams exposed by erosion. Having noticed its unique qualities, they went in search of more. Eventually, some of their number worked out that by burrowing into surface seams they could follow the flint below ground, and so the practice of mining the material was invented and developed.

There is no stranger-looking patch of landscape in Britain than Grime's Graves – as though 90-odd acres of the moon's pitted, pockmarked surface had somehow been made fertile and sown with grass. Around 7 miles north-west of the market town of Thetford, close by the Suffolk–Norfolk border, the land here was identified as a source of flint at least 5,000 years ago. The name 'Grime's Graves' is much more recent – bestowed by Anglo-Saxons at some time between the fifth and eleventh centuries. It has been loosely (imaginatively, in fact) translated from the Old English as 'the quarries dug by the masked man' – Grim being one of their gods, who concealed his face with a hood or a mask. It is interesting that those Anglo-Saxons even knew what they were looking at, but the pockmarks are indeed the effect of backfilled chalk rubble slumping down into the mineshafts from which it was hacked out so very long ago.

Among many other things, the Neolithic farmers were evidently geologists of a sort as well – and had certainly learned how to prospect for and find the brittle, glassy stone they wanted for their tools. During the course of perhaps a thousand years, multiple generations of miners sank more than 430 vertical shafts straight down into the chalk at Grime's Graves. It was no half-hearted endeavour. Many of them are in excess of 40 feet deep and as much as 30 feet wide. As they dug down, using picks made of red-deer antlers, the miners erected wooden scaffolds and platforms to enable the removal of the spoil, and then the flint, up to the surface. The chalk rubble was piled around the mouth of the shaft, held in place by timber revetments to stop it tumbling back down.

So specialized were the miners – so certain of what they were doing – they smashed through and largely ignored shallower layers of lower-quality flint on the way down to reach the thicker, richer seams below. What they were looking for was a layer of high-quality flint, like thousands of gallons of spilled toffee set hard. Whenever they reached that floor of flint, they followed it in every direction by opening horizontal tunnels and chambers to maintain access to the shining stone. Some of the spaces are so confined they could only have been exploited by children.

The flint was smashed out with stone hammers, and the great slabs of it were then hoisted topside, where rough-outs – the basic axe-shapes – were quickly fashioned. It seems likely these were then moved elsewhere, possibly over vast distances, for finishing in the hands of specialists all over the country. More than anything else flint was wanted for making axe heads – the essential tool needed by farmers to clear woodland to make way for open fields for crops and animals.

Grime's Graves is the only place in Britain where you can actually visit that Neolithic world. A few of the shafts and chambers have been excavated by archaeologists and left open. In so doing they have revealed that much more was going on at Grime's Graves than just industry.

Once each shaft was exhausted, all the available flint heaved up to the surface, it was carefully backfilled. On a practical level this would have helped keep the terrain in a stable condition, preventing subsidence and potentially dangerous collapses. But it seems too that the miners felt the need to undo the harm they had done to the land by burrowing inside it. Perhaps they regarded the flint as something else that grew from Mother Earth, yet more of her bounty. Having harvested a crop, they had then to seed the land to ensure regrowth. Archaeologists have concluded that no more than two or three shafts would have been open at any given time – yet more evidence of conscientious, methodical exploitation of a precious resource.

While the shafts and faces were open, the miners built hearths and little shrines down there in the dark, sometimes adorned with simple figures carved from lumps of the chalk. Before the backfilling began, other precious things were left behind as offerings and thank-yous. The archaeologists have found human and animal bones, finished axes and some of the antler picks that had been used as tools.

The Romans who came much later used the expression *quid pro quo* – 'this for that'. For the longest time it seems our ancestors understood and appreciated there was no such thing as a free lunch. If you wanted to take, then you had also to give. Long before our greedy consumption of everything, our mindless hollowing and harrowing of the Earth without a thought for the consequences, our forebears felt the need to keep an account, to remember what they owed and to try to pay it back. Just as some seed had to be kept to be sown in the spring, so it may have been deemed vital and right to return some of the flint, as well as other valuables, to ensure the continued productivity of the mines. At Grime's Graves they knew there was a price to be paid.

The scale of the mining makes plain it could not have been accomplished without serious commitment. For every miner working below, his efforts lit only by little lamps, exposed at all times to the threat of injury or death, there would have to have been many more people employed above, in the business of gathering and preparing food, making the antler picks and the rest of the tools needed below, preparing the rough-outs for export elsewhere. So hungry would the operation have been for antlers, archaeologists reckon captive herds of hundreds of animals must have been corralled nearby.

For weeks and months of the year the place we know as Grime's Graves would have thrummed with life – scores, hundreds of men, women and children living on site and working all hours to make the most of the opportunity presented by the flint.

While the terrain above ground is evocative in its own right, the field dimpled in every direction by the collapsed topmost layers of the truly colossal shafts, it is the underground gloom that offers an experience like nowhere else in the country. I do not care what anyone says, I believe fragments of the ancient past have snagged on to a few places, like strands of spider's web, or sheep's fleece caught on a nail. Down below in Grime's

Graves the air feels old, as though it has been inhaled and exhaled many times and now hangs exhausted. Here and there, lying against the chalk walls, are antler picks that were set aside by Neolithic miners 4,000 or 5,000 years ago. The archaeologists have left them where they found them, where they have always been.

Empires and kingdoms have risen and fallen. Kings and queens have come and gone. Wars have been won and lost. Most of the history that we know and care about has unfolded while those antler picks have lain slumped against the abandoned tunnels and chambers of Grime's Graves.

9

Great Langdale, Cumbria

Stone axes and the invention of Heaven

ALL OVER THE north of England, tucked away in folds in the landscape, are fossils of an old counting system. There are many variations, certainly dozens, and each sounds to our modern ears as unfamiliar as Sanskrit. Where those relics do survive, it is usually among people such as shepherds and the like – those that are or were in the business of counting stock. The one I learned by rote is Cumbrian and goes *yan, tan, ethera, tethera, pip, othera, bothera, edera, dedera, dik*. There you go – that is one to ten in a language with its roots in Old English and Norse, or perhaps even something Celtic, from Cornwall or Wales, and already ancient by the time the Romans arrived with their Latin more than 2,000 years ago.

Such truffles, rich and potent, make for distracting finds. At the very least they are reminders that modern Britain is a veneer stretched thin over other ways, older ways.

It was also in Cumbria, in the valley of Great Langdale, that I learned how our ancestors, the first farmers of these British Isles, seem to have invented for themselves nothing less than the concept of Heaven, or else a sophisticated idea of where that heaven might be found.

Great Langdale, a couple of miles from the town of Ambleside, is a classic U-shaped valley left behind during the last ice age by the bulldozing action of a glacier. Like much of the Lake District, Great Langdale is a landscape that inspires the imagination and encourages deep thoughts. From earliest times, our species has been moved again and again to try to make sense of, and simply to celebrate, the grandeur there. At the turn of the nineteenth century Wordsworth, Coleridge, Southey and the rest of the Lake Poets rendered their inspiration into words. But long, long before them came other people, and they made their record in the stone of the place.

Great Langdale is famous among archaeologists as the source of the raw material for a totemic style of Stone Age axe which was traded and exchanged all over Britain and Ireland. These axes occur in conspicuous numbers in the east of England, around Lincolnshire especially. Something like a quarter of all the polished Neolithic axes found in the British Isles so far are made of stone from just two mountains in Langdale.

The stone used for these axes is called tuff or, more poetically and descriptively, greenstone. Although those Neolithic farmers could not possibly have known it, greenstone is actually compressed volcanic ash – dust left over from the making of the world in ages past, transformed into mud and then solidified by great pressure and millions of years into rock. What those elder folk certainly did notice, however, was the naturally occurring patterns and variations in colour of the raw material they had at their disposal for the making of the tools and other items they needed. Some of the Langdale greenstone is veined and marbled with other colours – some light, some dark – that add a special beauty to the finished pieces. Because each lump of greenstone is made different by its own tracery of lines and inclusions, an axe fashioned by a master may have a completely unique fingerprint. Just as Japanese swordsmiths use repeated folding of their steel and then endless polishing to create the *hamon* – the characteristic wave form unique as a fingerprint that runs down the length of each blade – so the makers of the Langdale axes exploited the characteristics of their own raw material to produce pieces that could never be replicated.

What is strange, however, part of what is hard to understand, is that those veins are also imperfections – fault lines and weaknesses – and their makers would have known it.

An expert flint-knapper can take a piece of greenstone and make a rough-out in under an hour. Flakes are knocked away from the whole, using a harder stone, to create a long, narrow rectangular shape. It is the finishing that takes the time and the patience, and the artistry. Using first rough-grade abrasives and then progressively finer and finer sands and silts, the perfect final shape and polish is achieved over a period of perhaps hundreds of hours.

The result is a heart-stopper. Langdale axes from 5,000 years ago have on them the same deep, limpid lustre they had when they were first made. They can be big too – around a foot long – and heavy enough to require both hands to hold them. But on account of the marbling and variations that make each one so uniquely lovely, they might always have been useless for felling trees or any other kind of work. The first heavy blow struck would most likely have caused the implement to snap in two along one or other of the fault lines. And so the conclusion to be drawn is that at least some of the Langdale axes were made and valued not as tools but for a whole other set of reasons.

Much of the fabled greenstone comes from near the fractured, barren summits of just two mountains high above the valley of Great Langdale. They are Harrison Stickle and Pike o'Stickle, and since the exposed outcrops of desirable stone are around 2,000 feet above the valley floor, it takes an effort just to climb to them. On Pike o'Stickle, the axe men concentrated on what they could collect from a frighteningly precipitous ledge that promises injury or even death to the unwary. Strangest of all, from a practical point of view at least, there are perfectly good sources of greenstone lower down, in spots that are much easier to reach. By some measures, the lower stone may even be judged higher quality than that to be had from the near-death zone.

So what was going on? It seems clear that much of what mattered was the effort and danger required. During the Neolithic, the upper slopes of Great Langdale were probably not even inhabited full time. During the summer they may have provided high pastures for the grazing of cattle, and so it may have been during those few weeks that people made a point of embarking upon journeys that were as much rites of passage as mere runs to forage for workable stone.

The Neolithic was a time of change, when people were moving away from the old lifestyle of hunting and gathering and opting for settled farming. The whole approach to the landscape was changing too. Farming – the

need to clear and maintain fields – raised the spectre of ownership, property. Tombs, houses of the dead, were built as visible proof of long years
of occupation of the same fields. *This is mine – and I can prove it because
over there in that tomb my ancestors built are the bones of my father, my
grandfather . . .*

As the time of farming progressed, setting down ever deeper roots,
there were also changes in the way people seem to have treated their dead.
In the early years it was often about leaving the corpse exposed to be picked
clean by animals – or perhaps burying it briefly until the flesh was gone.
Thereafter, the bones of some people – just some – were gathered up and
stored inside the tombs. Later in the Neolithic, cremation became more
popular. Bodies were burned in great pyres until nothing remained but
ashes and bone fragments, which might be collected and stored or simply
scattered. Perhaps it was at this time, when the dead were being transformed from earthbound flesh and bone into smoke that could rise into
the sky, that the farmers began to pay more attention to the highest and
least-accessible places in their landscape. If the dead, or at least their spirits,
were rising into the sky, then maybe Heaven was up there too. A raw material obtained by making treacherous journeys into places as close as possible
to the sky may therefore have taken on a unique and priceless value.

An axe made from a piece of greenstone from up there, with its singu-
lar pattern of marbling, may have become a treasure to be passed down
through generations of a family. Such an axe may have had a name of its
own – like a Viking sword – and its own history. Having been made from
stone collected up in the sky, closest to Heaven, such an axe might have
been seen to embody some trace of the departed dead.

Anyone making for the Langdale Pikes would do well to start in the
village of Chapel Stile, a few miles to the north and west of Ambleside on
the B5343. As much as anything, Chapel Stile is known as the location of a
few colossal boulders formed of the same volcanic tuff, more or less, that
provided the raw material for the axes.

Giants like these, known to geologists as 'erratics', were left behind by
the same glacier that hollowed out the valley. The largest of them, Copt
Howe, is a worthwhile destination all on its own, without the need for the

lung-bursting climb up to the heights. For decades at least, rock climbers have practised their skills by scaling its smooth faces. As recently as the turn of the millennium, the great slab of its east face was found to be marked with ancient art. Given how faint the designs are, it is no wonder they were overlooked for so long. That said, once they are pointed out, they have an unassuming magic. It is best to go looking for them in the low angled light of morning, when the sun's shadow casts the shallow marks into relief. Seen then, they have some of the look of the sort of casual doodles you might make on a scrap of paper during a phone call. Much more time and effort was required, however, to render such designs in stone. There are little shallow circular scoops of the sort known to archaeologists as 'cup marks' – a regular feature of Neolithic art. Some of these have around them halos of concentric circles. There are other marks that look like half-moons, and also straight lines and what could be a chevron, filled in with pecked dots.

Some folk living nearby have speculated that they are quite modern – perhaps only Victorian – but most have about them the look and patina of great age. Specialists in rock art have suggested the concentric circle forms may have been made to depict tunnels – perhaps representations of the spinning portals to other worlds that are reported by people under the influence of hallucinogens. There is also another belief locally, that the marks may be a form of map giving directions to the axe quarries on the slopes of the pikes above. Whatever they are, it seems clear the artworks are connected to the Neolithic experience of coming to Great Langdale in preparation for hiking up into the high ground.

Fundamental to Aboriginal Australian understanding of their own land is the concept of 'the Dreaming'. I've had the idea explained to me more than once, by different tribal elders, and I don't mind telling you that repeating what I've been told is not unlike remembering a dream. In essence, it concerns a time before time, when the land was inhabited not by people but by the supernatural creatures that were their ancestors. It was during the Dreaming that the land took on its permanent shapes and forms – mountain ranges, lakes, rivers, valleys – and the ancestral creatures travelled far and wide, making special, sacred sites that were linked by paths of memory called songlines. As I have understood it, a person in possession of the songlines might move confidently across the landscape from special place to special place.

One afternoon in January 2016 I visited Montgomery Reef off the Kimberley coast of north-west Australia. The reef is an astonishing feature, covering more than 150 square miles and appearing out of the ocean when the tide drops. So quickly does the ocean fall away in that part of the world that thousands of waterfalls are briefly created, cascading down the sides of the reef as it appears to rise up out of the deep. We were watching the spectacle from a little aluminium boat, miscalculated the speed of the outgoing tide and became marooned. There was nothing to be done but wait for the tide to return and set us free. Aboard with us was a local elder called Donny Woolagoodja and while we lay waiting I asked him if I was part of the Dreaming as well, or was it just something for indigenous Australians?

'No, no,' he said. 'The world dreamed you as well, dreamed everything and everyone.'

It rates as one of the best things anyone has ever told me, and since he said it I have wondered if the songlines once reached all around the world, all the way to Great Langdale and everywhere else. Time and history have moved over Britain for so long and so powerfully they have erased the old lines and we have forgotten the songs. Only in the untouched vastness of places like the Kimberley does any of it survive.

But there are places in the landscape of the British Isles that seem, even now, like the work not of nature but of giant hands. At Copt Howe it is tempting to look at that ancient boulder and see it not as rubble left behind by a retreating glacier but as a great leftover building block. If the Neolithic farmers were making sense of the world by imagining a time before time, when supernatural creatures set some locations aside as more significant than others, then Copt Howe and the Langdale Pikes above would surely have seemed like places that had happened not by accident but by design. I try, and usually fail, to imagine such a time and such a place. But I can at least allow for the existence of people who watched the smoke and ash rising from their funeral fires and then wanted to honour that final journey by climbing as high as possible to collect the last stones touched by their dead on the way past and up.

10

West Kennet Long Barrow, Wiltshire

Burying the dead

SOMETIME DURING THE middle of the fourth millennium BC a commu-nity of farmers set about building a tomb for their dead at West Kennet, to honour some of those departed and to show their own inherent right to the land. The 'long barrow' they built here is one of the finest and most extravagant of a group archaeologists classify as the Cotswold–Severn tombs. Others of the type are scattered across that territory and yet none is more impressive. It is the best part of 330 feet long, a great tapering mound of chalk rubble.

It is useful to regard such creations as churches, cathedrals rather than houses or even just tombs. Like a Christian church, West Kennet is aligned east to west. The widest and most important end – the business end, if you will – is towards the east. A stone-lined passage, tall enough to walk through with head held high, leads inside from an impressive entrance. There is one chamber at the end of the passage and two either side. These are low-roofed and a person must crouch and crawl inside on hands and knees. No doubt the necessary lowering of the head, the humble crawling, was intended by the designers. Any who entered this space were stepping inside a place set apart, another world, the world of the ancestors. No doubt the hairs rose on the back of the neck and the breathing grew short and shallow as the faith-ful lowered their heads in the presence of the spirits of their dead.

Archaeologists found the remains of just forty-six people, men and women, inside West Kennet. The bones were disarticulated and gathered in separate piles of skulls, long bones and so on. Perhaps the bodies were laid out first, or buried elsewhere until the flesh was gone. When they were brought inside the tomb, they joined the wider community of the ancestors. The fact that only a relatively few individuals were placed inside surely means this was not the resting place of the whole community. Most people must have been buried, or their bodies otherwise disposed of, elsewhere. It was an open building, with people coming and going, for a long time – archaeologists are not agreed about how long. Like a church, people spent time inside. Maybe they prayed, asked for help from ancestors or from a god or gods, advice, an intervention in the world of the living. Maybe the bones were taken away for periods of time, for ceremonies elsewhere, and then returned.

The bones that were placed in West Kennet seem to have belonged to people who lived and died within one or two generations of each other. At some point a decision was taken to close the tomb for ever and it was then that a façade of massive boulders was erected across the east end, ceremonially blocking the entrance. Whatever had been going on inside the tomb – and for however long – that time had passed.

I defy anyone to enter that space now, stepping down past the great blocking boulders and into the damp-scented half-dark of the passage, without feeling the sensations that accompany entrance to a church or a temple. But imagine stepping there, stooping there, if you believed, truly believed, that the spirits of the ancestors were there too, watching and listening. As well as the individuals they had once been, they had come together as a single entity, the collected past of the people.

We take for granted the notion of a spirit, a soul that is separate from the body. Even if we do not believe in the existence of such, we are aware of the concept. But this was a great leap of imagination. No other species in the universe has achieved as much – conceiving the idea that a person might be more than that which can be seen and touched. It is at the root of the belief that sovereignty, the law, power is also separate. The power of the president passes from man to man. It exists in its own right, invisible and immortal. The king is dead, long live the king. The fading echo of that noble thought is there inside West Kennet.

11

Stonehenge, Wiltshire

Tracking the light

SOME 5,000 YEARS ago a community, or just a group of farming families that shared the same space on a broad chalk plateau, felt an urge to modify their landscape. For thousands of years people had been making their marks there or thereabouts. Some hunters had raised a few timber posts. Those stayed in place until they rotted away. Elsewhere some farmers had been at work digging ditches almost 2 miles long and using the spoil to create parallel banks alongside, making what archaeologists call a cursus.

Around 3100 BC, some others began digging a circular ditch in the location we know as Stonehenge. They dumped the rubble on the outer rim, creating a bright white bank. The whole thing was about 360 feet across. They dug holes around the edge of the circle. Archaeologists cannot agree whether those held timber posts or maybe stones that were subsequently removed for other reasons. Later still, around the middle of the third millennium BC, some ambitious and well-connected souls acquired some 200 tons of stones, bluestones from 150 miles away in the Preseli Hills of Pembrokeshire, and arranged them in two circles, one inside the other, towards the centre of the site. Years passed, countless sunrises and sunsets; generations were born and lived and died.

Later inhabitants of the plain saw fit to move aside the bluestones – each weighing over a ton – to make way for a circle of enormous rectangular sarsen stones topped with lintels. The raw material for all this was from much closer to home. A great crust of sarsen had once covered much of the land surface thereabouts, but these stones were huge and unwieldy, weighing as much as 40 tons each. The builders knew how to work with timber as well and took the trouble to fashion mortise and tenon joints to hold the lintels in place.

Endless opinions have been put forward about how the sarsens were shaped and prepared, why the designers demanded the unnecessary application of techniques required for working in wood. Some experts claim the stones were marked so their surfaces resembled the bark of the trees that had been cut and burned down long before. Were the builders paying homage to some distant time, remembered from generation to generation, when the first circle on the plain was a clearing in open woodland?

Inside that circle they raised a horseshoe of even bigger sarsen stones, topped with even bigger lintels. These are the trilithons, so familiar. The labour involved in it all was colossal and after all the years that have passed since that act of creation we are only really guessing about the purpose, the thinking behind it.

An entrance to the circle, the largest of the trilithons and a monolith outside the circle called the Heel Stone are all aligned on the path taken across the sky by the sun at midsummer and midwinter. In recent times some archaeologists have suggested people may have gathered at Stonehenge (the name means 'hanging stones', in reference to the lintels on the trilithons) in the depths of winter for ceremonies to do with burial and remembrance of the dead.

The most we can say with confidence is that the farmers had grown expert in tracking the movements of the lights in the sky. They depended upon the seasons for their crops – the planting in spring, the growth of summer, the harvest in the autumn. In winter they waited, lighting fires against the dark while the sun made its way back to them. Their ancestors had been hunters who commanded great territories and moved from place to place. Now they were farmers, tethered by the choices they had made and the obligations that had resulted, fixed in place to watch over their fields. So they watched the sun wander instead, the moon as well, and perhaps the planets. And as the sky moved around them they were aware of their place in the scheme of things. They had become the centre of the universe.

As well as so much else that is lost, we cannot ever know what the people who built it called the place we know as Stonehenge. In time, the name they had for it may have become known far and wide. People may have sought it out from a thousand miles away. The work on the place was never-ending, and when some or other generation turned their backs on it, it remained, as it had always been, unfinished.

12

Avebury, Wiltshire

Circles in time

THERE WERE TIMES in our past when it seems that the act of making mattered as much if not more than finishing. Making gives purpose to life and apparently our species learned that long ago. At the very least, making, creating, is a distraction from the thoughts that come when too much time is spent standing still, when reality and awareness of our powerlessness in the face of the vicissitudes of life rise like flood water. Better to get on with something in the meantime.

By the time the builders of the stone monument at Avebury in Wiltshire had completed the huge circle that would later enclose all else there, the earliest part of the great, deep ditch – the point at which they had begun to dig – was already silting up, chalky soil slumping, loosened by neglect, and yet no attempt was made to empty it again. It is as though it did not matter to the builders to reach the end of some fine day and know their creation was completed – in the way that matters to us. They simply set themselves huge tasks that would fill time not just for the few but for hundreds of people – maybe everyone they knew or had ever heard of. And not just for days or months, but for years, whole generations of time.

Avebury, constructed around 4,500 years ago, comprises three stone circles, two smaller enclosed within one larger. The greatest of the sarsen stones – silicified sandstone boulders found all over the chalk land of southern England – within the northern inner circle, a setting known as the cove, may weigh as much as 100 tons. A vast lump of a thing, hewn only by nature, much of it is out of sight and buried in the soil. Archaeologists have suggested it may have been in place long before any human work was even begun on the henge – the all-encompassing circular ditch and earthen bank – or anything else at Avebury. Its massive bulk may even have caught the eye of the hunters who knew the area long before the farmers came and then pointed it out to the new arrivals when their time came. Perhaps it is the keystone of the whole affair, its presence in the landscape attracting people, having them stop and stare, and eventually inspiring all that came after.

Henges and the stone circles that followed them might be conscious recreations of the forest clearings that had been gathering places first of all. When most of the trees were gone, cut down to make way for fields, the farmers may have felt the need for the places where they or their ancestors had once gathered – safe spaces out of the shadows, where fires might be lit and folk could talk, make plans. By setting such places aside from the rest, with ditches, banks and circles of stones, they might have satisfied a need for something they had lost when they cleared the wider landscape of trees.

The sarsen stones of Avebury have long been characterized as either slim, tall males or shorter, wider females. The giant at the heart of Avebury is the largest of the female stones – the matriarch, you might say. Surely it is impossible to avoid being affected by Avebury? The outer stone circle, surrounding the two smaller rings, is one of the largest in the world. Some estimates of the work involved run to more than a million man-hours. Tens of thousands of tons of chalk were dug out using only antler picks and muscle power. Each of the sarsen stones weighs tens of tons as well. Much of the site was destroyed by superstitious folk in more modern times, or the stones simply broken up and dragged away as building stone, and yet still it thrums with a latent charge of power. Visitors walk slowly, without being told. The urge to touch and stroke the stones is overwhelming, especially for kids. Even today, in a world filled with towering buildings, a stroll around the bottom of the ditch is enough to make a person feel small. V-shaped now, it would originally have been narrower and with sheer sides. From above, when the chalk was exposed, it would have had the look of a giant Polo-mint dropped on the grass. Best of all is to take children and watch where they go, the paths they find.

They say that by the medieval period people had forgotten how Avebury came to be. The ditch and bank, so vast as to be hard to take in, was dismissed as something natural – or even regarded as a corruption of the natural order and wrought by the Devil. The stones were mere boulders perhaps, like the rest of the shattered sarsen crust lying thereabouts and left over from creation. It took the eighteenth-century antiquarian William Stukeley to see it again and appreciate it as the work of humankind – even if he did think it a temple made by Druids.

There is nowhere and nothing as affecting as the works in these islands made by the first farmers. This part of Wiltshire is a hub of monuments. They have to be seen together, as parts of something grander than any one of them alone. For me they have more to give than even the pyramids of Egypt. The great pyramid at Giza, a so-called wonder of the ancient world, is all about the compulsive, autistic straight lines of the pharaohs and their architects. The Neolithic farmers of Avebury, however, were still in thrall to the feminine curves of the circle, fertile mounds above ground and fecund wombs below.

13

Silbury Hill, Wiltshire

Building something to endure

CLOSE BY WEST KENNET Long Barrow is another product of the Neolithic mania for building. Over 130 feet tall and with a footprint of nearly 6 acres, Silbury Hill is the largest man-made prehistoric mound in Europe. Like the ditches at Avebury and Stonehenge, the stuff of the hill was dug out with antler picks. It sits at the centre of the wide shallow dish created by all the years of labour. It is as big as those Egyptian pyramids that were built around the same time, roughly 4,500 years ago. Some estimates suggest the making of Silbury Hill may have occupied some part of people's time for hundreds of years. Consider, for the fun of it, that it was Henry VIII, on the day of his coronation in June 1509, who commissioned the building of the Millennium Dome on the banks of the Thames, which was then completed in the year 2000. That may be how long it took to make Silbury Hill.

Back in 2007, English Heritage were hard at work shoring up the hill. Centuries-old burrowings – from the top down and in from the sides – had made the structure unstable. The whole hill was beginning to collapse like a soufflé left out in the cold, and the restoration work was crucial. Before the last of the old tunnels was properly backfilled, I had the chance to stand at the heart of the mound, my feet on the ground surface last walked upon by those ancient farmers. It was a void that ought never to have existed, on loan from the heaped chalk, a debt soon to be called in. I breathed the borrowed, burrowed air and prayed for ghosts that never came.

We can hardly hope to know why it was built, what it meant to the generations who saw it rise, year on year. Although we cannot put ourselves into the minds of those people, the making of Silbury Hill, of Avebury, Stonehenge, West Kennet and the rest, still says something we can understand in our own way, in our own world. Right now in the twenty-first century, the lightning-fast advance of our own technology, our own scientific understanding of the world and the universe is dwarfing us as never before. We are being atomized – made smaller and smaller and forced to contemplate a view of reality in which we are utterly insignificant. Bonds of family are being broken down by social media, replaced with imaginary ties to distant strangers. Folk keep a thousand friends online and never meet any of them. Smartphones make the new clearings in the forest of the modern world, but sooner or later everyone is being told they are alone.

If our ancestors felt small beneath the sky, then we are learning to see ourselves only as incidental consequences of mindless natural processes devoid either of design or purpose. Chemical bonds, physical forces great and small, the thoughtless unfolding of evolution. According to much of the science and thought of our own time, these are the only making of us. That our ancestors bent their backs to making special places, to making places special, where something made sense, might unite us all across the ages. It mattered to them to give their time to making a mark that was real and tangible. In their own way, they too understood that they were small and that the world and the universe would go on without them, but they left something behind that insisted, 'We are here.'

14

The Amesbury Archer, Salisbury Museum, Wiltshire

Walking into history

O UR SPECIES IS especially well designed for walking, even over vast distances. It is something we have been practising for a long time – at least since three humans, or humans of a sort, walked across rain-sodden volcanic ash at a place in the Great Rift Valley in Tanzania that we know as Laetoli some three and a half million years ago. The little trio of souls were of a species classified as *Australopithecus afarensis*, a mouthful meaning 'the southern African ape', and their footprints reveal that they walked much like us – striking down with their heels and pushing off with their toes. Those quasimodos had feet quite like our own, or an approximation at least. While chimpanzees and gorillas have their big toes offset much like the thumb on a hand, those of our little relatives were in line with the rest of their toes, just like ours.

In our automated world in which we think nothing of travelling hundreds of miles in a single day by car, or thousands of miles in a jet plane, it is easy to underestimate the potential of just putting one foot in front of the other and repeating the act ad nauseam. The fact remains, however, that for hundreds of thousands of years – millions of years, even – Earth's various experiments with humankind successfully reached all four corners of the globe via shanks's pony.

It was pedestrians that reached Britain first. What is remarkable, what

I often think about, is just how far some of them might have walked to get here. By the Neolithic and later, it was no longer hunters drawn by great migrating herds of animals, but pioneers and pilgrims driven by ideas, pulled by their knowledge of the existence of special places. We built them, and they came.

In a book about places, it may seem odd to have people as destinations. We have already had the Red Lady of Paviland, in south Wales, the first fully modern inhabitant of this land that we know about. But the Amesbury Archer, stark and exposed in his display case in Salisbury Museum, is a must-see among dead men.

To some eyes he will appear forlorn, tragic and vulnerable. His bones have been laid out as they were found, and there is no doubting it is an intrusion of sorts, even a desecration, to make an exhibition of him in such a way. Surely those who laid him in the ground long ago thought they were sending him on his way to another place. At the very least they might have expected his remains to rest in peace, out of sight. So the fact that he lies now under glass in a white wooden box for all to see might be troubling for those opposed to the disturbance of graves. I only speak for myself when I say he seems to me like a time traveller, here in our time with a message from his own – about how much Britain has often, and perhaps always, mattered to the wider world.

He came back into the light in 2002 when archaeologists were summoned to investigate an area of land soon to be turned into a housing development, complete with a new school. The plot was already known as the location of a Roman cemetery, but it was when attention turned to two hitherto overlooked shallow depressions in one corner of the site that events took an unexpected turn.

At first glance it seemed possible that a pair of trees had been blown over at some point in the past, leaving hollows where their root bowls had been. Excavation, however, revealed them both to be graves and much older than their Johnny-come-lately Roman neighbours. Both burials were of men – one old and one young – who had lived and died during the early part of the Bronze Age around 4,500 years ago.

The larger grave, of the elder, had been lined with wood to create a coffin of sorts. Its occupant had been laid down on his left side, curled into a semblance of the foetal position. Also described as 'crouched burials', such inhumations are strangely affecting, since the posture evokes some-one sleeping. The idea of laying down a dead loved one and taking care to have them seem as if they are only asleep, or perhaps curled inside the womb of the Earth, is profoundly moving.

The man in question had been treated to a send-off of extraordinary attention and extravagance. Around his body, carefully placed, were five pots of a style and form known to archaeologists as 'beakers'. They always remind me of Bill and Ben flowerpots, but the thinking is that they were drinking vessels. Since they occur in graves all across Europe, they have gone down as the calling card, the defining artefact indeed, of an entire Beaker *culture*. As with 'civilization', 'culture' is one of archaeology's c-words and its use is always problematic.

Beakers were certainly part of the paraphernalia of the first people in Europe to use metal things. Usually their outer surfaces feature decora-tions applied to the still-soft clay with combs or pointed sticks. Whether they went into the graves brimming with water or beer or some other fluid is anybody's guess.

It seems likely our man was put into the ground fully dressed but that the passage of time has seen to the decay and disappearance of every last vestige of his clothing. Time has laid him bare in every conceivable way. On one forearm he bore a narrow, rectangular-shaped wrist-guard fash-ioned of black stone thin as a biscuit. Another of the same, made of red stone, was laid by his knees. It was these items – worn to protect the forearm from the painful recoil of a bow-string – that persuaded the archaeologists that he had been, among other things, an archer. As well as for protection, such guards were very likely worn as badges of high status.

Also sent into eternity with him were sixteen flint arrowheads, sug-gesting that a quiver full of arrows had been laid on top of him, perhaps along with a bow. Only the arrowheads had survived the ages. There were other flint tools, worn and used, and an antler spatula of the sort used for working and shaping that particular kind of stone. Some tusks collected from wild boar were in the mix as well, along with a little ring made of shale and possibly worn as a decoration on a belt around his waist. A bone pin found among his ribs might have been the fastening for a cloak.

So far, so Stone Age, but it was the remainder of his funerary finery, in addition to the tell-tale beakers, that marked him out as a celebrity – in his own time and in ours.

The people who laid to rest the Amesbury Archer (a name quickly latched on to by the news media) also saw to it that he had three little copper knives; two tiny, wondrously exquisite gold ornaments, fine as foil, for decorating plaited hair; and a well-used 'cushion stone' – a sort of portable anvil used for finishing and burnishing items made of metal.

The Amesbury Archer had almost certainly known how to work metal. If not, then he had kept company with someone who did. He was buried so long ago he was certainly one of the first masters of the new technology to have arrived in Britain. Whoever he was, his grave is the richest, the most extravagant early Bronze Age burial found in this country so far.

He is from that time when metalworking was in its infancy. The gold and copper he possessed would have been captivating and magical for those unfamiliar with the materials. As tools, however, copper knives are of limited use. Try cutting wood with one, or keeping a sharp edge on such a blade for more than minutes at a time, and it will quickly disappoint. Even the simplest flint blade is more effective in every practical sense.

Those trinkets were, however, the literal cutting edge of a new age. Imagine seeing a metal object for the first time, handling it. Think of watching a lump of gold or copper heated over a flame until it took on the texture of butter, before turning fully liquid. Anyone seeing such magic, such alchemy – liquid metal poured into a mould before becoming solid once more and having taken on a new shape – would know they had seen the truth of the world altered and remade.

The Amesbury Archer has also been the gift that kept on giving. Analysis of his skeleton told its own story – one of chronic pain. For one thing, he had at least one dental abscess, which would have been hellishly sore to live with. He was in his middle years when he died, maybe forty, forty-five, and at some point in his adulthood he had suffered a terrible injury to his left leg that took away his kneecap and left a wound that never healed. He would have been lame for the rest of his life, limping heavily and presumably walking only with the aid of a stick or a crutch.

He would never have known it, never been aware of it, but bones in his insteps that are disarticulated in the feet of most people were fused together in his. This was a birth defect, a genetic abnormality, but one so slight it would have had no outward sign or symptom, no consequences for him in life.

You are what you eat, and as infants our teeth and skeletons take on the stuff of the landscape where our food grows, where our drinking water flows. The constituent elements of the Archer's tooth enamel revealed he had spent his early childhood not in Britain but in a colder European climate – perhaps somewhere close to the Alps.

His leg wound would have seeped with infection and given off a bad smell. His breath would have reeked too, on account of the abscess. In spite of all that – the odours, the disability – he was greatly valued and esteemed by his own folk. He had grown to adulthood as much as a thousand miles away to the south and east and then embarked on his long, long journey into the west. We cannot know if he was wounded in his homeland – and then covered all that ground in spite of his handicap – or on the way or sometime after his arrival in our islands.

The second burial, close by the first, was not nearly so well appointed, nor as richly furnished, but the man laid within had exactly the same malformation of his feet. This was beyond coincidence and so the two must have been related. The same oxygen isotope analysis of this second man's teeth revealed he had had his childhood close by where he was eventually buried, so he had not grown up in the same place as his senior. Another pair of the same golden hair dressings were found close by his lower jaw – suggesting they had either been placed inside his dead mouth or worn on a cord tight around his neck. He was in his mid-twenties when he died, half the age of the elder.

Perhaps the Amesbury Archer travelled with family and an entourage. Perhaps he found a wife here in Britain and had a son with her, a son who inherited his peculiar feet. Radiocarbon dates are notoriously hard to interpret, but for what it's worth the Amesbury Archer appears to have died some years before the younger man. The village of Amesbury is just a couple of miles south-east of Stonehenge, and the dates make it clear both men were alive during the period when the great trilithons of sarsen stones were being raised there, the finishing touches to a monument centuries in the making and remaking. The two men (father and son?) may also have been alive when other monuments in the area – Woodhenge and Durrington Walls – were still in use as well.

By then the stone circles on Orkney – Brodgar and Stenness – were already old. The idea had come from there, after all. Work was under way to create an avenue of stones leading from Stonehenge to the River Avon. Archaeologists have wondered if that narrow way was not an attempt to recreate, in stone, the natural narrow isthmus of the Ness of Brodgar. It seems there were connections all over – between Orkney and the deep south of Britain, between Britain and the Alps. People restlessly on the move.

The wealth of the Archer's send-off has inspired some to wonder if he was one of the architects of that final phase of Stonehenge. The news media went so far as to dub him the 'King of Stonehenge' and fantasized that it was his contribution to that unique monument, his vision made real and in stone, that ensured him a unique send-off when he died.

Part of the fascination of the Amesbury Archer lies too in the distance he had travelled during his life. As Stonehenge was a work in progress for hundreds of years, no doubt its fame had spread far beyond these shores and this man may have been one of those, born hundreds, even thousands of miles away, who may have heard about it and set out to see it, to benefit from time spent in its shadow. Was the Amesbury Archer already a great man in his own right when he left his home close by the Alps? Did he have greatness thrust upon him after he arrived in Britain, on account of some spectacular contribution he made here? Did he come to a Lourdes in hopes of a cure for his ills? Was he, in the end, made into a king?

15

Cantre'r Gwaelod, Borth, Ceredigion

The Welsh Atlantis

WILLIAM BUCKLAND WENT to Paviland and the cliff called Yellow Top in hopes of proving the biblical flood of Genesis had really happened – that with the exception of the contents of Noah's Ark the world had been wiped clean of all life by the wrath of God. Although he was looking for casualties in the wrong place, and certainly in the wrong slice of geological time, he might have found something more to his liking on another part of the Welsh coast and less than 100 miles north of Goat's Hole Cave.

The village of Borth lies in Cardigan Bay, 7 miles north of the market town of Aberystwyth in the mid-Wales county of Ceredigion. The whole area is so thickly stirred with myth and legend it can feel like wading through treacle. Among the favourites and best told is the story of Cantre'r Gwaelod, the Welsh Atlantis.

Several versions of the tale survive and all have elements in common so that a person is forced to wonder if some fragments of truth are not folded into the mix along with all the rest. Cantre'r Gwaelod means 'the Lowland Hundred' and recalls a time when land there was parcelled into units that, depending on who you listen to, either contained a hundred settlements or might have been called upon to provide a hundred fighting men for the local king in time of war, or perhaps both.

By some accounts Cantre'r Gwaelod was, as recently as the sixth century, part of Gwyddno Garanhir's kingdom of Meirionnydd. That fabled region, close by the sea, was the real prize, coveted by all and sundry. Especially fertile, it was said any acre there was worth half a dozen elsewhere. Like anything and everything worth having, however, it demanded constant vigilance. Cantre'r Gwaelod was so low-lying its very survival depended upon the maintenance of dykes that protected it from the sea. At low tide a set of sluice gates was opened to allow the land to drain, and woe betide anyone who neglected to close them again before the waves returned.

One version of the legend places responsibility for the gates in the hands of a watchman named Seithennin and has him attend a party in Gwyddno's castle, where he drinks too much wine and then falls asleep at his post. Another gives the job to a lovely maiden called Mererid and casts Seithennin as a visiting king, a neighbour and rival of Gwyddno, who lures her into a tryst that has her quite forget her duties regarding the gates and the tide. Either way, the result is the same. Someone took their eye off the ball at the crucial moment. The tide rushed hungrily through the open sluice gates and that which was of incalculable value was lost for ever beneath the waves of Cardigan Bay. Gwyddno and his people had to run for their lives and later, having lost the Lowland Hundred (cast out, as it were, from their latter-day Eden), had to work for their living on poorer land to the east.

As you might expect, they do say in those parts that on quiet nights when the sea is calm you can hear the bells of the churches of Cantre'r Gwaelod tolling in the deep, calling back their folk.

A myth then in a land of myths, but there is a twist.

Borth today is a pretty little place, a quiet seaside village blessed with a long, golden curl of sandy beach. The estuary of the River Dyfi is close and visible from higher ground nearby. Any would-be visitor interested in glimpsing evidence of the Welsh Atlantis should consult some tide tables in advance – it is an especially low tide that is required. There is an element of luck involved as well, since the sand is always on the move and what might be revealed one week or one month will be entirely concealed from view the next.

But go at just the right time, when all the elements are lined up in your favour, and out on the sands there is a wonder to behold. I had the good fortune to walk out on to Borth beach just days after a series of spring storms had stripped away great swathes of sand. From a distance I thought I was seeing the carcasses of giant sea creatures – leatherback turtles come to grief in their hundreds, perhaps. Closer inspection revealed them to be the massive stumps of trees – the remains of a whole forest.

Oak, pine, alder, hazel and birch – all the makings of the sort of mixed woodland that cloaked Britain for the millennia before the coming of farming (or more particularly the coming of farmers, with their axes and with fire). Before there were waves in Cardigan Bay, there was a forest. When it was alive and growing, the coastline may have been as much as 20 miles further to the west. Analysis of the exposed timber reveals the trees died sometime between 4,500 and 6,000 years ago, overtaken by an ancient inundation by the sea. After the coming of the sea, peat grew on the saturated land until the ruined forest was submerged, like the Céide Fields, beneath an anaerobic blanket that held at bay all the processes of decay.

As you approach the stumps, it is easy to imagine they might be fossils – that they could have survived beneath the sea for so long only by having been turned to stone. But in fact the truth is stranger and the timber is still soft to the touch, still wood. The growth rings are clear to see and the overwhelming sensation is of being in the presence of trees that have only recently been felled. I would have sworn I could smell resin close by the pines. I wandered among them in a daze and could not stop hunkering down by one after another to feel their texture, which had about it, even after all those thousands of years, the stuff of life.

There is more submerged forest to be seen around 1½ miles to the north, at Ynyslas, which means 'the Blue Island'. There the peat is still much in evidence, the ancient trees and roots still partially or wholly submerged within the conditions that have preserved them for so long.

South of Borth, close to Clarach Bay, is a place called Wallog. Step on to the pebble beach there and you spot what looks like the early stages of the construction of a wide road leading straight out into the sea. It even seems to have a camber to it. This is Sarn Gynfelyn, a shingle spit left behind as the ice receded at the end of the last ice age, perhaps 15,000 years ago. Gynfelyn is the most southerly of three such *sarnau* that reach out into Cardigan Bay. It stretches for around 8 miles, most of it underwater, before terminating against a submerged reef.

Wholly natural features though the *sarnau* are, products of geological forces and processes, it is no wonder they seemed to our ancestors like massive man-made features – just the sort of walls and dykes that would have been required to keep the sea out of a kingdom like Cantre'r Gwaelod.

In January 2014, Borth beach was hit by yet more storms that stripped away acres of sand. Sensing an opportunity, two archaeologists took a stroll and found a stretch of ancient timber walkway. Built of short strips of coppiced branches fixed in place by evenly spaced vertical posts, it was laid down perhaps 4,000 years ago. Walkways of this sort were built by our ancestors whenever they had to adapt to moving around in environments that were becoming increasingly waterlogged.

The real wonder of Cantre'r Gwaelod, the Welsh Atlantis, is its demonstration of the reach of folk memory. However the legends may have come down to us, like fairytales for children the truth they contain feels as vital as the timber of those tree stumps. The story of the flood is universal – folded into the foundation myths of one civilization after another around the world. Inundations like that in Cardigan Bay may well have happened quickly – during the course of a single lifetime or even less. Loss of land to the sea is traumatic, forcing people to change their lives, to abandon territories colonized long before by their ancestors. Such events were always remembered and then passed down through the generations. In the face of climate change, global warming and the rest, present-day populations may well have to make similar adjustments. Maybe there is some comfort to be had in knowing that it has all happened before.

16

Geevor Tin Mine, Pendeen, Cornwall

The Cassiterides and the rise of bronze

TIN WAS COOKED and made in the hearts of stars much more massive than our sun. In terms of abundance it comes in at number 49 on the list of the ninety-odd elements occurring naturally in the crust of our Earth. Oxygen is number 1, aluminium number 3. In short, there is not, nor has there ever been, a lot of tin about.

In the ancient world – the one populated by Egyptians, Phoenicians, Greeks, Romans and the like – it was definitely hard to come by. They knew about deposits of the stuff in territory between those countries we call Germany and the Czech Republic, in the Iberian Peninsula and also in Brittany. It may have been available in a handful of other places besides. It seems quite conceivable, however, that in those long-lost days the most plentiful source of tin – that elusive metal upon which the ancient world depended for its bronze weapons and tools – was right here, in Britain's far south-west, in Devon and Cornwall. In the fifth century BC, the Greek historian Herodotus wrote about 'the Cassiterides', the tin islands, 'from which we are said to have our tin'. *Kassiteros* is the Greek word for tin, and as far as Herodotus was concerned those tin islands probably lay off the north-west coast of Europe. He was well travelled, having walked across much of the empire of the Persians, through Egypt and Babylon, Libya and Syria. He had also ventured north of the Danube and on into the east, along the north coast of the Black Sea, into Russia and across the Don, and on to Kazakhstan. He must have been gone from home for years and yet, as far as we can know, he never got anywhere near the Cassiterides. That he knew about them, wrote about them, suggests he must have acquired his knowledge from others who had – traders and other travellers.

To make matters even less convenient for all concerned, tin does not occur on Earth in a pure form – in nuggets like copper does, or gold. Instead it is always bonded to other elements and must be freed, by fiery heat, from within the black ore called cassiterite. The Cornish flag, with a white cross on a black background, honours not just Christianity but also the appearance of pure white tin from within black rock.

Copper was and is much more readily available than tin, coming in at number 26 on the list of elements – ahead of cerium at 27 and behind zinc at 25. As a material for tools it is fairly hopeless (too soft, as was surely known to the Amesbury Archer, owner of three copper knives), but when it is mixed with tin in the right proportions, magic happens, or rather bronze does.

When copper and tin are brought together in a ratio of about nine to one, the result is a wondrous, wonderful metal. Later in the story of the British Isles, and the world, it would be all about iron, by mass the most common element in the Earth's outer core. Iron is everywhere – in every farmer's field, common as muck. Anyone can dig around and find iron ore somewhere relatively close to hand. Bronze is elite, a treasure in its own right, and for thousands of years the civilizations of the ancient world were transfixed by it. Making it, having it, demanded sophistication of thought and action – aspiration and inspiration in equal parts.

Bronze is about connections between places and people, even over huge distances. If you needed copper or tin – or both – then you had to make contact somehow with those who had them. There was power to be had in dominating its few sources and influence to be wielded by having the ear of those who knew a man who could get it for you. Iron let people remain aloof from one another, but bronze forced them to come together and cooperate.

Tin, because it mixes so readily with other elements, is called by metallurgists a 'sociable' metal – it is pleasingly apposite.

Bronze looks better than iron, anyway – warm and golden when newly cast, instead of cold and grey. Flamboyant rather than utilitarian, bronze has panache. It is not merely beaten into shape, it is a marriage, a love match. Copper and tin, bride and groom, must lie on a bed of white-hot coals until they come together as one, a river too bright to look upon, before flowing, sparking and hissing in their union, into a mould from which, seconds later, a sword is drawn, still glowing and much too hot to touch until it is plunged into cold water.

Watch that living tongue of molten metal dart into the mould, its hot smell like something newly baked, and then see a glowing bronze sword drawn from that stone and instantly – *instantly* – you understand why the legend of King Arthur's Excalibur is eternal. No wonder they say he came from Tintagel in Cornwall. No wonder these British Isles – the Cassiterides, the tin islands – were burned into the consciousness of the world from the very beginning.

Dolly Pentreath, of Mousehole in Cornwall, died in 1777. She is generally regarded as having been the last native speaker of the Cornish language – the last for whom it was a first language. She told people she spoke not a word of English until she was in her twenties. You might say Cornish is a dead language, but more recently it has been resuscitated as people piece it together again from texts and old recordings.

In a pub in St Ives I met a local who was in the process of learning Cornish. Among other phrases I picked up that day (and I can only apologize here for my phonetic spelling) was 'Pinta coreff gweer, marplek.' This, I was assured, meant 'A pint of beer, please.'

Better yet – much better – I learned the Cornish name for St Michael's Mount. That lovely little tidal island, in Mount's Bay by Marazion in far south-west Cornwall, is thick with history in its own right. Most famously it is topped, wedding-cake style, by a monastery built by Benedictine monks first in the twelfth century and then again in the fourteenth after the first was destroyed by an earthquake. It is linked, in spirit at least, to Le Mont Saint-Michel, its prissier, fussier twin in Brittany.

But long, long before it bore the prosaic moniker of St Michael's Mount, Cornish speakers knew it as *Carreg luz en kuz* – 'the Hoar Rock in the Woods'. That means the Cornish language – fruit of the same branch that gives us Welsh, Irish and Gaelic – remembers a time before whichever post-glacial rise in sea level turned a rock surrounded by a forest into an island. Phoenician merchants moored their ships alongside St Michael's Mount 3,500 years ago while they took aboard cargoes of Cornish tin bound for the Mediterranean world and beyond. It has been an island for a very, very long time and yet the old language of the place, the first language of the place, remembers it all so differently. It is an example of how deep the roots of the British Isles are. Blackened with age, they reach down through everything, even the hardest rock, and have a hold on these islands that will not be broken.

Cassiterite, the tin ore, reaches down through the pitilessly hard granite of Cornwall like more black roots. It is likely that veins of it were spotted early on by people in boats and ships off the coast. Looking back at the cliffs they would have seen the tell-tale lines – usually black, sometimes purple. Where there was copper in the mix too, the giveaway of treasure within may have been streaks of green, verdigris. In any event, those who knew what they were looking for would have been drawn to Cornwall in search of those metals that were so precious to them.

Geevor Mine, beside wild cliffs overlooking the Atlantic Ocean, has nothing at all about it of the prehistoric. It was opened only towards the end of the eighteenth century, by a wholly modern world, but it offers a glimpse of a much older need, an older hunger.

Now Geevor is a tourist attraction and visitors can take a tour underground, down the shaft and into the tunnels and chambers. There, where water drips and flows ceaselessly and the light is that which you bring down from above, you may wonder at the working conditions that were endured right up into the modern era. The tiny spaces, constantly running with dark wet; the claustrophobic proximity of the sea itself. Geevor may not be prehistoric, but it is a burrowing among ancient roots.

Cassiterite often has a form of arsenic in its mix that oxidizes and leaks out into the air when the ore is exposed to the atmosphere or heated. As if the mining of the stuff were not dangerous enough already.

Once freed from the ore, though, tin is ethereally lovely. An ingot of it is as bright as silver and startlingly soft, so that it can be bent easily in the

The Ness of Brodgar, Orkney. Five thousand years ago a farming community embarked upon a building project. It would occupy them, and their descendants, for a millennium.

Cantre'r Gwaelod, Ceredigion – the Welsh Atlantis. Stumps of ancient trees, all that remains of a forest swallowed long ago by the sea.

Dún Aengus, Inishmore. An Iron Age fortress teeters on the brink of oblivion, at the edge of the world.

Roman baths, Bath – home to Sulis Minerva, goddess of wisdom and well-being.

Lullingstone Roman Villa, Kent, where a fourth-century Roman family hedged its bets, hiding Christian symbols within the pagan imagery of an elaborate mosaic.

*Bamburgh Castle, Northumberland
– Joyous Gard, refuge of Lancelot,
bravest and best of Arthur's knights.*

hands. Hold it close to your ear as you do so and you will hear what is called 'the cry of the tin' – a high-pitched squealing, as though the metal were complaining about the abuse.

All commercial mining stopped at Geevor in the early 1990s, due to the falling price of ore and the rising costs of keeping the place open. But put yourself there, with the booming of the ocean nearby and the smell of salt in the air and caught among the tussocky grass, and know that you are in the Cassiterides, right enough – the tin islands, imagined by Herodotus, known to the Phoenicians and the Romans, and upon which the ancient world depended for thousands of years. Without Cornish tin, the world would have worked out altogether differently.

17

Great Orme, Llandudno, Clwyd

The marriage of copper and tin

JUST AS THESE islands offered the old world its richest source of tin, so they possessed copper as well. A world lifting itself up with a scaffold of bronze looked north and west for the makings of a great deal of it. There were supplies of both metals in other places, but the archipelago set apart in the ocean at the edge of the known world offered them together.

The name the place has today was the choice of Vikings. In Old Norse, *ormr* was a worm or a serpent. Viewed from the prow of a longboat, the headland that thrusts north and west from the coast of what we know as north Wales might well have had something of the look of a giant serpent swimming out to sea.

Long before the Vikings – thousands of years before – people found copper in the bedrock there. The ancestors were accustomed to looking around them for sources of stone they could use for one thing or another. Once the technology of metalworking had been acquired, copper rose to prominence. Along that north-facing coastline those early geologists will have spotted the verdigris staining of copper deposits. No doubt some native copper – naturally occurring nuggets of the stuff – was available on the surface or revealed in waterways, but eventually a few of their number started chasing veins of green and blue malachite ore down into the darkness underground.

For people equipped in the main with beach pebbles and animal bones, mining into the limestone would have been painfully slow. Burrowing into rock, inch by inch, yard by yard, sounds like a labour for Sisyphus. Despite the hardship and the challenge, however, the copper mine at Great Orme yielded so much of the precious metal that it became the largest and most important in the world.

For long it was assumed there was no mining for metal ore in these isles until the arrival of the Romans in the first half of the first century AD. Radiocarbon dates obtained from bone tools unearthed in the Great Orme mine reveal it was already a busy and productive place nearly 4,000 years ago. Copper ore was still being mined there in the eighteenth and nineteenth centuries – activity that had hidden the ancient workings from view. It was only in the 1980s, when a site was being cleared to make a car park, that archaeologists and surveyors had the chance to explore what was there. Almost at once it became obvious that the modern mining had been preceded by millennia of earlier workings. It took five years of labour to empty, by hand, a Bronze Age chamber that had been deliberately backfilled with rock. Once it was cleared, it was revealed as the largest prehistoric man-made chamber anywhere in the world – every cubic foot of it dug out with nothing more than stones and bones. So far, something like 5 miles of tunnels have been mapped by archaeologists. The few hundred yards that are open to the public amount to just 3 per cent of what is known to be down there, and the full extent of the Bronze Age workings is yet to be revealed.

Since the miners simply followed the malachite ore, the tunnels twist and coil through the limestone like veins and arteries through a body. Clad in boilersuit and rubber boots, with a miner's hard hat and lamp on my head, I crawled through one such ancient burrow. No more than a couple of feet in diameter, it felt more like an excavation made by a rabbit or a badger than anything dug out by a fellow human being. As I struggled along, sometimes having to lie on my side or, worst of all, flat on my back with my nose brushing the roof, I tried to imagine what it must have been like for the man, woman or indeed – given the size of it – the child who had dug it out in the first place. Armed with no more than a lamp of animal fat, a few animal rib bones and a pebble small enough to be gripped in the hand, that poor soul spent hours, days, weeks nudging forward into the dark. At any time there must have been the threat of a roof collapse or of becoming jammed in a space too small to manoeuvre any further. As I type these words I can still remember the sound of the fabric of my boiler-suit scraping over the rock, my toes flailing inside my boots for purchase.

Mining was carried on at Great Orme for century after century. The archaeologists have calculated that during the Bronze Age around 1,700 tons of copper metal were produced from the ore there – enough to make ten million axe heads. There are good reasons for thinking the ancient mining operation within that giant, serpent-shaped headland was nothing less than the largest industrial site of the old world and its discovery caused scholars to rethink the entire period.

That ancient world – the one in thrall to bronze – needed the British Isles. Those in control of the tin in Cornwall, the copper in north Wales, would have grown rich and powerful. Tools and weapons made of our bronze would have been traded all across the European continent and beyond. Impressed though I am by the great age of it all, the scale of the enterprise, it is the magical transformation of ore into metal and how it would have appeared to someone seeing it for the first time 4,000 years ago that is most affecting. I put myself in the place of that someone, who had known only the making of tools of stone, bone, antler and wood – and imagine the impact that magic would have made.

18

The Dover Boat,
Dover Museum, Kent

Bronze Age shipbuilding

THE WHITE CLIFFS of Dover, made of the shells of trillions upon trillions of sea creatures that lived and died aeons ago in a long-lost sea, might be the most recognizable symbol of England. Since they are constantly eroded, nibbled like the end of a giant bar of Kendal Mint Cake, the white is always alabaster bright. Like nothing else could be, they are a symbol of home for millions of inhabitants of these islands. A first sight of them also leaves newcomers in no doubt about where they are headed – for the White Cliffs of Dover shine bright and clear in the imaginations even of those who have never seen them. Nat Burton, who co-wrote Vera Lynn's 1942 song about bluebirds flying over them, was an American who had never left home, but he still got the message.

If the cliffs were not symbol enough, they are topped at Dover itself by a castle built in the twelfth century by Henry II and known as the 'key to England'. Beneath the castle, and burrowed into the chalk for miles all around, are tunnels cut to house defenders of these islands through the ages. The cliff and castle are not just about England, either. The Battle of Britain – *Britain* – saw to that. When imagining a dogfight between a Spitfire and a Messerschmitt in that summer of 1940, it is hard not to picture cliffs of white below, as well as a blue sky above.

Just as the chalk is porous, allowing for much coming and going, so too is the port of Dover, the busiest ferry terminal in the world. Dover is synonymous with the idea of travelling, of having somewhere to go, some place to be. It is fitting, then, that the finest example of Bronze Age shipbuilding revealed so far was found preserved there in the shadow of those cliffs.

In 1992, when a new road was being built between Dover and Folkestone, archaeologists were called in to see if any worthwhile traces of Dover's past might be exposed in a deep trench that would, eventually, carry a pedestrian underpass. Sure enough, there were bits and bobs of a medieval town wall and then, beneath that, masonry from a Roman harbour. But as is often the case with rescue archaeology, when developers just want to get on with the job and the time for excavation is tight, the best was saved for last.

Protruding from the sticky, waterlogged clay that had preserved it for all of 3,500 years was the exposed edge of a timber boat. Hurriedly but carefully removed (cut into ten pieces, in fact, and later reassembled) was the unutterably mesmerizing wonder that became known as the Dover Boat. The ravages of time that had been held at bay by the clay were thwarted again by immersing the recovered pieces in liquid wax that permeated the timber. Freeze-dried and then placed within a giant, bespoke, air-conditioned display case, it may well last for ever. And just as well, because it is a priceless, irreplaceable glimpse of what our ancestors were all about a millennium and a half before the birth of Christ.

Like a stubborn tooth, the Dover Boat was not extracted entire; around half had to be left behind. It is estimated that the complete vessel was 60 feet long – and the 30 feet of it that sits now in splendid isolation in a darkly glowing glass box in Dover Museum is enough to take the breath away. It is what archaeologists call a sewn-plank boat. It is not a dug-out canoe, neither is it held together by pegs or nails like a more modern, clinker-built wooden vessel. Instead its makers cut and shaped four long oak planks and then literally sewed them together with 'withies' – thin branches of willow or similarly flexible wood. It is mesmerizing, because every inch, every foot of the thing, bears the imprint of its makers. The cut marks are plain to see, the efforts made with tools of stone and bronze.

The Dover Boat must have been commissioned by someone of high status and prestige. As well as the wherewithal for the making of it, he or she would have needed to command the services of strong men to power it. There is no evidence of a mast, and so it would have been rowed with oars. Much of the caulking that kept it watertight is still in place, but it would certainly have leaked just the same. Think of crossing the North Sea or the English Channel in a leaking craft, lying low in the water under the weight of rowers, passengers and cargo, probably with bailer in hand to help keep at bay the seeping seawater.

Just as there are places in the landscape that feel 'thin', where the divide between one world and the next seems slight, so an artefact like the Dover Boat seems to carry some trace of those that thought of her and made her. You might even say the thing is haunted, or that its own presence lingers like smoke from a fire just extinguished. While I stood and crouched beside her, I swear I felt her makers' ghosts close by. The hairs rose on my neck and arms and I strained as though to hear some whispered words. I am not making this up.

Marks on the timber and withies suggest that at some point its owner decided to be rid of it or else to give it back. Axes or other sharp edges had been used to cut through the ties, so that the whole was no longer intact. The vessel appeared to have been deliberately scuttled. Where the archaeologists found the boat, they saw traces of an ancient stream, long since silted up and lost. It seemed likely that, rather than an accidental loss, the boat had been rowed into some tributary and then sunk, drowned perhaps, or otherwise put out of sight and out of reach. Since it would have been a prized and expensive possession, its destruction may represent the settling of a debt. Having served its purpose in the world of humankind for long enough, its timbers were given back to the earth and water from which they had once sprung.

Just as it is today, the port of Dover has been a place of arrival and departure for thousands of years. Long before the town we know now, long before the coming of the Romans, Vikings and Normans, long before the avaricious eyes of any Napoleon Bonaparte or Adolf Hitler, the Dover Boat was waiting, knowing what it knows. No object from the story of the British Isles is more worthwhile. It is the single most moving, most affecting, most inspiring leftover from the past I have ever seen. As long as I live, whatever else I stand in the presence of, I will never forget it.

19

Llyn Fawr, Cynon Valley, Mid-Glamorgan

Reflections of another world

'FOR NOW, WE see through a glass darkly . . .' it says in the Bible, 'but then face to face. Now I know in part, but then shall I know even as also I am known.'

There is, and always has been, something strange and unfamiliar – magical, even – about the reflected world. In a reflection we see a world reversed, where left is right and right is left; a world the same, yet not the same.

The thinking goes that, among much else, those lines from 1 Corinthians 13:12 recall a time when mirrors were made not of glass but of polished metal – bronze or perhaps silver. Modern glass mirrors, coated on their backs with a thin film of aluminium, provide a bright and perfect image. Those made in antiquity, however, no matter how well polished the metal, could have offered up only a shaded reflection of reality. The image might have been recognizable enough, but always dark, and therefore different, as if of something slightly other.

In 2001, archaeologists excavating the wonderfully named site of Wetwang Slack in East Yorkshire discovered the remains of a woman buried along with a dismantled chariot. She and it had gone into the ground around 300 BC. Given the richness and complexity of her burial, she was undoubtedly of high status. Behind her head was found, among other treasures, a bronze mirror. It is possible it had to do with vanity, but it seems more likely that the mirror had been a tool she used for looking into another world. In the same way, Dr John Dee, astrologer, philosopher and mathematician, and remembered by history as magician to Queen Elizabeth I, kept a black mirror made of obsidian, now on display in the British Museum. It had come from the kingdom of the Aztecs, and Dee employed 'skryers', or mediums, to look into its dark surface in the hopes of communicating with angels and other spirits. It seems reasonable to imagine the often-indistinct reflections in such simple mirrors invoking all manner of ideas.

For most of our ancestors, though, a glimpse of their reflection could have been gleaned not from a mirror but only from the still surface of water – in bowls, or in puddles, quiet rivers and deep lakes.

Llyn Fawr, a reservoir now, was in ages past a natural lake, a dark mirror lying in the shadow cast by the steep north face of the ridge of Craig-y-Llyn. Work on the reservoir began in 1913 and it was discoveries made by the workmen then that put the place on the world map. In all, around sixty artefacts were found – every one a precious item that had been deliberately dispatched into the darkness of the lake as long ago as 800 years before the birth of Christ.

Most of them were made of bronze – axes, a spearhead, razors, sickles, horse-tack. Most extravagant of all was a huge cauldron, a beautiful and cleverly made exotic, probably an import from somewhere in central Europe and big enough to cook food for hundreds of people at a time. As well as those bronze items, there were also two made of iron – a sickle and a sword – so that the so-called Llyn Fawr Hoard seems to sit at a technological crossroads. Clearly the people were well used to bronze, but they were also in the process of adopting the new metal, for good or ill.

Depositing precious things in water was a tradition that lasted for hundreds of years at least. The explanation for it is still up for grabs, but most archaeologists agree it was about making offerings to the inhabitants of another realm – gods, spirits, ancestors – in return for good fortune, victory in battle. Sacrifices made now might shape the future, a time that does not yet exist, in our favour. The dark surface of a lake like Llyn Fawr may have been regarded as an entrance to that realm.

Although the Llyn Fawr artefacts were mostly in good condition when they went into the water, it was also common practice to bend such offerings in half, or even to break them into pieces. It seems to have been about making it clear that a time had come when they had to be put completely beyond the use of humankind. From that point on they were the possessions of gods, or ghosts, and therefore irrecoverable.

The best thing about a place like Llyn Fawr is that it brings us face to face with ancient thinking. The people who bothered to take some of their valuable belongings and send them to a watery grave – either placing them gently there or, like King Arthur, hurling them, over-arm, into the deep – were just like us in every physical sense. And yet their understanding of the cosmos and their place within it was quite different.

Perhaps the dark, calm surface of a lake – sometimes reflecting the sky, sometimes their own faces, sometimes just an implacable, impenetrable black plane – was regarded with trepidation, fear. Also fascinating is how the items were left there for eternity. Those who put them in the water knew they were there, so too their neighbours, their descendants. That such valuable treasures were left alone for all time – that it was accepted they had gone elsewhere and were out of reach – says a great deal about the depth and strength of the belief.

Overseeing all such practices – as far as we can tell from the works of Roman writers who came here in the first century BC – was a class of highly educated polymaths. According to no less a figure than Julius Caesar, behind the thrones of whichever kings ruled the territories of the late Bronze Age and early Iron Age British Isles were the Druids.

Caesar had already encountered their sort in Gaul. They were astronomers, healers, historians, mathematicians, philosophers, theologians. It appears they were even trained in a form of law. But he had learned from the Gaulish Druids that the wellspring of their thinking – their beating heart – lay here in the British Isles. According to Caesar, those Druids who wanted to finish their education, to reach the highest levels of their calling, came here for what might be regarded as their Master's degrees. 'This institution [Druidism] is supposed to have been devised in Britain, and to have been brought over from it into Gaul,' wrote Caesar. 'And now those who desire to gain a more accurate knowledge of that system generally proceed thither for the purpose of studying it.'

Llyn Fawr – and more particularly the hoard that made it famous – can only have come early in the story of the Druids. Caesar and the rest of the literate observers arrived here many hundreds of years after the ripples created by the last offering made to the mirror there had smoothed and gone. But it is a perfect setting. The surface of the water is ever-changing. The steep slope of Craig y Llyn casts a long shadow. By the time iron was replacing bronze as the material for weapons and tools of all sorts, there was another reason to come to these islands. Here was wisdom.

20

Dún Aengus and Dún Dúchathair Forts, Inishmore

At the end of the Earth

FOR THE LONGEST time, travellers and migrants, hunters and gatherers following the setting sun across Europe and then across these British Isles found the end of the line on the west coast of the island we know as Ireland. Whoever they were – whatever species or experiment with humankind, from *Homo erectus* to *Homo heidelbergensis* to *Homo neanderthalensis* to us – eventually they came there. Some had followed the herds of animals upon which their lives depended – horses, deer, mammoths. No doubt others only followed in the footsteps of their fellows who had gone that way before, but all were drawn inexorably towards this place and found in the end it was as far as they could go.

Some of them came early enough that it was possible to walk dry-shod into what was then still that peninsula of north-west Europe; for those who came later, it was necessary to put to sea in little boats that let them cross the Channel or some part of the North Sea to the island of Britain. Then from the coast of western Scotland there were ways to leapfrog from dry land to dry land across to Ireland. Those who reached its farthest coast must have let their arms drop to their sides at the impossible enormity of what lay before them, roaring and raging. Look out from Ireland's west coast and, now as then, 2,500 miles of Atlantic Ocean separate you from the next landfall on the eastern seaboard of North America. When the wind is blowing and the swell is big, I do not think the world-sea anywhere has bigger muscles, more dark intent, more justified determination in saying to us, 'That's far enough – stop right there.'

Some of the people who made their way here and stayed saw fit to build the forts of Dún Aengus and Dún Dúchathair on the Aran Islands, out in the sea to the west of Galway. It was 2,500 years ago and at that time those islands clung like barnacles to the outer edge of the Iron Age.

Inishmore – the largest of them – and then Inishmaan and Inisheer are like flat stones, or maybe oyster shells, set skimming by small boys and come to rest on the sea, all in a row, without sinking. Flat and treeless, they lie here at the mercy of the ocean, with a view towards the west unlike anywhere else in the British Isles. From the west-facing cliffs, the sea has the look of living flesh, albeit blue flesh – a snake's maybe, or a sea monster's, pulsing with the rhythms of life.

Travel to the fractured, battered western edge of Inishmore today and there you will find the ancient fort of Dún Aengus. It is a tourist attraction, and no wonder. You approach the place over shattered plains of limestone, flat as deliberate paving but worn out now. Greenery of one sort or another maintains a foothold here and there, but it is the flat, pale rock, level as a pavement, that you notice most. Ancient weak spots and fractures have been exploited by the elements to erode long straight cracks and gullies a foot deep where little plants take shelter. Geologists name the fissures 'grykes' and call the landscape 'karst' – descriptive of limestone that is being slowly dissolved by the carbon dioxide in rainwater. You can almost hear the place fizzing. Here and there little slabs of the same limestone have been broken from the bedrock and flipped upright by the wind, some of them catching in the cracks so that they look like the makings of a clumsy border, only knee high and set in place by someone who never returned to finish the job. All of it – the exposure to the ocean, the weather and the rock – has made for a particular sort of inhabitant on the Aran Isles and from time to time the more lyrical among them have described their feelings for the place.

'I was born on a storm-swept rock and hate the soft growth of sunbaked lands where there is no frost in men's bones,' wrote Liam Ó Flaithearta, poet, novelist and early communist, born on Inishmore in 1896. 'Swift thought and the flight of ravenous birds, and the squeal of hunted animals are, to me, reality.'

Or this from John Millington Synge, a posh Protestant lad from Rathfarnham, County Dublin, who recuperated on the Aran Islands after a bout of illness and wrote upon leaving: 'The sort of yearning I feel towards those lonely rocks is indescribably acute. The islands are fading already and I can hardly realise that the smell of the seaweed and the drone of the Atlantic are still moving around them.'

Dún Aengus was built around the middle of the first millennium BC. The process of possessing land there may have been started by people equipped with tools made of bronze and then finished by others who had by then acquired iron. What is visible now is largely the product of rebuilding by Victorian work gangs – a combined heritage-restoration and job-creation scheme. The brutalist wall of stone that dominates the landscape for miles around stands the best part of 20 feet high, with internal chambers, stairways and a wall-top wide enough for several people to walk abreast. Viewed from above, that massive C-shaped curl of drystone wall seems, at first sight, designed only to defend a lonely, barren patch of cliff top.

It looks like quite a prospect – to stand with your back to a 300-foot sheer cliff and the sea beyond and look out over that curving rampart towards the flat land and whoever or whatever was approaching across it. In fact, there is not just one surviving wall but four, each encompassing a wider area than the last so that from above they have the look of a set of irregularly placed, roughly concentric arches, or a comically raised eyebrow. In restoring it, the Victorians were sympathetic to the existing footprint and in the main made use only of the stones that had slumped from the original. Dún Aengus, as far as we can tell, is a faithful reconstruction of what was once there.

It is none the less a hard site to understand. A person might look at the set-up, the effort involved in the construction, and get the sense of some desperate last stand, when all else was lost and some ancient people had found their empire cut back to just the few acres of land they could hive off behind a massive wall, their backs protected by the thundering sea. You would have to wonder what on earth they thought they were defending themselves against.

Another of these so-called promontory forts, quite near but in an even more godforsaken spot, provides some clues to the mystery. Not far from Dún Aengus is Dún Dúchathair, 'the Black Fort'. Like Dún Aengus, it occupies a position that is beyond precarious. More karst, more grykes trail out on to a pointed, flat-topped headland shaped like a broken fingernail. The drop to the sea is sheer all round, a height of around 65 feet.

Incongruously, the neck of the headland is cut right across, as though by a grey torc, by another great wall of stone. Like Dún Aengus, the wall was restored by the Victorians – but again they were only tidying and making good again that which had already stood against the elements for two millennia and more. Here the feeling of bleakness is even stronger. Within the space set aside by the wall, there are the circular shapes of beehive chambers – spaces for living or storage. But the overwhelming feeling to be had inside Dún Dúchathair is futility. Why spend hundreds, thousands of hours erecting a wall to give you nothing but a fingertip of barren land thrust out towards the unforgiving ocean?

I had the great good fortune to visit the Black Fort with geologist Michael Williams. Now sadly passed away, Michael was professor of earth and ocean sciences at the National University of Ireland in Galway. He was one of those academics who breathed so much life into his subject, who was evidently having so much fun thinking about it all, that it made a person wish they had chosen his subject of study and not their own.

We walked around inside Dún Dúchathair and Michael showed me, near the cliff edge, great piles of slabs that appeared as though they had been dumped, unceremoniously, off the back of a lorry. In fact, he said, they had been tossed there by the sea. Many – and there were hundreds of them – weighed as much as 7 tons and yet they had been snapped off the cliff edge and flipped like tiddlywinks by the massive waves that so often afflict the western faces of the Aran Islands. They were, he explained, evidence of the rate (and the sheer scale) of erosion that has taken its toll on the promontory and the rest of the sea-facing land there for the last 2,500 years.

Michael pointed out the main obstacle in the way of understanding why Dún Dúchathair and Dún Aengus were built. 'The mistake we're making, I think, is looking at this fort in the context of today,' he said, 'whereas we should be looking at it in the context of, say, 2,500 years ago when it may have been built in the first place.'

Courtesy of the mighty Atlantic Ocean, the Aran Islands are being worn away at the ferocious rate of perhaps a foot and a half each year. In short, when those Iron Age farmers built their fort – a central, defensive point in the heart of their territory, perhaps – the cliff edge may have been as much as two thirds of a mile further to the west.

Dún Dúchathair, Dún Aengus – they are only the worn-down, ground-down stumps of the circular structures they once were. The ocean came for them. And it will not be stopped by anyone or anything.

21

The Roman Baths, Bath, Somerset

The arrival of the modern world

WHEN YOU GET right down to it, the Roman invasion of Britain was driven by two politicians on the make.

Disinclined to return to Rome after his conquest of Gaul, Gaius Julius Caesar took a first crack at the place in 55 BC. For a great general it was a poorly executed manoeuvre. Although word of his efforts across the great ocean earned him the praise of the senate back in Rome, as an invasion it amounted to little. He tried again the following year, made more of a dent in the hastily assembled defences of the Britons, but then turned his back on the islands for a second time. More trouble than they were worth.

For all that the British Isles remained unconquered, the connections to Rome were already established – and anyway pre-dated any of Caesar's designs on the place. The influence of Rome and the rest of the classical world had been as subtle and irresistible as the process of osmosis. Various tribes, notionally secure in their island fortress, had none the less seen the benefits of becoming clients of the empire, and so Roman ways had crept across the land like damp.

Less than a hundred years after Caesar's fumblings, in AD 41, Tiberius Claudius was made emperor after the assassination of his nephew, Caligula. Slightly built, deaf and with a limp, he hardly cut an impressive figure. Since he had gained power after what was effectively a palace coup, he felt the need of some gory glory to improve his standing in front of the proles, as well as in the eyes of men of power and influence.

Commius, chief of the Atrebates in territory we know as Hampshire, had been a willing accomplice and then a puppet of Caesar, who had encountered him first in Gaul and then used him as a go-between to try to secure the cooperation of the British tribes. When one of Commius's descendants, Verica, a ruler in his own right, came crying to Claudius about having been bullied off his throne by a rival tribe, the bellicose Catuvellauni, the new emperor saw an opportunity. In AD 43 he dispatched four legions – as many as 20,000 men – under the command of Aulus Plautius, an experienced general and senator. The Kentish locals put up a stout defence but were routed soon enough, as was everyone else.

Much of the heavy lifting was done by Vespasian, a young general then but en route to becoming emperor himself. Having been decisive in the early battles for control of the Medway and Thames rivers, Vespasian was tasked next with subduing the tribes of the south-west. In so doing he took control of the ports and harbours along the south coast, and also the tin, lead and silver mines of Somerset and Cornwall. Claudius followed in his army's victorious wake and was present for the capture of Colchester, the principal stronghold of the Catuvellauni. In the end, he spent only sixteen days in these islands before returning to Rome in triumph, but the die was cast. Although anything you might justifiably call conquest would take another thirty years and neither Scotland nor Ireland would ever be properly subdued, still the empire had added the province of Britannia to its demesne.

For the best part of the next four centuries, the shadow of Rome lay across the land. Fans of Roman history and archaeology will tell you the Roman occupation and settlement of Britain was the single most significant event in the story of these isles. They will tell you Britain is a Roman name, that the capital of the United Kingdom was first a Roman town (Londinium), that our language is more Roman than anything else. They will bang on about how we still use roads that were built by Romans and how our architecture was most profoundly influenced by that of the Romans. If provoked, they will use the c-word and tell you the Romans brought us civilization as well.

I take issue with all of the above and I will be the first to admit it is because I have always bridled, instinctively, at the notion of the British Isles owing quite so much to all that the Romans did for us.

For one thing, take the name Britain. It derives from Britannia, right enough, but the roots of that name lie in *Pretani* – most likely a Roman attempt at pronouncing whatever word the locals themselves already called their long island.

For the rest of it, I would say we give them so much credit because what they *do* represent is the arrival of what we recognize, consciously or unconsciously, as the modern world. They were all about hospital corners and filling in forms, keeping records and making reports for the attention of their superiors. I don't care what the consequences are when I say that in my mind they were, more than anything else, bureaucrats and desk-jockeys. I am not necessarily knocking bureaucrats and desk-jockeys, but I do question the implication that for all the hundreds of thousands of years before the arrival of Roman soldiers in AD 43, the inhabitants of these islands lacked a plan.

The fact is, influence flowed both ways and, as they were to demonstrate by their adoption of the Celtic goddess Sulis at Bath, the Romans were capable of being adaptable. So long as they paid their taxes and accepted the notion that the emperor in Rome was as good as god, the locals were largely left to carry on as before, and so they did.

It is in this way that the Romans are part of the story of the British Isles, and not the other way around.

The deep bones of Somerset's Mendip Hills are formed of carboniferous limestone. The stone itself is formed of ground-down shells and other hard parts of little creatures that lived millions of years ago in a warm sea. When they died, their bodies settled on the bottom, in vast quantities. Layer upon layer they were laid down, and for aeons. Weight of numbers bore down too, making of it all, in time, solid rock. As well as horizontal fault lines between the layers, vertical cracks (known to geologists as 'joints') formed within the matrix. Millions of years passed and the world shivered, shook and rearranged itself, so that what had been seabed became dry land instead. Thrust up into the world above, then weathered and worn by the elements, the limestone became the stuff of gently folded hills.

Thousands of years ago – no one knows how many thousands – rain fell upon those hills, as it always has. Down through the cracks and folds, that rainwater of long ago made its way deeper, ever deeper. Having seeped and spread, percolated and pervaded the limestone to a great depth – perhaps 8,000 feet or so below the surface – it began to warm up. Geothermal processes, powered by heat emanating from the planet's core, raised the temperature of the deep-buried water as high as 64 degrees Celsius – much too hot to touch, nearly enough to poach with.

Under its own pressure, water that fell once from a Stone Age sky now rises back up through the faulted rock, surrendering heat all the while, until it returns to the light of the present day at an altogether more pleasant temperature of around 45 degrees Celsius. In the whole of the British Isles this happens in just one place – right at the heart of the city we call Bath. It comes at a rate of a quarter of a million glasses a day.

(Tepid water rises at other spots – at Taff's Well in Cardiff; Buxton and Matlock in the Peak District; Mallow in the Republic of Ireland – but at no more than 28 degrees Celsius it's not water in which most folk would want to bathe.)

Surely for as long as people have walked the Somerset Levels, the hot springs here will have been revered as a source not just of warmth but of wonder. Imagine those times long before any settlement, when this was a wild, marshy terrain that became progressively soft underfoot. At all times, but especially during the colder months of the year, the springs would have been wreathed in coiling clouds of steam, adding an air of mystery or even foreboding. Anyone brave enough to penetrate the mists would have found water rising out of the very earth – hot to the touch and tinged red with the iron salts dissolved in it. All about the springs, pulsing pools of deep green, the ground would have been stained and coloured. It might have seemed the world was wounded there, bleeding.

In his *Historia Regum Britanniae* – History of the Kings of Britain – Geoffrey of Monmouth attributed the discovery of the springs to a princeling named Bladud in 863 BC. Educated in Athens, Bladud apparently returned home to Britain not just with a classical education but also with leprosy. Doom-laden, certain he could never be king while so blighted, he fled from his father's sight and became a keeper of pigs instead. He made his new home close by a steaming mire and noticed that whenever his pigs rolled in the warm mud there they emerged with blemish-free skin. Intrigued, Bladud stripped naked and did likewise, and after just a few visits found himself cured of his malaise. He returned home in triumph, assumed the kingship of his people and founded a fine city on the site of his miraculous recovery.

Whatever the truth of King Bladud, archaeological excavations have revealed that people have long been in the habit of leaving valuables at the springs – offerings to the source of the magic. Right up into the modern era the waters of Bath were famed for their curative powers – washing away all manner of ills, from rheumatism to piles, lumbago to gout.

By the time the Romans found the place, around the middle of the first century AD, the spring was holy to the people of the local Dobunni tribe. They knew the springs as watery gateways leading to the home of a goddess they called Sul or Sulis. She was concerned with health and well-being, as well as with wisdom and glimpses of the future. The place enthralled and fascinated the Romans, as it did everyone else, and when they heard about Sulis they realized at once that she had a great deal in common with their own goddess Minerva.

Among other things, those invaders and conquerors were pragmatists. Rather than seeking to replace the resident goddess, they appreciated instead the serendipity of their discovery and twinned her with their own to create Sulis Minerva. They were the first to build around the springs – in timber to start with – and to seek to control the water. As well as different baths for hot, warm and cold water, they raised a temple to the new goddess. It is no coincidence that, centuries later, a medieval abbey was built nearby as well, in hopes of currying favour with that same elemental healing power.

The baths became the number-one place at which to be seen. Roman citizens and locals alike socialized there, traders and merchants struck deals. There was food and drink to be had and entertainers to be watched. The temple next door was a place for animal sacrifice, where paid experts – augurs – might divine the future on a client's behalf.

Above all, the goddess was there to be consulted, prayed to, appealed to in times of strife. The Romans were in the habit of telling tales to her – scratching reports of crimes and slights they had suffered, however petty, on to little squares of lead which became known as curse tablets. These were then cast into the water in hopes that the goddess might intervene and punish the wrongdoer:

> 'May he who has stolen VILBIA from me become as liquid as water . . .'

> 'I curse him who has stolen, who has robbed Deomiorix from his house. Whoever stole his property, the god is to find him. Let him buy it back with his blood or his own life.'

Above the grand entrance to the temple was a carving of a gorgon's head – not female like Medusa, but a male of the species, his hair a writhing mass of serpents, his mouth open wide. This much survives, in fragments carefully mounted in a display. Once again the Romans had wedded one of their own ideas of a deity to a representation of a local river god. Wise enough, or just practical, they had allowed themselves to be changed by the place they had claimed as their own. As their culture passed slowly through the rock of the place, it was altered, purified perhaps – changed for the better.

In AD 306, Constantine was at York when his father Constantius, emperor of the west, died there. Although the soldiers proclaimed Constantine the new emperor, his position was anything but secure. Before the battle that settled things, by the Milvian Bridge just outside Rome in AD 312, Constantine looked up at the sun and saw a Christian cross above it and the words 'By this sign shall you conquer'. He duly ordered his men to put the same mark on their shields and they were indeed victorious. It was Constantine who summoned the Council of Nicaea, in Asia Minor, in AD 325, the same that came up with the Nicene Creed, the formal statement of Christian belief still used throughout the world today. It might therefore be said it was after having passed through the rock of the British Isles that

Constantine was of a mind to lay the foundations of what became the Catholic Church, which changed the world. If it had not been for York – Eboracum, as the Romans called it, the place of the yew trees – and Constantine, and all that followed after, what then . . . ?

Our image of the Romans is so clear, so fixed, so bolstered by amphorae and floor tiles, togas and villas, they are almost caricatures of themselves. Perhaps we latch on to them so readily because their lives remind us of our own – with jobs to go to, straight roads to walk along, central heating in their homes and taxes to pay to the Man. In any event, Roman Britain feels especially real at Bath – believable. The Roman structures are long gone, of course. The buildings that house the springs now are eighteenth century and after, the latest in a long line of redevelopments on the site. But the water now is much the same as the water then.

Their name for that marvellous place of warmth and healing was Aquae Sulis – 'the Waters of Sulis' – and there is a palpable connection to be made and felt from knowing the Romans knew that same warm flow and smelled that same faintly sulphurous smell. The curse tablets too are perfectly and completely human – glimpses of actual Roman pettiness and spite. There are not many places where a person can sense the righteous fury of a bather who has had his towel and clothes stolen, but Bath is one of them.

22

Sycamore Gap, Hadrian's Wall, Northumberland

The boundary of empire

Best to declare right now that Hadrian's Wall has never – never – marked the border between Scotland and England. Some folk living in Scotland today are passionate on this point. The mere mention of Hadrian's Wall in the context of the border between Scotland and England is enough to drive a fair few of them into an eye-popping rage. So understand this much right away: the border between Scotland and England is a contentious issue and has been for hundreds of years.

That said, Hadrian's Wall itself is a genuine marvel. It runs for 70-odd miles, up hill and down dale, all the way from where the River Tyne enters the North Sea in the east to the Solway Firth on the Irish Sea in the west – making it the largest Roman artefact anywhere in the world. It is also a UNESCO World Heritage Site. Marking the north-western frontier of the empire, it was commissioned by Emperor Hadrian and construction began in AD 122. The work was undertaken by soldiers from all three of the occupying legions and the bulk of it was completed within just six years. Apart from anything else, it is an engineering feat of note – and, even more than that, a stone-built, lime-washed white line underscoring Rome's ambition and sense of self. At no other place in their empire did they go to such lengths – literally and metaphorically – to mark a boundary between *us* and *them*.

Given the scale of the thing – and the patchiness of its condition over much of its length nowadays – it is important to pick the best place on the line to appreciate the wall's majesty and its audacity. From the B6318, known as the Military Road, the famous Sycamore Gap is clearly visible just to the east of Milecastle 39. The landscape there undulates like a cartoon of the Loch Ness Monster's humped back. While the wall was built by Roman soldiers, the sinuous rise and fall of the land is the work of the last ice age. Meltwater under great pressure, forced from beneath the ice sheet, carved deep channels into the underlying rock of the Whin Sill. As well as Sycamore Gap, there are depressions left by other runnels, including nearby Milking Gap and Rapishaw Gap. The milecastle nestles in another of them – and is fittingly referred to by most thereabouts as Castle Nick. Rising in natural splendour from the next dip along is the eponymous tree. It is one of the most photographed trees (and locations) in Northumberland, certainly, and probably in the whole of England. It was even named English Tree of the Year in the Woodland Trust's awards of 2016.

Rome attempted a more northerly boundary in Britannia a couple of decades later. This was the 39 miles of the Antonine Wall, built of slabs of turf on a stone foundation between the Firth of Forth in the east and the Firth of Clyde in the west. The sheer expense of maintaining an occupying force in the face of bellicose locals in a land with nothing to offer in the way of natural wealth, however, was deemed pointless soon enough. The Antonine Wall was abandoned after just twenty miserable years and Rome pulled back to her earlier line in the sand, where she stayed for the rest of her time here in these islands.

All the while the Romans held Britannia, and for centuries after they departed, there was no such place as Scotland and no such people as the Scots (for that matter, there was no such place as England, either, and no English). It was into the vacuum created by the absence of Rome that those other folk were drawn. The Scots came from Ireland. A ruling family from the territory of Antrim had established the kingdom of Dalriada by the fifth century AD, but Irish immigration had begun earlier still. What those incomers called themselves is anyone's guess. Scot, or Scotti, may have been a family name for some of them. In the mouths of the folk the incomers encountered in the northern part of old Britannia, 'Scot' referred first of all to seaborne raiders. It seems they were less than welcome – at least among the Celtic tribes that were in residence north of the wall when they arrived.

The Romans had lumped all the northern tribes together as one and called them Caledonii. The territory they occupied was therefore Caledonia. They likely chose the line of their wall for purely practical reasons. It traversed a narrow point on the long island and so required less time and manpower than other places. It was never supposed to act as an impenetrable barrier either. Rather it was intended as a declaration of ownership, and the various gateways along its length, defended by forts, functioned as useful places for collecting taxes from anyone travelling north or south.

But while it is true to say Hadrian's Wall never functioned as the national border between Scotland and England (the whole thing is contained now well within English territory), it is interesting to note that with eyes half closed it can seem close enough to the modern boundary. Almost 2,000 years ago and long, long before the existence of either polity, soldiers acting on instructions from Rome drew a line that cut the island into two parts – one northern, small and poor, the other southern, rich and a good deal larger.

Excavations have even identified a Bronze Age boundary line a few hundred feet south of the wall at Sycamore Gap – hinting at the possibility the Romans merely did what they always did and put their own stamp on something, a border of some description, that already mattered to the locals.

We are a mongrel people. Wave after wave of incomers made their way here. Some left after a while and others stayed for good. They all changed the place one way or another. The Scots came from Ireland. The English are descended from the Angles who came from somewhere across the North Sea. The Angles called the folk they found in the west Welisc, which means 'foreign', 'not us'. All our ancestors were immigrants once, all strangers to one another and to this place. Hadrian's Wall is a reminder that some of the lines separating us from one another were drawn not by us but by others.

23

Lullingstone Roman Villa, Kent

Layers of religion

A T SOME TIME in the last two decades of the first century AD, a wealthy family commissioned the building of a fine country house close by the River Darent in what would become the county of Kent.

They were either Roman citizens or Britons who had done well for themselves by adopting Roman ways. For three or four centuries the house was adapted and expanded until eventually it was truly vast even by Romano-British standards. Its largest footprint was in excess of 700 square yards. It had twenty rooms, underfloor central heating. In every way, it was a luxurious home – a real statement of power and status.

During the 1750s, labourers digging postholes to fence in a deer park discovered parts of a mosaic floor but thought no more about it. Only in the years following the Second World War did archaeologists properly turn their attention to the site, and between 1949 and 1961 their excavations revealed nothing less than the story of the arrival of Christianity in the British Isles.

The earliest inhabitants of Lullingstone Villa were pagans. They had a well in the floor of a cellar room – known as the cult room – and opposite it, watching over it, a painting of three water nymphs. Appease the nymphs and the water would remain fresh. By the third century AD, the nymphs had been painted over, replaced by two marble busts. These may have been likenesses of ancestors. Perhaps the villa was used as a country retreat by governors of Roman Britain – even a visiting emperor. In any event, the cult room was by then dedicated to the worship of hallowed spirits.

But all the while the family at Lullingstone went about the business of revering the dead, a new cult was abroad in the world and stretching inexorably towards and into the province of Britannia. During the fourth century, the floor of a large dining room at Lullingstone was decorated with two elaborate and expensive mosaics. The house owners were evidently well versed in classical mythology and commissioned the artists to depict Zeus, disguised as a bull and abducting Europa, and also Bellerophon, mounted on Pegasus and slaying the fire-breathing Chimera.

The mosaics are topped with Latin inscriptions and some scholars have suggested Christian messages are hidden there. By starting with the first letter of the second line and then taking every eighth letter that follows, it is possible to spell out the name 'Jesus'.

In a north-facing room of the villa, the archaeologists found the floor covered with thousands of fragments of what had been two wall paintings on a plaster backing. Painstakingly reconstructed and now on display in the British Museum, one shows six figures in attitudes of Christian prayer, while the other is the symbol called a chi-rho. This latter appears as a monogram, an elongated P spliced on to the top of an X. Using the Greek alphabet, X and P are the first two letters of the word Christ and were used by early Christians as a secret means of identifying themselves to one another.

The painted room was therefore what is known as a 'house-church' – a place set aside in the home for private, perhaps secret, worship. In later centuries the site was overlain by a Norman chapel, dating at least from 1115.

Lullingstone is unique in Britain and the earliest known example of Christian worship in these islands. The fascination lies in wondering whether the inhabitants of the house had, generation by generation, truly shifted their allegiance from the pagan Roman faith to the new cult of Christianity – or if they kept both forms of worship on the go, hedging their bets. Did they commission the mosaics with secret messages as a means of appearing pagan in front of pagan friends and neighbours while privately worshipping a new god? Or did they pay lip service to Christianity while, in the cellar underground, they might stay true to what they really believed?

We cannot know for certain. Emperor Constantine had ceased the persecution of Christians in AD 313. The mosaics and wall art at Lullingstone appear to have been made decades later. Perhaps the family feared the new faith was a passing fad and were ready to return to old ways the moment it fell out of fashion.

The villa, near the village of Eynsford, is displayed now, under cover. The mosaics are still there, still a wonder. More than anything else it is the scale of the house that impresses – alongside the possibility that some of the earliest Christian worship in Britain may have been quietly conducted within those walls.

24

Iona, Inner Hebrides

The coming of Christianity

GET TALKING TO the right person on the harbour side in Oban on Scotland's north-west coast, or maybe in one of the pubs or cafés in the streets nearby, and you might hear an especially good story.

Apparently, a couple of tourists, husband and wife (usually American – it depends who you hear it from), get out of their hire car one day and approach a group of fishermen standing by their boat, just chewing the fat.

'Can you tell me if this is the right place,' says the husband, 'to catch the boat to the island of Ten N. A.?'

The fishermen are more than happy to help, but the name of the destination puzzles them.

'To where?' asks one.

'To the island of Ten – N – A,' says the wife, enunciating slowly, carefully compensating for her accent.

The men exchange glances. They shake their heads and scuff their feet. An island without a name but with some kind of serial number instead?

'Sorry,' says one. 'That's a new one on me.'

'Tell you what,' says another, 'write it down for us – the name.'

Husband and wife duly fish in their pockets for writing materials and manage to find a pen. The wife locates one of those little folded pamphlets, the sort you pick up in tourist information offices advertising some place or other, and writes on the blank back of it in large, careful letters. She holds it up for the fishermen to read.

Light dawns on every face.

'Ah, right,' says one. 'You want IONA!'

Who cares if it's true? It's better than that. For one thing the story illustrates a couple of important points: first of all, the island of Iona has about it an air of mystery, as of somewhere that exists not in the real world but only in dreams. Second, even in the modern era it takes a bit of time and effort to get there.

The holy island, shaped like a worn and corroded arrowhead, lies just off the south-west tip of the much larger island of Mull. Any visit therefore requires not one but two ferry journeys. The shortest crossing to Mull is from the busy port of Oban. The Caledonian MacBrayne ferry takes you across to Craignure and from there it is an hour's careful drive, with passing places, from east to west to Fionnphort – pronounced Fee-on-a-fort. Visitors must then leave their cars behind for the ten-minute hop across the sometimes-choppy Sound of Iona.

It is all worth it. Among them all, Iona is my favourite place.

The much longer journey by which Christianity arrived in the West began in the cities and townships of the eastern Mediterranean in the first few centuries AD. In the beginning, the adherents of the new faith had stayed close to the birthplace of it all, so that the earliest version of Christianity remained mixed in with the rest of the mess of the so-called Holy Land. It was there and then that the necessary tradition of monasticism, the need to be apart from others, was first established. But the gospel of Jesus Christ was supposed to be taken to the ends of the Earth, and slowly it made its way into the shadow of the setting sun. It spread to the port of Marseilles in the western Mediterranean and then on to Tours in what would one day be central-western France.

When the most determined and committed of the monks felt the need to move on from that land, threatened as they were by the intolerance and depredations of unbelievers there, they headed north and took to small boats so that they might travel even further into the west, to places like Cornwall, Ireland and the furthest flung of the Scottish islands, where it had arrived by the fifth century.

Hardly anyone knows or remembers now, but it was in such scattered, lonely places that western Christianity found the finger and toeholds that would let it cling to the world for the hundred or so years that made all the difference. Elsewhere, everywhere, that faith was in decline, threatened with extinction, and while it only just held on to those western redoubts it was their very remoteness and isolation that ensured its survival. Western civilization is made of Christianity, of that there is no doubt, but for a century it was driven to the edge, caught there like a strand of spider's web upon a leaf tip. If it hadn't hung on there, it might have disappeared completely.

How might we imagine them now, those devout travellers who left behind the warmer lands of the south and east and kept their faces always into the west and north? It is all too easy to picture them as meek, hopeful of inheriting the Earth as Matthew had promised, heads down and shaved in some fashion or other, always turning the other cheek. That is to do them a disservice. Whoever they were, the monks that built and boarded little boats made of sprung saplings and stretched hides to cross to the British Isles were the toughest of the tough, the very SAS of evangelists. Hard bastards, all.

In the past the word 'meek' was understood differently. It was used to translate the Greek *praos* in Matthew's Gospel, which is a term that was also associated with the training of warhorses. American writer Sam Whatley has written about how, when the finest stallions were captured from the wild, they were transformed, like iron ore in the furnace, into lethal agents of destruction. Where before they had been jittery in response to danger, now they were fearless and ready to obey the rider's every command, however subtle. They would run down any foe, however he was armed, whatever the threat. When trained for battle in this way, they had been made *praos*, 'meek'.

Where those meek monks were going, there was no one to leech from, no benefits to be had and no houses to be borrowed or squatted in. They went where they went and did what they did because it was solitude they wanted and only their own God they trusted. They would fish, grow plants and crops and keep sheep for wool, build shelters from beach pebbles and driftwood, catch and slaughter seals. They had come in search of the ends of the Earth, *ultima Thule*, and there they would bask in the warmth of what they knew to be true.

I close my eyes and try to imagine such conviction, such faith. I think of other, similar men in other, similar places. If they and others like them had not come here to these islands, then everything and everywhere in the world would be different now in ways we cannot imagine.

Hardest of them all, those early Christians, without a doubt, was the one remembered as Columba. More precisely it is Colum Cille – 'the Dove of the Church' – but Columba is a nickname that took the place of whatever his mother ever called him. He was an Irishman, of the O'Neill clan, and it seems his violent, unforgiving approach to conversion to his faith had seen others put a stop to him back home. Whoever they were that thwarted him there, they must have been quite a bunch, and numerous, but for their own reasons they drove him away.

This was in the year AD 563, and if he had been lowly, no doubt he would have been snuffed out there and then, a sharp blade pulled across his throat or a heavy blow to the back of his head. But Columba was more likely high-born and so it came to pass that he was merely exiled with his followers and found sanctuary among the Gaels of western Scotland. Somehow or other he made friends there, among another stubborn lot – hard men and women given to belief in pagan gods and spirits in the trees and rivers. Against the odds, he won a hearing for his version of a new faith, and for his trouble and on account of his passion he was gifted the island of Iona to do with as he pleased. No doubt the local leaders were quite taken with the newcomer's skill of writing. Such men, chieftains and kings, are often fond of their own thoughts and words. A way of making them permanent – so that they might be distributed and read out to their subjects – may well have been the trick that sealed the deal and made Columba not just welcome but indispensable.

Here then was that Dove of the Church. We might think of him as a zealot, even a bloody terrorist. But his zeal had seen him driven from his home and forced to set down new roots on a tiny island made of rosy granite wreathed in talcum-white sand and washed by a sea as dark as port. It was an empty place then, or all but.

There is nothing I can write here that will affect a person as much as a visit to Iona. It is not about religion (or not only about religion) but rather about a place. The trip across Mull takes you past glowering hills that press down from above. Cross to Iona, however, and the effect is of emerging from under a weight into somewhere it is possible, irresistible, to stand tall and breathe in deep. Everyone, everywhere, talks a lot about the quality of light and its importance to the eye and to the soul, but on Iona it seems to spill around the island like a good idea or a soft wind. Mock if you will – until you go – but there the landscape, the light and the air conspire in a way that transcends any notion of any religion ever conceived by human-kind. Iona is quietly and wordlessly more – a sense of peace made only of the stuff of the world – earth, air, water.

There is no doubt Iona was a sacred place before Columba came, but still he made it his own, he and his ilk. One or more of the surviving Celtic manuscripts were made there – the Book of Kells, the Lindisfarne Gospels. No one knows now which came from where and some were surely made on Lindisfarne, that other holy island off the Northumberland coast. It does not matter. They are products of time spent long ago in tiny places on the edge of the world. They add up to some of the most wondrous art ever created at any time and in any place. Some of it was inspired, in part, by Iona – and if you go there you might understand why.

When the sun is shining, it is an unspeakably lovely place. Winter on any island to the west of Scotland, however, is a sight to behold, an experience to be had. The folk Columba brought with him, or drew to his side there, must have been a hardy sort. According to contemporary illustrations and descriptions, they shaved their heads from crown to forehead, leaving it long at the back, and wore hooded woollen cloaks they wove themselves. They cleared and prepared fields and vegetable plots and grew their own food. They kept animals as well and harvested what they could from the sea, including seals.

The monastery they built was made of timber – wattle and daub – and around it they dug a ditch and bank to enclose and thereby set aside their special place. Close by, on a rocky outcrop, Columba built a little wooden cell where he could be alone with his God. Inside it he prayed and wrote and made plans for the conversion of the world.

In 1957, archaeologist Charles Thomas opened up a trench on that outcrop, which is known as Tòrr an Aba, 'the Hill of the Abbot'. Though tradition had long connected Columba to the spot, in more recent times it had been all but dismissed as wishful thinking, just a good story for the tourists. But Thomas found traces of burnt hazel wood – the very species that would have been commonplace on the island in Columba's time – and kept the fragments in a matchbox.

In 2017 the radioactive carbon in those burnt remnants was dated. The wooden structure that had stood there on Tòrr an Aba had been built of wood cut down sometime between AD 540 and 650. Columba died on Iona in AD 597.

Tòrr an Aba is close by the much more modern, stone-built abbey so beloved of tourists. Stand on that rocky ridge of high ground now and it affords the perfect view of the whole place. The moody hills of Mull are right there and yet that larger island, and Scotland beyond, seem inconsequential, the lesser places, and kept at arm's length.

To find dots in the landscape, like that little wooden hut, associated with a named person from the distant past is incredibly rare. To me the thought that Tòrr an Aba was where Columba sat and wrote and went about his business is enough to make a shiver run. It is not about knowing he was Christian; rather it is about the fact *he* was *there* and that now I can go and stand on the same spot and so share the same space in the universe.

On Iona, they say there were once 360 stone crosses all fashioned in the Celtic style with a circle embracing and upholding the horizontal arms. The Celtic cross is profoundly different from those bearing the crucified Christ. The circle itself is just a simple architectural solution to a stonemason's problem: while a crosspiece carved of wood supports its own weight, the same form in stone needs the circle to support the horizontal arms and stop them snapping off. But more than that, the Celtic cross is an empty cross – Jesus is not hanging dead upon it but already risen and returned to life.

Only a handful of Iona's ancient crosses remain, the rest having been smashed and thrown into the sea by other zealots during the Reformation.

Close by the present abbey – built of stone long after Columba's place of wood and thatch had disappeared back into the soil – is a cobbled way called Sraid nam Marbh – 'the Street of the Dead'. It leads to the graveyard of St Oran, wherein it is said Scottish, Irish and even Norwegian kings are buried.

But all of it – the abbey, the crosses, the royal graves – is surplus to the point of Iona. It is and has surely always been a special place. No doubt Columba was drawn to it because, by the time he heard of it, it was already revered as somewhere apart that was good for the soul. Iona makes special everything that comes there. It is not about humankind or even Christian humankind. All that matters about Iona is simply there in the rock and the sea and the sky above.

25

Bamburgh Castle, Northumberland

A warrior named Arthur

SINCE THE MYTHICAL history of the British Isles is shot through with the legend of King Arthur, places in the landscape that seem touched by the tale are hard to resist. Belief in a hero-in-waiting – one sleeping under a hill until needed by his people – has lasted a while. Legends, myths and folklore run alongside historical facts, but these days they are mostly underground too, sleeping like Arthur. Having endured so long, however, they are also some of what the country understands about itself and therefore they are part of its story.

Bamburgh Castle, just 5 miles or so south of the holy island of Lindisfarne, has long been connected to Sir Lancelot, Arthur's favourite Knight of the Round Table. No single writer did more to make and fix our fantasy of King Arthur than the Englishman Thomas Malory – author of *Le Morte d'Arthur*, which he began to write while held captive in Newgate prison in London for his part in a failed Lancastrian attempt to overthrow King Edward IV in 1468 during the Wars of the Roses. According to Malory, Bamburgh was once Lancelot's fortress, a place he called Joyous Gard. It had been Dolorous Gard, but he changed its name from sad to happy following a visit by Arthur and his queen, Guinevere. After Lancelot's affair with Guinevere was discovered and she was sentenced to death for her betrayal, it was to Joyous Gard, according to Malory at least, that Lancelot carried his lover after stealing her away from her captors.

A glimpse of the Norman castle that sits now on that rocky knoll looking east towards the Farne Islands has the unmistakable shimmer of other world. In fact, its real roots are as strange, and as full of characters scarcely believable, as any tale told to beguile children.

Archaeologists have discovered evidence of prehistoric occupation of the land nearby and have found that the basalt rock beneath the castle has been occupied and used continuously for the past 2,000 years at least. It may once have been a base for Celtic Britons, but Anglo-Saxon invaders had it for themselves by sometime in the fifth century AD, making it the capital of their kingdom of Bernicia.

To read about the rise and fall of the various competing warlords at that time is to venture into a world as fantastical and unfamiliar as that imagined by Tolkien for his elves and orcs. A seventh-century Welsh poem called *Y Gododdin* recounts the ill-fated quest of a Brythonic-Celtic army that challenged the rise of the Anglo-Saxons. Apparently in an attempt to halt the northwards expansion of those foreign invaders, Mynyddog Mwynfawr, king of Gododdin, a northern territory encompassing a chunk of eastern and southern Scotland and northern England as far south as the River Wear, gathered 300 heroes to his banner. From all over Pictland, Strathclyde, Cumbria and even north-west Wales they rallied to him, and after a year of feasting and carousing they headed south to do battle with the kingdom of Bernicia at Catraeth, most likely near Catterick in North Yorkshire.

The result was an unmitigated disaster for Mynyddog and his men. All were slaughtered. In the aftermath, the victorious Anglo-Saxons invaded their enemy's territory, taking its capital, Din Eidyn (Edinburgh), for their own. The Gododdin had been the heirs and successors of the tribe the Romans called the Votadini, but after that battle they were no more.

The poem pays tribute to the vanquished:

Men went to Catraeth at dawn
All their fears had been put to flight
Three hundred clashed with ten thousands
They stained their spears ruddy with blood . . .

Whether they were truly outnumbered to such an outlandish extent is anyone's guess. No doubt the figure of 300 refers to all the grand men – knights, lords – and the sacrifice of the many hundreds or thousands of common foot soldiers simply did not merit a mention in the work of the poet.

If it was indeed written in the early years of the seventh century AD, then *Y Gododdin* also features the earliest mention of Arthur when in one verse a comparison is made between him and a British warrior named Gwawrddur: 'Though he was not Arthur/He made his strength a refuge . . .'

It is all so tantalizing – an ancient world of heroes and a glimpse of a warrior named Arthur whose bravery was already the benchmark against which the valour of other men might be measured.

Some parts of the historical truth involved souls who would have called Bamburgh their home or their capital. Finds of metalwork – including a little gold artefact in the form of a sinuous, coiling creature known as the Bamburgh Beast – seem to demonstrate that the place was home to wealthy, high-status folk. King Oswald – the Christian king who drew St Aidan from Iona to Lindisfarne – may have had his principal fortress there too.

According to the Venerable Bede – writing in the next century – and others, Oswald ruled then as the most powerful of all the various kings in England, until he was defeated and killed in battle by King Penda of Mercia in AD 642. His body was ritually dismembered, the limbs, head and torso hung up on spikes in mockery of the Crucifixion. Christianity was none the less unassailable in Northumbria by the end of the seventh century.

When the Great Heathen Army of the Vikings arrived in England in AD 865, led by Ivar the Boneless, Northumbria was first on their shopping list. Despite a united resistance under Earl Osbert and King Aelle, the kingdom fell the following year. According to folklore, Aelle suffered death by blood eagle – a fabled Viking practice of cracking a man's ribs away from his breastbone and spreading them back like a bird's wings. Maybe Aelle's gruesome fate was punishment for the death of Ivar.

During the Wars of the Roses, Bamburgh became the hub of the Lancastrian war effort. In 1464 the castle – by then the Lancastrians' last redoubt in Northumberland – was pounded into submission by heavy artillery. Since 1895 it has been the home of the Armstrong family. It was and remains an impressive, imposing, sometimes ethereal sight. Viewed from the coast, it looms above the sea and the sand dunes, heavy with history. Whatever the literal truth of King Arthur, it seems reasonable to imagine his name was spoken there, perhaps by people who knew him in life, and remembered.

For me, that part of the Northumbrian coast is a place that might have been tailor-made for legend. From the castle's battlements you can see the holy island of Lindisfarne, shivering ghost-like above the sea – perfect for the burial of a king, there to await the time of his return.

26
Lindisfarne, Northumberland
The holy isle in the east

As with a visit to Iona, the holy island of the west, much of the pleasure of seeing Lindisfarne, its fraternal twin in the east, lies in the journey to get there.

It is a tidal island, a carelessly thrown scrap of a thing lying just off the north-east shoulder of Northumberland and connected to it at low tide by a causeway slung poker-straight across the sand and mudflats. Viewed from above, Lindisfarne is the oddest shape – a tattered square but with the top-left corner stretched away from the rest like a gobbet of chewing gum. This lump, joined to the island by its narrow neck of sand, is called the Snook and is the point closest to the mainland.

Unless you are planning to stay the night – a highly recommended option, incidentally – then you need tide tables and half an eye on a time-piece. That said, the crossing alone is worth the trip. The distance is ample, the terrain flat enough to allow for all manner of optical illusions. Depending on the weather, the time of day and the light, the flit across the causeway can feel like a journey towards another Camelot, another Avalon. Even at low tide the sea is close, so that the crossing seems perilous, like skating on thin ice. And that is just the one-mile car journey . . .

Better yet is to set aside some extra time, perhaps a couple of hours, and follow the pilgrim's way on foot. A line of tall timber poles, evenly spaced as a dotted line from mainland to island, marks the 3-mile route. If attention to the tides is important for the crossing by car, then it is surely a matter of life and death for anyone walking over. The sea comes in wicked quick, faster than you might run, and underfoot the sand and mud can be soft and treacherous. For all that, and so long as you make sensible preparations, the walk is more than worthwhile. Ahead of you the island itself seems to float like a length of pale-green rope upon a mirror. The sky is big, its junction with the sea lost in mist, diffuse, so that the island seems claimed by both. The destination feels distant for almost the whole time too, until all at once it is within reach.

Historians still argue about whether Emperor Constantine was ever Christian in his heart. It has been suggested he was introduced to the faith in the early fourth century AD at the knee of his mother, an innkeeper's daughter named Helena from Naissus on the Danube, who had married the Roman emperor Constantius Chlorus. Perhaps Constantine made the cult legitimate only as an act of political expediency. Seeing it was on the rise, and perhaps unstoppable, he may have brought it inside the tent only with a view to somehow controlling it. In any event, the new faith spread throughout the empire from his time onwards.

As revealed by the mosaic at Lullingstone Villa, Christianity had reached Britain too at some time in the early part of the fourth century. It did well enough while the Romans remained here, but when, early in the fifth century, trouble at home persuaded them to pull their legions out of these islands, many of the locals revealed themselves as backsliders. The void left by the Romans was exploited by Angles, Jutes and Saxons, incomers from across the North Sea, and, since they were happily pagan, the old gods soon resurfaced here. Christianity was driven north to Scotland and to the western edges – into Wales and Cornwall, and even across the Channel, where exiles established the territory we know as Brittany.

Ireland had never been conquered by the Romans. Although the seed of Christianity may have blown across the sea from Roman Britain, the plant that grew there became a variant species. It was this Irish, Celtic form of the faith that made the return journey in the sixth and seventh centuries.

Oswald, King of Northumbria, had grown to manhood in exile on Iona in the early seventh century, shortly after Columba had brought Christianity to that part of the world. His predecessor on the throne, King Edwin, had chosen Christianity after listening to the advice of one of his friends. According to the Venerable Bede, writing a century later, that friend had told his king:

> Life is like a banquet hall. Inside is light and fire and warmth and feasting, but outside it is cold and dark. A sparrow flies in through a window at one end, flies the length of the hall, and out through a window at the other end. That is what life is like. At birth we emerge from the unknown, and for a brief while we are here on this earth, with a fair amount of comfort and happiness. But then we fly out into the cold and dark and unknown future. If this new religion can lighten that darkness for us, then let us follow it.

When Oswald came home to Northumberland to claim what was his, he brought with him from that western holy isle a holy man named Aidan and gave him Lindisfarne for his base of operations. Aidan – later St Aidan – had established a priory on the island by AD 635. If Bede's account is accurate, then it seems likely he would have been among the first to follow what became that muddy, splashy pilgrim's path: 'Whether in town or country, he always travelled on foot unless compelled by necessity to ride . . .'

Lindisfarne's most famous saint is Cuthbert, who was prior from AD 665. He died in 687 and was buried on the island. When, eleven years later, the monks decided he deserved a grander resting place, his sarcophagus was opened. The body within was found to be 'incorrupt' – or so the monks said – as though not a moment had passed since the hour of his death.

Visit Lindisfarne now and the island seems tucked away, almost out of sight. It can be a stretch to think it ever featured much in anyone's reckoning. But by the end of the eighth century it was quite the beacon – one of the brightest in Christendom – and it had come to the attention of men motivated by earthly desires. There was treasure on the island, and everyone knew it. Saintly souls may have adorned ornaments and holy relics there with gold and precious stones only to glorify them, but for those who served other gods entirely their gleam was irresistible.

On 8 June 793, men from Horoaland in western Norway brought their ships ashore on an east-facing beach on Lindisfarne, within sight of the priory. Those they found on the island, whether monks or lay people, they either murdered or rounded up to be sold elsewhere as slaves. All the valuables from within the buildings were carried off as well. The impact of this infamous Viking raid – remembered as the first of its kind in these islands – was felt all across the Christian world. The killing of defenceless holy men was appalling enough, but holy men in *that place* . . . on Lindisfarne . . .

By AD 875 the religious community had upped sticks and gone – taking St Cuthbert's remains with them for good measure. They wandered then for seven years before making a new home for themselves, and for him, at Chester-le-Street. In the tenth century they finally moved to Durham, where a shrine to Cuthbert was built in the cathedral.

The island the monks had imagined was finally reclaimed by more of their kind at the end of the eleventh century. The new tenants had come from Durham Cathedral and the priory they built then stood until the dissolution of the monasteries by Henry VIII four and a half centuries later. It was plundered soon after by the builders of the castle that sits, in fairytale splendour, on a knuckle of basalt known locally as Beblowe Craig. The original structure stood in ruins until the turn of the twentieth century, when it was acquired by Edward Hudson, publisher of *Country Life* magazine. His friend, the architect Edwin Lutyens (the same that would later design the Cenotaph in Whitehall), restored the place for him as a family home.

If you would visit Lindisfarne, then go prepared to let the tide do what the tide does. It is when the last of the tourists leaves, making for the causeway while they still can, that the place seems to exhale. Tidal islands, those that cannot quite decide whether they belong to the land or to the sea, have about them the atmosphere of other worlds. There is also something pleasing about the way mainland Britain is book-ended by two holy isles, one in the west and one in the east. Iona sees the last of each day's light, while Lindisfarne is washed in the first of it. Visit both and it is impossible to ignore the sensation of a connection, an invisible cord, between the two.

The advent of the people the world remembers as the Vikings was every bit as significant here as that of the Romans. They too changed everything – language, culture and the rest. The truth is, having arrived among us, they never left. They are with us yet and it is on Lindisfarne that their oldest fingerprints are to be found.

27

Brough of Birsay, Orkney

Trampled beneath Viking feet

JUST OFF THE north-west corner of Orkney's Mainland is the little tidal island called Brough of Birsay, a scrap of green like a solitary turf torn away by the tide. The word 'brough' has its roots in the Old Norse *borg*, which means 'fort', much like the more familiar 'burgh'. It is also close to 'broch', the name given to those enigmatic cooling-tower-shaped strongholds built in northern Scotland during the late Iron Age. 'Birsay' is Old Norse too and comes from the older *byrgisey*, which means 'a promontory or island connected to the main by a narrow neck of land'. Everything about the name implies a place that could or should be defended, or that might be expected to offer protection from harm.

As far as archaeologists can tell, the first inhabitants of the place were more of those early Christian hermits in search of peace and quiet, far from the madding crowd. During the seventh and eighth centuries AD it was home to farmers. They were the sort of people the Romans called Picts – the painted people, the people of the designs – the indigenous population descended from those who had, millennia before, concerned themselves with the building of great stone monuments like Brodgar and Stenness.

If those farmers did indeed feel safe and secure on their little island fastness, they were sadly mistaken. Whatever quality of life they had enjoyed, living in homes shaped much like larger versions of the circular cells the monks had inhabited in the earliest years, they had a terrible shock coming.

Sometime in the ninth century, Vikings arrived from Norway. While the first of their kind had come to the British Isles primarily to make smash-and-grab raids – striking without warning and making off with anything and everything of value – soon enough they came to stay, to colonize and to farm, to claim the land for their own.

Walk across the few hundred yards of causeway linking Mainland to Brough of Birsay during low water and you come face to face with the arrival in the Pictish nest of the Viking cuckoos. Archaeologists working there have found buried out of sight the foundations of the circular buildings that were home to the locals. Plainly visible now, however, are the long rectangular houses that were plonked on top of the old way of life by the new arrivals. All that had been there before, and for generations, was smothered and put away like an unwanted infant.

We cannot know what that first encounter was like. The Picts on the island were almost certainly Christian, while the Nordic incomers worshipped gods of war and thunder and the like. Fragments of a shattered Pictish stone, believed to be from the eighth century, were found during excavations in the 1930s. The restored original is in the National Museum of Scotland in Edinburgh now, but a replica stands on the island. On it are carved Pictish symbols – interpreted as a mirror, a crescent, a V-rod. There is also an eagle and a creature described either as a Pictish beast or a swimming elephant. This latter is, I would say, by far the most descriptive. There are also the figures of three men – warriors with shields, swords and spears, and the suggestion of long hairstyles. Two of the three are bearded and the one on the right, walking in the lead, may bear a crown. The one on the left, bringing up the rear, appears to be a callow, smooth-chinned boy. They are silent witnesses now, the shadows of the last of their kind.

The Vikings kept and made use of Pictish things – pottery, tools and so on. They also repurposed some of the circular houses as byres and storage sheds.

Brough of Birsay looks peaceful now. On a sunny day it is another little swatch of Heaven. But what happened there twelve or thirteen centuries ago was likely anything but. All over Orkney – and Shetland too, for that matter – that which had gone before was undone.

In 2006 I was involved in the ongoing People of the British Isles Project. The human genome had just recently been mapped and a team led by Professor Sir Walter Bodmer of Oxford University, a silverback in the nascent field, had invited thousands of volunteers to give blood for genetic testing. From Kent to the Outer Hebrides and from Cornwall to Orkney, people offered up samples to help the scientists glimpse the individual threads woven through the human tapestry of these islands.

Folk came forward with all sorts of notions about themselves, one family story after another claiming descent from these or from those. We had would-be Angles, Saxons, Normans, Picts, Celts, Romans. By far the most wistful and determined were those who earnestly believed they were the sons and daughters of Vikings. Some had family legends to prove it; others were convinced by no more than their blue eyes and fair hair. A few had an inherited deformity of the hand called Dupuytren's contracture. This last is commonly known as 'Viking Claw' and presents as a painful curling of the fingers towards the palm of the hand. Although once thought to be evidence of Viking genes, the disorder is now known to occur in populations all over northern Europe and even beyond. It is part of the human condition, but it is not exclusively Viking.

When we had to tell these people, as we usually did, that they were not of Viking stock after all, it was like delivering the worst medical news. I swear I saw more than one grown man cry on hearing he had no claim to the bloodline of Eric the Red or Svein Forkbeard, or to any other of that ilk.

Given the likely behaviour of Vikings in Orkney, Shetland and elsewhere, the passionate wish to be descended from the same was quite startling. What the project revealed on Orkney was nothing less than sinister. While a majority of modern native Orkney women showed descent from 'Pictish' folk, or at least from the indigenous inhabitants of the archipelago at the time of the Norse invasion, today's Orcadian men are almost always the descendants of Vikings. This evidence – woven through the flesh and blood of the people living there now – reveals a stark reality. Soon after the Vikings settled those islands, the local men, the Pictish men, stopped having any access to the local women. They were either driven off to settle elsewhere – on mainland Scotland perhaps – or simply ceased to draw breath altogether.

Genocide is a loaded word, but the genetic evidence is calm and unequivocal. From around the ninth century onwards, the only children being born on Orkney were the sons and daughters of Vikings.

'Orkney' is just about the only pre-Norse place name left in that part of the world; every other town, village, settlement, farm, valley, hill, river, harbour, cliff and bay was given a new Norse name. The word has been studied by etymologists. The Vikings called their new home Orkneyjar. *Orkn* is Old Norse for seal, while *eyjar* means islands – so 'the Islands of the Seals'. What seems likely, however, is that those Norse invaders had repurposed the old name of the place just as they re-used the houses, the quern stones, the loom weights and the rest of the belongings of those they had dispossessed.

Roman writers knew the islands as Orcades. The Gaels of Ireland had it as Inis Orc – 'the Islands of the Orcs'. Rather than some premonition of the works of J. R. R. Tolkien, however, *orc* is an old word for pig. In the distant past the tribes of the Orkney islands may have had animal totems. Perhaps the dominant clan knew themselves as the sons and daughters of the wild boar – so that the whole archipelago might once have been the 'Islands of the Wild Boar'. The thinking goes, therefore, that when the Vikings arrived and heard the first part of the place name, they recognized in it their own word for seal and simply called their new acquisition 'the Islands of the Seals'.

Just as some of their number had walked all over the native settlement on the little tidal island they renamed Brough of Birsay, so the rest of the indigenous culture was trampled underfoot. The Vikings had come, and they had come to stay.

28

St Wystan's Church, Repton, Derbyshire

Resting place for a saint, shelter for an army

THE VILLAGE OF Repton in Derbyshire has a population of around 3,000. It nestles on the edge of the floodplain of the River Trent and is home to Repton public school – alma mater of, among others, author Roald Dahl, *Top Gear* guru Jeremy Clarkson and athlete Harold Abrahams, who won gold in the 100-metres dash in the Paris Olympics of 1924 and whose story was one of those told in the Oscar-winning film *Chariots of Fire*.

The village is as pretty as it is old. Houses of stone and red brick, eaves drooping here and there with the weight of years. Its time at the heart of things is long past. The tide of all that is deemed to matter has pulled away, sucking and sighing, leaving Repton a backwater. Few would have reason to visit now, but it is worth the trip.

Where four main roads meet, close by the parish church of St Wystan's, there is a market cross, ancient and worn, octagonal in plan, with symmetrical flights of eight sandstone steps rising like wedding-cake layers and framing a smooth column topped by a stone ball. It sits on the spot where some claim Christianity was first preached in the Midlands of England. Whatever the truth of the tale, the market cross has the look of great age, as though the rivers of humanity and time flowing past it, along those ancient thoroughfares, have worn it smooth as a pebble.

Repton is a place that might lull the visitor into thinking that the way things are there now is the way they have always been. But more than eleven centuries ago Repton was the capital of the second most important kingdom in the land and a prized target for an invasion force bent on claiming the whole of that kingdom for their own. Anyone wishing to take a walk through fragments of that past time, that utterly different world, need do no more than stroll through the gates of St Wystan's Church and across the churchyard on close-cropped grass lain like a grandmother's blanket over her dead.

Wystan . . . even the name sounds like a whisper or a sigh. Wystan. Perhaps you heard it wrong and it is really wist*ful*, uttered with longing and vague regret. For it was this terrain, this hallowed ground that was, in AD 873, made into the winter quarters of the Mycel Heathen Here – the Great Heathen Army of Danish, Norwegian and Swedish Vikings who conquered all but one of the native kingdoms of the land that would, one day, know itself as England.

Beneath the floor of St Wystan's lies entombed another time entirely, and another place. The existing church is old enough by most standards, having been built between the thirteenth and fifteenth centuries. The abbey it replaced, or at least supplanted, was founded and raised during the seventh century. Some say it was ordained by St David of Wales and that work began there in AD 600. Others credit King Peada of Mercia, who converted to Christianity in 656 to win the hand of Alchflaed, daughter of King Oswiu of neighbouring Northumbria.

Whatever the truth of it, Repton Abbey came into being in a time before England existed, when Anglo-Saxon kingdoms grew up in fields left fallow by the end of the Roman occupation of Britain during the fifth century AD. It was the twelfth-century historian Henry of Huntingdon who first arrived at a count of seven Anglo-Saxon kingdoms in the early medieval period and it was he who also first called them 'the Heptarchy'. They were, as near as anyone can judge it, East Anglia, Essex, Sussex, Wessex, Northumbria, Kent and Mercia.

Repton Abbey was founded in that kingdom of Mercia, which was to rise to dominate its neighbours from around AD 600 onwards. Mercia is an old word and its roots are deep. It has in it traces of the Old English word *mierce*, which means 'men of the Marches'. 'Marches' is itself an old, almost forgotten term for border, and Mercia was bounded by foreigners from the west in the form of the Welsh. Its greatest king was Offa, who, during his rule from AD 757 to 796, built the mighty earthwork known as Offa's Dyke to separate his kingdom from the land of the Welsh.

Repton Abbey followed the rule of St Benedict and was a double monastery – home to both monks and nuns – ruled over by an abbess. Wystan is not the only name from that time that feels unfamiliar in our mouths. Peada . . . Alchflaed . . . Oswiu . . . The strangeness of the sounds by which they knew each other is a reminder, one of many, that their world is not ours and we do not belong there. The first abbess of Repton, whose name we know at any rate, was Werberga, daughter of Wulfhere, king of Mercia, and Ermelia, daughter of the king of Kent.

Repton was grand and most of its community were of the nobility – sons and daughters of aristocrats in search of closeness to their newly discovered Christian God. Mercia had been pagan and held out longest of all the kingdoms of the Heptarchy against the upstart faith. But when they knelt before the new God, they never rose away again.

Sometime in the first decades of the eighth century a baptistery was built. Since Christians are required to be born a second time, they have need of a second womb to contain the holy fluid of that rebirth. For that reason, the creation of a baptismal font – and an architecture to contain it – was of fundamental importance. At Repton, the baptistery was probably built over a natural spring. Archaeologists believe the first structure was dug into the ground, with a timber roof above. Whatever it looked like, it served its purpose for only a short time before it was converted into a burial chamber for royalty with stone columns supporting a stone roof. Kings being as they are, one or other of them had had the place made grander yet to suit his sense of himself.

The remains of King Aethelbald of Mercia were the first to be interred there, probably just his bones. After his death in 757 it is likely his corpse was buried elsewhere first, to allow the corruption of the flesh before the bones of his skeleton were washed and anointed prior to being placed in the mausoleum. A successor of Aethelbald, King Wiglaf, who died in 839, was buried there too.

It was with the murder of Wiglaf's grandson – our Wystan – that the burial chamber took on an altogether greater significance. The young heir to the kingdom was killed by his great-uncle in AD 840. Some nine years after the crime, Wystan's remains were moved into the crypt and before long miracles were reported: those who visited it while sick and ailing were cured. Poor dead Wystan was soon a saint and pilgrims began flooding to his resting place in such numbers that more staircases had to be built to cope with the flow.

But the saintly peace of Repton Abbey was shattered just twenty-five years later by the arrival of the Vikings. The raiders had attacked these British Isles before, arriving always and only during the summer months to carry off gold, silver and slaves. In AD 865 it was different. In that year, according to the *Anglo-Saxon Chronicle*, the Vikings arrived in numbers never before seen. This was the coming of the Great Heathen Army – and instead of staying just weeks or months, this time they came to conquer and to remain.

East Anglia fell to their swords and also Northumbria. By AD 873 they were in Repton. Mercia was conquered like all the rest and the invaders chose the abbey for their winter quarters. Forewarned of the advance of the heathens, the religious community had fled, taking the precious relics of St Wystan with them.

Only Alfred, King of Wessex, last of the Heptarchy, succeeded in stalling the Viking advance. After some reversals of his own, he brought their leader, Guthrum, to the bargaining table. Guthrum converted to Christianity and a whole tranche of the north was granted to him and his Danes as their own demesne – the Danelaw, where Danish law prevailed.

In time, the abbey at Repton was destroyed, but the crypt remained and is now fossilized within the fabric of the present parish church, a fragment of that moment when Vikings laid down roots that are here in the British Isles to this day.

During the 1970s and 1980s, archaeologists Martin and Birthe Biddle conducted extensive excavations of the churchyard at St Wystan's. One of their discoveries was a 6-foot skeleton they called the Repton Warrior. Alongside him was buried his great iron sword in a fleece-lined wooden scabbard bound in leather. In life, he had evidently been a leader among his fellows. Around his neck was a little silver hammer – a tribute to Thor, whose hammer was known as the mighty Mjölnir, miller of mountains. The Repton Warrior had died a rightful death, with wounds to his head and the likely severing of his femoral artery. It was the end every Viking man desired: blood-soaked, violent and guaranteeing entry to Valhalla and an eternity of feasting and fighting. Elsewhere in the grounds, the Biddles found a mass grave, the bones of hundreds of Vikings, men and women both (probably collected from many graves elsewhere, casualties of the invasion), laid out around a central grave that may have been that of Ivar the Boneless, one of the commanders of the Great Heathen Army. The sagas say Ivar died making war on the Anglo-Saxons. Otherwise a figure of myth and legend, he is made real by the discovery of those remains at Repton. His comrades chose the consecrated ground of the abbey for his final resting place and his presence there is part of what makes the place immortal.

Looking out from the roof of the church tower, a silver strip of water can be seen just beyond the churchyard, a relic of an older course of the River Trent. When the Danes chose Repton for their long winter, they arrived right down there in their longships. For security they threw up around their beachhead a D-shaped bank, with the river as its spine. The curving embankments terminated at each gable end of the old church, making of its doors a fortified gateway they could easily defend. Inside that space they lived and plotted, tending to their ships and sharpening their weapons for the wars ahead.

Architectural historian Nikolaus Pevsner described St Wystan's as 'one of the most precious survivals of Anglo-Saxon architecture in England'. And so it surely is. The stone steps leading down into the crypt are worn smooth as though by the flowing of another river – one made not of water but of people. The dimly lit interior is a place apart, a small square chamber with a roof made of three rows of three domed vaults held aloft by four pillars. John Betjeman described it as 'Holy air encased in stone'. Regardless of a person's stance on matters of religion and faith, the little pocket of fossilized time beneath St Wystan's Church is all of that. The proto-Indo-European root of 'holy', after all, means 'whole, uninjured' or 'that which must be preserved intact, that cannot be transgressed or violated'.

Repton's most sacred space is deserving of such protection. Just as moments spent inside the chamber of a Neolithic tomb seem to occur in a place adrift from the modern, so that crypt belongs to a world that is otherwise beyond our reach.

29

The Alfred Jewel, Ashmolean Museum, Oxford

An Anglo-Saxon treasure

PERHAPS THE SMALLEST of my destinations telling the story of the British Isles is the surface of the little teardrop of cloisonné enamel trapped beneath the rock crystal covering of the Alfred Jewel.

The jewel is housed in the 'England 400–1600' gallery on the Ashmolean's second floor. I have twice been filmed talking about it but have never been allowed to handle the thing. Once, I waxed lyrical while gazing at it in its glass display case. On the other occasion, I was allowed to handle one of the replicas commissioned at the turn of the twentieth century to mark the thousandth anniversary of Alfred's death. Even so – even across the void made of degrees of separation – it is a treasure that seems much more than the sum of all its precious parts.

It was found, in that way of most priceless artefacts, by a ploughman, in 1693 in a field at North Petherton in Somerset. This location is interesting in its own right, since it is just 6 miles from Athelney, where in AD 878 Alfred gathered his strength and will in preparation for the Battle of Edington, at which he defeated Guthrum and his Viking army and so halted their advance once and for all.

Specialists in the field of Anglo-Saxon finery happily describe the jewel as a high point, a zenith of the ambition, technical sophistication and sheer artistry of the craftsmen of that time. It measures about 2½ inches in length. The filigreed gold embellishing it is wrought with agonizing care and flair, patterns and flourishes so ornate they might have been piped like icing. The smith has given free rein to every twist and turn of his imagination until it seems everything possible with gold has been achieved. Around the edge are the words AELFRED MEC HEHT GEWYRCAN – 'Alfred ordered me to be made'. The whole terminates in the weird and wonderful head of a beast, its mouth agape. The cloisonné plaque behind the rock crystal features a male figure holding what look like flowers, one in each hand. Once it was thought to be Jesus, then King Alfred himself. More recently the figure has been interpreted as a representation of the sense of sight. As to purpose and function, it has been described as the headpiece for a crown and as a pendant, but the smart money now is on its having been the handle of a tool called an 'aestel' – a pointer for reading – which makes the depiction of the sense of sight entirely apposite. Once upon a time the beast's gaping maw would have held a length of wood or ivory. Aestels like these were sent, on Alfred's orders and at his own expense, to every bishopric in the land, together with a copy of a book by Pope Gregory the Great called *Pastoral Care*. It was a sort of medieval guide to good management practices, and Alfred thought it so important he had it translated from Latin into English so it might be appreciated by lay people as well as churchmen. The aestel would have been used to point out each word in turn as the book was read aloud for the edification of the illiterate masses.

For all that it is an undoubted 'precious', of the sort that might make a person 'gollum' with greedy desire, it is not the gold that makes me think it has a place in this story of the British Isles.

In *Caesar's Last Breath: The Epic Story of the Air Around Us*, Sam Kean wrote about how molecules of Julius Caesar's final exhalation, as he lay dying of his wounds on the floor of the Senate, are still around us, still there to be breathed and breathed again. So too traces, however infinitesimal, of everything from Cleopatra's perfume to the exhalations of dinosaurs.

Years ago, a good friend and I buried a time capsule on a hill near where we lived. Inside an airtight plastic box we put souvenirs – newspaper cuttings and such. We also drank half – precisely half – of a bottle of whisky. We sealed the box, re-corked the bottle and buried both. The plan was to return some day to look at the mementoes and drink the rest of the whisky. We have not done it yet, and perhaps we never will, but what I think about most is the air trapped in the box and in the half-empty bottle. It is the air of that day.

In my imagination, if nowhere else, some molecule or atom or particle of the world of Alfred the Great lies sandwiched between the crystal and the cloisonné of the jewel made in his name, like a flower between the pages of a book.

30

Hyde Abbey, Winchester, Hampshire

The burial of a king

WHEN MAKING SENSE of the stratigraphy of a trench – the order in which the different layers formed, one after another – archaeologists use the Latin phrase *terminus post quem*. It means 'the time after which'. If you find a grave with a coin in it bearing the date 1500, then it follows that the grave must have been dug at some point after that time – otherwise a coin dated 1500 would not yet have existed and could not have been in it. A 'TPQ' is a line in the sand.

The raid on the abbey at Lindisfarne by Danish Vikings in AD 793 was a *terminus post quem* for the Anglo-Saxons of the British Isles. You might also call it a 9/11 moment: the time after which everything was different.

For a generation after that utterly shocking and disorientating event, the Vikings of Denmark and of Norway were a fact of life in these islands. Up and down the east coast, in Orkney and Shetland, in the islands off Scotland's west coast, in Ireland, Northmen of one sort or another were raiding, killing and demanding gold and silver – protection money, really – in return for leaving people alone. Often it was holy places they targeted, abbeys and monasteries, but domestic settlements felt their wrath as well.

The next turning point came in 865 with the arrival in England of that Mycel Heathen Herc – the Great Heathen Army that conquered all the Anglo-Saxon kingdoms apart from King Alfred's Wessex.

Alfred may well have called himself 'King', but never 'Great'. Greatness was thrust upon him by those who came after. Every schoolchild learns (or used to) that Alfred protected his kingdom from further Viking attacks by creating the *burhs*, the network of defended towns, evenly spaced so that well-prepared units of his army could respond to any threat within a day. He began building a navy so he might tackle the foe at sea, if need be, and issued an updated system of laws. He championed education and insisted that only educated men should lead and govern. It is fair to say he is associated with much of the foundation of England, philosophical and practical, and of Britain.

His influence even crossed the Atlantic. In the years before he became the third President of the United States of America, Thomas Jefferson sought to restructure the State of Virginia along lines of which Alfred would have approved. In *Notes on the State of Virginia*, written in 1781, Jefferson suggested dividing that territory into 'hundreds' – the same unit established by Alfred for his kingdom, the same that applied in the case of Cantre'r Gwaelod, the Welsh Atlantis. Jefferson wrote: 'This bill proposes to lay off every county into small districts of five or six miles square, called hundreds, and in each of them to establish a school for teaching reading, writing and arithmetic.'

There are still those in America who take great pride in their Anglo-Saxon heritage, real or imagined. Without Alfred and his ways, there may have been no WASPs.

While he is remembered as Alfred the Great of England, in truth it was in the tenth century, the time of his son, Edward the Elder, and then his grandsons, that the Northmen were finally driven off for good, and that 'England' took on the shape and the scale it has today. But when Alfred died in 899 he was great enough. He was buried first in Winchester's old minster. He had intended to build a new one, but the work was actually undertaken and completed by Edward the Elder in the early 900s. Alfred's remains were moved from old to new, with due ceremony, but lay at peace in that new resting place only until 1110. By then the old line of Anglo-Saxon kings was at an end, replaced by those of Norman descent.

William the Conqueror's victory at Hastings and the Norman Conquest that followed was a final triumph for the Vikings in all but name. Normandy was land ceded to the Viking King Rollo by Charles the Simple of

France in 911 – it was literally the land of the Northmen. They had caused the French king so much grief he thought it best to buy them off with a territory big and rich enough to placate them once and for all. William was Rollo's descendant and so his conquest was in many ways the Vikings' last laugh – even if they were proper Frenchmen by then.

King Henry I – William's youngest son – had the monks build a new abbey for themselves at Winchester, outside the city walls, in Hyde Mead. Hyde Abbey was consecrated in 1110 and the remains of Alfred, together with those of his wife, Ealswitha, and Edward the Elder were carried the few miles from the New Minster to their new home.

Shakespeare's line from *Henry IV*, Part 2, 'Uneasy lies the head that wears a crown', might have been drafted with Alfred in mind. Having been buried three times and moved twice, his post-mortem peregrinations were not over yet.

Hyde Abbey, like all the rest, was dissolved by Henry VIII, and subsequently torn apart by locals in need of building stone. A bridewell – a combined prison and workhouse – was built on the site in the last quarter of the eighteenth century and the convicts who would call it home were brought in to help with the construction. The crypt containing the remains of the Anglo-Saxon royal family was smashed apart, like many others, and the bones scattered. Someone apparently did their best to collect them up again, from where they lay jumbled with other human remains, and they were reburied, after a fashion. In 1866 a *soi-disant* antiquarian called John Mellor conducted an excavation of sorts on the site and claimed to have rediscovered the royal bones. These he bundled up and sold to the Reverend William Williams, rector of nearby St Bartholomew's Church, who buried them in a little bespoke crypt in his churchyard.

In 2014, I was involved in a project to try to establish, once and for all, if any or all of the remains of Alfred and his family had indeed been among whatever was laid to rest there in that buried, brick-lined box. With touching reverence, the little unmarked grave was opened and the bones removed for testing. Much to everyone's disappointment, however, the resultant radiocarbon dates proved beyond any reasonable doubt that all of them were from more recent times than Alfred's – even as late as 1500.

We might have given up, but our bone expert, Dr Katie Tucker of Winchester University, took the trouble to re-examine bones collected during an amateur excavation of the Hyde Abbey site in 1999 and initially dismissed as animal remains. Katie found human bones in the mix, however, including part of a male pelvis. When a sample of the bone was tested, it returned a radiocarbon date that fixed its owner's time of death in the decades straddling the end of the ninth century and the start of the tenth – the time of Alfred's death. Since the only Anglo-Saxon remains known to have been buried at Hyde are those of Alfred and his family, it was reasonable to assume the pelvis had belonged either to Alfred or, slightly less likely, to his son, Edward the Elder.

St Bartholomew's Church is on King Alfred Place in Winchester. Close by and clearly visible is the gatehouse that once separated the inner and outer precincts of Hyde Abbey. Nothing else remains – nothing upstanding. The town jail that replaced the abbey is long gone too. Three dark marble slabs, laid flat among pale gravel and each bearing a simple cross, mark the supposed locations of the original graves of Alfred, Ealswitha and Edward, in places of honour before the high altar. The rest is parkland now.

It is the absence that is startling. Here was a great Benedictine abbey. Here too were the remains of one of only two English kings ever to have the word 'Great' added to their names. (The other was Cnut, a Viking and father of Harthacnut, who was half-brother of Edward the Confessor, who was succeeded by Harold Godwinson, last Anglo-Saxon king of England, who died at the Battle of Hastings. That Cnut and Alfred are paired by greatness seems fitting enough.)

If that hipbone is Alfred's, then he made it into the twenty-first century, quite literally, by the seat of his pants. Hyde Abbey in Winchester – or rather the empty space it left behind – is as close to him as a person might reasonably expect to get.

That empty space also has something profound to say about the Norman Conquest. Everyone knows about the Battle of Hastings, the arrow in Harold's eye, the Bayeux Tapestry depicting it all like a graphic novel. We read about how the conquest was really a boardroom takeover – with the proles carrying on much as before but under new management. The Normans had those proles build their castles and cathedrals – so much of the scaffolding that still holds the British Isles aloft today.

But what of the Anglo-Saxon ways that went before? They were scattered to the wind. Stand in the space vacated by Hyde Abbey and know that somewhere out there, lost beneath the grass, are the remains of an Anglo-Saxon royal family – perhaps the greatest branch of that tree. Lost, scattered, trampled underfoot. Here is conquest.

31

The Battle of Brunanburh

The north–south divide

F OR A BOOK about places, the Battle of Brunanburh presents an existential crisis. No story of these islands would be complete without an account of what happened that day in AD 937. That there would be one nation in the north of the long island and another in the south, rather than one kingdom encompassing all, was determined there and then. Brunanburh made certain the existence of a Scotland and an England. Destinies were set. The problem is that no one now knows where Brunanburh was.

Different writers and historians have championed their favourite locations over the years: Axminster in Devon, Barnsdale in South Yorkshire, Brinsworth by Rotherham. Burnley in Lancashire is on the River Brun and a popular contender (at least in those parts). Burnswark, near Lockerbie in south-west Scotland, is a prominent hill that has been fortified by different peoples, Romans and Picts, down through the ages. Burnswark sounds a bit like Bruneswerce, which was the name given to the battle by the twelfth-century chronicler Symeon of Durham. Other fields supposedly associated with the bloodshed are to be found in County Durham, in Lancashire and also in Wales. There is not even agreement on whether the battle was fought in the east or in the west. Perhaps it is claimed by so many because it mattered so much.

The king in the south, the land of the Angles, was Aethelstan, grandson of Alfred the Great. He had driven the Vikings out of Northumbria, completing the territory we would recognize as England. He had also forced an oath of submission from Constantine II, the king in the north – acceptance of the southern king as overlord. By AD 900 the northern kingdom was known as Alba, by the literate monks in their scriptoria at least. This Alba was a place where old conflicts between tribes of Picts and Gaels had finally been laid to rest after generations of strife, the two coming together to form one united entity under one king. The Gaels came originally from Ireland and had been given a nickname by those they landed among. They were regarded as pirates and the old word for such was *Scoti*, meaning marauders from the sea – so that Alba became a kingdom of Scots.

This Constantine, this king of Alba and his Scots, broke his word with Aethelstan and instead threw his lot in with Anlaf, the Danish Viking king of Dublin, and Owain, king of the Britons of Strathclyde. The Britons, and the Scots of Alba, marched south and joined then with Anlaf, who had brought his fighting men across the Irish Sea in their fabled longboats.

Aethelstan, together with his brother Edmund, marched an army north to meet them and the bloodbath that ensued was long remembered simply as the Great War. Even when the memory was fresh, the name of the place where it had happened was set aside. Many accounts survive, poems and songs too, in Old and Middle English, Welsh, Norse and Latin.

The most famous translation of the most famous Old English poem about it all – a fossil preserved in the *Anglo-Saxon Chronicle* – was made by Alfred, Lord Tennyson:

> *All the field with blood of the fighters flow'd . . .*
> *There lay many a man*
> *Marred by the javelin*
> *Men of the Northland*
> *Shot over shield*
> *There was the Scotsman*
> *Weary of war . . .*

It is a litany of death and unsparing in its reporting of how each fledgling nation was sorely wounded. High-born men and boys were harvested along with common foot soldiers. None was spared until the field was slippery with gore.

> *Mighty the Mercian*
> *Hard was his hand-play*
> *Sparing not any . . .*
> *Doom'd to the death . . .*
> *Five young kings put asleep by the sword stroke*
> *Seven strong earls of the army of Anlaf*
> *Fell on the war-field, numberless numbers . . .*

King Constantine's own son, nameless now, died on the field among the rest. Perhaps the ruler's tough old heart was broken then: he would step down from his throne just six years later and spend the rest of his life in monastic seclusion near St Andrews in Fife.

> *Slender warrant had*
> *He to be proud of . . .*
> *Leaving his son too*
> *Lost in the carnage*
> *Mangled to morsels*
> *A youngster in war.*

They fought until the sun set and the sky turned dark. Aethelstan claimed victory, but his army had been butchered too. From this point, what had been a confederation of Anglo-Saxon kingdoms would be the nation of England. Brunanburh had drawn a bloody line, curbed ambitions. There would be no further conquest in the north. For ever after there would be two centres of gravity on the long island.

> *Many a carcase they left to be carrion*
> *Many a livid one, many a sallow-skin*
> *Left for the white-tail'd eagle to tear it . . .*
> *Never had huger*

Slaughter of heroes
Slain by the sword edge . . .

More recently, a light has been turned on the town of Bromborough, on the Wirral Peninsula, as a likely location. Some early charters even give the name of the place as Brunanburh. The River Mersey, close by, would have been familiar to the Vikings of Ireland, sailors and seamen all, so it would have made sense as the place for Anlaf to arrive with his men.

The debate goes on. Perhaps in the case of the Battle of Brunanburh it does not matter to know the field, the hillside where all the blood was spilled. It was the Great War that settled the future of this place, the sword that sliced the land in two, leaving a scar that has never faded. And so the whole of the British Isles is the memorial of all that happened on that awful day.

It was the Athenian historian and general Thucydides, writing in the fifth century BC, who said it was not just in epitaphs on columns that profound and fateful deeds ought to be remembered: 'For the whole earth is the tomb of heroic men and their story is not graven only on stone over their clay but abides everywhere, woven into the stuff of other men's lives.'

32

Durham Cathedral

A mountain raised by men

B Y THE TIME of the building of Durham Cathedral, these islands were very different from the place where Silbury Hill was built – unrecognizably different. For all that had passed in those three millennia, and for all that was still to come, the ancient need to build, to mark, to establish a connection between Earth and Heaven above, had grown heavier yet.

The henges, the stone circles, the tombs – all had been expressions of humankind's need to find anchors in infinity. Our species had achieved something remarkable. We had conceived of some power that existed separately from even the best of us – a power that was overarching and eternal, that had existed before us and would continue without us. Durham Cathedral – looming, brooding Durham Cathedral – seems to me to invoke more potently than any other the presence of some greatness above.

Unlike Silbury Hill, the mostly Norman building that stands today within a lazy loop of the River Wear certainly went up during the course of a single lifetime. We know that much for sure. It also happened during a period of extraordinary dynamism and inspiration in western Europe.

The turning of the year 1000 had been traumatic for many folk. There had been a powerful belief that the passing of a thousand years since the birth of Christ would surely mean his return and so the ending of the world. But just as the year 2000 clicked around on Earth's odometer without incident, so 1000 may have been an anticlimax too, and without the fireworks. Within a hundred years of that date, however, our part of the world was positively thrumming with confidence, creativity and the blatant expression of all that is civilization.

After the depredations of the Vikings drove the monks away from Lindisfarne, carrying their dead saint, Cuthbert, with them, they made a new home at Chester-le-Street, outside Durham, and for 112 years Cuthbert languished there. He and they moved again as the tenth century was drawing to its close and settled in the space made by that meander of the Wear. No doubt they fancied the protection offered by the encircling coil of water. Out of timber they built a shrine for their saint. A stone building followed in time – the White Church, as it was known. King Cnut the Great came there and granted the monks more land. Soon there were so many pilgrims that the place grew rich and the town of Durham was the result.

It was as though the clouds had parted and everyone had looked up into a bright sky. They apparently found an energy they had not known before. It was a rush felt all over western Europe, and in these islands as strong as anywhere. If there was one, unifying reason for that elation, that freeing of spirits, it has been forgotten between then and now. Had the coming of the millennium's end been an awful burden right enough? When the new one dawned without supernatural incident of any sort, far less the intervention of a wrathful God, was there a collective exhalation of breath? We cannot know. Whatever the reason, whatever the inspiration for the new surge of energy, without doubt one of its most sublime manifestations was the building of Durham Cathedral, a job begun in 1093 by William de St-Calais, who had been made Bishop of Durham by William the Conqueror in 1080. William died in 1096, but work continued apace and most of what is there now was completed by 1133.

Even after all this time, Durham Cathedral is an astonishing place. I am no architect, but I sense that grandeur relies not on size alone but on proportion as well, and perhaps simplicity. Towering pillars, smoothly rounded arches, the ribbing of the ceiling of the nave like criss-crossed laces on the back of a lady's corset. They call it Romanesque in that it borrows shapes from Roman architecture, but whatever is going on in there has the effect of putting a person in their place. It is a mountainous, dominant presence from the outside as well, great cliffs of pale stone rearing high above the river.

Go there for lots of reasons: to contemplate the strange journey of St Cuthbert; to see the only surviving 1216 copy of Magna Carta – one that was drafted *tout de suite* after King John complained to the Pope that the original was making his life too hard. Mostly go to feel properly slight in the scheme of things, in the shadow cast by a mountain raised by mere men a thousand years ago.

33

Magna Carta and Lincoln Castle

The birth of democracy

IN 2014 I spent some weeks in Australia, in Canberra. It was in the run-up to the 100th anniversary of Gallipoli, the First World War campaign of 1915 that resonates so strongly in that part of the world. In New Parliament House, in a gallery on the first floor, I found a copy of Magna Carta.

Bought for £12,500 in 1952 by a Liberal coalition government led by Sir Robert Menzies, it is one of only four known copies of the so-called Inspeximus Issue of the Great Charter, made in 1297 and bearing the seal of Edward I. Of the other three, two are in London and one is on display in the National Archives in Washington DC. The Canberra copy is the only one in the southern hemisphere. Seeing it there, in a place of honour so far from home, gives a clear sense of just how much the very notion of Magna Carta really means to the democratic nations of the world.

Magna Carta was a very early declaration of the utterly revolutionary notion that not even a king was above the law. Its sixty-three clauses are out of date now, superseded by more recent legislation. It still enshrines the concept that no one should be imprisoned without trial, but apart from that its time as legal writ has passed. But the very name retains power, even for those who have not the faintest idea what its 3,500 words were ever about.

In the British Isles, the best place to see Magna Carta is Lincoln Castle. The Great Charter on display in Lincoln is a contemporary copy of the 1215 original – the same that King John argued about with his rebellious barons on a water meadow called Runnymede, by the Thames near Windsor. On paper – or rather on sheepskin – it was supposed to stop him abusing royal power in general and tax-raising powers in particular. The making of it is so familiar it features in a children's rhyme I remember learning at primary school:

> *Bad Prince John was a right royal tartar*
> *Til he made his mark on Magna Carta*
> *Ink, seal, table on Runnymede Green*
> *Anno Domini twelve fifteen.*

It is best to see it in Lincoln Castle because there, in a specially air-conditioned chamber, is the only place in the world where a 1215 original sits alongside a copy of the 1217 Charter of the Forest. This latter might arguably be the more important document and the copy in Lincoln is one of only two in existence. Within weeks of signing Magna Carta, King John persuaded Pope Innocent III to free him from any obligation to its sentiments on the grounds that he had only signed it under duress. To all intents and purposes, it was null and void. He died the following year and his son, Henry III, not only resurrected Magna Carta but also signed the Charter of the Forest, which was effectively a follow-up document enshrining the right of the common man to make use of the forests at the expense of the barons. Rather than dealing with the rights of the aristocracy, it considered ordinary people.

Once the 1215 Magna Carta had been written up, copies bearing the king's seal were sent to principal towns and cities. The one in Lincoln has on the back the original instruction that it should be delivered to 'Lincolnia'. Hugh of Wells, Bishop of Lincoln, was one of those who had signed the charter, and for centuries the city's copy languished in the archives of Lincoln Cathedral. During the Second World War it was sent to Fort Knox, Texas, for safekeeping. Only recently has it been put on public display in the castle.

Magna Carta in Lincoln, in Lincoln Castle especially, is a reminder somehow of the significance of the place. Even the name is as old as the hills. It was the Romans who made it *Lindum Colonia* – the Colony at Lindum – but they had only adapted and Latinized what the locals already called it. The Brythonic-Celtic form was *Linn-du*, which means 'the Dark Pool' (as Dublin, from *Dubh-linn*, is 'the Black Pool'). A hill sits high above a widening of the River Witham and it was there the Romans built their fort. Perhaps the hill cast the pool into shadow, or maybe the peaty soil gave the water a dark tinge.

The hill and the fort gave command of the point where the Fosse Way and Ermine Street, two major Roman roads, came together and Lindum was an important garrison town until the Ninth Legion was relocated to York around AD 71. Thereafter it became a colony town – one to which legionaries might retire at the end of their active service.

After the Romans withdrew from these islands, Lincoln was colonized by Vikings. It was the Scandinavian town that William the Conqueror appropriated and where he built his castle. When the central tower of the cathedral was completed in 1311, it was the tallest structure in the world – the first time anything man-made had exceeded the height of the Great Pyramid in Egypt. Lincoln held this distinction for two and half centuries, until the tower collapsed in a gale in 1549.

Magna Carta changed the world. Every nation that aspires to emulate our democracy invokes the spirit of that document signed and spurned more than eight centuries ago by a troublesome king. Without it the citizens of the United States of America would have some other Declaration of Independence, some lesser Constitution and Bill of Rights. Its ethos is there too in the Universal Declaration of Human Rights and, of course, in the Constitution of Australia.

34

Snaefell, Isle of Man

At the heart of the British Isles

THE ISLE OF Man coat of arms has on it the familiar three-legged motif and, below it, a Latin motto: *Quocunque jeceris stabit* – 'Whichever way it is thrown, it will stand'. The phrase has been associated with the Isle of Man since the seventeenth century, but the motif is much older. Properly described as a triskelion, it has been around for thousands of years, as in the triskelion in the form of three spirals joined at the centre etched into one of the monoliths of the 5,000-year-old Neolithic tomb of Newgrange in Ireland. Interpretations are, like a triskelion, manifold, and the best of them suggest that the symbol depicts continuous movement, the cycle of life, eternity.

Adrift in the Irish Sea, roughly equidistant from England and Ireland, the Isle of Man is an anomaly. Independent of Britain and yet not; technically a Crown dependency and yet with its own parliament – called the Tynwald and claimed by the islanders as the oldest of its kind in existence.

Man's oddness is in part a consequence of its having been cut off from the mainland – either Britain or Ireland – since the time when sea levels rose at the end of the last ice age. Since then it has been settled by most of the usual suspects. Hunters arrived by boat, then farmers. The Romans knew the place too, but may never have settled there. Sometime around AD 800 the Vikings came. From the thirteenth century onwards, its ownership was batted between the kings of Scotland and England.

As the Latin motto has it, the Isle of Man has been tossed around, metaphorically speaking, and yet still it stands, a place apart. Viewed from above, set in the context of the British Isles, it appears as near as dammit the centre of the whole archipelago. It is touched by all and yet retains a unique character.

Half an hour on the narrow-gauge railway from the village of Laxey on the island's east coast takes the visitor to the summit of Snaefell, at 2,036 feet. From there, on a clear day, they say you can see seven kingdoms – Man itself, England, Ireland, Scotland, Wales, the sea and Heaven above. On a day when the clouds roll in, it is still possible to sense the rest out there in the invisible. Man is often overlooked. Most will never visit. But it is the geographical heart of these islands and Snaefell is therefore their central point.

Queen Elizabeth is the head of state, known there as the Lord of Man. Since the island is independent, but not sovereign, it administers its own domestic affairs via the aforementioned Tynwald. Like the triskelion, it has three legs, or three chambers at least – the House of Keys, which is the elected body; the Legislative Council, whose members are elected by the House of Keys; and the Tynwald Court, which is formed of the first two coming together. Those that care to believe it say the Tynwald was established by Vikings in the tenth century. The word is certainly born of the Old Norse *thingvollr*, which means 'the field of assembly'.

There is something perfect, and apposite to a story of the British Isles, about finding, at the heart, somewhere that is stubbornly independent of all around it. You will find many who dismiss the place as a throwback, left behind; but if it is and has been, then on Man this feels like a virtue. The Manx language is a unique variant of the Gaelic the Irish brought there many centuries ago. Even the cats are different – the so-called Manx cat being tailless as a result of genetic mutation. The folklore on the island has it that their cat was the last to board the Ark, squeezing inside just as Noah closed the door and having its tail nipped off in the process.

Just as the Manx cat's tail is cut off from the body, so Man is cut off from some of what has happened elsewhere. Something of the past is there, or many different pasts. A walk along the prom in Douglas, the capital, takes you past buildings with names left behind in Victorian or Edwardian days – the Imperial, the Empress, the Savoy. There is simply something other-worldly about the whole place. Even the name of the island has mystery. Man is apparently from Manannán mac Lir, 'the Son of the Sea', the god tasked with ferrying the souls of the dead to the underworld. Either the island is named after him, or he is named after the island . . . you take your pick.

35

St Nectan's Glen, Trethevy, Cornwall

The invention of the future

SOME PLACES THAT matter to the telling of a story of these islands were made special by nature long before any involvement or effort of mankind.

In the Cornish hamlet of Trethevy, between the towns of Boscastle and Tintagel, lies St Nectan's Glen. The river that flows through it, ringing like a bell, bright as light, might stand for the careless passing of time itself. Time matters to us alone. Alone among all the living things, we are consciously preoccupied by its presence. We are the only species in the world, perhaps in the universe, that has been troubled enough to make and keep a record, to wonder not only where time comes from, but also where it might be going.

For us, this Cornish glen, this work of the world, bears the name of a Christian saint, but the glen mattered before his kind and will count as special for as long as our species cares to seek solace in places formed by forces other than those we wield ourselves. For all of these reasons, I could have placed this glen elsewhere in the narrative, anywhere perhaps. This is the order of events that makes sense to me. I place it here.

The saint in question was born in Wales sometime in the middle of the fifth century. He was the son of King Brythan, whose family had crossed the Irish Sea to Wales when he was still a youngster. While he was growing up, Nectan heard tales of St Anthony – Anthony the Great – who had lived as a hermit in the Egyptian desert. Inspired by thoughts of coming closer to his God by finding isolation of his own, Nectan set out with some companions aboard a boat they let drift where it might. It came ashore at Hartland in north Devon and for a while they made a home there in a forest. Still in search of more – or less – Nectan found his way to Cornwall and finally to a deep, wooded glen at what is now Trethevy. Tradition has it he built himself a little cell beside a deep pool hollowed out by the River Trevilet. They call the pool St Nectan's Kieve, after the local word for a tub or a bowl. The river has worn a hole through the kieve, through the Late Devonian slate of which it is formed, and from there it cascades as a splendid 60-foot waterfall before continuing on its way. The sea is not far and it is said Nectan would ring a bell to warn sailors whenever the weather turned foul.

As anyone might expect, the waters of the river are known for their healing properties. Its importance as a place of pilgrimage surely pre-dates St Nectan, however: people have been coming to the glen since time immemorial. The glen is certainly a lovely place, its rock walls thickly cloaked with moss and ferns. Below the clattering, shimmering fall, the water spreads shallow across a broad and level shelf of rock.

There visitors have taken to building little towers of flat stones, called fairy stacks. On the overhanging branches of trees are countless ribbons and other tokens, offerings left in place by people seeking help or guidance of one sort or another. Some seek a cure for physical ills, but most seem to come in hopes of finding a salve for wounds to the spirit, the soul. Etched into the rocks are names and messages written by those who came to remember loved ones. Most are as simple as could be: 'Mum x'. Photographs, some old, some new, are left behind to be consumed by the damp. Crystals, children's toys and other gifts are tucked into little clefts or balanced precariously just out of reach by those who have dared to climb up the slippery rocks. It is fair to say St Nectan's Glen is revered, made holy by people's faith and attention. Older than any church or stone circle or temple, it has drawn hopeful people for the longest time.

The Anglo-Saxon King Aethelstan is supposed to have heard about St Nectan in the days before the Battle of Brunanburh. A boy from Hartland, where the saint had first made landfall in England, had been afflicted by some or other plague. He took himself to the glen and prayed for a cure. His prayers were answered and he told the king to ask the saint for victory in the battle to come. Aethelstan did as he was told and at least lived to tell the tale.

As much as by anything else, or maybe more than, we are made by the stories we tell ourselves and each other. Part of that has been the making, or rather the noticing, of places that seem sacred. These islands are made in part of faith – or, if not of faith, then of a sense of obligation to something unseen but sensed just the same. Sometime in the ancient past our species experienced a revelation of sorts. People came to believe in the future. In every sense that matters, they invented the future as a concept. Having grasped the idea of a place that was real to them but which did not yet exist, one, or some, of our species had the realization that the future might be asked to be good – even commanded to be good. And so they made plans and performed rituals to affect the nature of it, so that when it arrived it might suit them. Part of this was making sacrifices of things they valued. Belongings, animals, food – sometimes members of their own kind – were paid forward. As well as settling debts by breaking and giving back swords, surrendering precious jewellery, scuttling priceless boats, they asked the future to be kind to them by offering up until *then* things that were urgently needed *now*.

'Cast thy bread upon the waters: for thou shalt find it after many days.' Those words from Ecclesiastes 11 are thousands of years old but probably record a way of thinking that is much older than Judaism or Christianity or any other formal religion still alive on the planet. It was a profound thought, perhaps the most profound of all thoughts, and for its proper enactment special places were sought and set aside. Eventually such places would be designed and built – clearings made by fire, henges, stone circles, temples, churches – but at first they were simply selected from what already existed in the world all about, formed by nature alone.

Stand quiet in St Nectan's Glen and it seems like a sacred place just because it is. Nectan was surely not the first to feel that way about it and it seems unlikely, at best, to believe it was his religion, his faith that made it so. More believable by far is that he was directed to the place by others who knew it already. The power of the glen is timeless – both older and younger than any formal religion. People have brought their hopes and cares there for the longest time and maybe always will.

These are the stories we are made of.

36

Arbroath Abbey, Angus

Light in the darkness

O N ACCOUNT OF the old French belief that all Englishmen were little better than monkeys, folk from Kent have the nickname 'long tails'. In Linlithgow, in the central belt of Scotland, the locals are 'black bitches'. I kid you not – something to do with a dog that was once chained to a post on an island and that features now on the town coat of arms, but no one is quite sure any more. In Arbroath they call themselves 'Reid Lichties'.

Some dozen or so miles out to sea from Arbroath lies a long, jagged reef called Inchcape. It was ever a dreadful hazard to ships, and local legend has it that for a while there was a bell on it to give some warning to sailors. For that reason the reef (and also the Stevenson lighthouse upon it, the oldest of its kind in these islands) is also known as the Bell Rock. Before the bell, there was, in another place, a light – a brazier kept burning by the monks of Arbroath Abbey in a great round window high in one wall of the south transept. The window is an empty socket now, open to the wind and rain, but the locals remember its importance and still call it 'the Round O'. It is because of the Round O and the red fire that once burned in it, that the citizens take the name Reid Lichties. By all accounts it watched, from its perch in the heart of the town, over landsmen as well as mariners. As an anonymous poet of the nineteenth century had it:

> *It was there where my father and mother both taught me*
> *To deal honest and fair, to be kindly and free*

And never to forget there's One Eye above us
That watches our actions where'er we may be.

So Arbroath Abbey was once a watchful place, and also a beacon, in keeping with the words in John 1:5: 'And the light shineth in darkness; and the darkness comprehended it not.'

It was also the richest abbey in Scotland. King William the Lion granted the necessary lands to a community of Benedictine monks in 1178 and when he died, in 1214, he was buried in front of its high altar. As well as the makings of great wealth, including the incomes from more than a score of parishes, he also gave into the brothers' care the Monymusk Reliquary. One of the most revered of Scotland's treasures, it is said to have held the remains (some of them, at least) of St Columba – the Dove of the Church, the same that founded the monastery on Iona. When Columba died in 597, he was buried on Iona, but fear of the Vikings led his followers to exhume his remains in 849 and they were divided then between religious communities in Ireland and Scotland.

Shaped like a gingerbread house, but made of bronze, silver and wood, the reliquary was said to ensure victory in battle, much like a latter-day Ark of the Covenant but without the bolts of holy fire. Columba had history as a bellicose individual after all, and it most likely made sense for the righteous to invoke his spirit in any time of battle against the sinful. The reliquary is said to have seen active service at the Battle of Bannockburn in 1314 and is now in pride of place among the collections of the National Museum of Scotland in Edinburgh.

The abbey itself took at least a lifetime to build – sixty years or more – but the finished article was so vast and so grand there was little need for enlargement or significant alteration in the centuries that followed. For all its size, today it feels tucked away out of sight, at one end of the High Street and beyond a grand, red-sandstone gatehouse. In older days it was plastered inside and clad on the outside with some sort of render. Those coverings are long gone and now the sandstone, harried for centuries by the salt air, is as pinkly red as a face freshly scrubbed.

Like the Temple of Orkney at the Ness of Brodgar, like little Iona where

Christianity took refuge while the Dark Ages waxed and waned, Arbroath and its abbey feel like places forgotten or overlooked. If the name registers at all, it might only be because of the smoked haddock delicacy – the 'Arbroath Smokie' – that they make there by the thousand each day. But this seeming irrelevance is only another trick of time, for Arbroath also had its hour, when it saw the drafting of a document that would resonate across the world. In time it would, like Magna Carta, inspire those who composed the American Declaration of Independence.

By 1320 Robert Bruce, King Robert I of the Scots, had been fighting to secure his crown and his throne for fourteen years. It was six years since his luminous victory at Bannockburn. Berwick, the last town in English hands, had fallen to him in 1318 and yet still the English king, Edward II, and his ally Pope John XXII refused to acknowledge him. In the eyes of the Church, Robert remained excommunicated – the murderer of John Comyn, Lord of Badenoch, before the high altar of Greyfriars Monastery in Dumfries in 1306. As far as the Pope was concerned, it was this *soi-disant* king of Scots who was to blame for all the strife with England. It was in such an atmosphere that Bernard de Linton, Chancellor of Scotland and Abbot of Arbroath, composed what we know as the Declaration of Arbroath.

In reality a letter to the Pope bearing the names and seals of fifty-one grand men of the realm, the declaration began with a history of Scotland up to the end of the thirteenth century. Scotland had long been an independent land, it said, free of the overlordship of England or anywhere else. It was Edward of England who was to blame for all the horrors that had unfolded: 'The insults that this prince has heaped upon us, the slaughters and devastations . . .'

But while Abbot Bernard praised Robert as the king who had rescued the land and its people, the real *declaration* concerned the consequences he would face if he let them down:

> To him we are bound . . . but if he should desist from what he has begun, and should show an inclination to subject us or our kingdom to the King of England . . . then we declare that we will use our utmost

effort to expel him from the throne . . . and we will choose another king to rule over us . . .

Imagine the audacity! In a world in which kings and queens held their power directly from God, Abbot Bernard dared to declare that this Robert Bruce, this King Robert who had already done so much, risked all and everyone he had ever loved in order to take and hold a kingdom, would be pulled from his throne and cast out if he proved unworthy:

for as long as a hundred Scotsmen are left alive, we will never be subject to the dominion of England. It is not for glory, nor for riches, nor for honours that we fight, but for freedom – this alone – which no good man surrenders but with his life.

As a final flourish (it being as well to be hung for a sheep as for a lamb), Bernard left the Pope in no doubt that from this moment on, having read the letter, any further bloodshed would be the Holy Father's fault and his alone:

If your Holiness does not sincerely believe these things . . . be well assured that the Almighty will impute to you that loss of life, that destruction of human souls, and all those various calamities which will follow.

The Declaration of Arbroath, written within the walls of the abbey there while the fire burned red in the Round O and the wind blew as cold and sharp as revenge, was truly a revolutionary document, an assertion of democracy in a world where previously the common man and woman had counted not at all. In truth, 'the people' were the landowning nobility rather than the rank and file, but it was still a bold move.

For all its undoubted panache, the letter had little immediate effect on the Pope. Before he died, Robert would be welcomed, like a lost lamb, back into the fold of the Church. It was another eight years, however, before the

Treaty of Edinburgh–Northampton brought about the formal acknowledgement of Robert as king of an independent Scotland.

Today the abbey seems to wait for something, quiet at the heart of the city. The only reid licht now is made of sunlight on worn sandstone walls. But it was a beacon once – saving souls upon the sea as well as on land – and the thoughts composed there helped illuminate the whole world.

37

Glastonbury Tor, Somerset

A place of legends

Back in 2011, I was the warm-up act for U2 at Glastonbury.

Maybe you had to read that line more than once. No one would blame you for dismissing, as nonsense, the suggestion that before Bono and The Edge hit the Pyramid Stage, Glastonbury 2011 was all about me.

In fact . . . I made a little film that year about the legends surrounding Glastonbury and its Tor and it was broadcast as part of the BBC's live coverage of the festival. Immediately after my insert had gone out on the box, Radio 1 DJ Jo Wiley told the watching millions I reminded her of Frank Gallagher (unkempt and disreputable patriarch of *Shameless*, thanks for that) and introduced U2.

Dig beneath the surface of any myth, peel away the layers made of telling and retelling, and chances are you will find a little bit of truth, however unlikely or unexpected.

Glastonbury Tor is another stage, one set for magic and mystery. Like an elongated jelly mould, that ethereal sandstone hill rises some 500 feet out of the surrounding fenland. Its sides appear sculpted, the effect of a set of seven level terraces stepped into the slopes. Quite how or why those terraces came to be remains unclear. Either they were made by nature or by people, but even now there is no agreement among geologists and archaeologists and the rest. There is even an abiding tradition that it was the very existence of Glastonbury Tor, with its tiered shape, that inspired the

Neolithic farmers of Wiltshire to build the gigantic, eccentric wedding-cake mound that is Silbury Hill.

The tor is topped by a pale stone tower, three storeys high – all that remains of what was once the church of St Michael. The first church of that name on the site lasted from the eleventh century until 1275, when it was destroyed by an earthquake. Its replacement stood from the fourteenth century until 1539, when reformist zealots unleashed by Henry VIII pulled down all but the tower, which, defiant, still sticks up from the grass.

Walk through the nearby town of Glastonbury and the myths and make-believe are so thick in the air you practically have to swat them away from your face. It seems as if every other shop is selling crystals or statuettes of dragons, rune stones or Tarot cards. The smell of smouldering incense sticks is everywhere, and up and down the streets (especially in summer, but at other times besides) stroll all manner of colourful characters. Glastonbury exerts a magnetic pull, and people do come.

It has been that way for hundreds of years, if not longer. In 1184 the local Benedictine abbey was wrecked by fire. As good luck would have it (you might say), the monks made a wonderful discovery while they set their backs to the job of building themselves a replacement. While digging foundation trenches for new walls, they found a dressed stone. Underneath was a lead cross bearing a Latin inscription: *Hic iacet sepultus inclitus rex Arturius in insula Avalonia* – 'Here lies entombed the famous King Arthur in the island of Avalon'.

Beneath the cross was a huge coffin, carved from a substantial part of an oak tree, and inside it two skeletons. One was of a man of great size and the other that of a slender woman. Here then were the mortal remains of the legendary King Arthur and his lovely queen, Guinevere.

By any measure it was a top result for the brothers. Whether or not it was a shameless fiction and publicity stunt, a person must decide for him or herself, but at a stroke Glastonbury was on the map of the wider Christian world. Given that the tomb of the martyred Thomas Becket in Canterbury on the other side of the country was already drawing pilgrims like flies, the discovery of the grave of Arthur and Guinevere was set to make Glastonbury every bit as big a pull. And it did. Soon the faithful were flocking to the place. In 1278 King Edward I came with his own queen, Eleanor of Castile, to witness the reburial of the royal and ancient bones in an elaborate ceremony. Glastonbury quickly became internationally famous. Here was Avalon, and Arthur.

But of course, that is only part of the legend of the place. The story goes that just twenty years after the crucifixion of Jesus Christ, Joseph of Arimathea came to Glastonbury. Joseph was Jesus's great-uncle and folklore even has it that he had earlier brought the young Christ himself to spend time acquiring wisdom among the Druids of the west. According to the Gospels, he provided the tomb in which Jesus's body lay until he rose from the dead. Better yet, Joseph is said to have brought with him to Glastonbury from Palestine the Holy Grail, the cup from which Christ had drunk wine at the Last Supper and in which his blood and sweat had later been collected while he hung dying on the cross. This Joseph buried, for safekeeping, at the foot of the tor. He then climbed up the slope of nearby Wearyall Hill and, near the summit, thrust his staff into the ground. This took root at once as the thorn tree that flowers in Glastonbury to this day – in the spring, like all hawthorns, and also and uniquely at Christmas time.

It is all so fantastical – and so medieval. It seems easy to dismiss and yet . . . and yet it has to be asked why so much legend has collected around that one spot – like the nacre that grows around a grain of sand to make an iridescent pearl.

Curiously enough, archaeologists and geologists have learned that, 2,000 years ago, Glastonbury Tor really was surrounded by water, at least some of the time. Back then, and before the advent of modern drainage, the fens and marshes flooded every winter. The waters of the Bristol Channel encroached all around until the tor would have been made a temporary island. An older, Welsh name for the tor is Ineswitrin, or Ynys Wydryn, which means 'the Island of Glass' and may recall a time when its appearance suggested a hill sitting upon a mirror.

The south-west corner of England was a destination, 2,000 years ago, for ships that followed the coastlines all the way from the Mediterranean world to western Europe. It is certainly reasonable to suggest that people from as far afield as Palestine might have come here in search of the tin for which that part of Britain was famous from as early as the Bronze Age. Was Joseph of Arimathea among them, aboard a ship that ventured into the Bristol Channel and all the way to the Island of Glass? Who can say?

In any event, from the twelfth century onwards, the monks were loudly claiming to all and sundry that Glastonbury was where Christianity had first arrived in these islands. This was a time in history when Christian pilgrimage was more popular than ever before and in order to take advantage – to make a destination hot on the list of favoured destinations – claims had to be as captivating and irresistible as possible. Whatever they found or did not find, those monks of Glastonbury laid the wonder on as thick as the mortar with which they built their new church. Their home was not just Avalon, last resting place of England's most romantic king and his ethereally lovely wife, but also the place where Christianity in these isles had begun. Better yet, the faith had arrived in Glastonbury while the memory of the living Jesus was still fresh in the mind of one who had known and loved him as a man, as well as God.

When the Reformation was in full flood, Glastonbury became a place of horror and fear. On 15 November 1539, eighty-year-old Richard Whiting, Abbot of Glastonbury, was dragged up on to the summit of the tor. There, along with two of his brother monks, he was hanged, drawn and quartered. The mutilated bodies of all three were then hung up on the tower of St Michael's Church in an ugly, shameful mockery of the Crucifixion.

In spite of it all – or because of it all – Glastonbury is an undeniably captivating location. The sculpted tor with its tower; the twice-flowering hawthorn – *Crataegus monogyna biflora* – so conveniently symbolic of life in the midst of deathly winter. There is even a spring, the Chalice Well, that flows with water stained red. It is only iron from the rock beneath, but given the legend of the buried Grail, itself stained with the blood of Christ, it is all wonderfully serendipitous. Surrounded by its ancient yew trees, the spring provides some 25,000 gallons of its strange, metallic-tasting water every day. Even in times of drought, when the people might have gone thirsty, it keeps flowing.

For as long as there have been people here on Earth and on these islands, they have needed and wanted places to gather, places to revere as special. As a species, we have needed to hear and tell stories that give us a sense of who we are, where we came from, what life might be about. Whatever the truth of it – whatever does or does not lie buried there – Glastonbury Tor is evidently one of those places.

38

The Fortingall Yew, Perthshire

Europe's oldest living thing

A Latin harsh with Aramaicisms
poured from his lips incessantly; it made
no sense, for surely he was mad. The glade
of birches shamed his rags, in paroxysms
he stumbled, toga'd, furred, blear, brittle, grey.
They told us he sat here beneath the yew
even in downpours; ate dog-scraps. Crows flew
from prehistoric stone to stone all day–
'See him now.' He crawled to the cattle-trough
at dusk, jumbled the water till it sloshed
and spilled into the hoof-mush in blue strands,
slapped with useless despair each sodden cuff,
and washed his hands, and watched his hands, and washed
his hands, and watched his hands, and washed his hands.

EDWIN MORGAN, 'Pilate at Fortingall', 1984

IN SCOTLAND THERE is an old story that has Pontius Pilate born in Fortingall in Perthshire. There is no proof of it, none whatever, but as the man himself is supposed to have said during the trial of Jesus Christ, 'What is truth?'

Pilate was certainly the procurator of Judaea between AD 26 and 36. More credible sources suggest he was a Spaniard or a German. He may simply have been a born-Roman from somewhere in the territory we know as Italy. But still the legend of a Scottish birth persists.

Although the Romans' attempts to conquer Britannia in 55 and 54 BC under Julius Caesar ended in failure, in the decades that followed and up until the successful invasion by Claudius in AD 43, Rome is believed to have maintained contacts in the archipelago. Her agents were *in situ* all the while, striking deals and forging alliances with the tribes. It is not unreasonable to imagine she had a man or two in the territory she would come to know as Caledonia. If so, then a relationship, a love affair even, between a Roman man and a Caledonian woman is also possible. It is this scenario that would allow for an infant Pontius being born in Fortingall.

There are references to a chief Metellanus in Glen Lyon who may have been feted by Roman envoys keen to forge a relationship with a powerful man in the north. Perhaps it was one of the women of his tribe who became mother to a Roman child. What she might have made of Rome when her husband was recalled and the little family travelled away into the east is anyone's guess.

Glasgow-born poet Edwin Morgan knew the story too and so imagined the man returning to his birthplace in old age. Tormented by his part in condemning Christ to crucifixion and death, he still seeks to wash the guilt, the blood, from his hands.

If Pontius Pilate really was born in Fortingall, then he would have known the yew tree that grows there. Scientists expert in the study of trees happily allow that the Fortingall Yew is at least 3,000 years old. Some of them accept it may be as much as 9,000 years old and therefore the oldest living thing in all of Europe. If any of that is true, then the tree was already old when Pilate was a boy. Perhaps he sat in its shadow and listened while his father told him tales of empire.

Like St Nectan's Glen, the Fortingall Yew is a work of nature. If it is as old as some folk say, ought it not to appear many pages back? If it has been growing for nine millennia, should it not feature first when this place of ours was not even an archipelago, but still a peninsula of western Europe? For me the yew tree that grows in Fortingall represents something more and older than the sum of its particles. For me it is out of time. Like Arthur C. Clarke's monolith, it seems to me it has always been there, casting its shadow over all that our species has done. Like us and everything else on this planet, that tree is made of the stuff of stars that burned out long ago. Those elements are fixed for now in its roots and branches, its leaves and berries, but in some way they are for ever. They have been around since their stars died and, once that tree has given up the ghost at last, they will recombine as something else, something else in Fortingall.

The modern village of Fortingall nestles at the eastern end of Glen Lyon – the glen Sir Walter Scott called the 'longest, loneliest and loveliest . . . in Scotland'. From Fortingall the glen stretches for 25 miles into the west, all the way to Loch Lyon. There are good reasons for believing the glen has mattered to folk living there or thereabouts for thousands of years. Archaeologists have found traces of settlement during the Neolithic as well as in the Bronze and Iron Ages. Some 10 miles or so down the road, beyond Craig Dianaidh and between Slatich and Camus Urachan, is a little hill called Tom a' Mhoid – 'the Moot Hill'. On it sits an ancient stone roughly carved with a cross. This is St Adamnan's Cross (pronounced Athavnan), and it is close by a stone with a deep hole cut or worn in it where that man of God (who also wrote the hagiography of St Columba, his predecessor as Abbot of Iona) is said to have chased the plague out of the glen. Elsewhere is a grassy mound called Càrn nam Marbh, 'the Cairn of the Dead', which marks the mass grave of villagers taken by a later outbreak of disease. Tradition has it that an elderly woman, passed over by the plague, was the only one fit enough to tend the dead. They say it was she who carried the bodies one by one, dug the pit and raised stones above it for their marker.

Before any of that, all of that, there was the yew tree. Its presence may have been the inspiration for everything else. By the time Christianity was being preached in the glen by St Adamnan or whoever, that already ancient tree may have meant the place was considered sacred.

The Fortingall of today is largely the product of improvements dating from the latter part of the nineteenth century when wealthy ship-owner and philanthropist Sir Donald Currie bought large tracts of land there. He was generous and spent goodly sums building churches, schools and the like. The present church was built between 1900 and 1902 – a mere stripling indeed, the stuff of the blinking of an eye when compared to the tree close by. No doubt the location of the church was determined by that ancient incumbent. In the church grounds are a worn stone font, cross-marked slabs and bits and pieces of crosses that may be Pictish in origin. Long before the church, from some time in the seventh century, there was a monastery on the spot.

The Fortingall Yew, impressive though it still is, has been diminished in recent centuries. In 1769 its girth was measured and found to be 52 feet. This circumference is marked on the ground with pegs, but souvenir hunters have taken a toll since then. The magic of the species, though, is that whatever happens to the growth above ground, new life springs always from the roots below.

Standing by the yew now, you might consider the passage of time. If it really is 9,000 years old, then every scrap of history we know about – from a time before even the advent of the first farmers, a lost world when hunters stalked red deer through the dappled light of the wild wood – has happened in its shadow.

39

Cambuskenneth Abbey, Stirling

The Battle of Bannockburn

FOR ALL THE fervour and fascination surrounding the name of Bannockburn, as a place in the real world the battlefield has always proved elusive. I have been part of two attempts to use archaeology to pinpoint the site of the fighting, and any number of historians have had a stab at finding the seat of the fire that still warms the hearts of Scottish nationalists and patriots alike. In spite of furious debates, endless digging and ferreting around, metal-detecting, divining with coat hangers and a great deal of wild conjecture, not much in the way of hard evidence has ever come to light. To put it another way, from the would-be visitor's point of view there has always been precious little to see.

This is a shame. The Battle of Bannockburn was, for Scots, the defining moment in the long Wars of Scottish Independence. The fight did not start there – neither did it finish – but the victory in the shadow of Stirling Castle was an immortal roar of defiance.

Brown road signs lead to a patch of high ground a couple of miles south of the city centre. It was there, by the side of what is now the Glasgow Road, that King Robert I and his lieutenants are said to have watched the approach of the English army. Tradition has it he had raised his standard there, a rallying point – and the site would certainly have afforded a good view south along a road first built by the Romans and now leading to the castle.

For years it was thought the fighting had been nearby as well, and so it made sense, in 1964, to put a heritage centre on the site in advance of the 650th anniversary of the battle. A huge rotunda of concrete blocks was built then too, as a memorial of sorts, alongside a twice-life-size statue of the king by sculptor Charles d'Orville Pilkington Jackson. The statue is a splendid thing – Robert fierce in helmet and chain mail, mounted upon an even fiercer warhorse. In 2014, in preparation for the 700th anniversary, the old heritage centre was replaced with a high-tech offering that uses 3D trickery to recreate the spectacle of the conflict. It is fantastic fun – complete with galloping holograms of mounted men, hails of arrows real enough to demand dodging, and a battle room where you can take a hand in fighting the battle all over again. But no soldiers ever fought anywhere near there.

The English army had come north to relieve the Scottish siege of Stirling Castle. The fortress, high on its rock, was held by an English garrison, but Edward Bruce – the king's brother and in command of the siege – had promised his enemy he would back off and leave if an English army marched to within a mile of the place by Midsummer's Day 1314. King Edward II – son of the much more formidable Edward I – sent a large force to meet the terms of the deal. King Robert was less than thrilled. He had been fighting a successful guerrilla war for years, striking without warning. Now his brother had committed him to taking up a position at a pre-arranged place and time when on paper at least he simply lacked the necessary numbers.

Thrilled or not, he brought his army into position and prepared the ground – famously digging pits filled with sharpened stakes, Vietnam War-style – to halt the advance of the dreaded English heavy cavalry. There was a first, inconclusive clash on 23 June. After it, the Englishmen made camp on the flat floodplain by the River Forth – what they now call the Carse. Early next morning, King Robert led his men in a surprise attack. The English had expected him, and them, to disappear overnight, back into the shadows, but he launched a headlong assault instead. Hemmed in by the various meanders of the River Forth and two of its tributaries, the Pelstream and the Bannock Burn, the English cavalry were unable to deploy. The silvered coils of the rivers that had offered them protection in

*St Wystan's Church, Derbyshire.
Holy air encased in stone, a
precious surviving fragment of
the world of the Anglo-Saxons.*

Durham Cathedral, where men lifted their gaze from earthly concerns and looked towards Heaven above.

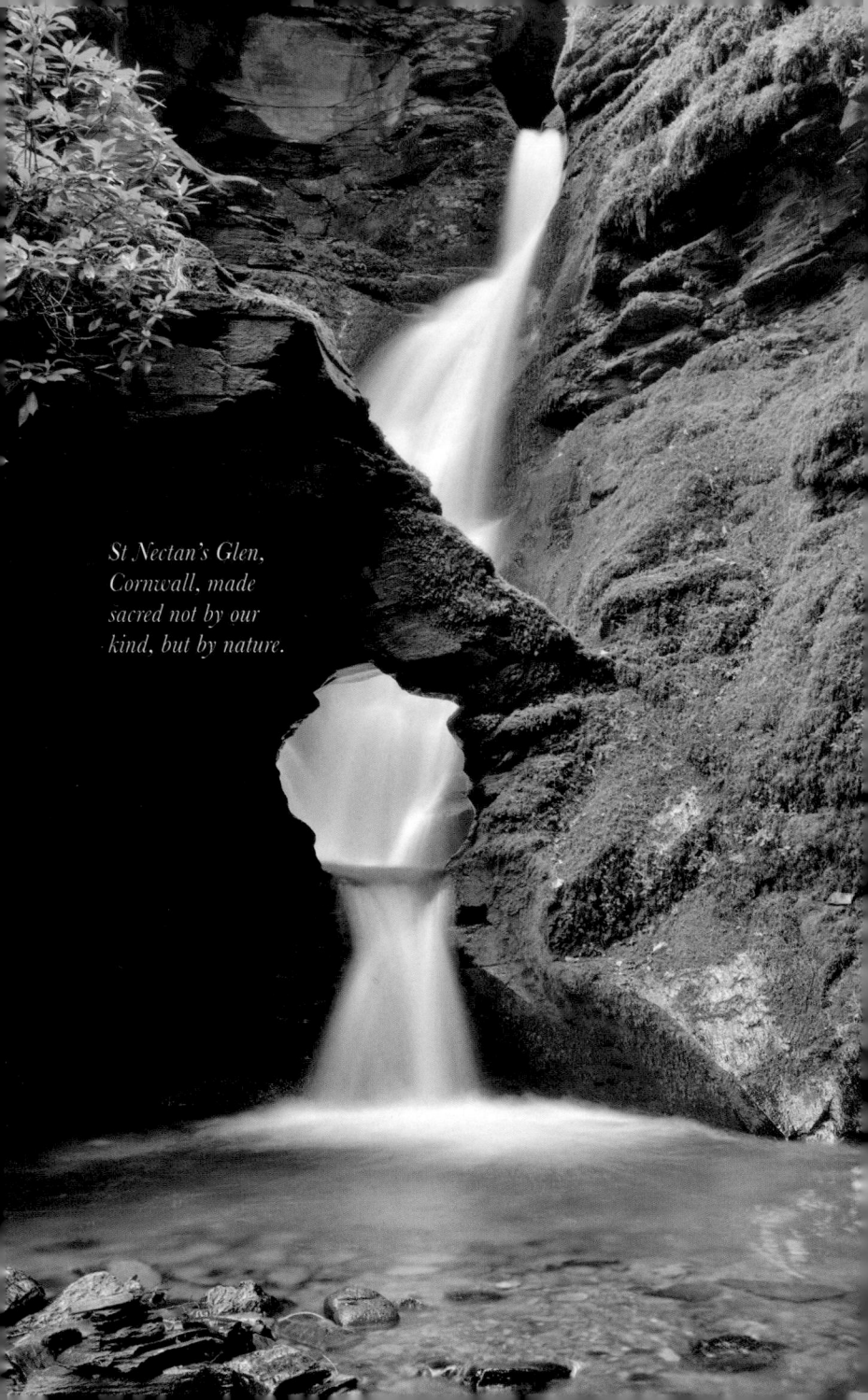

*St Nectan's Glen,
Cornwall, made
sacred not by our
kind, but by nature.*

The Fortingall Yew, Perthshire.
Before kings and kingdoms, empires
and emperors, before any of it, a tree
grew at the end of a sacred glen.

Harlech Castle, Gwynedd. A clenched fist of masonry, a place of last stands and legends.

*Stirling Castle – the brooch that pins
Scotland's Lowlands to her Highlands.*

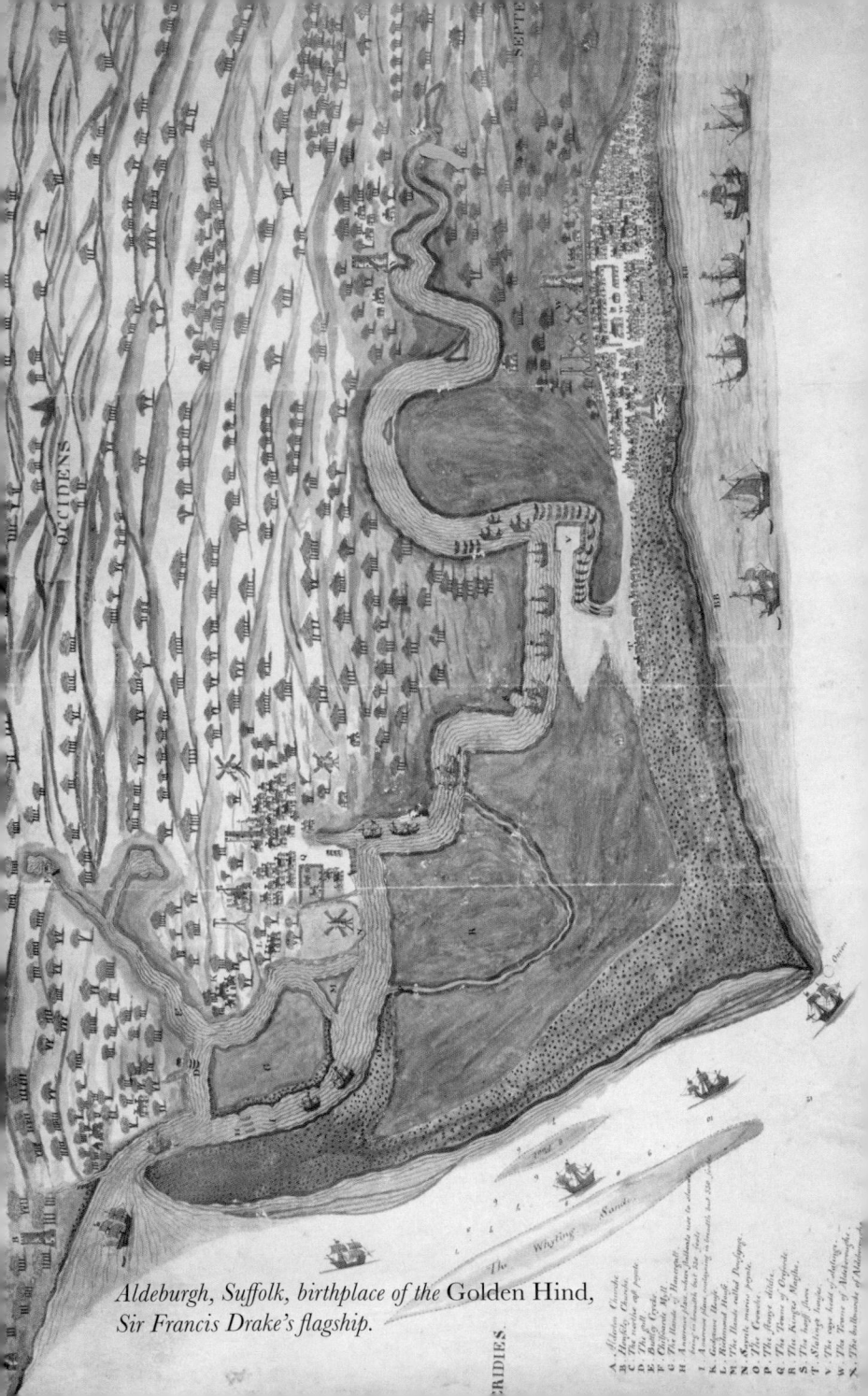

Aldeburgh, Suffolk, birthplace of the **Golden Hind**,
Sir Francis Drake's flagship.

the dark made nooses for their necks in the morning. The Scots, armed with long pikes and advancing shoulder to shoulder like one huge angry porcupine, were able to press their advantage. The mass of the English army turned and ran – uncounted hundreds, even thousands of them, drowning in the various waterways as they tried in vain to escape. They say the water ran thick and red – that so many English dead blocked the streams a Scotsman might walk across them dry-shod. It was a stunning victory for the Scots. King Robert's army had been dwarfed by the English force, but his tactics and audacity had carried the day.

Courtesy of the most recent archaeological projects around Stirling Castle, we nowadays have a far better idea about where that hellish clash at dawn on 24 June 1314 took place. A would-be sightseer must now come down off the high ground at the visitor centre and make instead for the Carse. East of St Ninian's Kirk, the Pelstream is still visible. In 1314 it presented steep banks overgrown with brush and trees. The Bannock Burn survives too, and it is still possible to follow its path across the Dryfield of Balquhidcrock. Now more or less tamed by drainage, in 1314 it was a fast-flowing tidal stream and therefore a terrifying obstacle for men on the run, weighed down with chain mail.

A large-scale metal-detector survey led by archaeologists from Glasgow University in 2014 found three artefacts likely to have been dropped during the battle. It sounds, and is, a pitiful hoard. But after 700 years buried in acidic soils, any find from that day is miraculous. A medieval iron spur, worn by an armoured man, was unearthed on land between the Pelstream and the Bannock Burn. An iron stirrup was found on the east bank of the burn and also a copper-alloy cross pendant decorated with gold, silver and blue enamel. Of a style popular in the fourteenth century, it may have been part of the adornment of an English nobleman's horse, torn away and lost during the rout.

Within shouting distance of the Battle of Bannockburn (and also the battles of Stirling Bridge on 11 September 1297, where the name of William Wallace was made legend, and Sauchieburn on 11 June 1488, which saw the death of James III) is Cambuskenneth Abbey. The name means either 'the Creek' or 'the Haven of Kenneth' and remembers yet another battle there, in the ninth century, when King Kenneth I, often called first king of Scotland, defeated an army of Picts.

As it flows across the flat Carse, the Forth meanders in the laziest of manners, making loops and coils like a silver necklace dropped in the grass. Within one of those, on a space that is all but an island, in the twelfth century King David I granted land to a community of Arrouaisian priests and had them pray there for his immortal soul. The place was torn apart after the Reformation, but a fine, three-storey bell tower – the only campanile of its sort in Scotland – was left mostly intact. Perhaps it was too useful as a lookout over the surrounding flat land. An upstanding gothic archway close by appears at first like an elaborate gateway to a little cemetery but was once the west door to the abbey church.

There in the shadow of the tower, looking towards the loop of river, it is easy to imagine the ground is little changed from the days of King Robert. The abbey was well known to him. It was there, in June 1304, that he signed his name to a bond 'of mutual friendship and alliance against all men' with William Lamberton, Bishop of St Andrews. Loss of independence for Scotland would have put the Scottish Church under the control of the Archbishops of Canterbury and York. Bishops like Lamberton fancied Robert as the king most likely to maintain their separateness, and by the bond signed at Cambuskenneth he was promising their support. It was also a treasonous document, and both men agreed that whoever failed to live up to it would pay the other the fantastic sum of £10,000.

It was there in the abbey that King Robert held a parliament in November 1314 where, among other things, he seized the lands of those Scots lords who in June had either stayed away or fought against him. In 1326, in a chamber known by then as Parliament Hall, he established the rights of succession that gave Scotland its long line of Stewart kings.

Rivalry and discord between Scotland and England has been a recurring theme in the story of the British Isles. Before the existence of either, there was Brunanburh. Bannockburn was another letting of the same bad blood. While tens of thousands of men hacked at one other with steel blades, the priests of Cambuskenneth could do no more than pray. The abbey had been Edward Bruce's base for his siege of the castle in the months before the battle, and King Robert parked his baggage train there. The same metal-detector survey that found the spur, stirrup and cross also discovered an English silver penny at Cambuskenneth. Minted in London during the late thirteenth or early fourteenth century, it would have amounted to a month's pay for one of Edward's soldiers. Perhaps it was a tiny fragment of the booty, the spoils of war taken back to the baggage train by Robert's army.

After the Reformation, stone from the abbey buildings was carried off and used elsewhere – notably for a house built near the castle for John Erskine, Earl of Mar.

History hangs in the air at Cambuskenneth, so that you might feel it brushing against your face. Folk living thereabouts talk of seeing ghosts. The bell tower is like a bone sticking up through the turf, a stubborn remnant of other days, bloody days.

40

Westminster Abbey, London

Wars of the Roses

THERE ARE MORE than 3,000 tombs in Westminster Abbey containing the remains of dead folk, and 450 monuments remembering more that are buried elsewhere. It is a reliquary, a shrine for the British Isles, a grand box of memories. Kings and queens – eighteen of them – servants of the abbey and of the realm. Geoffrey Chaucer, who died in 1400, was first among the many gathered up into Poets' Corner. Brave knights and soldiers. Musicians and artists. Heroes. Charles Dickens and Sir Isaac Newton have their graves in the abbey. William Shakespeare and Winston Churchill have memorials.

Of all the gravestones set into the floor the only one that may never be walked upon is that of the Unknown Warrior of the First World War, scooped up from a battlefield cemetery on the Western Front. 'Thus are commemorated the many multitudes who during the Great War . . . gave the most that man can give life itself,' it says on his stone. 'They buried him among the kings because he had done good toward God and toward his house.'

Who knows what molecules hang in the sacred air of Westminster Abbey. Edward the Confessor built himself an abbey on Thorney Island in the Thames in 1050. His Palace of Westminster was nearby and he wanted, when his time came, to be buried close to home. Little remains of what he ordered built, but the door on the right as you enter the Chapter House is a surviving fragment. Made from an oak tree cut down sometime in the middle of the eleventh century – when William the Conqueror was still in his late teens or early twenties – it is the oldest door in Britain.

William the Conqueror sought to legitimize his rule over England and the English by having himself crowned in Edward's abbey. He was the first king of England to do so, and he set a trend. Henry III built the abbey we see today, from the mid-1240s onwards. He was a huge fan of Edward, a saint by then, but he kept next to nothing of what had been there before – just that door, really. It must have mattered. When it was in Edward's abbey it was bigger – as much as 9 feet tall rather than the mere 6-footer it is now. Maybe it was connected to some remembered moment or time from Edward's life – perhaps the door to whichever room the monks chose for the laying out of Edward's body or where prayers were said for the dead king. In any case, although he was making everything else new, Henry kept that door and had it cut to fit the space between the Chapter House and the abbey cloisters.

Edward's remains were exhumed and made the centrepiece of the new abbey. Henry was one of those who carried the coffin to its resting place within a lavish shrine of gold and jewels. In years to come, more kings and queens were buried around him – Edward I and Eleanor of Castile, Richard II and Anne of Bohemia, Edward III and Philippa of Hainault. Henry III is there too, and Henry V.

Coiling invisible from the tomb of Edward III are the tendrils that bore the bitter fruit of England's Wars of the Roses in the middle years of the fifteenth century. The battles fought in the name of Lancaster and York, two rival houses of the Plantagenet family, bloodied fields from one end of England to the other. It was the longest and most violent run of civil wars in English history. The crown changed hands five times and tens of thousands of men died forgotten deaths. And yet it can be hard to find anywhere in the landscape that stands for all of that.

Something in my wiring means it matters to me to find physical connections to events. Places to stand, things to touch. My dad's dad was wounded more than once fighting in the First World War. He came home with a piece of metal lodged in the flesh between his left ear and his skull. I could feel the edge of it if I ran a fingertip over the surface there. That Grandpa had a fragment of the Great War in his head was amazing to me. He had brought the war home and so was my real-life connection to all the unbelievable stuff that had happened to millions of men between 1914 and 1918.

So when I read a story from history, I wonder where I can go to feel closer to it.

Westminster Abbey may be as good a place as any to look for the Wars of the Roses. It is a filing cabinet of death, a hard drive burned with names.

The wars were all the fault of Henry VI, great-great-grandson of Edward III. If he had been a stronger man, a better king, none of it need ever have happened. His father, Henry V, of Agincourt and all that, would have been a tough act to follow for any prince. As it was, Henry VI was mentally and emotionally fragile, the wrong sort of man to be a medieval king.

Abbot Bernard of Arbroath had declared in 1320 that an unfit king – one who could not wield power in the best interests of the people – would be cast out and replaced. But while that might be easy to say, the doing was another matter. The Wars of the Roses were an inevitable consequence of leaving a lame duck on the throne because he seemed too well-meaning and kindly to overthrow.

Henry let things slide, failed to govern effectively. Factions formed in the darkness close by him, and old rivalries turned poisonous. His cousin and sometime advisor, Richard, Duke of York, chose to claim the throne for himself, and all hell broke loose. By 1460 Richard's head was on a spike at the Micklegate in York. His son declared himself King Edward IV and sought revenge as well as the crown. The great charnel house of the wars – Towton, on Palm Sunday 1461 – was his own creation. No quarter was given and none expected because by then it was a fight to the death.

Thousands died on nondescript fields outside the Yorkshire village of that name, perhaps tens of thousands. A worn, easily overlooked stone cross by the side of the B127 road marks more or less the centre of the battlefield. The armies formed up on a line from east to west; the Yorkists would have been towards the south, the Lancastrians to the north. Historians used to say the soldiers fought for hours that day, from dawn until dark. The tally of dead was put anywhere between 20,000 and 40,000. More recently archaeologists and others have decided none of that was possible.

The physical reality of fighting with heavy swords in the midst of a snow-storm surely meant men were exhausted far sooner, fought and brought to a standstill. An apparent absence of mass graves might mean fewer died. But Towton was remembered as a horror – another Brunanburh. It seems fair to imagine it was a butcher's yard by the time they were finished and that a generation was scarred by what they had seen and done.

Francis Bacon described the Plantagenets as 'a race dipped in their own blood'. There was more claret to come. The Lancastrians kept harrying Edward, but he held them at bay until his own death in 1483. His brother, Richard III, lost it, crown and all, at the Battle of Bosworth Field in 1485, to the vaguely Lancastrian Henry Tudor, first of his line.

Henry Tudor reigned as Henry VII. He extended the abbey eastwards by building the Lady Chapel, described by those who know best as the finest example of Tudor Gothic architecture in these islands. It may be the brightest jewel in the abbey, with a ceiling they call a pendant fan vault and that looks as though it was iced like an upside-down wedding cake. Henry is buried there, in a tomb designed by the Italian sculptor Pietro Torrigiano, who lost his temper with Michelangelo when they were at art school together and broke his nose.

Best of all is the tomb tucked away in a side room off the Lady Chapel. Here is Lady Margaret Beaufort, Henry Tudor's mother. She was married off to Edmund Tudor, half-brother of Henry VI, when she was just twelve years old. Even by the standards of the day she was a child bride, but Edmund took her into his bed just the same. She had Henry, her only child, when she was thirteen and her husband died of the plague the same year, leaving her a widow. Margaret was a tiny little thing, more like a bird than a woman, yet she fought all her life, and like a lion, for her son. She lived to see him made king – and also his son, Henry VIII.

If there are ghosts in Westminster, she is there among them, tough old broad. The bronze likeness over her bones is unsparing and shows a face lined with all the enervating toll of a fight that lasted a lifetime. But it was her son who was the ultimate winner of the Wars of the Roses and she is the mother of the Tudor line of kings and queens. If her ghost walks among the rest, then she might well feel truly proud of herself.

41

Harlech Castle, Gwynedd

Last stand of the brave

MYTH-MAKING IS PART of human nature. Where a story matters a great deal to its audience, or its storyteller, the facts may be played with over time – augmented and modified. When certain facts no longer deliver the effect intended by the storyteller, or if they may not please the audience, they might be dropped altogether, replaced with new material. What remains is neither truth nor fiction but a blending of both.

The 1964 war film *Zulu* was a massive box-office hit. It presented a version of the events that unfolded in and around a British Army supply station called Rorke's Drift in Natal in southern Africa during the course of a couple of days in January 1879. Around 150 British and colonial soldiers were attacked there by perhaps 4,000 warriors of the Zulu nation. Despite the overwhelming odds, the defenders dug in and successfully repelled wave after wave of attackers. Queen Victoria was so impressed by the bravery of her men that she awarded an unprecedented total of eleven Victoria Crosses – the highest accolade for British fighting men. A highlight of the movie sees Welshman Private Owen, played by singer Ivor Emmanuel, respond to a song being sung by the massed Zulu army.

'Think the Welsh can't do better than that, Owen?' asks commanding officer Lieutenant John Chard, played by Stanley Baker, as the deep tones of African voices roll and rumble across the veldt.

'Well, they've got a very good bass section, mind,' says Owen. 'But no top tenors, that's for sure.' And so he clears his throat and begins to sing 'Men of Harlech'.

Since the film portrays the defenders of Rorke's Drift as mostly Welshmen, all the soldiers know the words of the anthem and one by one they join in until their voices rise to do battle with the chanting of their foe. Even thinking about it now makes all the hairs rise up on my neck. It is part of the magic of the storytelling.

The problem for historians, however, is that Rorke's Drift was defended by soldiers of the 24th Regiment of Foot, a majority of whom were Englishmen. Only a small proportion of the total at that time – perhaps 10 or 15 per cent – were Welsh. There were also Scots and Irishmen. Even more awkward for movie fans is the fact there is no record whatever of anyone singing during the battle. If they did, then the regimental song at the time was not 'Men of Harlech' but 'The Warwickshire Lad'.

Zulu is myth-making at its very best. I have been watching it, off and on, since sometime in my childhood and its hold on my imagination is profound. I have helped survey and excavate some of the battlefields of the Anglo-Zulu War of 1879, of which the defence of Rorke's Drift was a part, and have read several heavyweight books on the subject. I know almost as much as anyone about what really happened there and yet some deep-buried part of me continues to believe the fiction of the movie at the same time. I have a great deal of respect for the power of the myth.

That spine-tingling, hackle-raising anthem 'Men of Harlech' remembers and celebrates events that played out in Harlech Castle in the county of Gwynedd in north-west Wales during the Wars of the Roses. The truth of those moments is buried too, slumbering beneath the weight of yet more myth-making.

Harlech was and remains a clenched fist of a place, built between 1283 and 1285 on the orders of Edward I of England. Llywelyn ap Gruffudd, the last sovereign Prince of Wales, had defied Edward and paid for his temerity with his life. The English king had gloried in his conquest of Gwynedd, taking away from there all the royal insignia and also a fragment of the True Cross that had been held by her kings and princes for hundreds of years. Edward was determined to subdue Wales and the Welsh for all time and so built an 'iron ring' of castles to defend his garrisons and strangle the living daylights out of any opposition.

The construction of Harlech, on the coast of the historic county of Merionethshire, was overseen by James of St George, Master of the King's Works. Remembered and revered as a military engineer of unsurpassed genius and ingenuity, James of St George exploited the defensive character-istics of 'walls within walls'. Harlech is therefore a castle within a castle, defended and defended again by great cliffs of masonry rising from its spur of rock. Even now it looks impregnable, beyond all reach, stubborn and pale against the dull mercury of the Irish Sea beyond. While the waves had Harlech's back, its front was defended by stone walls a dozen feet thick. The east gatehouse in particular feels almost absurdly strong. Best of all, the secret of the success of Harlech was a defended staircase leading 200 feet down a cliff face to what was then sea level. From there the defenders within could be supplied by ship and so prolong any siege almost indefin-itely. The water gate is dry now – left behind by a dropping of the sea level that has taken place during the last seven centuries – so that Harlech Castle is a kind of rock pool left waiting for a returning tide.

The defences were first tested in 1294. Edward was busy again then. Just two years before, he had overseen the placement of John Balliol on the throne of Scotland and had had the feckless soul swear allegiance to his English overlord. He had France in his sights as well, yet still found the time and energy to put down a revolt in Wales. Madog ap Llywelyn, a dis-tant cousin of the last prince, raised an army and set about attacking towns and castles held by the English – including Criccieth and Aberystwyth, both of which had also been remodelled by James of St George. Inside Harlech were just forty fighting men and yet they held off Madog and all that he could bring to bear against them.

Owain Glyndŵr, rebel and self-styled Prince of Wales, sought to cast off the English yoke in the first decade of the fifteenth century. English Harlech held out stubbornly, but after weeks of siege it fell to his forces in early 1404. Glyndŵr made it his home and held a parliament there in 1405. The grinding resilience of English intent could not be withstood for ever, though, and by late 1408 or early 1409 the castle was back in English hands.

It was half a century later, during the Wars of the Roses, that another last stand at Harlech provided the proper stuff of legend. After the Yorkist victory at the Battle of Northampton on 10 July 1460, Margaret of Anjou, wife and queen of the Lancastrian King Henry VI, fled the field and ran with her entourage all the way to Harlech. For the best part of the next eight years the castle was a monument to Lancastrian defiance, resisting all Yorkist attempts to winkle out the defenders. Soon enough it was the Lancastrians' last redoubt, all the rest of their strongholds in England and Wales having surrendered. Finally, in 1468 the Yorkist King Edward IV sent a huge force, perhaps 10,000-strong, against its walls. This stage of the siege was too cruel, and even the water gate was not enough to prevent the inevitable. After a month, the defenders were starved into submission. History was done with them, but not the myth-makers. Those were the defenders later immortalized in song as 'The Men of Harlech', whose stubborn bravery became a standard to which all men of valour might aspire.

> March ye men of Harlech bold, Unfurl your banners in the field
> Be brave as were your sires of old, And like them never yield!
> What tho' evry hill and dale, Echoes now with war's alarms
> Celtic hearts can never quail, When Cambria calls to arms.

Last stands have ever been the stuff of legend and Harlech, like the supply station at Rorke's Drift, has been fixed for ever in the canon. It stood defiant a final time during the English Civil War, before falling at last to Oliver Cromwell's forces in 1647. The music of the song was not composed until sometime in the late eighteenth century and then a first version of the lyrics was published in *Gems of Welsh Melody* in 1860.

From the top of the castle's tallest tower, the view out over the sea or the streets of the town, or across to the mountains of Snowdonia, is enough to swell the hardest heart. Harlech is a UNESCO World Heritage site now and the monumental nature of the defences makes it easy to see why. The almost sheer faces of the rock seem defence enough. James of St George certainly knew what he was about, and the way he reinforced the only vulnerable approach, to the main gate, is still so emphatic as to make you draw breath. To walk beneath not one but three portcullis gates is to understand just why Harlech was a thorn in the side of so many would-be conquerors.

42

Morecambe Bay Sands, Lancashire

Lost in the mire

FOR ALL THE man-forged horrors committed here in these islands, and they are best left uncounted, the geographies themselves feel safe enough, and placid. Volcanic eruptions and serious seismic events are lost in the past. The great tsunami wave that washed and scoured away lives and land up and down the long island's eastern seaboard is forgotten by all but geologists. It is not even the stuff of folklore. Courtesy of the North Atlantic Drift, we have a climate that is soft, free in the main from life-threatening extremes. Aside from the odd adder on a path on a sunny day – hidden treasure, a flicker of diamonds on dark – we have no dangerous wildlife any more. It is worth remembering, however, that there are places in our landscape where a person can put him- or herself, knowingly or not, into harm's way. These British Isles have swallowed more history than anyone can remember. Lost in the mire of unreliable memory are whole peoples, whole empires – their sunken hides turning dark as tea and crushed flat by all the weight of time.

There is, too, at least one stretch of sand and sediment that serves as a reminder that the process of disappearing is still at work.

Morecambe Bay, between north Lancashire and south Cumbria, has been both a place of ethereal, scintillating beauty and a serious threat to life for hundreds, if not thousands, of years. Born at the end of the last ice age, it is our largest area of intertidal sand and mudflats – 120 square miles of the sort of lone and level sands that would swallow whole any statue of Ozymandias, King of Kings. In all, five rivers drain into the Irish Sea there – the Kent, the Keer, the Leven, the Lune and the Wyre – sculpting the sand and mud so that from above the bay has the look of a pale curtain torn ragged by the wind.

Dumped by retreating ice sheets, the sediments there are tens of metres deep. The river channels move like snakes in slow motion, sinuously altering their place day by day, month by month. The tide comes in faster than a horse can gallop, they say – certainly quicker than you or your family could run. You might be standing hand in hand with loved ones admiring the view, with a toddler on your shoulders maybe, while behind you all a channel is swiftly filling with cold seawater and cutting off your retreat to shore. Although across the great distances of the bay the surface appears level as a table top, the tidal range can be as much as 30 feet, meaning the incoming tide is not just too fast to outrun, it also creates deep water. It is altogether treacherous and lethally dangerous.

A few years back I spent a day in the bay with the venerable Cedric Robinson, the Queen's Guide to the Sands. Such was the loss of life endured by people having to cross the bay that appeals for help were made to the Crown during the 1500s and in 1548, during the first year of the reign of Edward VI, only son of Henry VIII, an official guide was appointed. Cedric is the twenty-fifth to bear the title, having been in post since 1963. He is paid £15 a year by the Duchy of Lancaster and, more usefully, is entitled to live, for the duration of his tenure, in Guides Cottage in Grange-over-Sands, overlooking the bay.

A lifetime of experience makes Cedric the very best person with whom to venture out on to that vast and lovely expanse, and I walked with him as he marked the route for his next guided tour from Arnside to Kents Bank, a distance of about 8 miles. We carried with us a supply of 'brobs' – branches of laurel. One at a time he placed them as markers, forcing their cut ends into the soft sand where they quickly anchored as though rooted there. Laurel has always been the choice because the leaves stay on the branch even when they have turned brown, making them more visible than species that wither to bare branches.

Under Cedric's supervision I also investigated the phenomenon of the infamous Morecambe Bay quicksand. When high tides deposit sediment into deep hollows, the mixture of mud and sand may be so saturated it cannot support a person's weight. Such trouble spots, randomly located, are known locally as 'melgraves' but a more apt description of the effect of all that water and sand is 'cow belly'. Walk out on to a melgrave and the whole surface wobbles disconcertingly; I felt as if I was on the skin formed over the top of a giant rice pudding. Spend more than a moment there and you begin to sink. Once your feet and ankles are submerged, stepping clear of the glaur is already difficult. Sink down as far as knee depth and freeing yourself becomes a physical impossibility. Without mechanical assistance, such as a winch, you are doomed – fixed in place to await the incoming tide that will drown you. It sounds unlikely that something so simple might pose such a threat, but I write from experience. The suction of the saturated sediment is frighteningly strong, irresistible. Put hands in to pull at your feet and they are grasped too, so that now you are bent double while you await the waves.

Cedric has led hundreds of thousands of visitors safely across the sands. He explained that the infinite moods and looks of the bay are all products of wind, tide and weather – and that it is a combination of high tides, heavy rain and strong wind that transforms the environment into some place deadly. In 2004 a group of twenty-three Chinese immigrants drowned while cockle-picking. The cockle beds are as old as the hills and since time immemorial people have come to grief while harvesting them. Countless dead have been consumed by the sand, never to be seen again. Nowadays climate change is making the place even more unpredictable and dangerous. Submerged out there too are innumerable vehicles – from horse-drawn carts to 4x4s – swallowed whole without a trace or any hope of recovery.

From all around the bay it is possible to glimpse the fourteenth-century pile of Piel Castle. Stubbornly planted on the southern tip of Piel Island, at the north-west limit of the bay, it was built by the abbot and monks of Furness. It was a dubious place, its loyalty to the Crown debatable. The monks exported wool and other valuables to the Continent from Piel without paying much of anything in the way of taxes. On 4 June 1487, it was the mustering station for one last roll of the Yorkist dice. Tudor Henry VII was king by then – a usurper in the eyes of many, if not most – and so a final gasp of Yorkist resistance gathered like a forlorn gust of wind behind an unlikely would-be king. Lambert Simnel was the ten-year-old son of an Oxford craftsman, but a group of conspirators paraded him as Edward, Earl of Warwick, nephew of Edward IV and therefore a rightful claimant to the throne. The brief campaign that followed – with an 8,000-strong army of pressed men and mercenaries – was the bitter end of the Wars of the Roses. There was a pitched battle in due course, at Stoke Field near Newark, and Henry's army trampled the threat into the grass. The rebel leaders were killed, most of them messily butchered, but miraculously Henry saw Simnel for the hapless puppet that he was and took him to work for him as a kitchen servant and then a falconer. He eventually married and lived into the reign of Henry VIII.

In 1933 the elegant Midland Hotel was opened in Morecambe – an art-deco masterpiece complete with works by acclaimed artist Eric Gill. Believe it or believe it not, Morecambe and the bay were known in those just-forgotten days as the 'Naples of the North'. Signing their names in the register at the Midland then were 1930s glitterati like Coco Chanel, Noël Coward and Laurence Olivier.

The shifting sands of Morecambe have swallowed every last trace of those times – luminous stars and boy-kings all. Look upon my works, ye mighty, and despair. It is a landscape that has a great deal to teach about threats to the unwary and the temporary nature of all but the rock of the Earth.

43

St George's Guildhall and the Hanse House, King's Lynn, Norfolk

European trade links

THE EUROPEAN UNION is hardly the first free-trade organization to have sought to rise above national borders. All of eight centuries ago the members of trades guilds living and working in cities along the Baltic Coast began cooperating with one another in ways that would be broadly familiar to the nabobs and panjandrums of modern Brussels, the de facto capital of the EU.

The precursor of all that we know now in twenty-first-century Europe was the Hanseatic League, which began to crystallize into a recognizable structure from as early as the late 1100s. Vikings from Sweden and Gotland had sailed and rowed their longships across the Baltic and then down the River Volga. The peoples they encountered there called them the *Rus* – which means 'the men who row' – and in time the whole vast territory would take its name, Russia, from those bold pioneers.

The trading links established then formed the framework for all that came later. From the thirteenth century onwards, the craftsmen of the guilds, or *Hansa*, forged links that spread out from the city of Lübeck on the Baltic – east as far as Novgorod and west as far as the British Isles. (A letter signed in the East Lothian town of Haddington by William Wallace, apparently in the aftermath of his victory at the Battle of Stirling Bridge in 1297, was sent to 'the Senate and commoners of Lubeck and Hamburg' to let them know that a newly independent Scotland was open for business with the League.)

The Norfolk market town known then as Lynn – now King's Lynn – grew up on land close by the point where the River Great Ouse flows into the Wash. In 1204, Lynn was given a royal charter by King John. Then, during the thirteenth and fourteenth centuries, it developed to become the third most important port in England and, along with only seven others in the country, Lynn was made part of the Hanseatic League. Ships sailing in and out of such nodes were assured protection from piracy and guild members could expect to have their voices heard during the negotiations for international trade agreements. Lynn was soon busy with traders from all over northern Europe. Herring, iron, pitch, timber and wax arrived in the port, and cloth, grain, lead, wool and skins were dispatched from there to ports elsewhere.

Just as the Romans had dominated trade in the Mediterranean Sea in their own time, so the league exercised similar dominance in the north for more than three centuries. But rather than force, their influence was based largely on trade and supranational cooperation. Between July 1322 and October 1323, more than £6,000 worth of trade goods passed through Lynn – a colossal sum for the time. Merchants from the German cities even owned properties in the town. During the Wars of the Roses, financial support from the Hanseatic League helped the ambitions and campaigns of Edward and his House of York.

King's Lynn today still features evidence of all that international influence. On St Margaret's Lane stands the Hanseatic Warehouse – also known as the Hanse House – which was built around 1480 by foreign merchants granted permission to store their wares. It is not only unique in England but also a rare find anywhere in Europe. St George's Guildhall, on King Street, was built in 1406. At over 100 feet long, nearly 30 feet wide and two storeys tall it is the largest and most complete of its kind in the whole country. As well as meetings of the local guilds, the hall was used for the performance of plays. Local legend has it that William Shakespeare used the venue for one of his own productions in 1593.

It is all a reminder of another, earlier, time when folk of the British Isles looked east for trade. It was the discovery of the New World in the west that sounded the death knell for the Hanseatic League, ushering in a 180-degree shift of interest that would see the power of the Baltic cities steadily wane.

44

Stirling Castle

Scotland's silver brooch

WE IN THE Oliver family consider Stirling Castle our own personal property, so there. Since 1927, anyone living within the space defined by what is called 'the Old Burgh boundary' – the ancient city limits, if you will – has had free entry to the place. As long as we remember to take something with our address on it – like a gas bill, for instance – we are in, buckshee. But whatever Historic Scotland is charging for a ticket now, it is worth it. Stirling Castle is just the best.

They say Stirling, and more specifically the castle, is the silver brooch that hitches the Highlands of Scotland to the Lowlands. As usual there is truth even in that sentimental statement. In ages past, before the drainage that came with modern farming, the few miles around the castle rock provided the only dry passage for men or beasts. On either side, to east and west, was miserable morass. Right up into the modern era any warlord or general needing to march an army north or south had to pass close by the rock. Hold the rock and you controlled all comings and goings. The Romans appreciated as much and built a road leading straight to it, but if they bothered to raise a fort on it, not a trace remains.

The rock on which it stands – like nearby Abbey Craig, upon which sits the National Wallace Monument – is what geologists call a 'crag and tail'. When a glacier of the last ice age ground its way across that part of the world, it hit stumbling blocks of hard volcanic basalt. Those stubborn plugs defied the bulldozing power that lowered the softer material all around them and so remained proud. The hard crags also shielded and protected the softer material immediately behind them and it is this that forms the sloping ramps called the tails. Edinburgh Castle – more famous but not nearly as good – sits atop another of the same, with the tail there providing the slope of the Royal Mile.

King Malcolm Canmore – who killed Macbeth to avenge the murder of his father, Duncan – had a fortification on the site in the eleventh century. From that time on, Stirling Castle is shot right through Scotland's story, and therefore through the story of the British Isles. Kings and queens were born there, christened and crowned there, died there. Edward I pounded its walls with a colossal trebuchet – an outsize catapult – he called War Wolf, to punish Scottish defiance of his will. The garrison had already surrendered, but he battered the place to smithereens for his own amusement and because he could. William Wallace had it for a while. Robert Bruce fought the Battle of Bannockburn to keep it and then smashed it down so it might not ever again fall into English hands. On and on it goes. James II of Scotland lost his temper with the young Earl of Douglas there, murdered him and flung his still-warm body out of a window.

James III was born in the castle in 1451. James IV built the Great Hall, famous for its hammerbeam roof (built without a single nail) and for being, then and for a long time thereafter, the largest indoor space in Scotland. After his death at Flodden in 1513, his son, James V, completed the construction of most of what stands on the rock today. To please his French queen, Marie de Guise, he had French artisans build her a glamorous Renaissance palace. Houses in the nearby King's Park have plum trees in their gardens, and local legend has it they are descended from others planted in what was then open parkland by a Scottish king anxious to provide food his French wife might like. Their daughter, Mary Stewart – who would be Queen of Scots – was hidden from Henry VIII behind the castle's walls until she could be got away to the elegant sanctuary of the French court, aged five.

The old horror had wanted Mary as a bride for his infant son, Edward, but in spite of 'the rough wooing' he dealt Scotland – murdering, raping and burning – he never got her. Cut through the topmost battlements is a little circular spy-hole her guardians made for her – so a toddler queen might peek out at her demesne without fear of her ginger curls being spotted by Henry's agents prowling below.

In due course her own son, fathered by the disastrous Henry Stewart, Lord Darnley, was christened in the Chapel Royal. Soon after his birth she told one of her advisors 'this is the prince whom I hope shall first unite the two kingdoms of England and Scotland'.

The Scotland in which James was born was Protestant, and yet the rites at his christening, on 17 December 1566, were Catholic. Elizabeth I was his godmother, but stayed away. Darnley had been part of the recent murder of David Riccio, Mary's favourite courtier, and was as far from Mary's favour as it was possible to be. He too ducked the ceremony, skulking in corners, and would be murdered the following year in Kirk o'Field in Edinburgh. He was heir to the Lennox Stewarts and claimed by some as a rightful king of Scotland and yet hardly a soul remembers him as such today. Instead of king, or even king consort, he is just Darnley, little more than a cipher. By custom, the priest ought to have spat into baby James's mouth, but Mary forbade it. No expense was spared, so they say, and the event was marked with the first recorded fireworks display in Scotland.

In more recent years the castle has been the regimental headquarters of the Argyll and Sutherland Highlanders. They had the Great Hall for a barracks, but by 1999 they had moved out and the whole place was restored to glory, the exterior limewashed to golden brilliance so that it shines now like a crown. The interior of the fabulous palace built for French Marie has been restored too and is a wonder to behold – colours so bright it almost hurts to look at them.

Something of the world before survives in Stirling Castle. Because so much of it is what Jameses IV and V made real, their decades hang around the place like dust sheets over furniture worth preserving. Of those two kings – in fact, of all the men, women and children of Stirling Castle – I am most affected by James IV.

In the first year of the sixteenth century, a wandering friar called John Damian presented himself before James at Stirling Castle, claiming among other things that he was an alchemist. James evidently liked him and let him stay. He financed the experiments and also lost money to him at cards and marbles. Years passed, however, and no base metals were ever transformed. Possibly in a bid to divert attention from his failings, Damian said he would fly from the castle walls. A crowd gathered. Damian donned a pair of wings covered in feathers and duly leaped into space from the battlements. Either by luck or good judgement, he landed in a soft but stinking pile of muck. His leg was broken, but he was still alive.

If it ever happened, it ought surely to have reminded a well-read man like King James of the Greek legend of Icarus, who flew too close to the sun on similar wings and fell to his death.

In 1513, James embarked upon a grand adventure of his own. Placing too much faith in technology, and in his own prowess, he set in train a sequence of events that would – directly and indirectly – change the destiny of Scotland and of these British Isles.

45

Flodden Field, Northumberland

The Flowers of the Forest all withered away

THE MELODY OF 'The Flowers of the Forest' has lasted longer than any words. Recorded countless times, played at funerals, services of remembrance, woven into at least one film score, it is a tune you will have heard, even if you did not know its name at the time. It was composed as a lament for the dead of the Battle of Flodden, but no one knows exactly when. While the battle was fought on 9 September 1513, more than a hundred years would pass before the musical score was first written down and published. If there were words to go with it, they had been forgotten by then. The familiar lyrics – recorded by everyone from Kenneth McKellar to Dick Gaughan to Isla St Clair – were composed by Jean Elliot, a Scottish poet, in the middle years of the eighteenth century:

> I've heard them liltin' at the ewe milking
> Lassies are liltin' before dawn o' day
> Now there's a moanin' on ilka green loanin'
> The Flow'rs o' the Forest are a' wede awa'.

So it is with the battle itself. The emotion has survived – the sadness, the melody – much longer and more clearly than any understanding of why events had to unfold as they did.

We have the bones of it. Scotland's king at the time was James IV. Since he was drawn to science and the arts, he has been called a 'Renaissance king'. He employed at least one alchemist and financed experiments to find the 'quintessence' – the legendary fifth element. He wore a cilice, some sort of spiked belt, around his waist as painful penance for his part, murky at best, in the death of his father, James III, at the Battle of Sauchieburn, outside Stirling, in June 1488.

In 1503 he married Margaret Tudor, daughter of Henry VII of England. The two kings had signed a Treaty of Perpetual Peace the year before, and the royal wedding was supposed to underscore their commitment to avoiding internecine strife. If only life were so simple.

James was also bound to France and her king, Louis XII, by the ties remembered by many Scots as the Auld Alliance and forgotten by most French as the Treaty of Paris. Henry VIII succeeded his father in 1509 and by 1513 was making plans to take an invasion fleet across the Channel. James duly honoured his obligations to his auld ally and rounded up the biggest army ever led into England by a Scottish king.

Margaret Tudor was understandably torn and bemoaned 'the unnatural spectacle of seeing my husband arrayed in mortal combat against my brother'.

It went James's way for a while. With his huge host, tens of thousands strong, he crossed the River Tweed into England near Coldstream. The castles of Norham, Etal and Ford fell quickly into his hands. His critics claimed he dallied at Ford with Elizabeth, Lady Heron.

With Henry fighting in France, the defence of the realm was in the hands of Thomas Howard, Earl of Surrey and Lieutenant General of the army in the north. James eventually dug in on top of a hill called Flodden, close by the village of Branxton. When Surrey, old and toughened by years of war, found him there, tucked behind heavy guns, he sent a herald to protest that chivalry demanded their forces meet in pitched battle on an open plain. James shrugged him off at first and so Surrey began marching his army around behind – into a position that, among other things, would block the way north. Seeing his path towards home imperilled, James moved to intercept his foe and was first to the high ground of nearby Branxton Hill.

English guns pounded the Scots soldiers there, until finally they clattered downhill in formations bristling with 18-foot-long pikes. These were weapons with which James, the Renaissance man and technophile, had recently fallen in love. Swiss in origin, they had been taken up next by the French – and it was from Louis that James had taken delivery of a consignment of the things. Effective in the hands of men well-practised and over level ground, they were a hopeless encumbrance for beginners running down a grassy slope made slick by rain.

Soon the Scots were throwing away their unwieldy pikes and drawing swords instead. They collided head-on with Englishmen armed with billhooks – huge axe heads on the ends of 8-foot shafts. Cruelly efficient, essentially modified farming tools, the bills were soon making butcher meat of the Scots. There were English bowmen too – and it was one of those that cut down King James with a shot to the face as he fought valiantly to within yards of Surrey himself. Had he reached and felled the old warhorse, it would all have been so different.

In the end, it was a catastrophe for Scotland and the Scots. Alongside the king fell scores of the great and the good of the land, named men, together with uncounted thousands of foot soldiers who were quickly forgotten. These then were the flowers of the forest – all withered away, as the song says.

What followed for Scotland, after the tears dried and the wailing turned to silence, was a century riven by a lack of any self-confidence. The domain of King James IV had been a country on the up. His death, and the terrible winnowing of the great men of the realm, left the place diminished, withering in the shadow of all that might have been. His son was just a year and a half old when he was crowned in the Chapel Royal of Stirling Castle. Instead of by a Renaissance king, the land was now ruled by regents, and always vulnerable to the machinations of both England and France.

Scots remember Bannockburn and forget Flodden. It seems to many that all that had been gained by Robert Bruce in 1314 was carelessly squandered 199 years later by a vainglorious prince. Flodden was also a loss of footing that let the country be swept further downstream towards eventual union with England. James's marriage to Margaret Tudor, a splicing of the English rose and the Scots thistle, would ultimately prove crucial. When

Elizabeth I died childless, it was James VI, great-grandson of James IV, who took her place on the English throne.

But in the short term Flodden broke Scotland's heart. In towns close by the battlefield they remember what happened, or a version of it at least. At Coldstream, where the Scots crossed the border into England, there is an annual remembrance as part of the town's Civic Week. In Selkirk, 30 miles from the battlefield, the annual Common Ridings culminate in a re-enactment of the moment news of the calamity reached the town.

Locals there will tell you four score Selkirk men marched away to the war of 1513 – and only one came home. His name was Fletcher and when folk gathered round him he could not bring himself to speak of what had happened to his townsmen, far less to Scotland. Instead he merely held aloft his banner and then lowered it to the ground in wordless tribute. This tragic moment is replayed every year while the town band plays 'The Flowers of the Forest'.

I have noticed over the years that Flodden is a battle people have usually heard of but struggle to place in the scheme of things. Maybe it's because it sounds a lot like Culloden or Flanders. It was remembered and commemorated, but in quiet ways. Little Mary, Queen of Scots, was crowned in Stirling Castle on 9 September 1543, thirty years to the day after Flodden and the death of her grandfather.

I once helped excavate part of the battlefield. We deployed a team of metal-detectorists and one of them found an English cannonball still plugged in the soft soil of Branxton Hill. It was solid lead, a little smaller than a cricket ball but many times heavier. Given its location, where it had been lying for the best part of half a millennium, it was likely fired towards the massed Scottish pikemen, standing shoulder to shoulder in formations called schiltrons and waiting for the off. Moving it from hand to hand, feeling the awful heft of the thing, it was easy to imagine the damage it may have caused to blood and bone.

The villagers of Branxton bought their old red BT phone box for £1 and turned it into arguably the world's smallest visitor centre. It has a map showing the routes both armies took to the battle, and leaflets to take away. From Branxton village, the battlefield is well signposted. On top of a rise called Piper's Hill is a plain granite cross that was raised as a memorial in 1910. It has on it: 'To the brave of both nations'.

There the visitor is close by where the English army formed up. The slope of Branxton Hill, down which the Scots advanced, is straight in front, towards the south. In some ways it is all just gently rolling farmland, typical of Northumberland. But when you have in your mind's eye the image of tens of thousands of men, armed with weapons cruel and rushing towards each other headlong, the scene takes on an awful grandeur.

Nearby is the little church of St Paul's, where James's body rested for a while after the battle. Inside there survives an elegant chancel arch that would have been part of the fabric at the time. The rest is largely Victorian.

Flodden is a place it matters to see – the scene of a battle that defined the futures of two nations, a link in the chain that would bring England and Scotland together, a glimpse of the reality of the sort of place, common or garden, where men have fought and died in such terrible numbers. It is also a place where a person might think about the difference one man or one woman can make – by their presence or by their absence.

46
Aldeburgh, Suffolk

The Golden Hind and sailing round the globe

LIKE HAPPISBURGH IN Norfolk, sometime home of the million-year-old footprints, Aldeburgh in Suffolk endures the less-than-tender attentions of the North Sea. What shelter it does have from the wind and waves is in the form of a spit of shingle of that grade that is hard to walk upon. Two steps forward, one step back. Remnants of a fishing industry cling as stubbornly as the lichen that has formed on the timbers of little boats abandoned above the high-water mark. It is a place of sharp colours and contrasts – brightly painted hulls, the square lines of the parish church standing tall among red roofs on white houses, big sky and the constant accompaniment of the gunmetal sea tirelessly rearranging the pebbles with a sound like the rattling of bones.

The town takes its name from the River Alde, which flows behind and parallel to the shingle before entering the sea a few miles further south. There must once have been a fort there too, a *burgh*, but it is gone now, swallowed mouthful by mouthful by the always hungry sea. Up until the early part of the twentieth century there was another village nearby, called Slaughden, and it is all but gone too, consumed by the waves. There is still a working boatyard – R. F. Upson & Co. – all that remains of what was once a thriving industry in those parts. There is a yacht club too, and a Martello Tower, one of around 140 built for protection against a Napoleonic invasion that never came.

Aldeburgh's most famous former resident is the composer Benjamin

Britten. Born in Lowestoft, he moved to Aldeburgh in 1947 and along with a couple of friends set up the Aldeburgh Music Festival, which is still held every year. In the early nineteenth century Aldeburgh-born poet George Crabbe had written a series of poems called *The Borough* about the life and times of the place. Britten took one of them – 'Peter Grimes' – and used it as the basis for his opera of the same name, nowadays regarded as the most important British opera ever written.

Through it all flows the North Sea, sometimes calm and considered, at others predatory and proprietary. When audiences around the world listen to *Peter Grimes*, it is the music of the North Sea they hear ghosting in the background, the calls of seabirds in flight, the rise and fall of the wind. Aldeburgh was made by the sea and will likely be unmade by it in time.

The town's high point came in the sixteenth century when it was an important east-coast port. Shipbuilding was going like a fair too. A map of 1588, the time of the threat of Spanish, rather than French, invasion, shows Aldeburgh as a busy cluster of hundreds of houses arrayed along four or five parallel streets. Two- and three-masted ships ply their way along the coast, and the river appears almost jammed with yet more vessels.

It was the silting up of the river that choked the old life out of the town. Once it was too shallow for ships, Aldeburgh went into decline and never recovered. Visit now and it feels like the sort of seaside destination that was popular one or even two generations ago. Aldeburgh is on that part of the south-east coast that feels remote even though it isn't. London is less than 90 miles away but might as well be on another continent. For a Scot, or perhaps for anyone born and raised in these islands, it also feels perfectly English, like the backdrop for some words by John Betjeman.

But for all that, a job of work that was completed here more than 400 years ago reached out and influenced the whole world. It was in Aldeburgh that the keel was laid down for the building of a ship called, for a while at least, the *Pelican*. In 1577 she set sail as the flagship of a squadron of five vessels destined to circumnavigate the globe. Only the *Pelican* returned from that three-year odyssey and by then her captain, one Francis Drake, had given her a new name. Drake's principal sponsor for the voyage was

Sir Christopher Hatton and since his crest had on it a gilded female red deer, Drake renamed his vessel the *Golden Hind*.

She was classed as a galleon, 70 feet long, 20 feet wide and weighing around 150 tons – a tiny thing by modern standards. She was five decks deep and three-masted, and accommodation aboard was cramped and miserable.

Drake's objective, with the blessing and encouragement of Her Majesty Queen Elizabeth I, was to sail first to South America and then pass through the Strait of Magellan. By the time the *Golden Hind* had made it through to the vastness of the Pacific Ocean, she was alone. The rest of the vessels were lost or had turned back.

The west coast of South America had been Spanish territory for decades, rich in treasure. On 1 March 1579, Drake captured the *Nuestra Señora de la Concepción* and found her so loaded with treasure it took his men days to carry it aboard their own ship. Later in the voyage he claimed a chunk of the coast of California for Elizabeth, naming it New Albion for good measure. The little ship from Aldeburgh sailed as far north as Vancouver Island before turning back. After a spell in San Francisco Bay, she crossed the Pacific, then the Indian Ocean, rounded the Cape of Good Hope and returned to Plymouth 'very richly fraught with gold, silver, pearls and precious stones'.

The profit from the voyage was 4,600 per cent – a return of £47 on every £1 invested by the sponsors. Queen Elizabeth, who may or may not have bothered to put up any of her own money, pocketed so much loot she was able to pay off England's national debt in one go. There was even enough left over to let her kick-start the Levant Company, key to establishing English foreign trade with the Ottoman Empire and the near east. Legend has it that Elizabeth knighted Drake on the deck of his ship.

The *Golden Hind*, all the way from Aldeburgh, had therefore made a vital contribution to the opening up of the wider world to English trade. Her captain was the first from these islands to circumnavigate the globe. Only the Portuguese explorer Ferdinand Magellan had done as much – and time would show that England, and then Britain, would do much more.

47

Tilbury Fort and Tudor Jetty, Tilbury, Essex

Elizabeth I and the Spanish Armada

THE LEFTOVERS FROM the past are all around, in the air above and on the earth below, dissolved in the water. Nothing is lost to this Earth, or not entirely. Soft bodies of ancient and tiny lives lived in warm and shallow oceans of long ago were made liquid for a while. They have been rock and stone ever since – transformed by pressure and time into the flint and chert from which the oldest people, the first people, hunters and farmers, made their tools. Ash from volcanic eruptions in ages past settled and was buried and crushed and made into greenstone for Langdale axes. Some of the footprints being made along shores in silt and mud right now, this very instant, might be filled and saved for finding by more like us, many years hence, although only if our clumsy species is luckier than seems likely.

If molecules of Caesar's last breath are still with us – if one or two have travelled together, conjoined twins, and found their way to where you are reading this now – consider too what else, who else, might be in the mix and about to be taken into your lungs, heart, blood. If molecules of forgotten breaths are there, then surely so are ancient sounds – the hissing, static residue of the Big Bang and the cooking of the universe. I have read of radio transmissions, frantic calls made by Spitfire pilots locked in dogfights with Messerschmitts, still bouncing through the upper reaches of the atmosphere, trapped by the Heaviside layer and growing fainter.

Tilbury Fort is right opposite Gravesend on the Thames. Take the ferry across the river and it is a walk of no more than a quarter of a mile. There are guns there still, but modern. It has an incongruous look about it and you cannot miss it. When the river is at its lowest, the sulphur reek of the river's mud seems thick enough to taste.

Henry VIII was first to put a fort on the site. Among the many he upset by splitting from his first wife, Katherine of Aragon, his brother's widow, was her nephew Charles V, the Holy Roman Emperor. With the encouragement of Pope Clement VII, in 1538 Charles made an alliance with France. Fearing invasion, Henry began building defences and, since the Thames was a vital link to the wider world and vulnerable to attack, he commissioned forts along its banks. The one at Tilbury was a simple affair – a stout blockhouse of stone and brick protected by irregularly shaped ditches and revetments. There were guns, too, but none of it was ever used in anger. The threat of invasion passed like one of Henry's sour moods.

The Thames has always been worth protecting, however, and down through the centuries kings, queens and governments have kept an eye on Tilbury – adding more and more, brick by brick. Somewhere underneath the modern defences, shaped like half a snowflake, are the remains of whatever Henry put in place.

His daughter Elizabeth (born to Anne Boleyn – the one who caused all the trouble for Katherine, and with her nephew and with the Pope) found need of the fort at Tilbury as well.

On 8 February 1587, in the great hall of Fotheringhay Castle in Northamptonshire, the executioner set aside his axe and stooped to pick up the severed head of Mary, Queen of Scots. The baby crowned on the thirtieth anniversary of her grandfather's death in battle, the toddler who had looked out at her Scottish kingdom through a little hole cut in the battlements of Stirling Castle, had grown into a troubled and troublesome queen. She had been lovely for a while. Tall, long-limbed and red-haired; clever and witty, good at sports. When the axe man bent to pick up her head, he did not know he was clutching only at a red wig. The severed head rolled away from beneath it and all gasped when they saw the dead face, withered and old beneath thin and greying hair. It was a killing that shook the world.

A monarch might be assassinated, perhaps, poisoned for preference – but a public beheading like that afforded common criminals?

Elizabeth had ordered her cousin's execution, a final solution after nineteen years of holding her prisoner, a constant threat to her Protestant throne. King Philip II of Spain was among the many who were appalled. He had regarded Mary's claim on the English throne as superior, legitimate, unlike that of Elizabeth, Henry's bastard. With her execution, the hope of returning a Catholic to the English throne was gone. His only option was to invade England and replace Elizabeth with someone more to his liking – perhaps even himself.

By the end of July 1588 his Armada was in the Channel. Elizabeth organized her defences. The navy was dispatched to intercept the foe, and on 8 August she boarded a barge bound for Tilbury. It was her intention to speak to her troops, rally them and give them heart. She stepped ashore, on to the timbers and paving of the jetty that served the fort. There are numerous accounts of what she wore that day – a dress of white velvet, feathers in her hair. In her hand she held a silver baton and for armour she had a silver cuirass – a soldier's breastplate. She arrived among her men mounted upon a white charger but soon jumped down and moved among them with only a light bodyguard for protection. It was brave, since it was rumoured Philip had put assassins there.

At the fort, or nearby, Elizabeth addressed her forces. It was one of the most famous speeches ever made, one of the most legendary and mythologized moments in all of English history:

> My loving people. We have been persuaded by some that are careful of
> our safety, to take heed how we commit our selves to armed multi-
> tudes, for fear of treachery; but I assure you I do not desire to live to
> distrust my faithful and loving people. Let tyrants fear. I have always
> so behaved myself that, under God, I have placed my chiefest strength
> and safeguard in the loyal hearts and good-will of my subjects; and
> therefore I am come amongst you, as you see, at this time, not for my
> recreation and disport, but being resolved, in the midst and heat of
> the battle, to live and die amongst you all; to lay down for my God,

and for my kingdom, and my people, my honour and my blood, even
in the dust.

I know I have the body but of a weak and feeble woman; but I have
the heart and stomach of a king, and of a king of England too, and
think foul scorn that Parma or Spain, or any prince of Europe, should
dare to invade the borders of my realm; to which rather than any dis-
honour shall grow by me, I myself will take up arms, I myself will
be your general, judge, and rewarder of every one of your virtues in
the field.

I know already, for your forwardness you have deserved rewards
and crowns; and We do assure you in the word of a prince, they shall
be duly paid you. In the mean time, my lieutenant general shall be in
my stead, than whom never prince commanded a more noble or
worthy subject; not doubting but by your obedience to my general, by
your concord in the camp, and your valour in the field, we shall
shortly have a famous victory over those enemies of my God, of my
kingdom, and of my people.

History shows it was wind and weather that made most difference
in the end. The valour and blood of the thousands – perhaps 20,000 – that
had thrilled to Elizabeth's words at Tilbury had not been needed. They
would have been the last line of defence in the event of a landing by Spanish foot soldiers, but their weapons stayed cold and their hearts never beat
faster than when they listened to their queen that day. Sir Francis Drake
and the rest of them did their duty. There were fire ships to put fear into the
hearts of the enemy, but mostly the job of scattering the Spanish fleet was
completed by a storm – which then saw most of them having to circumnavigate the whole of Scotland and Ireland before a few could limp home
to think again.

For Elizabeth it was not just a famous victory, it was the shaping of a
legend. From then on her place in the hearts of her people, and in immortality, was assured.

Right by the fort, down among that fragrant mud- and lichen-slimed
rubble of the Thames foreshore, the Tudor jetty Elizabeth walked upon is

still there. Thames mud is magical stuff. Its anaerobic properties give a hard time to the sorts of bacteria that would otherwise busy themselves with the elegant processes of decomposition, so that anything enfolded in it is in some defiance of time. The Tudor timbers are only partly covered, however, and their protection is not complete. None the less, enough survives of the piles and the rest. The narrow jetty is clearly visible – the same that Elizabeth knew and trod upon, on that day of all days, when she stepped ashore from her barge. Perhaps the words she would shortly speak were going around in her head as she walked, minding her feet and being careful not to slip or stumble and so alarm her subjects with any glimpse of weakness, frailty.

Does any molecule of the breath that carried her words survive there? Why not?

48

The Giant's Causeway and Lacada Point, Antrim Coast

The wreck of the Girona

BETWEEN 50 MILLION and 60 million years ago – when all the big dinosaurs were gone and the little mammals were emerging, blinking and snuffling from the shadows to take over the world – the rock that would one day be Ireland was ablaze with volcanoes. It was during a geological epoch called the Palaeocene, and Ireland was not Ireland yet. All of what would eventually be Europe was still lost within a supercontinent geologists call Laurasia. Like the rest of that huge mass, the odds and sods that would end up being the British Isles were somewhere in the northern hemisphere, but that is about as much as can be said.

Lava found its way up through rents and tears in beds of chalk laid down long before, and spread like dark melted chocolate to form a vast plain covering hundreds of thousands of square miles. As it slowly cooled, some of it cracked – vertically as well as horizontally. In the case of the patch earmarked for the Irish Antrim of the future, some of the cooling and cracking produced a honeycomb mass of mostly six-sided columns. The part that is visible today near the village of Bushmills is famous the world over as the Giant's Causeway.

Irish legend has it the work was done not by geological forces but by a giant called Finn McCool, who built the causeway so he could cross the Irish Sea to fight a Scottish giant called Benandonner. This is a better story and an easier explanation for a feature that certainly looks made, if not by men's hands, then by a giant's. Like fire, the sea has the power to stop people, make them sit down, turn around and watch it, and at the Giant's Causeway there are always figures sitting upon the handy bar-stool tops of columns, just looking out to sea. The causeway also has the feel of an auditorium, seats set haphazardly but facing the performance on a stage made of sea and sky.

In the summer of 1588, the latest would-be arrivals to these islands were thousands of soldiers and sailors lately dispatched by Philip II of Spain. Determined to make their own mark on England – to replace Protestant heresy there with the faith of the one true church – they had departed Lisbon, and then La Coruña, aboard 130 ships and headed north into English waters. It was an ill-starred enterprise from start to finish. Galled by the English navy in the Channel, they were driven before a storm that sent them up the eastern seaboard of England and then Scotland. Unknown numbers of men drowned in stormy waters. Many of those that made it ashore in the north and west of Ireland were butchered in the shallows by the locals. Fellow Catholics or no, they were seen to have it coming.

Second in command of the Armada was a Spanish grandee named Don Alonso Martínez de Leiva en la Rioja, Knight of Santiago and Commander of Alcuescar. He was Philip's favourite, a soldier of wild and dangerous reputation, and the young nobles flocked to him, desperate to be by his side in the fight and on the victorious march through London. He had set out aboard the *Rata Santa Maria Encoronada*, once a merchantman but for the Enterprise of England transformed into a ship of war. She bristled with thirty-five cannon and had left the port at La Coruña with hundreds of soldiers, seamen and officers. All but a handful of the Armada's noblemen were among them – together with all the gold and bejewelled finery they had brought for their parade towards and into Westminster Abbey.

After the inconclusive fighting and then the storm, the *Encoronada* had finally limped into Blacksod Bay in County Mayo, where, still pounded by the weather, she was driven on to rocks. Don Alonso had his men strip the ship of everything of value, then they took her guns and marched inland, where they found a ruined fortress and dug in. Soon there were two more ships taking refuge in the bay. The best of them, the *Duquesa Santa Ana*, caught the Don's eye and he ordered his men to load aboard her everything that had been saved from the *Encoronada* – plate, apparel, money, jewels, weapons and armour.

If those Spaniards thought their new ship would bring them a change of luck, then they were mistaken. Once clear of Blacksod Bay, they were driven north again – back the way they had come. For three days and nights they fought the elements and their unwieldy vessel. With painful slowness, they tacked from Inishkea to Erris Head, rolling sickeningly in the towering swell until they were driven against a coastline held by a war-lord named McSweeney Ne Doe, a vassal of the fearsome O'Neil clan. They dropped anchor at a place called Lougherris, but so great was the force of the tempest the cable was snapped like a straw. A lone seaman made it ashore with a line and the *Santa Ana* was held in place (by providence, per-haps) long enough for all left alive to clamber out and swim to shore carrying whatever valuables they could bear.

Don Alonso stayed aboard until the end, insisting every other soul depart before him. As he was about to jump into a waiting currach, the dying ship bucked and rolled beneath him and he was flung against a cap-stan, breaking a leg. The *Santa Ana* broke her back in the shallows and, carrying the injured Don, the Spaniards climbed the sand dune at the back of the bay and saw the dull, flat slab of Kiltoorish Lake and an island with a jagged ruin of a castle perched upon it. In small boats they ferried them-selves and their possessions to the island and dug themselves in among the castle's walls.

For nine days they waited, while the rain poured down and their supplies dwindled. On the tenth day, they saw Irishmen approaching them – McSweeney's men, who brought word that, as fellow Catholics, they were welcome. Better yet, the little delegation had news of another Spanish warship. It was a galleass, named *Girona*. In all the Armada, there had been only four galleasses, from the squadron of Naples. Part galley and part galleon, they were as slender and elegant as Viking longships, and as fearsome. With eighteen oars a side, square sails on the foremast and the mainmast and a lateen on the mizzen, they were as fast and as manoeuvrable in action as they were lovely to behold. These were the vessels upon which so much had turned at the Battle of Lepanto, seventeen years before, when a Christian alliance had utterly destroyed an Ottoman fleet.

The *Girona* had been soundly thrashed after weeks in the North Sea and in the Atlantic, but she was still dangerous. She bristled with guns of bronze and iron – cannon, demi-cannon, demi-culverins, esmerils, perriers, sakers and demi-sakers. She had left Naples loaded with powder and more than 8,000 cannonballs, and most of it was intact.

McSweeney's men showed them the way, south from Ardara and through the valleys to the bay at Killybegs where the galleass lay at anchor. They even provided something like a sedan-chair in which Don Alonso could be carried.

Just before dawn on 26 October 1588, the *Girona* departed the safe harbour of Killybegs, but she was overfull. Don Alonso had been ashore in Ireland for a month and around him had gathered an unlikely company. As well as hundreds of Spanish soldiers and sailors, nobles and their servants, adventurers and renegades, there were all the persons required for such an endeavour – tradesmen, barbers, tailors, surgeons and advisors. There were others besides – Irish Catholics on the make, priests and monks to shepherd souls. In all, Don Alonso had given passage to 1,333 men and boys.

Despite the lack of space aboard, the nobles and gentlemen kept their treasure – their jewellery as well as their coins. It was one thing to lose a war and quite another to lose a fortune. There was hardly space enough for a man to stand, far less lie down, and all aboard felt the sickening sensations of a vessel lying too low in the water.

On the night of 27 October, the wind and waves drove the galleass on to rocks beneath a headland called Lacada, barely a mile east of the Giant's Causeway and that stage set always for drama. Lacada might sound Spanish, but comes in fact from the Irish *leac fhada*, which means 'the Long Grey Stone'. Broken in two, the *Girona* spilled her passengers into the drink. A handful survived, perhaps as many as nine. They stumbled ashore and climbed cliffs to find Dunluce Castle, home to a local warlord called

Sorley Boy MacDonnell. He gave the survivors shelter while he helped himself to whatever the waves tossed ashore. The corpses that washed up with all the rest were buried in nearby St Cuthbert's Graveyard. Perhaps Don Alonso, Knight of Santiago, was among them.

The rest of the *Girona's* cargo remained out of reach and out of sight until 1967, when the wreck was found by Belgian diver and adventurer Robert Sténuit. During the course of the next two years, he and his team hauled up the greatest hoard of treasure ever recovered from a vessel of the Spanish Armada.

Their haul was nothing less than a marvel and much of it is on display now in the Ulster Museum in Belfast. Mounds of gold coins, chains by the bucket-load, jewellery, all manner of the paraphernalia of a ship of war. A little gold salamander, once set with precious stones and worn in hopes of protection against fire, is especially fine; so too a set of cameo rings bearing the likenesses of Byzantine Roman emperors; and a cross of the Knights of Santiago. Best of all, I think, is a little gold ring in the form of a belt with the buckle undone, in a sign of submission, surely a keepsake from a lover. On one terminal a tiny hand clasps a heart. Around the band are inscribed the words, *No Tengo Mas Que Darte* – I Have Nothing More To Give Thee.

I interviewed Mr Sténuit about the *Girona*. He said the ring was among the final finds, and we wondered together if the sentiment engraved on it was a message from the sea, and the wreck, and the dead.

The Spanish Armada, Elizabeth's triumph, the framing of a legend that gave England a sense of identity and right – after more than four centuries, it can all seem like too much to believe, to take in. But stand at Lacada Point and look down at the waves breaking over jagged reefs, feel the howling wind that whips the waves into white tops and think of a thousand men and boys flailing in the dark. Noblemen and poor men, far from the warm soil of Spain. Scattered beneath them, finding hiding places on the seabed, was all the finery of a peacock army – for all the good it did them. There, the fate of them all feels real.

49

Hampton Court Palace, Surrey

The King James Bible

Like Westminster Abbey, Lincoln Castle and a slew of other destinations, Hampton Court Palace is a place where multiple strands of our history converge before moving on again in different directions. Follow a thread of the story of the British Isles and you will eventually have to pass through its corridors and gardens.

Going back from our own time, in 1944 it was in a tent in a camp set up in Bushy Park – adjacent to Hampton Court and formed of three earlier open spaces set aside by Henry VIII as the palace hunting grounds – that General Dwight D. Eisenhower planned the D-Day Landings. In the late seventeenth century William and Mary employed Christopher Wren to transform the Tudor palace into something more in keeping with the fashion of their time. William Shakespeare and his company of actors, the King's Men, performed in the Great Hall for Scottish King James.

But perhaps it is the bloated, corrupted shadow of Henry VIII that falls darkest over the red bricks and fussy gardens. He married Katherine Parr, his sixth and last wife, in the Chapel Royal at Hampton Court. Much of what he is famous or notorious for had already happened there too. His letter to the Pope threatening to break with the Roman Church was written in that palace. Edward, his only son, was born and baptized there. Jane Seymour, the prince's mother, died in the palace three weeks later. Henry divorced Anne of Cleves at Hampton Court and then married the teenaged Katherine Howard. When he found out she had been no virgin before her wedding and allegedly no faithful wife after, he had her imprisoned within its walls. She escaped for a few moments and ran screaming for him through its corridors. She never got to him, though, and was tried and executed soon after.

In spite of all the twisted and twisting intrigue of Tudor times, Hampton Court really does look the part of a royal palace. So many royal addresses only look impressive or menacing – hardly ever the sort of gaffs a person might fancy living in. Buck House looks like a dull grey office block. Edinburgh Castle is a dour tenement block upon a black rock. Of the fabled residences on the Thames, only Windsor Castle and the Tower of London survive – except Hampton Court, and Hampton Court has panache.

It started out as a property of the Knights Hospitaller, but was acquired in the early 1500s by Cardinal Thomas Wolsey – butcher's boy from Ipswich turned favourite of Henry VIII. In his pomp he was Lord Chancellor, the king's most powerful minister, and he built the first version of Hampton Court as a pad befitting one such as he. Like so many others, he fell from Henry's favour. Scenting his own blood flowing by him in the river beyond his windows, he offered up his palace as a gift to the king in 1528. For all the good it did him. He was broken and dead two years later.

However he ended up regarding his former Lord Chancellor, Henry definitely liked Hampton Court. For a start it was in the ideal spot. Just a dozen miles from Westminster on the river that was, of course, the best way of getting into London, it was also far enough away to offer peace and quiet. It was Henry who had the Great Hall built, with its astonishing hammerbeam roof, as well as much else. As the king grew ever bigger, so did Hampton Court. Apparently he was so impatient to have the whole job completed that the labourers and craftsmen had to work through the nights by candlelight.

Like others of his family name, Henry was a successful sovereign and a hopeless stud dog. It was his inability to produce strapping boys that had him work his way through so many wives. And it was his treatment of the first of them – his brother's widow, Katherine of Aragon – that caused him the most trouble. Among the legion that opposed his divorce from his

Spanish queen was William Tyndale, infamous translator of the Bible. Henry, fuelled by his customary spite, had him hunted down as a heretic. Tyndale was on the Continent when he was captured on Henry's behalf by agents of Charles V, the Holy Roman Emperor, and in 1536 he was duly tried and executed. His last words before he was strangled to death were apparently, 'Lord, Open the King of England's eyes.'

Tyndale's was not the first Bible in English. John Wycliffe had produced more than one in the last years of the fourteenth century – and, even before his efforts, the job had been done, more or less, by earlier scholars. Tyndale's stood out because it was the first version translated into English from the original Hebrew and Greek texts. Within a few years of his execution, Henry had commissioned his own translation, called the Great Bible because the finished product was physically on the large side. Big man, big palace, big Bible.

The Bible is therefore the brightest thread that passes through Hampton Court Palace. Henry died, rotten inside and out. Poor Edward followed him into the shades after just a few years. Catholic Mary was next, Henry's only surviving legitimate heir, daughter of his first wife. Long before any threat of an invasion, and the Tilbury speech and the galleass *Girona*, Mary had married Prince Philip of Spain, only son of Charles V, who in later years would become Philip II of Armada fame. It was a marriage to settle matters political, but still they went through the motions of the flesh. She had a first false pregnancy. Fearing she was being punished by God for tolerating heresy in her realm, Mary burned Protestants at the stake and was rewarded with a second uncomfortable emptiness in her womb. It was likely cancer, and it killed her. She was succeeded by her half-sister, Elizabeth, who was glorious. But though she won the adoration of her subjects, Good Queen Bess provided them no heir of her own. At least she was Protestant though.

In 1603, when after her death Elizabeth's cousin James VI of Scotland was made James I of England as well, the work of tidying and purifying the Church was still on the go. James was thirty-seven when he came to the English throne, the orphan king. He had been christened Catholic but raised in the Scottish Presbyterian form of the Protestant faith. When he arrived in England, representatives of more than one flavour of Christian ity waited anxiously to see how he would treat the various faithful.

The English Puritans got to him early on and, in a document called the 'Millenary' Petition, suggested the new king might benefit from 'a conference among the learned'. The result was the Hampton Court Conference of January 1604, a loud and chaotic gathering attended by King James himself, the bishops, leading Puritans and a host of royal officials.

In terms of making changes to the Anglican Church, the gathering, in the king's Privy Chamber in Clock Court, accomplished little. The Puritans had wanted to see the back of bishops, but James was of a mind to keep them. What was decided and decreed by the king, however – and what changed the Western world thereafter in countless ways – was yet another translation of the Bible.

The resultant King James Bible was the work of many hands and minds – perhaps fifty-four scholars in all – and several places. In the Bodleian Library in Oxford, learned men pored over existing translations – Tyndale's, Wycliffe's, others – as they sought to give new shapes and rhythms to old verses. The final edit was done beneath the candy-bright roof beams of the Jerusalem Chamber in Westminster Abbey. In Stationers' Hall, by St Paul's Cathedral, the product of all the work was read aloud, line by line, to see that it sounded good enough. It took the best part of the year 1610 to hear it. But the poetic, musical flow of the words is there too in Hampton Court, by the lazy bend of the Thames where the idea was conceived.

The King James Bible, the KJB, the Authorized Version or AV, is the cornerstone of English literature. It provides countless examples of the phrases we use every day – 'rise and shine', 'the powers that be', 'the apple of his eye', 'a man after his own heart', 'signs of the times'.

It was daily reading of his KJB that informed and shaped the speeches William Wilberforce, MP for Hull, would make in the Commons nearly 200 years later in hopes of ending slavery. It was the elegance of the humanity expressed within its pages that empowered the formation of what we understand as modern democracy. The concept of the essential equality of all human beings led not only to the freedom of African slaves but also to the emancipation of women. It crossed the Atlantic and inspired the freedoms built into the foundations of the United States of America. For three and a half centuries after it was created, it was *the* translation of the Bible into English. It has been the bestselling book in the history of the world.

50

The Globe Theatre, Bankside, London

A stage for Shakespeare

Such an assault upon the senses would it have been, I doubt many of us could have borne William Shakespeare's London for more than a moment. By most of our prissy, sterile standards, the city of the bard was a cesspit ripe with every stink of animal and human. Like a bitch's womb of unborn pups, the capital was stuffed with wrestling, restless life, all in a heaving tangle. Not a body washed, not a mouth rinsed; the halt and the maimed suffering in plain view of the handsome in their finery.

People's lives were pressed together, rich and poor alike. Even the city's structures were oppressive. Streets were more crowded and claustrophobic than any we have known, made almost into tunnels by the overhanging tiers of buildings' upper floors coming together overhead until they more or less touched. In the absence of any kind of plumbing or sewerage, everything unspeakable was tipped from above into the streets below and left to stew. In winter at least the cold might have kept the reek at bay, a frozen crust upon the top of it. But in summer we might dread to imagine – the smells like a vision, every conceivable odour of every conceived body, waste of every sort all about and all the time. Every life was lived inside a fetid miasma – 'a foul and pestilent congregation of vapours' right enough.

The populace had burst beyond the constriction of the ancient city wall only a century before Shakespeare's birth. Above and about the seven gates through that wall were hung the rotting body parts of dismembered criminals, enemies of the Crown. Building within 3 miles of the boundary was banned by law, but the relevant edicts were routinely flouted. Since a demolition order might come at any moment, however, all was cheaply constructed, with the result that it was slums of the worst sort that slumped against the ancient masonry. That London, squalid shanties and all, was comparatively little – 3 miles from east to west and no more than 2 from north to south. Accurate figures are hard to come by, or altogether nonexistent, but it's fair to imagine 200,000 people calling the place home then. The bulk of them were cheek by jowl behind the wall, hemmed in and clustered round the forbidding fortress of the Norman Tower, thronging Old St Paul's Cathedral and all the streets, lanes and alleyways in between.

England's second largest city then was Norwich, with just 15,000 souls. In all of Europe, only Paris and Naples were as big as or bigger than London. For all that the place was crowded, a ceaseless winnowing was at work all the while as well. By the latter years of the sixteenth century, England's population was permanently under siege from all manner of illness and disease. Every few years the cesspit ran with plague – an enervating pattern of infection that had held for three centuries at least. London drew towards itself, from the surrounding counties, a constant flow of immigrants, which was just as well. In addition to the plague, there was a host of other ills keeping the population always in retreat – fevers, fluxes, 'frenzies and foul evils'; consumption, dysentery, measles, rickets, scurvy and many more maladies less well described, far less understood.

The hundreds and thousands that made their way to London in hopes of a better life were soon grist to the mills of primitive manufacturing. London was the greatest industrial centre in the land and much of the work, like brewing and tanning, only added to the stench.

Nothing yet built there by man was as commanding or omnipresent as the River Thames. In spite of all the vile outpourings flowing into it from septic rivers and streams, or heaved in from its banks, fishermen still pulled a cornucopia from its depths – all manner of fish as well as porpoises and the occasional whale. The only crossing then was London Bridge, just as crowded and built-up as every other inch of space. While traitors' arms, legs and torsos were hung about the city gates, their heads were displayed on sharpened stakes at the Southwark end of the bridge.

It was into this enveloping, overwhelming world that William Shakespeare made his entrance. For such a towering figure, a North Star in the firmament, we know precious little about him, really. He figures in the historical record on just a handful of occasions. He was baptized in Stratford-upon-Avon on 26 April 1564; towards the end of November 1582 he applied for a marriage licence – presumably with Anne Hathaway in mind. This Anne, eight years his senior, gave birth to their eldest daughter, Susanna, in May 1583, and then twins, Hamnet and Judith, in February 1585. By 1592 Shakespeare was identified as an actor and playwright in London. Success brought him the wherewithal to buy land and houses in Stratford, and in 1613 he bought a house in London too. He signed a will and when he died he was laid down in the chancel of Holy Trinity Church in Stratford, the same in which he had been baptized.

He conjured into being a million words of plays and poetry, and yet left next to nothing scratched in his own hand. We have just a few of his signatures. There is a play called *Sir Thomas More* (about the saint whose bones lie among others beneath the stones of St Peter's Church in the Tower of London). Some experts insist a handwritten revision of it is Shakespeare's own, but there is no consensus.

When he came to London, he was surely drawn to Bankside, south of the Thames and west of London Bridge. Here, without the wall, the land was beyond the jurisdiction of the city's governors. The mayor and his ilk objected to theatres and the actors who populated them. In such a stiffly religious era as the Elizabethan, many plays were considered Godless, wanton. Such forces of law and order as did exist feared trouble from the crowds that gathered to watch them being performed, while employers suspected their workers might be distracted from honest labour. In a place like Bankside, therefore, among the other dens of iniquity that loitered where the law was not – pubs, brothels, gambling houses, pits for cockfights and bear-baiting – those given to the seedy ways of the acting profession might meet to plan their entertainments.

By the late 1590s Shakespeare was a member of a troupe of actors called the Lord Chamberlain's Men. They had had the use of a theatre in Shoreditch called simply The Theatre, but in 1597 their lease ran out. The wooden structure of the place was owned by James Burbage and his sons Cuthbert and Richard, the latter of whom was the company's leading actor. They reasoned that, since it was only the lease on the land beneath their stage that had run out, they could solve their problem by moving the stage elsewhere. Three days after Christmas 1598, they set to work. The Theatre was taken apart like a piece of flat-pack furniture and reassembled on a new site in Bankside. Called The Globe, the new venue was a great success. Shakespeare was a shareholder in the venture, as well as an actor and playwright, and for fourteen years audiences packed the place to see, among other efforts, productions of *Hamlet*, *Macbeth*, *King Lear*, *Othello* and *Twelfth Night*.

Disaster struck during a performance of *Henry VIII* in June 1613, when wadding fired from a cannon as a stage effect set light to the building's thatched roof. Audience and actors escaped unhurt, but the theatre burned to the ground. A second Globe was built on the same site the following year and business resumed until 1642, when the Long Parliament of the Puritans ordered the closure of all London's theatres. The relevant ordinance described plays as nothing but 'lascivious Mirth and Levity' and the actors who performed them little better than vagrants. That second Globe was demolished by 1644.

And so it would have remained without the intervention of American actor and director Sam Wanamaker, who, from 1969 until his death in 1993, dedicated a monumental effort to having a third Globe Theatre built as close as possible to the site of the original – a recreation of the space that Shakespeare himself had known. It is an oddity for certain – a whitewashed polygon topped with a tonsure of mossy thatch – but busy every day with tourists and school parties.

The legend of Shakespeare is told and retold. Scholars have obsessed about him and still do. There have been those who claim his plays were written not by him but by others. What matters is that the man lived and those plays were written. The King James Bible, the works of William Shakespeare – the language of those creations has moved and shaped the whole world. That Shakespeare made his exit so elegantly and completely, leaving only words behind, is perfect somehow. The words, however they were written, are immortal.

Walk around outside the white walls, or pay to stand or sit for a performance beneath the same sky that Shakespeare knew. Watch and listen to the Thames still flowing by. The vibrations made by Shakespeare's plays must be there or thereabouts. 'For 'tis your thoughts that now must deck our kings. Carry them here and there, jumping o'er times, turning the accomplishment of many years into an hourglass . . .'

51

Dunashad Castle and Lot's Wife, Baltimore, County Cork

The white slave trade

I N 1215, THE same year King John signed Magna Carta at Runnymede on the banks of the River Thames, a castle was built on a rocky outcrop in a corner of south-west Ireland, overlooking a sheltered bay. It was constructed by Norman conquerors in the Norman style, a solid grey block of a thing, but its owner had adopted some Irish ways by then and called his fortress Dún na Séad, or Dunashad, 'the Fortress of the Jewels'. He called himself MacSleimhne, or Sleynie. It was the Irish Gaelic form of Fitz-Stephen, and he was descended from Robert FitzStephen, who had arrived in Ireland with the Norman–Welsh lord Richard de Clare – 'Strongbow', 2nd Earl of Pembroke and legendary leader of the Norman conquest of Ireland.

Sleynie and his kin did well until 1261 and the Battle of Callan, where they were crushed and swept out of sight by the vengeful warriors of the O'Driscoll clan, who had been dispossessed nearly fifty years before.

Dunashad is still the most permanent-looking structure in the area – visible from all over. Given what happened thereabouts on the night of 20 June 1631, it is remarkable there is anything or anyone there at all.

The O'Driscolls held sway for the best part of four centuries, growing rich in the process. Their prosperity came to an end at the turn of the seventeenth century when they backed Catholic Spain against Protestant England. After the failure of his Armada in 1588, Philip of Spain tried to rouse the rebel Irish to make fresh trouble for Elizabeth. The Spanish and Irish were roundly smashed at the climactic Battle of Kinsale in 1601. Fineen O'Driscoll, leader of his clan, had handed his castle to the Spanish commander and in the aftermath of the battle it was surrendered to the English as spoils of war.

Fineen had been a friend to Queen Elizabeth and so managed to get himself a royal pardon. He joined forces then with an Englishman, Thomas Crooke, and established an English colony on some of his ancestral lands. The castle of Dunashad, already old, a blackened tooth, became the focal point and the new settlement was called Baltimore, a corruption of the Irish for 'Town of the Big House'. The colony was part of wider English plans to take control of Ireland by replacing the obstreperous Catholic locals with Protestants loyal to the English Crown. This was the Plantation of Ireland – begun by Henry VIII and continued by Elizabeth and then by James VI and I.

All of its history meant that, by that fateful night in 1631, Baltimore was an isolated English enclave surrounded by a population that wished them ill. What followed sounds so outlandish it might as well be fiction – but in truth it offers a glimpse of a terror, often overlooked now, that afflicted Christian Europe for hundreds of years.

Prowling offshore from Baltimore that night was a ship, or ships, led by a renegade Dutchman whose name had once been Jan Janszoon van Haarlem. Some thirteen years earlier he had turned Turk, as they said in those days: converted to Islam and changed his name to Murat Reis, which means 'Captain Murat'. He operated out of Morocco, with the blessing of the Ottoman sultan in Istanbul, and had grown rich from piracy and slavery. In 1627 he led two raids to Iceland and seized 400 men, women and children to be sold as slaves.

This was the time of the tyranny of the so-called Barbary corsairs. From their bases all over North Africa they raided the European coastlines for 300 years or more. By some estimates, between the sixteenth and nineteenth centuries Muslim pirates took as many as 1.25 million white Christians to the slave markets of Algiers, Tunis and Tripoli.

The English settlers of Baltimore may have been victims of a Catholic plot to see the back of them once and for all. After the Battle of Kinsale, most of the O'Driscolls had fled into exile in Spain, and so another theory has it that it was those dispossessed relatives of Fineen, bitter at losing any legitimate hopes of inheriting the land around Baltimore, who invited Murat and his men to help themselves to the town's population of English cuckoos. Whatever the truth of it, the raiders that descended on Baltimore that night left hardly a soul behind. Definite figures are hard to come by, but the town was emptied. Over a hundred men, women and children were driven on to Murat's ships and away. Some accounts have it that as many Irish were taken at the same time, just to make the trip worthwhile. No more than three of the English settlers made it home again, their relatives having paid ransoms for their return. For the rest, their kidnap opened a door to futures so alien as to be impossible to believe, then as now. For the men, it might have meant spending the rest of their lives as galley slaves, never setting foot on dry land again. The women may have become house servants or concubines. The children would have been brought up as Muslims, separated from all kin and raised to lifetimes of servitude far from any home they had ever known.

The slavery of white Europeans at the hands of Muslims is often forgotten, swamped by the notoriety of the trade in black Africans. The latter may have dwarfed the former by perhaps as much as twelve to one, but it is worth remembering that the horror of slavery has been experienced by all of humankind at one time or another.

Baltimore is in County Cork, a part of Ireland I feel sure I have only ever seen through rain and mist. Folk in those parts describe such weather as soft. It is a lovely part of the world for all that, lush and green. Countless bays and coves for pirate hiding places. On the high ground above the town stands a 50-foot-tall white-painted stone beacon, put there at the end of the eighteenth century as an aid to shipping. It is known locally as Lot's Wife, after the Biblical figure who was turned into a pillar of salt as punishment for looking back at the home she was leaving behind against her will.

Those people stolen away by Murat and his pirates, shackled in irons and flung below deck into stinking holds, probably had no chance to do the same.

52

Greyfriars Kirkyard, Edinburgh

A covenant for the faithful

GREYFRIARS BOBBY IS a name and a story that has travelled the length and breadth of the British Isles and right around the world. The most popular version has it that in the late 1850s a shepherd named John Gray, who later became a night watchman for the Edinburgh police, had as his companion an especially devoted Skye terrier he called Bobby. So attached was the little dog that even when Gray died and was buried in the kirkyard of Greyfriars Church on the edge of Edinburgh's Old Town, he chose to spend his days on his master's grave. Apparently he stayed at his post for fourteen years until his own death and burial in unconsecrated ground just inside the kirkyard gates.

No doubt the truth was different, the details having varied with each telling, but in essence it is a parable about fidelity. Whatever else a person is supposed to take away from the hearing of it, they should at least be moved by the unshakeable faith of one hapless little dog. However lowly a creature, his heart was true. Tourists from all over the world make a point of visiting the statue of his likeness that now stands close by the kirkyard gates, where the southern end of George IV Bridge meets Candle-maker Row.

Greyfriars Kirkyard was a response by Edinburgh's city fathers, at the end of the sixteenth century, to a chronic shortage of space for burials around the church of St Giles on the High Street. In summer the smell of corruption was overwhelming, so a new burial ground was established on the southern edge of the city in the vicinity of what had been a monastery for grey-robed friars faithful to the ways of St Francis.

In the February of 1638 the kirkyard was the scene of one of the most significant moments in Scottish history. It was there among the stones and tombs that thousands gathered to pledge fidelity everlasting, as they saw it, to their own master.

The previous year had seen the publication of the new Book of Common Prayer for Scotland. Its creation had been overseen by King Charles I and also by William Laud, the man he had appointed as Archbishop of Canterbury. In the century before, however, Scotland's churches had reformed under the leadership of John Knox. Compared to English Protestantism, the new brand of religion was austere. White-painted walls, plain wooden communion tables. No fuss, just faith. By the seventeenth century, many Presbyterian Scots were so enraptured with the intense nature of their personal relationships with the Almighty, they were in no mood to listen to anyone with ideas about changing the nature of the conversation – not even a king.

Scots faithful to the reformed Presbyterian Church regarded English, Anglican Protestantism as a 'Synagogue of Satan'. Let them do what they do, but God help the man that sought to impose those Popish ways on Scotland and the Scots. Charles I was that man. Whereas his father, James VI and I, had grown up in Scotland and understood the twists and turns of the Scottish psyche, other than his first three years Charles had grown up in London and so lacked his father's experience of the place and his insight. When his 'black popish superstitious service book' arrived on pulpits around that reformed land, he reaped something of a whirlwind.

More than anything else about Anglicanism, Scots Presbyterians despised the existence of bishops. The congregation spoke directly to God with no intercession, and royally appointed bishops therefore could not and would not be tolerated. Charles loved his bishops, however, so the two sides were set upon a collision course. There were other matters – English moves interpreted by Presbyterians as backsliding towards Catholicism with all its pomp, idolatry and superstition – so that when James Hannay, Dean of St Giles', began preaching from the new book on 23 July 1637, he provoked a riot. Tradition has it that a tough old bird named Jenny Geddes waited until Hannay had read out the first line before standing, picking up her wooden stool and flinging it at his head.

'Wha daur say Mass in ma lug?' she cried – Who dares say Mass in my ear?

The unrest and downright rebellion spread rapidly from church to church, from parish to parish. A rebel parliament was formed and, among other matters, organized the writing of a contract between God and the righteous. Drawing much of its inspiration from the Scottish Confession of Faith, which had been signed in 1581 by Charles's father, James VI, it was a promise to defend 'the true Religion'. The new contract's authors – church minister Alexander Henderson and lawyer Archibald Johnston of Wariston – set down demands for a free Scottish parliament and a general assembly. Although they paid lip service to obedience to an anointed king, they made clear above all else that the Church in Scotland would not tolerate the rule of bishops acting in the king's name. It was a direct challenge to the nature and extent of Charles's power.

The document was called the National Covenant – a deliberate reflection of the original Covenant between God and his people after the Flood. By 28 February 1638 it was available for signing in the kirkyard at Greyfriars and the faithful turned out in their thousands. Copies were made and circulated throughout the land so that everyone had the chance to commit themselves. As well as those making their mark out of genuine, personal faith, there were others who had it forced upon them. Those were febrile, fanatical times, and everyone felt watched and judged by everyone else.

Around a thousand copies of the National Covenant have survived. They are remarkable artefacts, each and every one. As well as the signatures of high-born men and women, there are also the names of common folk – servants and ploughmen, tradesmen and clerks, fishwives and charwomen. There are names signed with a practised, educated hand and many more scratched as though by children. Those that had not learned to write at all were invited simply to make an X. Some names were signed in blood. Confident or clumsy, literate or not, those names and marks are priceless. Never before had the rank and file of the Scottish population been invited to record their consent upon such a document. For the first time, the everyday soul was noted as weighing the same as that of a lord or his lady.

Charles treated the signatories – called Covenanters – as traitors. Scotland, the land of his birth, was in open revolt against him and his divine right to rule as he wished.

The blood that had flowed as ink for signing the parchment was only the first. When in 1639 Charles sent an army to bring the Covenanters to heel, the result was the First Bishops' War. The rebellious Scots were victorious and so war spread south, east and west until all of these islands were harrowed by it. In 1643, when the English Parliamentarians needed Scottish help to fight the king's forces in the bitter Civil War, they signed up to the Solemn League and Covenant, a document that enshrined the central concepts of the National Covenant.

Though the king was defeated in the end, and put to death, the matter of religion was not at rest. Not at all. After Charles came Oliver Cromwell, and after him, in 1660, the Restoration, when Charles II was set upon his father's throne. When the new king declared that he and he alone had final say in matters spiritual as well as civil, he kindled a fire that would scorch Scotland and the Scots for the best part of the next three decades as Covenanters were hounded, tortured and killed.

A copy of the National Covenant is on display in St Giles' Cathedral, signed by James Graham, 1st Marquess of Montrose, who was a Covenanter first and then changed sides to fight for the king.

Today Greyfriars Kirkyard is a peaceful place near the heart of the city. As well as Bobby and his master, all manner of Edinburgh worthies have their graves and tombs there. It is humbling to walk here and imagine a time when people in these islands were ready to face all manner of unspeakable torments and deaths rather than deny their faith.

53

Lansdown Hill, Bath

Civil war

Fᴿᴏᴍ ᴛʜᴇ ɴᴏʀᴛʜ-ꜰᴀᴄɪɴɢ edge of the Lansdown escarpment the land drops steeply away for hundreds of feet. On the far side of the valley is Freezing Hill, and beyond that Tog Hill. The way up or down is a struggle. The slope is thick with trees and undergrowth now, obscuring a view that three and a half centuries and more ago would have been clear for miles. A few hundred yards back from the edge, running more or less east to west across green fields, is a length of drystone wall. On the evening of 5 July 1643 it provided some little shelter for hundreds of soldiers, exhausted by hours of fighting.

These were Parliamentarians, tasked with preventing a larger force of Royalist infantry and cavalry from taking possession of the nearby city of Bath. The two armies had fought back and forth over the hillside all day. Tired hands pulled desperately at the stones of the wall to make scooped depressions all along the line of it. Into those spaces were manoeuvred their artillery pieces, barrels looming over an open field of fire, ready to continue the slaughter. The day must have seemed endless.

The English Civil War pitted a king who regarded his subjects as unruly children against a parliament that felt entitled to be treated like grown-ups. Charles I had believed his father, James VI and I, when he said a king was a little god with a divine right to rule. But while Charles was hardly the first king with a god complex, he lacked the charisma to carry it off. Since King John and Magna Carta, the English parliament had grown in confidence as well as influence. Gone were the days when a monarch might act with impunity. God might set kings and queens upon thrones, but in order actually to get things done they required money. Successful monarchs therefore tended to be those with the guile and charm to persuade their wealthy subjects, some of them powerful in their own right, to finance whatever escapades they had in mind.

By the late 1630s and early 1640s, more and more members of the English parliament expected their king to accept that they had a right to some say in how the realm was governed. Since Charles simply expected them to gather – without a quibble, far less a condition – the taxes he required and desired, things could not end well. All too soon his high-handed attitude and complete lack of elan were causing trouble from one end of these islands to the other. It was not just an English war. The trouble in England was just one part of a conflict that moved across the whole archipelago like a great storm. Some historians prefer to put all the strife under the umbrella of the more broadly encompassing title of the War of the Three Kingdoms.

Before the troubles in England there had been unrest in Ireland, and in Scotland Charles had pushed his subjects beyond breaking point by meddling with the manner in which they worshipped their God. The king tried to use force to get his way, but his army was beaten off. When he grudgingly went cap in hand to the English parliament for more money to try again, its members sought to exploit his financial difficulties by demanding he accept some constraints on his power. Charles threw his toys out of his pram. He left London in high dudgeon and headed for the north of England, where he felt more appreciated. He raised an army and parliament did likewise.

At first, most of the country tried to keep out of the dispute, but by the summer of 1642 factions and paranoia had spread all over the land until everyone felt compelled to pick a side. In terms of numbers, the opposing camps were equally matched. The king's support came, in the main, from the countryside, while the towns and cities tended to lean towards parliament. There were some skirmishes, a first pitched battle at Edgehill in Warwickshire that October, but nothing decisive.

By the summer of 1643 Charles had his headquarters in Oxford. A large Royalist force in the south-west, commanded by Sir Ralph Hopton, was moving east to join up with the king and push towards London. Parliament could not allow that to happen, and a force under Sir William Waller stood ready in the area around Bath. Hopton had the numbers – as many as 4,000 infantry and 2,500 mounted men. Desperate to bolster the city's defences, parliament dispatched a force of cavalry from London under the command of Sir Arthur Haselrig. They were a blast from the past, heavily armoured cuirassiers protected by metal plate from chin to knee and soon nicknamed 'the Lobsters'. For all that they were anachronisms, or nearly – dressed for a style of war that was soon to be out of fashion – they were well trained and well led. Waller now had the necessary mounted men, but only half the infantry force of that available to his rival. Ah, his rival . . .

Hopton and Waller reveal all the acute sadness of the English Civil War – indeed of any civil war. They had known each other since childhood and were the very best of friends. They had attended the same church and sat together in parliament. Before the outbreak of fighting they had shared many of the same views about what was best for the land and the nation. But while Waller found his true calling in the parliamentarian cause, Hopton felt he could not turn his back on his king. The lifelong friends took up arms against one another.

In the weeks before their respective forces clashed at Lansdown, Hopton wrote to Waller requesting a face-to-face meeting. Knowing a line was already drawn between them, unbreakable as a drystone wall, Waller saw no point. Instead he sent a letter that expresses all of the heartbreak of that war:

To my noble friend Sir Ralph Hopton at Wells.

Sir,

The experience I have of your worth and the happiness I have enjoyed in your friendship are wounding considerations when I look at this present distance between us. Certainly my affection to you is so unchangeable that hostility itself cannot violate my friendship, but I must be true wherein the cause I serve. That great God, which is the searcher of my heart, knows with what a sad sense I go about this service, and with what a perfect hatred I detest this war without an enemy; but I look upon it as an Opus Domini and that is enough to silence all passion in me. The God of peace in his good time will send us peace. In the meantime, we are upon the stage and must act those parts that are assigned to us in this tragedy. Let us do so in a way of honour and without personal animosities. Whatever the outcome I will never willingly relinquish the title of Your most affectionate friend. William Waller.

On 5 July both armies had raced for the high ground of Lansdown Hill. Waller got there first and ordered his men to dig in, throwing up earthen defences. Nothing, though, could prevent bloodshed. Cavalry charged and were stalled. Cornish foot soldiers, loyal to the king and armed with pikes 18 feet long – the same as those that had so failed James IV and his Scots at Flodden – struggled up the slope and over the top into withering fire. They were recklessly brave. Waller sent his cavalry to drive them back. To the fore of the pikemen, already a legend, was the luxuriantly named Sir Bevil Grenville. He was among the many felled by the swinging blades of the cavalrymen. Somehow his Cornishmen held on, furiously stubborn, and Waller felt he had no option but to withdraw his forces to the shelter of a drystone wall to his rear. By then hundreds lay dead on the field, and yet still it was not over.

Darkness came, but the firefight continued. Neither side wanted to move out of cover and commit flesh and bone to a fresh assault. Finally, Waller ordered his men to set smouldering match cords on top of the wall – creating the illusion of armed men still on watch – and then led them silently away into the shadows. Hopton and his Royalists were left in command of the field, but it had been a pyrrhic victory.

The Civil War ended in 1651 in victory for parliament and the execution of the king. That was a pyrrhic victory too. Having been a Royalist to the end, Hopton was among the many that fled into exile. He died in

Bruges, of fever, in 1652. Waller remained an MP but the reality of Oliver Cromwell and his Commonwealth turned his stomach and in time he would campaign for the restoration of the monarchy. He died in 1668. Waller's letter to Hopton is the last known contact between the pair. As far as anyone knows, they never saw or heard from each other again.

On Lansdown Hill the wall is still there; nowadays it is known as Waller's Wall. Close inspection seems to reveal places where holes were once made in its fabric and then later repaired. Nearby, among the trees at the lip of the slope, stands a monument to Sir Bevil Grenville. It is badly worn now and in any case only really commemorates one man. The wall stands for more, rough and cold beneath the hand. A dividing line that has a person choose a side upon which to stand.

<h1 style="text-align:center">*54*</h1>

Sedgemoor Battlefield, Somerset

The Pitchfork Rebellion

I remember how boldly an abundance of men talked for the Duke of
Monmouth when he first landed; but if half of them had as boldly
joined him sword in hand, he had never been routed . . .

DANIEL DEFOE, 1660–1731

THE BATTLE FOUGHT at Sedgemoor in Somerset on 6 July 1685 was the
last of any note on English soil.

James Scott, Duke of Monmouth, eldest of the bastard sons sired by
King Charles II, had landed on the beach at Lyme Regis in Dorset in early
June with eighty-three men and a cache of arms. He had not arrived in the
West Country by chance – rather he knew it as a hotbed of religious non-
conformists and troublemakers. His objective was the English throne.
Charles was dead, succeeded by his Catholic brother, James II, and there
was an appetite for a Protestant usurper. Monmouth fitted the bill.

In 1680 he had indulged himself with what amounted to a Royal Progress through the counties of the West Country, revelling in his popularity
among the locals. None seemed to care that he was illegitimate. He was a
king's son and, more importantly, a Protestant. In the end he had pushed
his luck, though, sniping about Catholic James – then Duke of York – and
even about Charles himself. Realizing he had said too much, he took
himself off to the Continent and into the company of other prominent
Protestants, such as Archibald Campbell, 1st Marquess of Argyll. Monmouth was in Holland when news reached him of his father's death in

Lacada Point, Antrim, resting place of the Spanish Armada's last treasure ship.

The Globe Theatre, London …
'turning the accomplishment of
many years into an hourglass'.

The Globe

St Giles' Cathedral, Edinburgh, the Heart of Midlothian and the heart of Edinburgh.

Schiehallion, Perthshire. The mountain of the constant storm, where we learned the weight of the world.

The Iron Bridge, Shropshire, forged in the first fires of the Industrial Revolution.

TO BE SOLD & LET
BY PUBLIC AUCTION,
On MONDAY the 18th of MAY, 1829,
UNDER THE TREES.

FOR SALE,
THE THREE FOLLOWING
SLAVES,
VIZ.

HANNIBAL, about 30 Years old, an excellent House Servant, of Good Character.
WILLIAM, about 35 Years old, a Labourer.
NANCY, an excellent House Servant and Nurse.

The MEN belonging to "LEECH'S" Estate, and the WOMAN to Mrs. D. SMITH

TO BE LET,
On the usual conditions of the Hirer finding them in Food, Clothing, and Medical Assistance,
THE FOLLOWING
MALE and FEMALE
SLAVES,
OF GOOD CHARACTERS.

ROBERT BAGLEY, about 20 Years old, a good House Servant.
WILLIAM BAGLEY, about 18 Years old, a Labourer.
JOHN ARMS, about 18 Years old.
JACK ANTONIA, about 40 Years old, a Labourer.
PHILIP, an Excellent Fisherman.
HARRY, about 27 Years old, a good House Servant.
LUCY, a Young Woman of good Character, used to House Work and the Nursery.
ELIZA, an Excellent Washerwoman.
CLARA, an Excellent Washerwoman.
FANNY, about 14 Years old, House Servant.
SARAH, about 14 Years old, House Servant.

Also for Sale, at Eleven o'Clock,
Fine Rice, Gram, Paddy, Books, Muslins, Needles, Pins, Ribbons &c. &c.

AT ONE O'CLOCK, THAT CELEBRATED ENGLISH HORSE
BLUCHER,

Wilberforce House, Kingston upon Hull.
'A trade founded in iniquity and carried
out as this was must be abolished.'

HMS Victory, *Portsmouth — Nelson's flagship and the oldest warship in the world still on active service.*

The Brontë Parsonage, Haworth. The cradling of genius in a landscape made of weather and rock.

February 1685, and soon he was listening to Argyll and others telling him the English throne was rightfully his. Argyll proposed to raise an army in Scotland and urged Monmouth to do the same in England.

As soon as Monmouth splashed ashore at Lyme Regis with his followers, the malcontents of the West Country began rallying to his side. He quickly assembled a ragtag force of perhaps 8,000. They were poor men, and poorly armed – they were quickly dubbed the 'Pitchfork Rebels'. In Taunton, Monmouth had himself proclaimed king, and by the end of the month his uncle, King James, had raised an army of his own.

Young Daniel Defoe was among the relative handful of Protestants that hastened from London to Monmouth's side. With success as an author still ahead of him, he was an opportunist. Among other jobs, he had bred civet cats for the perfume trade. The year before Monmouth's landing in Dorset he had married a relatively wealthy heiress called Mary Tuffley. Her dowry was at least as attractive as she, and her cash had enabled him to settle his debts.

Defoe and a handful of like-minded friends were among Monmouth's motley army when they reached the patchwork of farmland between the villages of Bridgwater and Westonzoyland in Somerset in early July. The Pitchfork Rebels had done well enough earlier in their campaign in the face of local militia, but by then a professional force was bearing down upon them. The king's troops were under the command of Louis de Duras, Earl of Feversham, but when it mattered the telling tactical moves would be made by Major General John Churchill. He would later rise to glory during the War of the Spanish Succession and win the title of Duke of Marlborough along with a vast palace called Blenheim, but it was at Sedgemoor that he first demonstrated his prowess as a leader of men.

The fire was going out of the rebels. King James had let it be known he would pardon any man who laid down his arms and abandoned the cause. This inducement, coupled with waning enthusiasm and the prospect of facing professional soldiers, meant many had already deserted. Rather than quit the scene himself, Monmouth chose to roll the dice and trust to fate. As darkness fell on 5 July, he led his men on a night march, hoping to surprise the royal army. The intervening terrain, however, was cut through by deep drainage ditches – called rhynes – and in the darkness the rebels failed to find any way across the worst of it. A pistol shot rang out too – by mistake or by treachery – and the element of surprise was lost.

The sun began to rise and the royal army with it, deploying in good order. Monmouth's rebels were no contest for cavalry and disciplined musketry. Churchill led a telling assault across the field of Sedgemoor that soon routed those men armed with pitchforks and the like. Along with all the rest, Monmouth fled, but he was captured two days later, hiding in a ditch, and taken to London, where he begged for his life before his uncle the king. It was not to be. He was parted from his head on Tower Hill on 15 July.

The rebels were sorely treated too. Those who survived the battle were rounded up and brought in batches before kangaroo courts presided over in the main by one Judge Jeffreys. These were the 'Bloody Assizes', when perhaps as many as 400 men were hanged or butchered for their treason. Another 800 were transported in chains to the colonies, there to work as slaves on the sugar plantations.

Defoe did rather better, of course. He fled the field and hid out in a church. It is even rumoured that a name on a gravestone in the churchyard – Robinson Crusoe – caught his eye and stayed in his memory. When he came to write the book, he also drew upon what he had heard of the experiences of a fellow rebel called Dr Henry Pitman. Not so lucky as Defoe, Pitman had been captured and sent to a plantation in the Caribbean. He escaped, Papillon-style, and spent time on the island of La Tortuga, off the coast of Venezuela, before making it all the way back to London.

King James may have been victorious, but not for long. Just three years after the battle he would be ousted from his throne by the Glorious Revolution.

Sedgemoor today is much as Monmouth left it, still pastureland after all the years, the fields still cut by deep ditches. The battlefield, marked by information boards and by a memorial of pale-grey stone, seems too small to have hosted so much incident. It almost feels claustrophobic, hedges pressing in from the sides and the sky from above. The horrors meted out by Jeffreys at his Bloody Assizes are still remembered by people there and if ghosts walk the fields, as it is said they do, it would be no surprise.

55

St Giles' Cathedral, Edinburgh

The Treaty of Union

FOLDED AWAY WITHIN the story of the British Isles is the marriage of Scotland and England. A couple that had fought like cat and dog for years were brought together in some kind of matrimony on 1 May 1707. In terms of weddings, you might say it was a registry office do – a legal functionary or two, some paperwork to be signed. The bride was unhappy, could not even afford a dress. The groom was every bit as disinclined and in no doubt he was being married for his money. From somewhere out of sight came the distant sound of tolling bells.

By a stroke of the pen, rather than the sword, the previously separate and independent parliaments of England and Scotland had been replaced by the Parliament of Great Britain. This was the reality of the Treaty of Union. The countries had shared a monarch since 1603, but it was the coming together of their parliaments that made a United Kingdom of them. Resented by a majority of Scots and hardly any more welcome in England, in time the marriage would prove the best thing that had ever happened to either.

Not to put too fine a point on it, Scotland was broke. The last decade of the seventeenth century had been blighted by the 'ill years', made of seven years of bad harvests. Disaster followed hardship when the Darien Company attempted to establish a Scottish colony in Panama in Central America. The dream was to grow rich by creating and controlling a short-cut between the Atlantic and Pacific Oceans. The promise of wealth attracted feverish interest until something between a quarter and a half of all the liquid capital in Scotland was invested in the scheme. The necessary ships set sail, and between 1698 and 1700 the pioneers sought to establish themselves in what proved to be a flyblown, malarial swamp. Everything went wrong. Instead of the right clothes and equipment for a tropical environment, they had taken wigs and woollens. From start to finish it was hubristic farce. All was lost – many lives along with every last sou of the money.

For its own part, England simply wanted a final solution to what it considered the Scottish problem. After the Glorious Revolution ousted James II from the throne, he was succeeded by his Protestant daughter Mary and her husband William of Orange. As they were childless, their heir was James's younger daughter, Anne – a Stuart, right enough, and Protestant. In all she had eighteen pregnancies, but not one of her children survived into adulthood. By 1700 the last of them was dead and the next in line to the throne after her was her younger half-brother, the Catholic James Francis Edward Stuart – the man who would be the Old Pretender, father of Bonnie Prince Charlie. Rather than risk a Catholic on the throne, Anne accepted the English parliament's idea of offering the prize of England, Ireland and Scotland to a distant cousin. Sophia, Electress of Hanover, a granddaughter of James VI and I, was a Protestant Stuart with a Protestant son, George. By all accounts Anne could hardly bear the sight of them, but by the Act of Settlement of 1701 it was agreed George would follow her on to the throne. The Scots were livid. They had not been consulted – just presented with a fait accompli. They could hardly complain, though, or not in all seriousness at least. The prospect of a Catholic king was not what the majority of Scots wanted either, not in their heart of hearts.

Cool (and self-interested) heads in Scotland reasoned that the nation's options were limited, and stark. She could strike out on her own, into a cold, hard world – or contemplate what had previously been unthinkable and cosy up to the Auld Enemy. In the end, the latter choice won out. England was rich, with lucrative trade links overseas. For as long as Scotland remained apart, with its own parliament, the door to all the foreign booty would remain legally closed. If the Scots got into bed with their southern neighbour, all manner of opportunities might present themselves. The final sweetener came in the form of cold, hard cash. Many Scottish nobles had been ruined, or nearly, by Darien. In return for backing the proposed union, thousands of English pounds were sent north to nudge some influential Scots over the finishing line.

The die was cast. The Scottish Privy Council proclaimed the formal dissolution of the Scottish parliament on 28 April 1707. By similar means the English parliament was done away with too. There could be only one – and it was the Parliament of Great Britain. Scotland had to make do with just a sprinkling of Members, but those with their eyes on the prize deemed it a compromise worth making. Although their numbers were small, at least they were finally inside the tent pissing out.

On the first day of May, the Act of Union came into force. Beneath the crown spire of St Giles' Cathedral in Edinburgh a new carillon of bells played an old Scottish folk tune, 'Why Am I So Sad, On This My Wedding Day?'

Seated proudly in the middle of the Royal Mile, St Giles' is at the heart of Edinburgh. Set into the pavement close by its west door is the Heart of Midlothian, a heart-shaped mosaic of cobbles that marks the site of the old Tolbooth, once a place of execution. It is also near Parliament House, where sat the parliament of Scotland. All in all it was a fitting place from which to give voice to the lamentation of troubled people. Momentous change had come, and many found it hard if not impossible to contemplate the new future joined in wedlock to all they had previously feared and despised.

Given that cathedral means 'the Church of the Bishop's Seat', and since the Church of Scotland has no bishops, the word is literally out of place, an anachronism. Some folk in Edinburgh call it by other names – the High Kirk, or the Mother Church of Presbyterianism. During the 900 years of its existence, it has witnessed no end of drama.

Throughout the medieval period, Scotland's kings and queens had attended Catholic Mass at St Giles'. By the time Mary, Queen of Scots, returned to the land of her birth in 1561, Scotland was Protestant. She generally avoided the place, but her son, James VI, was a regular – often heckling the minister there about theology. It was here that, in 1637, James's son Charles I tried to force his new prayer book on the Scots.

One upheaval after another had afflicted Scotland, and St Giles' was always there in the background, or the foreground.

Alexander Henderson, who had helped compose the National Covenant, was later a minister of St Giles'. James Graham, 1st Marquess of Montrose, had signed the Covenant but later fought for the king. He was captured and executed outside St Giles' in 1650. His king was dead by then, on another butcher's block. Witnesses reported how Montrose met his end dressed 'like a bridegroom', wearing a black suit, a scarlet cloak and ribboned shoes. Another wedding then, another groom resigned to his fate. St Giles' was so often a witness to Scotland's sadnesses. In the last moments remaining to him, Montrose recited a poem he had composed while he sat in the condemned cell:

Open all my veins, that I may swim
To Thee, my Saviour, in that crimson lake.

Montrose's great enemy had been Archibald Campbell, 1st Marquess of Argyll and leader of the Covenanter army. When Charles II was restored to the throne in 1660, he ordered a state funeral for Montrose in St Giles'. Argyll was charged with treason the following year and beheaded on the same spot as his old adversary.

Much of what visitors see inside the cathedral is the result of restorations and renovations in the eighteenth and nineteenth centuries. What had been a clutter of little chapels and partitioned spaces was opened up, so that for the first time since the seventeenth century it had the cavernous interior intended by its medieval architects. During the Victorian era there was a mood to put a salve on all the old hurts. First Montrose was given a fine, ornate monument, complete with effigy, and the same was provided for Argyll soon after.

St Giles' is still a focal point of the Old Town, still a quietly beating heart at the centre of Edinburgh, Scotland's capital.

56

Culloden, Inverness

The Jacobites' last stand

WE NO LONGER have much truck here in these islands with political or religious extremism. Monarchs, governments and political or religious groups of whichever hue have all had a go over the centuries – religious fundamentalism and the persecution that attends it, communism, fascism. But none of it persuades the mass of the people of the British Isles any longer. An upcoming generation will still do as it's told for a while, turning a blind eye, wearing the T-shirts with the right slogans, even trotting out the dogma. But when it comes to dressing up in black shirts and goose-stepping through London's East End, or singing 'The Red Flag' and demanding revolution, the mass of folk on these islands generally end up laughing up their sleeves at the latest preposterousness and then get back to minding their own business. We've been around long enough to have seen it all before. Any one generation might be fooled by their first hearing of some old song, but the depth of history here means sooner or later the newest batch of charlatans and madmen gets rumbled. J. R. R. Tolkien had us as hobbits – resilient little people who would grudgingly break off from tending their gardens just long enough to topple the roaring monster, foreign or domestic.

This sangfroid in the face of loud mouths and strutting popinjays is the product of harsh lessons learned one after another and over and over again. So much has happened here – and we have kept track of most of it – there is rarely anything new for us now. We recognize would-be butchers, deluded fantasists, zealots, troublemakers and rabble-rousers because, in our time, we have been all of those things – and to each other as well as to the inhabitants of foreign lands. We have been abused and abuser both.

Of all the bloodlettings that have stained these islands, few carry a stronger latent charge than the Battle of Culloden. Even now the lessons of those dreadful moments on a moor north-east of Inverness are still to be learned by some. An alarming number of people continue to think it was a clash between Scotland and England, or Highlanders and Lowlanders, when it was neither. Others revere Charles Edward Stuart, the so-called Bonnie Prince, as though he were someone who gave so much as a damn about the Scots and Scotland, when in fact his only dream was to take the British throne in London. In fact, the Jacobite Rebellion, to which Culloden was a bloody full stop, was part of a pan-European civil war involving Britain and her allies against her old European enemies France and Spain.

It was not even as simple as Catholic versus Protestant. The 1745 Jacobite rising in Scotland – on the surface an attempt, like its predecessors since 1689, to restore the Catholic Stuarts to the throne of the United Kingdom – was a sideshow of the War of the Austrian Succession. Protestant Britain's principal ally in that fight was Habsburg Austria, which was Catholic.

As usual, Great Britain and France were on opposite sides. While the Hanoverian government of King George II supported Maria Theresa's claim to the Habsburg throne, France and Prussia opposed her, citing ancient Salic Law that prohibited women from inheriting thrones. Hostilities had broken out on the Continent in 1740 and the war would involve most of the European powers before its end in 1748. It was in hopes of fomenting a rebellion in Scotland that France spoke up, and not for the first time, in support of the Catholic Stuart claim on the British throne. Charles Edward Stuart, the Young Pretender, was dispatched to the Scottish Highlands to stir up the sort of trouble that might force Britain to abandon the war on the Continent in order to deal with dangerous trouble at home.

In the short term, then, the Protestant Hanoverian government's victory at Culloden silenced the domestic threat of Catholic troublemaking.

When Britain embarked upon the Seven Years War in 1756 – fighting France, Spain, Russia and Sweden – at least the government had no need to fear Popish trouble at home. By the end of that larger conflict, Britain's rule by the House of Hanover was secure beyond doubt, as was her control of an empire spanning North America, the Caribbean and India.

Myth-making by Sir Walter Scott and others later served to varnish Jacobite bones with a gloss of tragic nobility, while simultaneously demonizing the red-coated British soldiers as fascist myrmidons. It glossed over uncomfortable truths about how more Scots had fought for Hanover and the Duke of Cumberland at Culloden than for Bonnie Prince Charlie and the exiled House of Stuart.

Little by little, though, and year by year, the truth of what happened there is finally crystallizing. The myth of the brave but doomed Highlander in his plaid, pitched against the evil 'Butcher Cumberland' and his red-coated lackeys, is steadily being eroded.

Culloden battlefield itself has shimmered and altered like a mirage over the last forty years as well. Within my own memory the Clan Graves had a road running right through them. This has long since been taken away and the area grassed over until it feels more like a graveyard. For long the only visitor centre was in a drystone cottage called Old Leanach. A better effort was made with a purpose-built centre installed in the 1970s – and then in 2007 this too was replaced as part of a multi-million-pound effort to return the whole site to a condition closer to that the protagonists would have known on 16 April 1746.

In spite of all the meddling and tinkering that has gone on during the two and half centuries that have passed since the fighting stopped (and I've done my share), there is no doubting the enduring emotional impact of the battlefield. More than 130,000 people visited the new centre in its first year of opening. Many of them – tens of thousands – would have brought their own needs and wants to the place. Culloden is a canvas upon which dreamers sketch out their own dreams and fantasists live out their fantasies. Japanese tourists come in search of kinship with what they consider to be a fellow warrior race. They have absorbed the legend of the Highlander and sense in him *Bushido* – the way of the warrior as practised by their own samurai. Nationalist Scots come with their Saltire flags, many with faces painted blue in tribute to Australian actor Mel Gibson's portrayal of William Wallace in *Braveheart*. His triumphant Battle of Stirling Bridge was fought for other reasons in another world, four and a half centuries before and hundreds of miles south, but at a place like Culloden a strange mixing takes place and the ghosts of a thousand broken dreams find communion, and tears are shed for all of it.

The opposing battle lines are marked with flags, and carefully laid-out paths lead visitors in the footsteps of the two rival armies. As with all battlefields, it is hard to walk the ground in peace and quiet and imagine the place as a killing field. The fighting lasted less than an hour. The hand-to-hand, face-to-face stuff, with swords and pistols, muskets and bayonets, point-blank grapeshot and mortars, may have taken no more than half that long. The most recent archaeological investigations have suggested the outcome was a close-run thing – even though the Jacobites were significantly outnumbered on the day. The rebels played to their strengths – quickly closing the distance in hopes of bringing terror and butchery to their foe as they had done before. Cumberland's troops had learned the lessons of Jacobite victories at Prestonpans and Falkirk Muir, however, and so knew they had to stand and fight in the face of the fabled Highland Charge, depending on discipline and teamwork. However many hellish minutes it lasted, government age and guile triumphed over the youth and innocence of Bonnie Prince Charlie's rebel army.

Cumberland oversaw a brutal retribution in the weeks and months that followed. The Highlanders and Highlands were stamped on – men, women and children taught that fomenting or supporting rebellion carried a death sentence, and that even innocent bystanders would not be spared punishment. It was a tactic the British government would deploy over and over (against the Native Americans, to name but one other people), until the lesson was later learned that lasting victory is best achieved by winning hearts and minds.

The Clan Graves are a focal point – grassy mounds, some marked with boulders bearing individual clan names and raised by landowner Duncan Forbes in the 1880s. No doubt there really are Jacobite dead there or thereabouts, buried in mass graves in the aftermath by folk that knew them.

Culloden was the last pitched battle on British soil – meaning the last time two armies actually confronted one another across an open field at a prearranged place and time. Ever since the time of John Balliol, king of Scotland in the last decade of the thirteenth century, Scotland had been used by the French whenever it suited them to make trouble with England. Charles Edward Stuart, supported by the French King Louis XV, was just the latest glove puppet. But he was the last of them that mattered. Red-coated soldiers would be at French throats over and over after 1746, but they would never have to watch their backs in quite the same way again.

57

Staithes, North Yorkshire

The grocer's boy and the lure of the sea

IN ITS HEYDAY in the nineteenth century, the North Yorkshire village of Staithes was one of the busiest fishing ports on England's north-east coast, with an eighty-strong fleet. As many as 400 men earned their livings there, setting out from the beach in locally built, distinctively crafted boats called cobles. Since they headed out into the swell in all weathers, such vessels had to have high, upturned prows for protection from the waves, and owed at least some of their design to Viking longboats of the sort that had, long ago, preyed upon that coastline at will. Fresh catches of fish and shellfish were loaded on to trains at Staithes station and transported to fish markets up and down the country.

Now only a fragment of that industry survives, a handful of boats working part time. More than fishing has moved on and left Staithes behind. At one time miners dug nearby for alum, a chemical compound used to fix dye colours to fabrics, until that industry failed following the discovery of cheaper, synthetic alternatives. There were sources of jet too, and potash, but all of that lies in the past as well. The geology thereabouts is part of the so-called Dinosaur Coast and still today trophy hunters come in search of fossils.

During the late nineteenth and early twentieth centuries, Staithes was home to an artists' colony. Inspired by French Impressionists like Paul Cézanne and Claude Monet, a group of around twenty-five British artists were attracted to that exposed east coast and toughed it out in the face of wind and rain. Instead of the rarefied calm of the studio, they preferred to practise their art *en plein air* – in the open air – and were dedicated to the quick, almost spontaneous capture of the effects of natural light. Among them were Dame Laura Knight, later the first woman given full membership of the Royal Academy, and Frank Henry Mason, whose art-deco railway posters are still instantly recognizable today.

The village is so tucked away as to seem deliberately hidden – like a purpose-built den for smugglers. Roxby Beck, a fast-flowing river, joins the North Sea there. It is on both sides of its valley that the houses and cottages jostle for space, red- and grey-roofed and piled on top of one another as though in search of shelter and warmth. The side of the valley with its back to the sea is formed by a sheer-sided cliff of crumbly sandstone. A bridge connects to the opposite bank, where there is more room, and it is here that most of the buildings are huddled and piled, higgledy-piggledy like Lego bricks.

There was indeed smuggling in Staithes once – another industry gone over the hill into history. Half the houses are second homes and now it is mostly a haunt of tourists. But no wonder – it is a lovely spot, like a dream of a fishing village, a Brigadoon for the seaside.

Some places in the landscape seem to matter just because they do – if for no other reason than that the combination of light and sharp air and constantly changing weather conspires to make a visitor feel better. Staithes is made all the more rewarding by the fact that it would be so easy to drive right by the end of the road leading down to the village without even noticing it was there.

But besides all this, Staithes also has its own claim on world history. It was to the hustle and bustle of the fishing port that one James Cook moved at the age of sixteen. He had been born near Middlesbrough but moved to Staithes in 1745 to take up a post as a shop boy. He tried it for a year and a half but proved unsuited, not just to shop work but to life ashore. The grocery business's loss, however, was exploration's gain. Historians have speculated that it was the glimpses of the sea to be had from the shop window, the comings and goings of the fishing boats, that inspired young James to seek his future and fortune elsewhere. The owners of the shop were a couple by the name of Sanderson. Apparently sensitive to the lad's dissatisfaction, they arranged for him to move to the nearby port of Whitby, where friends of theirs with a fleet of colliers took him on as a merchant navy apprentice.

Just as Sir Francis Drake's flagship, the *Golden Hind*, set out from Aldeburgh on the Suffolk coast, so the career of Captain Cook began in another haven tucked away out of sight of most of the world.

58

Whitby, North Yorkshire

Captain Cook and HMS Endeavour

I MAKE NO APOLOGY for mentioning James Cook a second time. We are an island race for certain and so have depended on the sea like nothing else, and for the longest time. It was those who ventured out upon the world-ocean with a view to making sense of it that set the course of our islands' future. Among them all, no navigator ever shone brighter than Cook.

Young James, failed grocer's boy and would-be mariner, was just eighteen years old when he arrived in the seaside town of Whitby to serve an apprenticeship with local coal merchant John Walker. It was 1746, the same year the last Jacobite rebellion was put to death on the heather moorland of Culloden and Prince Charles Edward Stuart fled to France. Bonnie but broken, Charles's bold adventures were over. Cook's were about to begin.

As was customary, he put his name to a contract. The terms had been written out twice upon the same page. Cook signed one and his master the other. The page was then torn in two, making a jagged edge, and each party retained his own half. If needs be, they might be brought together at a future date to prove they were the genuine article, the unique halves fitting neatly together. Contracts of that sort, with toothed edges, were therefore said to be indented – and an apprentice taken on such terms was *indentured*.

Ship-owner and collier Captain John Walker saw to it that the likely lad studied all the subjects he would require for a life at sea – mathematics, navigation, astronomy and the like. Walker was also a devout Quaker. No doubt he knew by heart verses 23 and 24 of Psalm 107: 'They that go down to the sea in ships, that do business in great waters; These see the works of the Lord, and his wonders in the deep.'

Local tradition in Whitby has it that Cook had a room in a house on Grape Street. He happily served out the three years demanded by his indenture on coal ships plying up and down the east coast between the Rivers Tyne and Thames. He was a merchant navy man by then, but in 1755 he joined His Majesty's Royal Navy. Always ambitious, he knew that service in the military might lead to speedy advance up through the ranks, and he was right. Within two years he had passed his master's exams and was soon commanding vessels of his own off the coast of North America. Still he longed for more, and in the years before his famous voyages of exploration began he penned words that would hardly look out of place in the captain's log of the *Starship Enterprise*. He wanted, he wrote, to go not just 'farther than any man has been before me, but as far I think as it is possible for a man to go'.

In 1768 Cook was given command of His Majesty's Bark *Endeavour*. She had been built as a collier – in Whitby, fittingly enough – and originally named the *Earl of Pembroke*. She was an able workhorse – flat-bottomed so she might be sailed into shallow water for loading and unloading or for any running repairs. It was a pedigree that would serve her well in distant waters.

Cook was set a course for immortality by the ambitions of the Royal Society in London. Immersed in the business of clarifying Earth's relationship to the rest of the bodies in the solar system, the fellows were fully aware that in 1769 the planet Venus would pass across the face of the sun, a tiny mote on the great golden eye. Measurements taken during a so-called Transit of Venus – from as many different points on Earth as possible – would enable the necessary calculations of relative distances between planets, so plans were duly laid.

The *Earl of Pembroke* was acquired, a gift of King George III, and refitted for a voyage into the South Pacific. Cook was a lieutenant, but his superiors had noticed his talents with the chart and sextant and he was made commander of the voyage. By the time they set sail, the ship had been renamed, her hull caulked and sheathed to protect her from the depredations of the worms known to populate tropical waters.

When ready for the voyage, *Endeavour* was packed to the gunwales and space was hard to come by. For a cabin mate, Cook had the botanist Sir Joseph Banks. Banks was as wealthy as he was learned. A landowner of note, he was the principal financier of the expedition and so it was deemed only proper he should share the best of the available accommodation aboard ship. The cabin was large by the standards of what the crew accepted as their due, but hardly spacious. Cook and Banks were both tall and rangy, so the time they spent together must have been interesting at least.

It was the first of three odysseys for Cook. What he and Banks accomplished on that voyage into the unknown was as noteworthy as the giant steps taken by Neil Armstrong and *Apollo 11* 200 years later. The Pacific then was unknown and unimaginably distant from these islands. While the moon would prove utterly devoid of life, what Cook, Banks and their fellow travellers encountered must surely have struck them as nothing less than alien life.

Endeavour departed Plymouth in August 1768. After crossing the Atlantic Ocean into the west and rounding Cape Horn, they arrived off Tahiti in time for that Transit of Venus. From there onwards it was all discovery, in territory hitherto uncharted. The hold of the *Endeavour* was soon filled by Banks with specimens outlandish and wondrous. At his insistence, space aboard was found for a Tahitian noble named Tupaia. He had impressive knowledge of what would become known as Polynesia – 'the Place of Many Islands' – and stayed with the *Endeavour* until his death in 1770, in Batavia, modern Jakarta.

The expedition reached New Zealand by October 1769 and then Australia in April of the following year. As well as tracking the path of Venus across the face of the sun, Cook had been tasked with settling the matter of the fabled unknown southern continent – *Terra Australis Incognita*. Both the Greeks and the Romans had supposed there must be lands in the south to counterbalance all the continents north of the equator, and by the time of Cook's voyage at least two European vessels had encountered some fragments of the truth of it. Cook has gone down in history as the first to lay claim to the place, however, and he made the first charts of Australia's eastern seaboard between Botany Bay and the Great Barrier Reef. He almost came unstuck there, the ship's hull torn open by coral. Luckily for Cook – and he was lucky, as well as a genius – *Endeavour's* flattened hull lent itself to the necessary hurried repairs.

Cook, Banks and their crew eventually arrived back in Plymouth on 10 July 1771. They had been gone three years and the consequences of their voyage would change the world.

It is hard to overstate Cook's abilities as a navigator, as an adventurer. He had travelled as far from his apprenticeship in Whitby as it is possible to imagine. He had had his first glimpses of a life at sea from a grocer's shop window in the village of Staithes, and through that keyhole he had passed into the wide world. Subsequent journeys would bring him into contact with Hawaii, and islanders there who at first mistook his sails for clouds come down from Heaven itself. They heard the ship's cannon fire and thought it the thunderous voice of their god Lono. Cook was welcomed at first, a visitor touched by the divine, but his later return, in February 1779, would see him beaten to death and parts of his body eaten. Most of his remains were handed over to his men, but some bones were kept ever after in a bowl dressed with feathers and carried high during ceremonies to honour the gods.

It all sounds too outlandish to believe – the stuff of fiction – but Cook's adventures were real enough, the *Endeavour* too. The space shuttle *Endeavour* was named in her honour, spelled in the English manner rather than the American. On her first flight into space she carried a fragment of her namesake's hull in her cockpit, all the way from Whitby.

Whitby today is, and I choose the word deliberately and with love, a strange place. The name is likely Old Norse, meaning 'the White Town'. It is picturesque all right, a child's drawing of an English fishing village. It is also a geological oddity, cradled between two cliffs of quite different character. On the east, the rock is thick with fossils of ammonites and belemnites, plesiosaurs and ichthyosaurs. There is jet there too, of course   Whitby jet   made of fossilized Monkey Puzzle trees from the Jurassic and used in Victorian days for black jewellery worn by those in mourning. The west cliffs, topped by the arch made of a whale's jawbone, are sandstone, riddled with the fossils of yet more plants and trees but from other times entirely.

The Irish writer Bram Stoker came to Whitby in 1890 and stayed at Mrs Veazey's guesthouse on Royal Crescent. He was apparently captivated by the cliffs and by the winding cobbled streets lined with red-roofed cottages. His writer's eye was caught too by the cliff-top ruins of Whitby Abbey, built by Benedictine monks in the eleventh century. Nearby is the parish church of St Mary, reached by 199 worn stone steps from the beach below. It was all too Gothic to ignore. When he came to write his famous novel, Stoker had it that Count Dracula, of Wallachia, arrived into Whitby harbour on a ship, the *Demeter*. All the crew had vanished during the voyage. Only her captain's corpse remained, lashed to the ship's wheel. As she ran aground at the foot of the East Cliffs, a massive black hound leaped ashore and bounded up the steps towards the church. A dog is one of the forms that might be taken by a vampire . . .

As one legend departed Whitby into the west, so another arrived there from out of the east.

59

Salisbury Crags and Arthur's Seat, Edinburgh

James Hutton, father of geology

'Lord pity the arse that's clagged [fixed] to a head that will hunt stones.' So wrote James Hutton, the man lauded as the father of geology, in 1774. He was in Bath when he recorded his sore bottom – presumably saddle-sore – but the idea that had put him on horseback and sent him in search of proof had come to him in his home town of Edinburgh.

He was a lucky man – lucky to have been born wealthy enough to spend his days thinking instead of working, and in Edinburgh during the several decades of the late eighteenth and early nineteenth centuries known as the Scottish Enlightenment. That city – small, cold, cramped and filthy as it was then – was the brightest source of the light. It drew thinkers like moths. Benjamin Franklin was a regular visitor. It was said a person might stand 'at the Mercat Cross and, in half an hour, shake 50 men of genius by the hand'. No less a thinker than Voltaire said at the time, 'It is to Scotland that we look for our ideas of civilisation.'

Hutton grew up in a world still in thrall to the notion that man and the Earth were the same age – around 6,000 years old. Archbishop James Ussher is usually credited with totting up the age of the world in the seventeenth century, after a painstaking reading of the Old Testament. By his calculation it all began at six o'clock on the evening of 22 October 4004 BC.

But Hutton lived in a city where the bare bones of the world were exposed for all to see. Salisbury Crags, Arthur's Seat and the great crag and tail upon which squats Edinburgh Castle are all leftovers from ancient volcanic activity. He had no way of calculating how ancient, but he had walked the ground and seen how different types of rock overlay one another. He decided the planet must be in a state of constant flux – that old rock was eroded by the elements and washed to the sea only to be replaced by new rock made deep in the heat of the planet's core.

Rather than the Earth being 6,000 years old, Hutton came to believe it 'had no vestige of a beginning and no prospect of an end'.

These were the foundations of uniformitarianism – the theory that the present-day forces shaping the planet and the wider universe had also held sway in the past and would continue to do so in future. Hutton wrote: 'We are thus led to see a circulation in the matter of this globe, and a system of beautiful economy in the works of nature.'

A lifetime before Charles Darwin published *On the Origin of Species*, Hutton also explained the variety of living things:

> If an organised body is not in the situation and circumstances best adapted to its sustenance and propagation, then, in conceiving an indefinite variety among the individuals of that species, we must be assured, that, on the one hand, those which depart most from the best adapted constitution, will be most liable to perish, while, on the other hand, those organised bodies, which most approach to the best constitution for the present circumstances, will be best adapted to continue, in preserving themselves and multiplying the individuals of their race.

Hutton was no atheist, a deist rather. He had no truck with any literal reading of Scripture either, such as had inspired Archbishop Ussher to say the Earth was only 6,000 years old. He was no creationist, but he certainly believed in a benevolent, non-interventionist creator.

The best starting point for a visit to Salisbury Crags and Arthur's Seat is from the gates of Holyrood Palace at the foot of Edinburgh's Royal Mile. The crags loom over the lanes and closes of the Old Town, where all those men of genius lived cheek by jowl while the Enlightenment burned bright. The climb to the summit of Arthur's Seat is the stuff of no more than an hour and yet it is a walk through the burned-out heart of a volcano. Hexagonal basalt columns, exactly the same as those of the Giant's Causeway, form the feature known as Samson's Ribs. The exposed face of Hutton's Section – the very foundation of modern structural geology – is easily found too.

In the end, it is simply important to remember that Hutton found, on Salisbury Crags and Arthur's Seat, the answers to questions no one else had ever even thought to ask. He realized that there around him was evidence of the process by which all new land is created. Like Rome, Edinburgh is built on seven hills. Hutton saw that they had been volcanoes and that here was how all the world was made – thrust up from the furnaces of the Earth as molten lava. He was among the first to contemplate deep time and in so doing grasped at the fringes of the truth of our predicament. He made room for understanding dinosaurs and ice ages, even for the Big Bang, and confronted us with our insignificance in the face of eternity.

60

The Statue of General James Wolfe, Royal Observatory, Greenwich

At the centre of time and place

THERE ARE MANY reasons for following the worn and winding path up to Flamsteed House and the Royal Observatory. For one thing, there is the Greenwich Meridian Line. As the tour guides on every open-top bus and Thames riverboat will tell you, straddle that steel strip set into the building's courtyard and you have one foot in the world's western hemisphere and the other in the eastern. For another, there is the Shepherd Gate Clock, hung on the wall outside the observatory, the first in all the world to reveal Greenwich Mean Time (GMT) to the general public. On top of the building there is the red Time Ball that drops down its pole every day at precisely 1 p.m. On display inside the museum is one of the watches John Harrison built, known as the H4, the first reliably to tell the time aboard a ship at sea and enable mariners to calculate longitude. For those in search of time and place, the Royal Observatory is the very spot.

The hilltop on which the Royal Observatory stands was once home to a fortress built by a younger brother of Henry V. Henry VIII had it as a hunting lodge and, given its proximity to nearby Greenwich Palace, where he was born, he apparently found it a useful location for stashing whoever was his mistress of the moment. When Charles II ordered the building of an observatory for the calculations that would make for better maps, it was Christopher Wren who suggested the site as the ideal home for the starry men with their optic glasses. Work began in 1675, and for most of the next two centuries the goings-on inside were mainly the preserve of those men of science, watching stars and planets, making charts that were ever more precise.

Time-keeping grew more precise too, but the inhabitants of most towns the length and breadth of these islands had their own 'time', based simply on the position of the sun as they saw it in their own patches of sky. The same was true in the wider world. Just as they preferred their own opinions, most men trusted their own idea of the time of day. It was not until the expansion of the railway network in the middle decades of the nineteenth century that anyone saw the need to have a universally agreed time. Before then there was barely even a consensus on the length of an hour, or even when each day should start and finish. But once trains were on the move across the land and people felt the need of reliable timetables in order to make proper use of them, some sort of general agreement became a necessity. In 1847, so that folk might be standing on the plat-forms when the trains arrived in the stations, Greenwich Mean Time was adopted all over these lands.

This was the time shown on the Shepherd Gate Clock, itself a slave to a master timepiece inside the building. From 1852 onwards, the time on the Shepherd master clock, designed and installed by English clockmaker Charles Shepherd, was sent via the telegraph network to London, Belfast, Glasgow, Edinburgh and other cities besides. By 1866 GMT was being relayed to America, by transatlantic cable, to keep them straight as well. In 1884, delegates from twenty-five countries assembled in Washington for the International Meridian Conference to decide from which point on the globe the nations of the world might count 0° of longitude, the beginning and end of the world. Great Britain and the USA were already using Green-wich for that purpose by then, and by the end of the conflab all but two of the other twenty-three were doing likewise. Brazil withheld its vote – France too, but then they would, wouldn't they?

Greenwich has been the centre of the world for time and place ever since. Go there and know with absolute certainty not just where you are but also when. In truth, however, the best reason for making your way to the Royal Observatory is its proximity to the statue of Major General Sir James Wolfe, installed in 1930 just beyond the gates, a gift to the people of Britain from the people of Canada. There in its shadow is a different gift, and a better one I would say.

Wolfe was born in Westerham in Kent in 1727, the eldest son of Lieutenant-General Edward Wolfe. The family moved to Macartney House on the edge of Greenwich Park in 1738. James, despite being physically frail and prone to ill-health, was commissioned in the army at the age of fourteen and distinguished himself during the suppression of the Jacobite Rebellion. His name and memory were later made immortal and luminous by his victory over the French forces at Quebec in 1759 during the Seven Years War. After months of deadlock, he had his forces ascend the formidable cliffs called the Heights of Abraham so that they might launch a surprise attack against the foe. Wolfe was mortally wounded at the moment of victory. The French commander, the Marquis de Montcalm, was also killed, and it was his descendant who presided over the unveiling of the likeness of Wolfe.

The great soldier is depicted atop a tall plinth of pale stone, its pockmarks the result of German bombing in 1940. Wolfe wears a belted coat, long cloak and a tricorne hat, and his right hand holds a telescope – appropriate both to his famous victory and to this place – while his left is placed lightly on his hip.

Stand beside the statue and you are rewarded with absolutely the best view to be had of London. This is what makes a visit there truly worthwhile, and enlightening in its own way. In the foreground is Wolfe's beloved Greenwich – the buildings of the Royal Naval College designed, like so much else, by Wren – and the silvered sweep of the Thames. Beyond is the great city itself.

On any given day, the Royal Observatory is crowded with tourists and visitors. They watch the clocks, they take turns having their photos taken with one foot in the east and the other in the west, they potter in the museum. In the end, it seems most time is spent with Wolfe – whether they know him or not – and with that view he commands.

Some of what was true of Wolfe is also true of these islands. He was hardly the physical type to achieve so much, to lead so well. He was the son of a military man, born of the fight, but he had to work, to toughen up, rise above his physical limitations, his frailties, earn and maintain respect. He understood the need to have faith in himself. He had, too, a sense of his own mortality, that he would not last longer than he was needed. Legend has it that as he was being rowed down the St Lawrence River, in the quiet darkness before the day of his victory, he quoted a line from Thomas Gray's *Elegy Written in a Country Churchyard*: 'The paths of glory lead but to the grave.'

In his own time, J. M. W. Turner immortalized the vista from above Greenwich as it was in the early 1800s. Still today it draws us in, and holds us there. There is no understanding the story of these islands without at least attempting to take in London, which has so much to tell. Beyond the gates of that observatory, of all places, time seems to stand still. All London is laid before you and that gift of time is well spent picking out one land-mark after another. Made just small enough to take in with a single glance, the whole city appears tabletop-sized. While standing still, it is possible to see how much has been achieved, how much might be lost. It is all places we have made. The most obvious now are the most recent: the London Eye, the O2, the Shard, the clustered glass towers of Canary Wharf, the towers they call the Gherkin and the Walkie-Talkie. Woven through it all, just as the Thames runs through it like a silver thread, are 2,000 years of other striving, and all of it in need of a general's vigilance. It seems so vulnerable, laid out on a flat dish of river-borne silt, ready for the taking. There is even a shining path leading into its heart. From the vantage point of Wolfe's statue, London almost seems to make sense. Almost. We must keep watch.

61

Schiehallion, Perthshire

Measuring the weight of the Earth

LOOK AT A map of Scotland and point, pin-the-tail-on-the-donkey style, at the centre of the country. Your finger will in all likelihood have landed not far from the mountain in Perthshire called Schiehallion. Some guidebooks have it that the name – pronounced *She-hally-on* – is a corruption of the Gaelic for 'Fairy Hill of the Caledonians'. Others say it means 'Constant Storm'. It is one of the sentinels keeping watch over the famed wilderness of Rannoch Moor, where clans roamed, often visiting unforgivable cruelties and horrors upon one another.

At just over 3,500 feet high, Schiehallion is a Munro – one of the 282 Scottish peaks measuring 3,000 feet or more. From most viewpoints it appears as a whale-backed ridge, but seen from the west, across the mirror of Loch Rannoch, it looks like a perfectly symmetrical cone or a volcano. It was this aspect, this shape that brought the mountain to the attention of eighteenth-century scientists looking for a place where they might calculate the weight of the Earth.

From at least the Neolithic period and the time of the Ness of Brodgar and the Stones of Stenness and such, the inhabitants of the British Isles devoted some of their time to watching the movement of the lights in the sky. Maybe the more observant among them realized the difference between planets and stars. The stone circles were certainly raised to help those early astronomers keep track of it all. They had noticed the regular, repeating patterns drawn by the sun and the moon and took to aligning stones on solstices, equinoxes. Sometimes they took care too with the positioning of the entrances to the tombs they built for their dead, so that the sunrise of significant days – midwinter, midsummer – might illuminate the passageways and chambers. Whatever else their studies meant to them, it seems reasonable to surmise they were given to grand thoughts.

For the longest time, Earth was assumed to sit stationary at the centre of all the motion – the fixed point in the universe about which everything revolved. Some observers imagined our planet within a vast outer shell, a pearl within an oyster shell through which were pierced many pinpricks that let in light from beyond. In the second century, Ptolemy thought the planets were caught up in a circular dance with invisible partners, the waltzing pairs spinning together around our Earth. In 1543, Copernicus realized the essential truth – that it was the sun at the centre, with all else, us included, revolving around it.

During the second half of the seventeenth century, Isaac Newton observed that the force causing an apple to fall straight to the ground from its tree was the same as that holding the planets in their orbits around the sun. With the kind of genius that makes me wonder why I bother getting out of bed in the morning, he concluded that each object in the universe, however large or small, exerted a pull on every other. In the case of anything smaller than a planet, however, he supposed the effect of the force would be too slight to see or feel, far less to measure. He imagined a plumb line suspended close to a mountain would be pulled away from the vertical by the magnetic mass of all that rock, but he was convinced no suitably vast mountain existed on Earth to produce the effect on a scale he could appreciate.

'Nay, whole mountains will not be sufficient to produce any sensible effect,' he wrote in his *Principia*. 'A mountain of an hemispherical figure, three miles high and six broad, will not, by its attraction, draw the pendulum two minutes out of the true perpendicular; and it is only in the great bodies of the planets that these forces are to be perceived.'

It also occurred to him that the force in question, gravity, must be proportional to the mass – that is, the weight – of each object in question. But how then to weigh the sun, the planets or even the Earth he stood upon and so establish the constant nature of gravity?

In 1772 the Royal Society sent a surveyor named Charles Mason (famous for his part in drawing the Mason–Dixon Line, recognized at one time as the boundary between the slave-owning states of the American south and the free states of the north) to find a mountain that might prove Newton wrong . . . and also right: right about the pull of a mountain and wrong about the impossibility of measuring its effect here on Earth. The peak he selected was Schiehallion. The man chosen for the job of conducting the experiment with the plumb line, however, was the Astronomer Royal, the Reverend Nevil Maskelyne, and in the spring of 1774 he left Greenwich bound for the forbidding north. It is an indication of just how much of a challenge the journey was that rather than travel by road he sailed as far as Perth. Edinburgh might have been burning bright with the intellectual fire of the Scottish Enlightenment by then, but outside the city the country was regarded by many as bleak, poor and downright dangerous. The clan system that had enforced an order of sorts had broken down in the wake of the defeat and destruction of Jacobitism. For a southerner like Maskelyne, the maths was comprehensible enough but the wilds of Scotland were beyond his ken.

Schiehallion is of a similar height to Snowdon, the highest peak in Wales, but from a distance it is hard accurately to appreciate its scale. It stands alone, a solitary peak surrounded by lower, gentler terrain. Because it is easily accessible for a large part of the population, it is regarded as a good introduction to Munro-bagging (as they call the hobby of climbing as many as possible). In the context of such peaks it is a relatively gentle hike, but it still climbs like a mountain. In parts the ascent feels lung-bursting and, on account of all the shattered rock underfoot, definitely the sort of terrain upon which a person might twist or break an ankle.

Consider then the experience of Maskelyne as he and his team lugged their kit up on to the high ground, close to the summit, and then cleared by hand a level terrace. Along with all the stuff required for measuring and surveying – ropes, chains, theodolite, telescope and the like – they had also to build a bothy and tower to contain it all. Undaunted by the weather (which was apparently especially foul that year), he remained at his post from July to November. In all, thousands of measurements were taken. In addition to finding that a plumb line was indeed attracted by the mountain – and to an extent that could be measured – his recording of so many spot-heights around the slopes provided a bonus. The job of making sense of all the numbers fell to English mathematician and surveyor Charles Hutton. Since they amounted at first sight to nothing more than a confusing jumble of numbers, Hutton found it helpful to join together all the dots marking the same height and so inadvertently invented the contour lines that appear on Ordnance Survey maps to this day.

The essential maths was done back in Greenwich, but all of the effort had been worthwhile. Earth was subsequently found to weigh around five million, million tons. From that standpoint, Maskelyne and Hutton also calculated the mass of the sun and our moon, and of several of the other planets and their moons as well. More modern calculations, using computers and satellites and the rest, arrive at a similar, though more accurate, figure. In a final nod to the brilliance of Newton it is worth noting that, although he had doubted the utility of a mountain experiment, he did make his own estimate of the weight of the Earth – and came as close to the right number as makes no difference.

It was here in the British Isles then that some of the essential work of calculating the nature of our world's relationship to every other object in the universe was done, and for the first time. A fundamental answer was found among the frost-shattered quartzite glittering on Schiehallion's flanks.

62

The Iron Bridge, Coalbrookdale, Shropshire

The birth of the Industrial Revolution

A s you might guess from the name, the area around Coalbrookdale in Shropshire was long known for its supplies of buried minerals. Both coal and iron ore were plentiful. For a long time there was a community of monks at nearby Much Wenlock Priory and by the time it was dissolved by Henry VIII, around 1536, there was already a 'bloomsmithy' nearby, smelting iron. The Coal Brook is a tributary of the River Severn and so provided all the water that might be required by any emergent industry. Along the banks of the gorge were useful sources of sand, clay and limestone. All the ingredients for modern endeavour were there, just waiting.

From the late seventeenth century onwards, the British Isles were simmering with the steadily building heat of technological change and advance. Creative and industrious types were experimenting with all sorts, including ever more efficient ways of making and working iron and steel. In 1708 an exemplar of the sort arrived in Coalbrookdale, drawn by the mineral riches. His name was Abraham Darby. Born in Staffordshire and raised as a Quaker, he had served an apprenticeship at a factory in Birmingham making mills for grinding malt for the beer industry. There he had seen the use of coke as fuel.

At that time, the smelting of iron from ore depended upon burning charcoal. Since charcoal was in turn dependent on timber, it was in a supply limited always by the rate of growth of the nation's forests. Darby settled on Coalbrookdale as a source of coal that might be coked – that is, heated in a furnace until impurities like sulphur were driven off – to produce coke in great quantities.

Maybe by luck, maybe by good judgement, he had alighted on a source of coal that happened to be naturally low in sulphur. Once he got his furnaces up and running, the coke he produced was of high quality – and so too, then, his iron. Darby was soon making good money turning out pots and cauldrons and the like for the local community and beyond. His family and descendants took up the mantle after he died, and in 1768 the thriving business came into the hands of his 18-year-old grandson, Abraham Darby III.

Thanks to the ironworks, industry had grown in the surrounding area. More people were coming and going, and eventually the presence of the Severn Gorge, separating the parishes of Madeley and Benthall, began to feel like a limiting factor. There were calls for a bridge to span the gap and in 1773 a Shrewsbury architect named Thomas Pritchard came forward with a revolutionary idea. Surely, he said, the newly abundant cast iron could and should be used to build the necessary bridge. Darby Junior, likewise convinced of the limitless applications of his product, agreed. Together they preached the need for an *iron* bridge across the Severn, and in 1777 work began.

In the foundry, foreman pattern-maker Thomas Gregory had produced detailed drawings of how the desired result might be achieved. Used to working with wood as well as with iron, he employed the technology of mortise and tenon joints, as well as dovetails and wedges, to create the necessary parts. Most were made individually, and so while they appear uniform at first sight, each was in fact shaped to fit a specific gap in the jigsaw puzzle whole – much as though they had been hand-finished by craftsmen, which in a sense they were. As well as spanning the Severn, Pritchard and Darby also forged a lasting union between technologies ancient and modern.

Like stone, cast iron is strong under the forces of compression but weak in response to tension. Wrought iron has flexibility, but cast iron is only brittle. Pritchard's design, featuring a single, sweeping arch, was therefore ideal, since all the weight of the structure would crush downwards. Pritchard did not live to see the completion of his creation – a delicate-seeming 100-foot span supported by five semicircular ribs. After he died in 1778, the job of overseeing the work fell to Darby himself.

In 1997, researchers working in a museum in Stockholm found a little watercolour painting by artist Elias Martin that shows the work in progress. A timber structure was used to raise the ribs – each made in two pieces – from the deck of a boat positioned on the river beneath. The bridge was completed in 1779 and opened to traffic in 1781, and in no time the name of that place of so much innovation had changed to Ironbridge.

That fruit of Pritchard's ingenuity and Darby's industry was the first cast-iron bridge built anywhere in the world. Finally closed to motor traffic in 1934 and listed as a Scheduled Ancient Monument, it represents the great conceptual leap that bridged not just the Severn Gorge but past and future.

Coalbrookdale and Ironbridge are often cited together as the birth-place of the Industrial Revolution. Since the technology of smelting iron was already ancient by then, and broadly similar innovations were in a fledgling state elsewhere, such a claim might be overstating reality. In truth, the Industrial Revolution, like the Iron Bridge itself, comprised many component parts, made in many different places. There is still magic in the sight of that elegant span none the less.

Once kindled, the fires of technological advance spread rapidly – much more quickly than any innovations that had come before – and all around the world. The Iron Bridge spans another space besides. The American War of Independence began in 1775, two years before the building of the bridge was begun. The entire construction phase took place within the duration of that conflict. By the time of the Peace of Paris that ended the hostilities in 1783, the bridge had been in use for two years and the world was an altogether different place. In 1776 the Second Continental Congress produced the United States Declaration of Independence and a whole new future for the world had been forged.

63

Burns House, Dumfries

The worldwide reach of Robert Burns

Is there anywhere a breed like the Scots that has travelled so far, to so many parts of the world, and there stamped its mark?

Among much else they took with them on their exodus and odysseys, the memory of the birth of Scotland's national bard, Robert Burns, was held as dear and kept as close as anything.

On or near his birthday, on 25 January, there are celebrations of his life in every corner of the globe. From Switzerland to Singapore, from the Canny Man pub in Hong Kong to the Dunedin Burns Club on New Zealand's South Island, from the Abu Dhabi St Andrew's Society to the Caledonia Society in Hawaii and just about everywhere in between, you will find a Burns Night party in the last week in January.

And so, if the Scots are the best travelled, is it not also fair and true to say that, among all the poets who have ever lived and rhymed, Robert Burns is the best loved? It would be hard to argue the contrary.

The words of 'Auld Lang Syne' (say it Syne, not Zyne, I beg of you) are known off by heart not just by ex-pat Scots sobbing into their whisky glasses but also by Russians and Romans, New York WASPs and New Delhi Hindus, Australians and Icelanders. There is not, and likely never will be again, anyone else like Burns.

As well as about absent friends, he wrote meaningfully and immortally about most else besides:

My love is like a red, red rose . . . The best laid schemes o' mice an' men gang aft agley . . . Oh, would some power the gift tae gie us/To see ourselves as others see us . . . But pleasures are like poppies spread . . . Had we never loved sae kindly/Had we never loved sae blindly . . . It's comin' yet for a' that/That Man to Man, the world o'er/Shall brothers be for a' that . . .

Most books, I'm sure, would make space for William Shakespeare and leave out Burns, but I cannot in all conscience write a story of the British Isles without my countryman. I had part of my childhood in Ayr, close by Alloway where he was born in 1759. Burns Cottage, described by the man himself as 'the auld cleg biggin', is kept as a museum now by the National Trust for Scotland. I did the rest of my growing up in Dumfries and it was in a house there that Burns died on 21 July 1796, aged just thirty-seven.

Burns and his wife, Jean Armour, and their many children moved into a simple, double-fronted house built of locally quarried red sandstone, on what was then Mill Street. Since his death it has been renamed Burns Street, of course. The house is looked after by Dumfries Town Council and it is a museum now. His writing desk is there, so too some examples of his work in his own hand. Visitors will surely be struck by how small the house seems, how cramped the rooms, but for Robert and Jean it was a big step up from the nearby two-roomed flat they had moved from. Now there was a front room for guests, with a long case clock in the corner, a study too. They lived well, kept a housemaid. They often ate game, and wellwishers sometimes sent them fresh oysters by the barrel-load.

Part of Burns' appeal, even now, is that he was everyman. He was mercurial – changing his mind and his opinions as the mood moved him. He loved women and a sociable drink with his friends. He had some success with his writing while he lived, but never anything like enough and far less than he was due. Farming was his mainstay but did not suit him. He took a job as an exciseman – collecting taxes on imported liquor – but just as promotion came close to giving him real financial security, rumours about disloyalty to the Crown held him back.

Legend says Burns was born in a blizzard. He wrote about how the brevity of life was there in the span of a snowflake:

Or like the snow falls in the river
A moment white then melts forever.

He himself proved as fragile as the falling snow, and as fleeting. He may have been suffering from a rheumatic heart when his physician, one Dr Maxwell, advised him to seek a cure for his ills by bathing in the cold, silty waters of the Solway Firth. He did as he was told, spending time at a spot called the Brow Well. There he waded fully clothed into the water up to his armpits and then, after suffering it as long as he could, had to let his clothes dry on him. He drank of the iron-stained waters as well, from an iron mug on a chain.

It was no cure at all. Burns died soon after. He was buried in a simple grave in a corner of the kirkyard of St Michael's, just a few hundred yards from the family home, on the same day that his son Maxwell was born. At first his grave was marked only by a simple stone slab – all Jean could afford. She welcomed visitors to their home, which she kept as a memorial to her late husband. On 18 August 1803, it was the poets Samuel Taylor Coleridge and William Wordsworth who came calling. John Keats made his own pilgrimage in 1818 and the American writer Nathaniel Hawthorne came at some time in the 1850s.

Eventually funds were raised to build a grand mausoleum in a more prominent position in the churchyard. It was completed by 1817 and Burns' coffin was moved there with full civic honours. When Jean died in 1834 she was laid beside him.

Burns is a symbol of the reach of all that is best about Scotland, about Britain. His words have travelled the world, touching and uplifting hearts. In his own way, he made the world a better place.

64

Whitehaven, Cumbria

John Paul Jones and the land of the free

A LONG WITH JUST about everything else worth having, we gave birth to the United States of America. Say what you will to the contrary, but the foundations of that great nation were laid by Britons. The fifty-six signatories of the Declaration of Independence, the document that drew so much of its sentiment from the Declaration of Arbroath, were British subjects. When they fomented rebellion and war, it was against their own government. Rebels, yes – angry and dissatisfied with their treatment by the British Crown – but they were *British* rebels.

The man honoured as the father and founder of the US Navy was born in the village of Arbigland, in the parish of Kirkbean in Scotland, on 6 July 1747. Christened John Paul, he was the son of the head gardener of the estate at Arbigland. The life of the landlubber was not for him, and aged thirteen he joined the crew of a coastal sloop bound for Whitehaven. There he signed on for a seven-year apprenticeship with the merchant navy and was soon gazing out at the coastlines of Barbados and Virginia. He had an elder brother in the colonies and spent time ashore with him at his home in Fredericksburg. As an adult, he would write that America was 'my favourite country from the age of 13 when I first saw it'.

In his time, while still learning his craft as a mariner, he served aboard slave ships and by the age of twenty-one he was captaining merchant ships criss-crossing the Atlantic. During the early 1770s he had run-ins with the law as well. While captain of a vessel named the *Betsy*, he caused the death of a mutineer and, rather than face the consequences, chose instead to make himself a fugitive from British justice. By 1774 he had taken the name Jones as his surname and he was John Paul Jones by the time of the outbreak of the Revolutionary War. He was made captain of the Continental Navy – the seagoing force hastily assembled by George Washington. In fact, he was the very first so commissioned after the signing of the Declaration of Independence in 1776.

In November 1777 he sailed out of Portsmouth, New Hampshire, at the helm of the *Ranger*, a sloop-of-war. After crossing the Atlantic to Brest in northern France, from there he set a course up the west coast of England. It was his intention to make as much trouble as possible for his erstwhile homeland and by 23 April 1778 he had the *Ranger* lying in wait off Whitehaven. It's likely he chose the place not out of any specific malice but only because he knew it well and could find his way into the harbour under cover of darkness.

Had his crew been more than a rabble, Jones might have been able to do real damage. His plan had been to launch a lightning raid, take and spike the town's guns and set fire to a fleet of heavily laden coal ships moored in the harbour. As it was, his men were more interested in finding their way to the local taverns, and while Captain Jones led a force that kindled a blaze aboard one British vessel, the locals were soon on the scene and able to extinguish the flames before they properly took hold. Rather than putting Whitehaven to the torch, the raid had been a damp squib. The news of an attack on the British coastline by an American warship, however, spread like a bushfire. Word reached London and forty ships of the Royal Navy were promptly recalled from service off the coast of the rebellious colonies and put on alert back home. Captain Jones continued to cause damage, capturing merchant vessels, and by the time he returned to America he was a legend.

He had even greater success the following year, leading a flotilla into battle against the British off Flamborough Head on the Yorkshire coast. It was there, with Jones aboard his ship the *Bonhomme Richard* and in the heat of the fight, that Captain Pearson, of a vessel called *Serapis*, suggested he might surrender. John Paul Jones' reply, 'I have not yet begun to fight', became the unofficial motto of the US Navy ever after.

It was a sheen on his legend, but his name had already been made immortal by his audacity at Whitehaven. Every year since 1999 a US Navy warship has made a pilgrimage to the town. There her captain and crew are treated as honoured guests and peace is formally proclaimed between the two nations. On the quayside, there is a statue depicting the spiking of the guns. All in all, it feels almost too much to believe. But it's true enough. John Paul Jones is a hero and legend to Americans – a freedom fighter, father of their navy. Here he is regarded as a rebel at best, a traitor at worst. However he is best remembered, he was a son of these islands and he had a hand in the making of the land of the free.

65

Merchant City, Glasgow

Tobacco lords and an infamous trade

MR DARCY – HERO OF Jane Austen's *Pride and Prejudice* – is rich beyond the dreams of avarice on an annual income of £10,000. His wealth is enough to give all of the Bennet ladies – Elizabeth included – an attack of the vapours. Fitzwilliam Darcy is only a fictional creation, of course. Had he been flesh and blood, he would have been more or less contemporary with John Glassford, one of the real-life 'tobacco lords' of Glasgow. In a typical year, Glassford saw a turnover of half a million pounds sterling.

He was just one of a group of merchants, based in Glasgow, who dominated the trade in tobacco from places like Virginia towards the end of the eighteenth century. Their wealth would have made them the Bill Gates and Jeff Bezos figures of their day, but every pound and dollar was made on the backs of African slaves. The vessels that brought back the tobacco plants, dried and ready for sale, had carried a human cargo on the outward journey. Ships sailed from British ports to Africa, where men, women and children were bought from chiefs growing rich in their own right by selling their own people. The vessels making the journey west were known as 'black birders' and were apparently so foul they could be smelled from miles away. Once the Africans were unloaded, the holds were cleaned out and loaded afresh with either tobacco or perhaps cotton or sugar for the trip east.

None of that human misery was thought about or fretted over.

Glasgow – like Liverpool, Bristol, Dublin and other cities – grew immensely wealthy from the triangle of trade. Glasgow's Merchant City was formed of the great warehouses the so-called tobacco lords built between Buchanan Street and High Street to house their wares. They were and are splendid indeed – veritable cathedrals to commerce. It is said the grid pattern of streets and blocks pioneered in Glasgow was subsequently exported to Manhattan Island for the building of New York.

The legacy of the traders left other reminders of their presence. Andrew Buchanan, Archibald Ingram, James Dunlop and the mighty John Glassford are all remembered in street names. Antigua Street, Jamaica Street, Tobago Street and Virginia Street recall some of their overseas holdings.

William Cunninghame was another of them. At the height of his powers he acquired a plot of land on a muddy track called Cow Lane. There he built what was then the most lavish and spectacular private home in the city. Cow Lane was renamed Queen Street and the bill for his grand residence was . . . £10,000 – all of Mr Darcy's earnings for a whole year. Nowadays his former home is familiar to Glasgow residents as the GOMA – the Gallery of Modern Art. Where one wealthy man and his family once lived, now visitors step quietly and view masterpieces.

Cunninghame and others like him used real business acumen to grow richer yet. Instead of slaves, they began shipping out luxury goods – furniture, tableware, silver cutlery, crystal glasses. The tobacco growers saw the finery and, in their vanity and greed, felt the need to have it in their homes. Merchants like Cunninghame then extended lines of credit to the growers – allowing them to take possession of the shiny things on the understanding they would settle their accounts later on. All too soon the hapless farmers were hugely in debt so that their creditors could drive harder and harder bargains when it came to buying up their tobacco.

The warehouses they built, the streets that connected them, were not known as the Merchant City while the tobacco lords were in residence. That name came later. Nowadays the buildings have all been repurposed – as offices, private apartments, shops. It is still the commercial heart of Glasgow and a walk around those towering blocks is through a place with an infamous, if largely forgotten, past.

66

Fishguard, Pembrokeshire

The last invasion of Britain

STOP A HUNDRED people in Britain and ask them the year and place of the last invasion of Britain, and most will say 1066 and Hastings. Such answers might be forgivable, but they would be wrong just the same.

Just as the Battle of Brunanburh in 937 is forgotten by most – despite it being the clash that fossilized our long island as one split between an identity in the north and another, quite different, in the south – so too the events that unfolded in south-west Wales in February 1797 are all but overlooked.

Europe was deep in the gruesome turmoil unleashed by the French Revolution of 1789. Citizen Louis Capet, formerly King Louis XVI, had lost his head to the guillotine in the January of 1793. His queen, Marie Antoinette, met the same fate nine months later and as many as 40,000 Frenchmen and women were similarly dealt with. Neighbouring monarchies reeled at the horror and sought to turn back time, to undo the Republic and restore the rightful way of things.

The French Revolutionary Wars swept like a storm, back and forth, across the country and the continent. In June 1795 a combined force of émigré French and British troops landed at Quiberon on the southern coast of the Brittany peninsula in hopes of crushing the revolt once and for all. By the end of the following month those would-be invaders and righters of wrongs had been utterly destroyed. Along with many prisoners, the soldiers of the French First Republic captured vast quantities of equipment, including arms and uniforms. Many of the invaders' red tunics were taken and dyed black, then used to dress the 1,400 or so men of La Seconde Légion des Francs. Given their dark attire, they were soon better known as La Légion noire – the Black Legion.

By 1796 the French were seeking to strike against Great Britain on our own turf and so prepared a three-pronged invasion. Knowing full well that rebellion was stirring in Ireland among those opposed to British rule, a 15,000-strong French force under the command of General Lazare Hoche was loaded aboard ships at Brest that December and dispatched for a proposed landing in Bantry Bay in Ireland's south-west. In the event, the whole affair was a debacle. Beset by the worst storms in years, the fleet was scattered in all directions. The Royal Navy was aware of the French presence but never able fully to engage them. In the end, the weather did the job. It had spared Elizabeth I's England, and now it did the same for the whole United Kingdom. The French lost a dozen ships and thousands of men drowned or captured. By then a similar disaster had already befallen a second force, which had departed Dunkirk that November bound for Newcastle upon Tyne. Their objective was to destroy shipping in the area, but more bad weather off the coast of the Netherlands forced them to return to port.

By February 1797 only one prong of three remained – the Black Legion under the command of an embittered *chef de brigade*, Irish-American General William Tate. Apparently the son of Irish parents killed in the American War of Independence, Tate had Irish republican sympathies and so was minded to seek revenge upon the British. The 1,400 men he commanded were by most accounts a crew most motley. Around a hard core of perhaps 600 professional, if ill-disciplined, soldiers was pressed a rabble of French thugs and convicts seized from prisons in Brest and Le Havre and forced into uniform. Their original destination was Bristol, then Britain's second most important city, but no sooner had Tate and his men departed Brest than yet more contrary winds had him change his plans. His objective had been to sack Bristol and then turn on Wales, and so he moved immediately to the second part of the plan.

On the morning of 22 February, the locals of Fishguard in Pembroke-shire awoke to find four warships anchored off their coast. They were flying British colours, but closer examination of the nature of their rigging revealed them for what they were – a French invasion force.

It was hardly the first time that part of south-west Wales had been eyed hungrily by men of violence. Centuries before, it had been Viking raiders who targeted the area, drawn in no small part by the wealth of nearby St David's Cathedral. Far-flung it may be, yet that peninsula has long been one of the most culturally rich landscapes in all of Wales. St David, the national patron saint, founded a church and monastery by the River Alun sometime in the sixth century. His was an austere view of the world. All was about asceticism, the setting aside of all earthly pleasures and posses-sions. The monks were allowed only water and salted bread. But in spite of the saint's aspirations, the religious community grew rich. The tiny city that bears his name is the smallest in Wales and yet in time the church was wealthy enough to attract the attentions of seaborne pirates. In hopes of concealing it from avaricious eyes, the cathedral was built in a hollow, but the Vikings found it just the same, again and again.

The men that came ashore in February 1797 were intent on inflicting as much harm, but proved singularly incapable of operating as an army, pro-fessional or otherwise. Having established the nationality of the blow-ins, the locals fired a single shot towards the flotilla from a cannon in the town's fort. The ball flew wide, but it was enough to persuade Tate to make his landing not at Fishguard itself but on to the rocks at Carregwastad Point on the nearby Pencaer Peninsula. His ships were among the newest in France and the men were well armed. By the end of that first day they were safely ashore and camped on the outskirts of Fishguard.

It was then that the French conscripts, the pressed men, showed their true colours. Many deserted or mutinied. Others spent their time raiding local homes in search of food and alcohol – and since a Portuguese cargo vessel full of port and brandy had recently been wrecked nearby, there was plenty of the latter.

Local volunteer soldiers under a Lieutenant-Colonel Thomas Knox were quickly deployed, followed within hours by a force of British reservists and militia commanded by John Campbell, Lord Cawdor. The invaders outnumbered the local side by a considerable margin, but the drunkenness and indiscipline of much of the French force meant their invasion descended into farce. A woman named Jemima Nicholas captured a dozen of them, single-handed, armed only with a pitchfork. Folklore has it too that the arrival of other local women, dressed in traditional garb of tall black hats and red cloaks, had the Frenchmen thinking they were British Grenadiers.

Within forty-eight hours of landing, Tate was forced into an unconditional surrender. He and his men were later exchanged for British prisoners of war held on the Continent. Farcical or not, when news of the affair reached London there was a run on the bank. Account holders rushed to demand gold in place of their banknotes, but there was not enough bullion to go round. From that day on, it has been the case that British banknotes are quite literally not worth the paper they are printed on.

The town today is wrapped around with the history it has seen and felt. It is made of two halves – Fishguard and Lower Fishguard. The latter is older, the original hamlet from which the rest grew in time. The Welsh name is Abergwaun, meaning 'the Mouth of the Gwaun River'. Fishguard is a corruption of the Norse *fisgardr*, which refers to a place for catching fish. Pestered by Vikings, then by Normans, it bears hints and traces all about – including the remains of a motte-and-bailey castle. For all it has known, for all that nearly happened, it is quiet now and pretty.

The events at Fishguard in 1797 have gone down in history as something of a joke. Had the invasion force been of a higher calibre – rather than cast-off soldiers and criminals – they might well have posed a serious threat. As it was, the storm of the French Revolution had blown flotsam and jetsam as far as Britain's western seaboard.

67

Wilberforce House, Kingston upon Hull

The abolition of slavery

O F ALL THE names associated with the abolition of slavery, that of William Wilberforce, MP for Kingston upon Hull, is surely the most familiar. He was born on 24 August 1759 in a fine house on the city's High Street. It was built in the 1650s for one Hugh Lister, a merchant occupied with the business of exporting Derbyshire lead to Holland, and acquired by William Wilberforce, grandfather to the great campaigner, in 1732.

The younger William Wilberforce was born in a small bedroom next to the grand wood-panelled banqueting room on the first floor. He was a sickly little boy and short-sighted. He attended Hull Grammar School before reduced circumstances following the death of his father, Robert Wilberforce, had his mother send him to live with relatives in London.

So much of the wealth of these islands was built on slavery, though it was hardly our invention. Egyptians, Greeks and Romans – all of them made slaves of others too. Muslim Arabs were up to their knees in the misery of it all from around the ninth century, capturing, buying and selling white Europeans as well as black Africans. The West African chiefs were as guilty as anybody else. As economic historian Niall Ferguson has pointed out: 'The rulers of western Africa prior to the European empires were not running some kind of scout camp. They were engaged in the slave trade.' It is here today, all around the world in many forms. Slaves for sex, slaves to take care of their owners' homes and children. Slaves to harvest fruit and vegetables from our fields.

But if the British did not start it, we certainly got stuck into the cruel horror of it all and grew fat on the colossal profits. During the eighteenth century, it is estimated, around 50,000 African slaves were shipped across the Atlantic every year. No one kept count of the number that died on the way.

Illustrations from the time, on display now in the Wilberforce House Museum, show the inventive way in which space below decks in the so-called 'black birders' was maximized. At first glance you might think you were looking at hundreds of spent matches arrayed in a cigar box. And then you realize you are looking at people, shackled and crammed together without an inch to spare.

Wilberforce attended Cambridge University, where he met and made friends with William Pitt the Younger. By the age of twenty-one he was MP for Hull and during the 1780s underwent a profound conversion to evangelical Christianity, which opened his eyes to the plight of the oppressed and the downtrodden. Every day thereafter, it seems, his copy of the King James Bible was never far from his hand. That book of books, commissioned by the first to call himself king of a Great Britain and set in motion in the Palace of Hampton Court, was a cornerstone of the cleansing of the greatest stain on humanity.

It was in 1787 that Wilberforce first met Thomas Clarkson. The friendship forged between the two men at that time would last for the rest of their lives, and it was Clarkson's commitment to the abolition of slavery that gave real focus to that of Wilberforce. The two men worked and campaigned together tirelessly.

In a speech to the House in 1789, Wilberforce said of the Atlantic Slave Trade:

The number of deaths speaks for itself and makes all such enquiry superfluous. As soon as ever I had arrived thus far in my investigation of the slave trade, I confess to you, sir, so enormous, so dreadful, so irremediable did its wickedness appear that my own mind was completely made up for the abolition. A trade founded in iniquity and carried out as this was must be abolished. Let the policy be what it might. Let the consequences be what they would. I, from this time, determined that I would never rest 'til I had effected its abolition.

On 25 March 1807, Wilberforce reached his first milestone. On that day in the House of Commons, the Abolition of the Slave Trade Act banned the buying and selling of those already enslaved. It had been carried by 283 votes to 16. It was not until 26 July 1833 that Parliament finally passed a Bill to end slavery itself throughout the empire. Wilberforce lived long enough to hear the news, but died just three days later. One month later the Abolition of Slavery Act was passed by the House of Lords and came into effect the following year.

Wilberforce House is the only seventeenth-century house remaining in High Street, but two adjacent Georgian houses became part of the Wilberforce Museum in 1957. The whole story of his life's work is told within. In the front garden a statue of the man bears the words, 'No Englishman has ever done more to evoke the conscience of the British people and to elevate and ennoble British life.' This is interesting in itself – not English people or English life by then, but British.

Wilberforce is buried in the north transept of Westminster Abbey, close by his friend William Pitt. Behind his old house is a space set aside now as the Nelson Mandela Peace Garden, created in 1983. It seems likely Mr Wilberforce would have approved.

68

Bettyhill, Sutherland

The Highland Clearances

I VISITED THE VILLAGE of Bettyhill in Sutherland in the Scottish Highlands at the end of a long day in 2005. A group of us had walked a few miles of the A836 road from Altnaharra, following the route taken nearly 200 years before by tenant farmers cleared from their land to make way for sheep. All together in our group there were around 200 descendants of those long-ago victims of the infamous Highland Clearances. As one said at the time, the road had likely not been so busy with folk on foot in many a long day.

As we walked we talked about why it had all happened, what it must have been like for those evicted from all they had known, who had watched their homes burned behind them so they had no reason ever to go back. I was in thoughtful mood as we reached the village, and some of us headed into a hotel for a quiet pint. It was all the more surprising then to find the public bar jammed to the rafters with a stag party, baying and roaring as a stripper, naked as the day she was born, sat grinding in the lap of a young chap who looked as though the lager in his hand was not his first of the day. It was all so unexpected that for a few seconds I felt I had walked out of one world and into another. Maybe the ghosts of the Clearances looked down and laughed at my feelings of dislocation.

Stag-dos and strippers notwithstanding, Bettyhill sits in one of the most heartrendingly beautiful and peaceful parts of Scotland. Just to the west is the long golden sweep of Torrisdale Bay, popular with surfers.

The River Naver that empties into the North Sea there has been famous for salmon. All around are deserted hills and glens, the stuff of pictures that come to mind when you think of the Highlands. But of course, the glens were not always empty. We made them like that. An old way of life was put to death in the last decades of the eighteenth century and first decades of the nineteenth, and the tumbledown traces of houses and field walls dotted through the landscape are its scoured bones. A friend of mine said years ago that she looks out at some desolate Highland hill-sides and for a moment the distant sheep, moving among the ruins of abandoned blackhouses, seem like maggots crawling over a corpse. It is a potent image.

During the century between 1760 and 1860, an estimated quarter of a million people were forced out of the Highlands. It was not just the Highlands that were cleared either – the Lowlands experienced some of the same as landowners all over Scotland turned their backs on their tenants and on centuries of tradition in pursuit of cash. Highland or Lowland, the Clearances amounted to one of the biggest mass movements of people in all of British history. In places like Sutherland it was nothing less than the systematic demolition of an ancient culture.

On the lands owned by the Countess of Sutherland and her husband, the Marquess of Stafford, it was especially brutal. Elizabeth Sutherland Leveson-Gower, the 19th Countess, presided over an estate of 1.5 million acres, the biggest in Europe. She looked out over her land and saw too many people doing too little with their time. Ideas that had formed in the south had travelled north by a kind of social osmosis. For too long, it seemed, tenant farmers had lived by subsistence, doing just enough to get by and living lives that left them looking as unkempt as their herds of scruffy little cattle. God forbid the rest of their time might be spent by the fireside, maybe nursing a whisky and playing tunes on a fiddle. Landed types, many living idle lives themselves, found unbearable the seeming sloth of others, and a few of their number evolved schemes of improvement. For a start, the land would surely be made to yield more money for its owners if most of it was populated not by people but by sheep. The people could and would be moved – out of the glens and off to the coast where they might learn to fish, collect seaweed for fertilizer and soap, and generally make themselves busy and productive.

To ensure they did more than just revert to old ways, growing a few crops to feed themselves and their families, the land on the coast was apportioned in plots so small – no more than 2 or 3 acres per family – there was no hope of growing enough or of keeping enough animals. There would be no choice but to put to sea as well, or to wade into the shallows in search of the beds of kelp and such. It was a land-management technique known as 'pinching' and all of it would, it was thought, maximize the profits of the estate. Little of that grandiose philosophy is remembered now. On account of the trauma experienced by so many, the original intentions have been lost. What has lasted in the popular memory – for the descendants of those cleared to Bettyhill, for instance – is anger, hurt and sadness.

Since time immemorial the clan system had prevailed in the hills and glens. The Gaelic *clann* means 'children', and the clan chief was therefore regarded as a kind of father, supposedly with the best interests of his people at heart. The clansmen farmed and kept animals on the clan lands and paid rent in coin or in kind. The chief in turn wielded life-and-death authority, settled disputes and led his people in battle when necessary. Concepts of ownership of the land were hazy for the longest time, and it was only in the seventeenth and eighteenth centuries, as chiefs had more and more contact with English landlords raised to the feudal system, that ideas began to change and crystallize. Since an individual clansman seldom had written title to the land he farmed (had arguably never needed such), he found himself hopelessly vulnerable in the face of any chief who wanted him to clear the way for a flock of sheep.

So when Elizabeth, Countess of Sutherland, decided to improve her land, her tenants were defenceless. The actual clearing was organized and led by her factor, Patrick Sellar. So vicious was he about the whole business, he would eventually stand trial for manslaughter after the death of one elderly tenant summarily dragged from her home. Although he was acquitted, there was no denying his casual brutality. The clearance of Sutherland lands was forced through in double-quick time. The countess even had the audacity, and the vanity, to name the town she had planned for the coast by Torrisdale Bay after herself. Between 1814 and 1821 more than 500 families were forcibly evicted from the glen leading to Bettyhill, some thirty villages wiped off the map in the process.

The folk I walked with that day had inherited their forefathers' sense of injustice. For some of them the hurt was still close to the surface, even after all the years. It is a fine road to walk, for all that. The first sight of the sea and Torrisdale Bay seems like a gift. But whatever the plans of the countess and her ilk, Bettyhill is today a tiny place. She spent her money building roads instead of harbours and so the fishing industry never took off. The sheep farming did little better. Ironically, it eventually faltered in the face of competition from New Zealand and Australia, the very lands that had opened their arms to so many of the cleared farmers.

By the time he died, her husband had been created 1st Duke of Sutherland. The countess saw to it that a memorial was raised to him – a fine statue atop a 100-foot column on the summit of Ben Bhraggie, above the town of Golspie. It has on it a whole screed about what a caring landlord he had been – that he had 'provided useful employment for the active labourer, opened wide his hand to the distresses of the widow, the sick and the traveller'. It also notes it was, in part, local subscriptions that paid for the monument: 'a mourning and grateful tenantry'.

Scotland had a tradition of emigration before the Clearances, but that experiment with human engineering gave it a fresh impetus. At the turn of the nineteenth century, the Sutherland Highlanders had been raised from the same valleys and had marched away to the Napoleonic Wars. Scotland would haemorrhage her people again and again as those with the means and the gumption jumped rather than be pushed. It is part of the story of that part of the British Isles.

As Rudyard Kipling had it:

There dwells a wife by the Northern Gate
And a careworn wife is she
She breeds a breed o' rovin' men
And casts them over sea.

69

Burnham Thorpe, Norfolk

The birthplace of Horatio Nelson

THE RECEIVED WISDOM is that it's best to stay away from personal heroes, for fear of disappointment. One of mine – Horatio Nelson – has, at the time of writing, come in for some belated character assassination, his name and reputation dragged through the mud of racism. Across the Atlantic, statues to leaders of the Confederate Army – Generals Robert E. Lee, Thomas 'Stonewall' Jackson and others – have been torn down by those who say such works honour a regime that enslaved African Americans. Since what happens first in the United States often travels here too, our own hero of Trafalgar has been labelled a hearty accomplice to the same crime. At least one English journalist has called him a white supremacist.

Archaeologists and historians are careful not to be fooled into thinking we can ever put ourselves into the minds of those who lived in the past, even the recent past. Nelson was a product of a Georgian world that is out of reach like all the rest. Revere him or not, it is still worth walking around some of the places where he spent time. We cannot hope fully to understand him. None of his footprints have been preserved, pressed into the Norfolk mud like those of ancient hunters, but there are glimpses to be had of the places that moulded him.

The village of Burnham Thorpe, just a mile inland from the north Norfolk coast, is where he first drew breath on 29 September 1758, the sixth of eleven children born to Edmund and Catherine, the local parson and his wife. It is one of those settlements – flinty cottages, red-tiled roofs, white-washed walls – that let a person know they are probably on the east coast, whether or not they can see any road signs.

The old rectory where Nelson was actually born was pulled down after Edmund's death in 1802. A new parsonage was built close to the footprint, grander than the original by all accounts. On a wall there is a bronze plaque, dark with patina and verdigris. Beneath the hero's name it reads: 'The old rectory in which the Admiral was born stood twenty yards back from this wall . . .'

What does survive, in the private garden of the younger building, is some of Nelson's own handiwork. Having joined the Royal Navy aged twelve, serving first under the command of his mother's uncle, he was gone from Burnham Thorpe for a long time. He saw service in the Baltic, in Canada and the West Indies. In 1787 he married Frances – Fanny – Nisbet and, during a period of peace with France, the couple returned to England. Captain Nelson was, as they say in the senior service, 'cast on the beach' – that is, laid off on half pay. By 1788 the Nelsons were back in the village of his birth, and back in the old rectory. It was a frustrating period for one so ambitious, and he spent at least some of his time pestering contacts and patrons in hopes of an early return to gainful employment. For five years none came his way, and it was during the lull that he created, with the help of a gardener called Williamson, a frankly bizarre ship-shaped pond in the garden of the house. Fed by a diversion of the nearby River Burn, it is over 30 feet long, with a square-ended stern and a pointed bow. To say it reveals what was really on his mind at the time is an understatement.

Arguably his most famous monument in the village is the Lord Nelson pub. It opened as the Plough in 1636 but was later renamed in honour of the local boy made good. In 1793 he was recalled to active duty and given command of HMS *Agamemnon*, supposedly his favourite ship of all. So excited was he by the prospect of going back to sea, he hosted a dinner for the locals – and when news later reached them of his victory at the Battle of the Nile in 1798 they renamed the pub the Lord Nelson. I had a pint in there around 2008 and it was a wonderful place: dark wood panelling, narrow creaking corridors, cosy bars and cosier snugs. Smoking bans and business rates being as they are, even such a venerable venue has lately fallen victim to market forces. I contacted the present owners, Greene King Brewers, who told me the pub had closed its doors in 2016 and that there were no immediate plans to reopen.

It seems a meagre reminder of a star so bright as Nelson's. He lost the sight in his right eye during the Siege of Calvi on Corsica in 1794, and the use of his right arm at the Battle of Santa Cruz de Tenerife three years later. It was during his posting to Naples, after the Battle of the Nile, that he met and fell in love with his soulmate, Emma, Lady Hamilton, wife of William Hamilton, His Majesty's Minister Plenipotentiary to the Kingdom of the Two Sicilies.

Emma had been mistress to and cast aside by Hamilton's nephew, Charles Francis Greville. Her new husband was sixty when they wed and she just twenty-six. They were a glamorous couple – he charming and erudite, she beautiful and beguiling. They hosted parties where Emma, a veteran of the theatres of Drury Lane, would entertain their guests by performing her 'Attitudes' – dressing up and striking poses to bring to mind all manner of characters, such as Medea from Greek legend, or Mary Magdalene. When Nelson entered their orbit, both Hamiltons were entranced by him. When William died, he was in his wife's arms and holding Nelson's hand. In 1801, while still in their respective marriages, Nelson and Emma had a daughter together, Horatia.

During the Battle of Copenhagen that same year, his senior officer Sir Hyde Parker put up a signal ordering Nelson to cease his action. Ever the aggressor when his blood was up, Nelson put his telescope to his blind eye and said to those around him, 'I really do not see the signal' – an economy with the *actualité* that gifted us 'turning a blind eye'.

Horatio Nelson lived in a world in which the British were the latest exponents of the ancient wrong of slavery. But by his actions, the cause for which he would eventually give his life, Nelson ensured the freedom of the ocean sea and for ever hobbled the ambitions of a tyrant. Like much of the Norfolk coastline, he is being eroded, his immortal contribution somehow diminished. His subordinates, inferiors all, have sought to wound him anew more than two centuries after his death. There have been calls to pull down his statue from its column in Trafalgar Square. Even the pub in his home town, bearing his name, is cast on the beach, awaiting better times. It matters therefore to seek his memory, such as it survives, in Burnham Thorpe. Nearby is the beach at Burnham Overy Staithe. No doubt he walked there – as a young boy, dreaming of the wider world, and then again as a Royal Navy captain, while he awaited his return to the sea.

In 1804, with Trafalgar just beyond his horizon, Nelson wrote about his village from the desk in his cabin aboard HMS *Victory* as she cruised by the island of Ushant off the Brittany coast: 'Most probably, I shall never see dear, dear Burnham again. And I have the satisfaction in thinking that my bones will probably lie with my father's in the village that gave me birth.'

His father's church, All Saints, has both parents' graves but not his own. In 1881 the Lords of the Admiralty presented the church with a lectern made with oak from the *Victory*, his flagship at Trafalgar. The Nelson ensign, white with a red cross and the Union Jack in one quadrant, flies from the square tower, as it has since the First Sea Lord gave his permission in 1913. Only St Martin-in-the-Fields in London shares the same honour. All about, the soft wet green of Norfolk spreads away in every direction. Overhead the sky is as big as it ever was, and Nelson matters as much as he ever did.

70

HMS *Victory*, Portsmouth Historic Dockyard

Nelson's flagship and the Battle of Trafalgar

IN *CIVILISATION*, ART historian Kenneth Clark wrote: 'if one wants a symbol of Atlantic man that distinguishes him from Mediterranean man, a symbol to set aside the Greek temple, it is the Viking ship'.

He was right. Here on the Atlantic coast it is command of the seaways that has mattered most. In terms of both ambition and technology, the Viking longship was the great forwards leap of its time. But if there is to be a symbol of British dominance of the world-ocean, the achievement and the spirit that enabled the British Empire, then I say it is the wide-bellied, bull-headed hull of HMS *Victory*.

Her keel, made from the trunks of seven elm trees, was laid at Chatham Dockyard on 23 July 1759. More than 150 workers used 6,000 trees in total, almost all of them oaks, to build her frame. Oak trees are the unsung heroes of the Royal Navy of the seventeenth, eighteenth and nineteenth centuries. It has been estimated that timber from 50,000 trees was afloat in the form of the twenty-seven ships of the line Nelson commanded at the Battle of Trafalgar – representing two million years of growth. Much of the oak went on single pieces, like her 30-foot high sternpost. More went into her outer planking and at the waterline her timbers were 2 feet thick. Some 3,000 feet of strong, supple fir and spruce provided her decks, masts and yardarms; 27 miles of rigging served 4 acres of sail; and 2 tons of nails and bolts shaped from copper and iron helped hold her together. Even with all our modern technology it is unlikely we could even attempt to build a vessel of such a size, of such manoeuvrability, from timber. The skills required are gone, along with so much else our ancestors worked so hard to acquire, to master and to finesse. *Victory* was completed by 1765 but since she was not needed right away, most of her next thirteen years were spent berthed in the River Medway.

She almost never left the dockyard at all. On the eve of her launch, ship foreman Hartley Larkin realized that not only was she the largest ship built so far for the Royal Navy, she was also some 9½ inches wider than the gates of her dock. With a party of government and navy high-ups due for a lavish launch party, Larkin led a team of men armed with axes and saws to swiftly hack away the extra inches from the gates' timbers. With no room to spare, the great vessel squeaked through into the river – a painful, messy birth.

Victory went into active service in 1778 and took part in both the American War of Independence and the French Revolutionary Wars, but it was the looming threat posed by Napoleon that set her on course for legend. Although she had been built when Horatio Nelson was just a lad at school in Norfolk, and had more recently languished as a hospital ship, she was none the less a hero-in-waiting. When the need arose, she was awoken from her slumbers back in the Medway and made ready once more.

The ship had featured a paint scheme dominated by the colours black and red, but as part of her refitting for tackling the combined fleets of France and Spain she was given a cosmetic makeover to go along with all the structural work to ready her for fighting in the new century. Today, in her permanent berth in Portsmouth Historic Dockyard, the bright orange-and-black chequerboard appearance of her hull is undoubtedly striking. Recent work by restorers has suggested Vice-Admiral Nelson never saw *Victory* with quite as much of a President Trump tan. Having painstakingly peeled away her many layers of paint, undressing the old girl back to her birthday suit, they have concluded she faced the French and Spanish with more of a pale yellow complexion.

Whatever her hue, she was Nelson's flagship by May 1803. The Battle of

Trafalgar on 21 October 1805 was a slow-motion nightmare for the crews involved. Light winds meant that from first sighting one another it took six hours for the fleets to come within fighting distance. *Victory* was a full half hour behind the first contact, scores of her men dead and her steering already damaged by enemy fire, but when she broke through the centre of the enemy line she unloaded a devastating broadside into the stern of the French flagship *Bucentaure*. Within moments, the eighty-gun French ship of the line had lost 200 dead and wounded, splintered and scattered like skittles in a bowling alley. Once in the thick of it, *Victory* was exposed to the fire of several more enemy ships and it was in no small part the arrival of HMS *Temeraire*, directly behind her, that made the crucial difference to her survival. Remembered as the *Fighting Temeraire*, and immortalized in oils by J. M. W. Turner, she was commanded at Trafalgar by Captain Eliab Harvey. The English poet and critic John Ruskin added his own burnish to *Temeraire*'s legend, describing:

> those sides that were wet with the long runlets of English life-blood . . . gleaming goodly crimson down to the cast and clash of the washing foam – those pale masts that stayed themselves up against the war-ruin, shaking out their ensigns through the thunder till sail and ensign drooped . . .

Much as Nelson had imagined and intended, the fighting descended into chaotic pell-mell stuff – every ship, captain and sailor knowing their commander expected them each to fight their own war. In spite of *Temeraire* and Harvey, in spite of every man doing his duty, in spite of all of it, the unthinkable happened. At around a quarter past one in the afternoon, a sniper high in the masts of the French ship *Redoutable*, cheek by jowl with *Victory*, fired a musket ball through Nelson's chest and into his spine. A man long convinced of a necessary rendezvous with death, Nelson knew it for a mortal wound. When his men carried him down into the damp stink of the cockpit, on the orlop deck closest to the keel, he declared as much to the surgeon. 'Ah, Mr Beatty! You can do nothing for me,' he said. 'I have but a short time to live. My back is shot through.'

There among the rest of *Victory*'s many wounded he lingered, in terrible pain, for several hours, dying at around 4.30 p.m. Whether he ever asked for a kiss from Captain Thomas Hardy is lost among the legend. Perhaps he spoke rather of 'kismet', meaning destiny. He lived long enough to know the battle was won and England safe. His body was preserved in a barrel of brandy and word of his death reached London, and the Admiralty, before he did. Though he had imagined he would be laid to rest beside his father in the churchyard of All Saints back in Burnham Thorpe, he was buried in St Paul's Cathedral on 9 January 1806.

As with Captain James Cook, I feel the need to mention Nelson twice, such is our debt to him. We take the freedom of the seas – *mare liberum* – for granted. There are no lines upon the world's oceans. No one owns them. Had Trafalgar ended with victory for Napoleon, everything might have been, surely would have been, different. At the very least, from that moment on Napoleon knew that, whatever else might happen, he was landlocked. He might master the continent, but never the ocean.

Victory is the oldest warship in the world still on active service. Though she sits in Portsmouth Historic Dockyard, she is the flagship of the First Sea Lord. In 2005 I was part of celebrations marking the 200th anniversary of the Battle of Trafalgar. Some of them were on the gun deck of the *Victory* and I swear there is nowhere more evocative of a time and a way of life. Much of her outer shell is new – part of her ongoing conservation. Below decks, down where the water laps thick and dark against her timbers, she is still Nelson's and she stands for what the United Kingdom of Great Britain and Ireland used to be.

71

The Smalls Lighthouse, Pembrokeshire

Safeguarding life at sea

WINSTON CHURCHILL DESCRIBED us as an island race. He admired our demonstrable steadfastness in the face of threat from abroad, our willingness to go to whatever lengths circumstances demanded to make and keep the place safe.

Our existence here on these storm-swept rocks has made us mariners as well. In order to survive and thrive, we have depended upon mastery of the seaways. And so this island race has also led the way in seeking to preserve life at sea and around our coastline. The National Institution for the Preservation of Life from Shipwreck was founded by volunteers in 1824. Due in no small part to the unfortunate acronym, the name was later changed to the Royal National Lifeboat Institution, but the original ethos has been preserved. The RNLI is still a charity, dependent upon donations from a suitably grateful public.

The provision of lighthouses is even older. In 1514, Henry VIII granted a Royal Charter under the name of 'The Master, Wardens, and Assistants of the Guild, Fraternity, or Brotherhood of the most glorious and undivided Trinity, and of St Clement in the Parish of Deptford-Strond in the County of Kent'. First in charge of the new body was Thomas Spert, master of the *Mary Rose*. Known now as Trinity House, it was all a response to complaints about dangerous practices and habits among boatmen on the

River Thames. In 1566, Henry's daughter Queen Elizabeth I extended the role of the brotherhood by giving them responsibility for 'beacons, marks and signs for the sea . . . whereby the dangers may be avoided'.

We have therefore been looking out for those in peril on the sea for a long time.

In Scotland the role of providing lights and lighthouses falls to the Northern Lighthouse Trust, formed in 1786. It is almost legend in these parts that the lighthouses around Scotland's coastline were the work of one family – the so-called 'Lighthouse' Stevensons. The patriarch was Robert Stevenson, appointed Sole Engineer in 1808 and responsible for building fifteen lighthouses, including one of the most famous of all – the Bell Rock, off the coast of Aberdeenshire. It was Robert, and his sons and grandsons, who perfected the building of the towers with precisely shaped, interlocking granite blocks – like three-dimensional jigsaw pieces – which, when fitted together, made for a structure that proved indestructible in the face of any storm. In all they built ninety-seven lighthouses around Scotland, while at the same time creating all manner of optics and other apparatus to improve their effectiveness.

Lighthouses are so much a part of our coastal landscapes they seem almost to have grown there, or to have always been there. They are also a testament to the tradition of British engineering that would reshape the world. Robert Louis Stevenson, grandson of Robert senior, wrote that engineering 'was not a science then. It was a living art, and it visibly grew under the eyes and between the hands of its practitioners.'

In 2005 I spent the night in one of the most notorious lighthouses of them all – that which perches upon the Smalls, a stump of basalt 20 miles off the west coast of Pembrokeshire in south Wales. The second lighthouse in this spot, it was designed by the English engineer James Douglass and its light was switched on in 1861. It has all the look of a Stevenson lighthouse – that distinctive shape like the trunk of an oak tree, first used by John Smeaton in the Eddystone lighthouse off the Cornish coast and then developed by Robert Stevenson. It was automated in 1987 and was the first in these islands to use wind and solar power. I arrived by helicopter on to a purpose-built pad on top of the light chamber and climbed down inside through a hatch in the roof. When the chopper took off again, the sense of isolation was profound.

Outside, down on the rock, the stumps of great wooden posts could be seen, blackened with age. Those are all that remain of an outlandish structure conceived and built in 1776 by a musical-instrument maker from Liverpool named Henry Whiteside. Like one of the Martian machines from *The War of the Worlds*, it stood 70-odd feet above the rock on legs of oak. On top was a two-storey cabin with accommodation for two keepers below and the chamber for the oil-fired light above. Outlandish or not, after a few teething problems and subsequent reinforcements it would stand up to the westerly winds for more than seventy years.

Smalls Lighthouse was made infamous during the winter of 1800–01. As was customary then, two men were on station – Thomas Howell and Thomas Griffith. It was well known that the pair were always arguing, and so when Griffith was taken ill and died, Howell feared he might be charged with murder. Rather than dispose of the body, as he might have wished, he built a coffin and put Griffith inside it so as to preserve the evidence. Bad weather set in, a storm that lasted weeks and then months. Sickened by the smell of corruption, Howell moved the coffin outside on to the balcony. Freak waves broke it open so that Griffiths' body was exposed and when a rescue ship finally arrived, its horrified crew were greeted by the sight of his dead arm waving in the wind as though beckoning. Inside they found Howell – quite mad, his hair turned white.

It was the tragedy of the Smalls that changed lighthouse protocols for ever. After that horror, Trinity House would insist always on a three-man crew. If one should be lost, or otherwise compromised, the other two would at least have each other for company while they dealt with the problem.

The Smalls Lighthouse today – replacement that it is for Whiteside's original – has a forlorn feel all of its own. Down on the rock I had to keep an eye on a friend in the tower above at all times. The rocks barely break the surface of the water and the threat of being washed away by a wave was ever present. That night, while we lay in our bunks, the sea pounded below, relentless as pain. The thought of weeks or even months isolated and trapped, Rapunzel-style, in our ivory tower was almost too much to bear.

There are no lighthouse keepers now, of course. When in 1998 the last of the structures was automated (North Foreland on the eastern tip of the Isle of Thanet), a centuries-old tradition went over the hill into history. Bella Bathurst, author of *The Lighthouse Stevensons*, has observed that it is the first profession ever to have been made totally redundant.

But the lighthouses remain, sentinels still. The British Isles have been a beacon of hope for the world. Even now, uncounted thousands are trying to make their way here, drawn by our way of life. For hundreds of years, we have kept all sorts of lights burning in the dark, like the beacon in the high round window at Arbroath Abbey. HMS *Victory* might be a symbol of Britain. I say our lighthouses symbolize what it has meant to be *British*.

72

The Brontë Parsonage, Haworth, West Yorkshire

Genius born of hardship and rock

T HE BRITISH ISLES are made separate and special by their geography. With the wild Atlantic Ocean at their backs and the multitude of strangers on the Continent held at bay only by narrow ribbons of grey sea, they have made a challenging cradle.

The Brontë sisters – Charlotte, Emily and Anne – were born in Thornton, near Bradford. They spent the most productive years of their lives in the mill town of Haworth after their father, Patrick, was appointed curate there. With the wild Yorkshire moors behind and separated from the busy life of the village only by the walls and garden of the parsonage, they kindled between them a genius that would shape and change the world of literature.

After a century and a half, our view of the Brontës is almost a caricature – three spinsterly ladies oppressed by their time and venting their frustrations in the form of novels they published under made-up men's names. It seems more accurate to see them as tough, strong-willed survivors who weathered the deaths of their mother, Maria, and two of their sisters. They certainly benefited from an intellectual inheritance. Their father had filled the house with books – by Byron, Scott, Shakespeare and more – and the sisters had free access to all of them. Patrick liked to talk about literature and politics, and since he was mostly in the company of his daughters, he held his conversations with them.

The parsonage that was their home is a museum now. It is an elegant Georgian house, large enough to suggest grandeur but small enough to feel homely. The rooms within are cramped by modern standards, but it is easy to picture the authors there. It is their furniture in the rooms, their clothes and possessions displayed around the place. The dresses are so tiny that the effect is almost of being in a doll's house. Charlotte stood just 4 feet 8 inches tall, doll-like right enough. Walk from room to room and remember it was there that the trio imagined all the characters and incidents of *Wuthering Heights*, *The Tenant of Wildfell Hall*, *Jane Eyre* and more. Irish novelist George Moore wrote in 1924 that Anne's *Agnes Grey* was 'the most perfect prose narrative in English letters' and that, had her life and talent not been cut short, her achievements might have eclipsed even those of Jane Austen.

But long life was not to be – not for Anne or any of her siblings. By 1849 Anne was dead, at twenty-nine, of tuberculosis. Emily had been carried off by the same disease five months earlier, aged thirty, just after their brother, talented but troubled Branwell, aged thirty-one. A few years later Charlotte married and in 1855 became pregnant with her first child. She might have been the Brontës' happy ending, but no. She was taken either by tuberculosis like her sisters or complications related to her pregnancy and died aged thirty-eight. Patrick had outlived his wife and all his children.

Their deaths were hardly unusual for the time and place. Haworth was growing fast, driven on by the Industrial Revolution. Housing was poor for most – cold, damp, cramped and unsanitary. Cholera was commonplace and the long lists of children's names on the gravestones in the cemetery by the parsonage reveal the reality of child mortality.

But the Brontë sisters were not passive victims. For one thing, they were closely bound to one another, offering support and encouragement. Anne's novels in particular laid bare the realities of life for women of their station – hobbled by social convention. *The Tenant of Wildfell Hall* was even scandalous, portraying the damage done to a family by a husband's alcoholism and violence.

If the village provided the grist to the mills of the sisters' imaginations – the realities of life, harsh and unrelenting then the rest of their inspiration surely came from the moors above. A well-signposted walk leads away from the church that contains the Brontë family vault and up into the wild and wuthering (a word that means 'stormy weather' in those parts) moors.

A couple of miles of easy walking bring the visitor to the so-called Brontë Falls. Writing in November 1854, Charlotte described a trip she made to the spot with her husband, Arthur Bell Nicholls:

> I intended to have written a line yesterday, but just as I was sitting down for that purpose, Arthur called to me to take a walk. We set off, not intending to go far; but though wild and cloudy it was fine in the morning; when we got about half-a-mile on the moors, Arthur suggested the idea of the waterfall; after the melted snow, he said it would be fine. I had often wished to see it in its winter power, so we walked on. It was fine indeed; a perfect torrent racing over the rocks, white and beautiful!

Further on is the ruined farmhouse of Top Withens claimed by Brontë fans as the inspiration for Heathcliff's home in *Wuthering Heights*. There is no basis for the association bar the atmosphere of the place. Describing the house she had imagined, Emily wrote:

> Pure, bracing ventilation they must have up here at all times, indeed; one may guess the power of the north wind blowing over the edge, by the excessive slant of a few stunted firs at the end of the house; and by a range of gaunt thorns all stretching their limbs one way, as if craving the alms of the sun.

It is all desolate beauty, as of a face worn and aged by years but still lovely on account of the bones beneath the skin. The moors thereabouts are famed too for their birdlife. From spring until midsummer there are glimpses to be had of raptors, peregrines and merlins, sharp black silhouettes against the blue. Among the heather and grass there are the nests of curlews and golden plovers, life jealously guarded while the wind blows.

The Brontë Parsonage, Haworth, the moors above – it is all a metaphor for Britain itself. A landscape made of weather and rock, yet giving birth to stubborn genius and creativity. A place always on the edge of hardship, where bright fires were kindled and tended that lit up the world.

73

The Jurassic Coast,
Lyme Regis, Dorset

Mary Anning, fossil hunter

IT IS HARD to picture the Cobb at Lyme Regis without seeing a woman in a dark, hooded cloak at its end, with wind and waves stirring around her. It is the scene from the 1981 adaptation of *The French Lieutenant's Woman*, with Meryl Streep as the woman in question, and it fixed the west Dorset seaside town's ancient breakwater in the nation's consciousness for ever. Those who have read Jane Austen's *Persuasion* might remember too the tumble taken by Louisa Musgrove when she jumps off the steps of the Cobb and suffers a concussion.

The Cobb has been there since at least 1313 – the year before Edward II was humiliated at Bannockburn by Robert Bruce. Like a child's arm protecting a jotter from a neighbour's prying eyes, it curls protectively.

If the thought of Lyme Regis and the Cobb brings the image of a woman to mind, then it is appropriate. But the town should be famous first and foremost not for a fictional woman but for the real one known to science as 'the Mother of Palaeontology' – fossil hunter Mary Anning. Born in 1799, she learned her craft from her father, Richard, a carpenter and cabinetmaker. Richard and his wife, Mary, had ten children, but only young Mary and her elder brother, Joseph, survived into adulthood.

The Annings' home was close enough to the sea that it was sometimes flooded by storms. Richard was in the habit of noticing and collecting the fossils revealed by such events and the whole family were involved in cleaning the finds and readying them for sale to tourists. It was just as well that Richard showed Mary and Joseph as much as he did, because he died in 1810, leaving the family with painful debts and no obvious means of supporting themselves. To supplement what little help was available in the form of relief from the Overseers of the Parish Poor, Mary and Joseph made a business out of selling the fossils they found on the beach at low tide. In time, the tongue twister 'She sells seashells on the sea shore' would be written about Mary.

Lyme Regis lies on the stretch known to geologists as the Jurassic Coast. The stretch of cliffs between the town and the neighbouring village of Charmouth to the east is composed of sediments left over from around 190 million years ago. At that time, the land that would be Europe, including England, Ireland and Wales, was submerged beneath a warm, shallow sea. The whole of it was much closer to the equator – near to where North Africa lies now. That long-lost sea deposited layers of clay and limestone, which, exposed to the elements and the waves as they are now, erode very rapidly. Fossil ammonites, belemnites and the like have been spilling on to the beach like dropped coins ever since.

It was Mary and her brother who put the place on the map, however. Between 1811 and 1812 they uncovered remains that were subsequently identified as the world's first fossil of an ichthyosaurus. Bits and pieces of other examples of the same bizarre creature – like a cross between a fish and a dolphin and as much as 50 feet long – had been found before, but theirs was complete and came to the attention of the eminent British surgeon Sir Everard Home. It was he who identified the creature and announced the discovery to the Royal Society in 1814.

Neither Mary nor her brother was mentioned, far less credited, in the scientific paper published by Home at the same time. Instead, the Annings – poor and uneducated, therefore mostly beneath the contempt of great men of science – were merely paid for their find. Struggling on the breadline as they were, the cash was welcome enough.

Joseph eventually abandoned the search for fossils, leaving Mary to go on alone. For years she endured all manner of physical hardships in pursuit of her treasures, often working in foul weather in precarious locations at the foot of unstable cliffs. On one occasion a collapse killed her pet dog. But still she carried on – also finding the time and perseverance to work through scientific journals that gradually enabled her to develop expert knowledge of her own.

In addition to several more ichthyosaurus skeletons and many examples of other species, in 1824 she trumped all of it with the discovery of the world's first plesiosaurus – another large marine animal and the one often invoked as an explanation for sightings of a monster in Scotland's Loch Ness. In 1828 she discovered the first pterodactyl to be found outside Germany.

Already famous – and increasingly receiving due respect from the scientific community – Mary became a tourist attraction in her own right. People came to Lyme Regis not just to see fossils but in hopes of meeting the famous 'fossilist'.

One such, Lady Harriet Silvester, wrote in 1824:

> The extraordinary thing in this young woman is that she has made herself so thoroughly acquainted with the science, that the moment she finds any bones she knows to what tribe they belong. She fixes the bones on a frame with cement and then makes drawings and has them engraved. It is certainly a wonderful instance of divine favour – that this poor, ignorant girl should be so blessed, for by reading and application she has arrived to that degree of knowledge as to be in the habit of writing and talking with professors and other clever men on the subject, and they all acknowledge that she understands more of the science than anyone else in this kingdom . . .

We scratch our lives on the topmost layer of time. Beneath our feet is all that came before, layer on layer. It is worth remembering that all Mary's discoveries and endeavours came at a time when the mass of people still accepted the literal truth of the book of Genesis. From poverty, uneducated other than by her own efforts, she was none the less part of the breaking down of the great wall of ignorance that had separated mankind from a true understanding of the real age of the planet and the elegant processes of evolution that had given birth to its creatures.

Mary Anning died of breast cancer in 1847, not long after she was made an honorary member of the Geological Society; women would not be officially accepted into the society until 1904. Her real monument is in the array of her fossil discoveries, which still feature in institutions like the British Museum and the Natural History Museum in London. The business of comprehending the story of planet Earth was under way, and Mary Anning was one of its most important students.

74

Tolpuddle, Dorset

The struggle for workers' rights

IN THE DORSET village of Tolpuddle, the largest sycamore tree in the south-west of England grows on the smallest village green. Like the Fortingall Yew and that other sycamore nestled in its hollow by Hadrian's Wall, the branches of the Tolpuddle tree provide shelter for a few moments in time. It is legend now that in the early 1830s some poor farm labourers took to gathering in its shadow to discuss how best to improve the desperate conditions of their employment. They were brothers George and James Loveless, James Hammett, James Brine, and father and son Thomas and John Standfield.

Agricultural revolution had been working its way throughout the land for several decades. A wind of change was blowing and old ways of doing things were coming adrift from their ties, snapping in the gusts. New machines could outdo the muscle power of men and, as a result, wages had been cut and jobs were growing scarcer. Economic depression brought more unemployment. The spectre of poverty rose dark and menacing. Many men and women rose too, in rebellion – smashing the new-fangled machines and beating up the bosses. In 1830, across southern and eastern England, threatening letters were sent to landowners and their overseers, signed by 'Captain Swing'. He was a fiction, but the threat was real and soon the militia were called in to stamp out the so-called Swing Rebellion. Hundreds of men were arrested. First threatened with hanging, most of them were transported to Australia as enslaved labour for the fledgling colonies.

Workers were already in the business of learning to gather together in unions, or friendly societies as some were called, so that they might bring collective power to bear in their demands for better conditions and an end to pay cuts. In 1833 in Tolpuddle, George Loveless emerged as the leader of one such society, dedicated to shaping a better life for workers thereabouts. At a time when landowners were seeking to cut wages back to as little as 6 shillings a week, the Tolpuddle men refused to work for less than 10. Loveless was a Methodist, a lay preacher by some accounts. At first he and a handful of like-minded souls met in a little, roughly built Methodist chapel. It was important to give members of the fledgling union a sense of brotherhood and so they concocted an induction ritual. As an act of faith, each new member would place his hand upon a Bible and then swear an oath while looking at a painting of a skeleton, a reminder of their short span, their own mortality.

Alarmed by the Swing Rebellion – so recently crushed – the authorities moved to make life hard for any workers still with a mind to get up on their hind legs in the face of the landowners and bosses. As the Tolpuddle men sought to keep their activities out of sight, meeting indoors in lamplit places became less attractive. Soon it was in the shadow of the sycamore tree on the village green that George Loveless and his companions came together to talk and make plans.

The formation of such a society, a union by any other name, was not in itself illegal – indeed in February 1834 the Grand National Consolidated Trades Union was formed in London. But while joining forces was within the law, there were archaic prohibitions against the swearing of secret oaths. Loveless and his fellows sought to affiliate with the newly formed confederation in the capital but they were undone simply by the way in which they had sworn fellowship to one another. Since it was known the Tolpuddle men had their ritual with Bible and skeleton, there were sufficient grounds to arrest and charge them.

Their trial at Dorchester Assizes in March 1834 was quick, their convictions a foregone conclusion. All six men were found guilty of administering an unlawful oath and sentenced to seven years' transportation. They arrived in Australia in the summer of that year.

What the authorities had not counted on, however, was the public outcry throughout the country that followed their condemning. There were marches in the streets, petitions signed by hundreds of thousands of workers. Parliament, recently reformed, began to fear it had been caught out of step with the people. All the while the protests raged, the families of the so-called Tolpuddle Martyrs were provided with financial and practical support by members of other trade unions, donations freely given. Such was the sustained volume of opposition to the treatment of the men that in 1836 they were issued free pardons. Amazingly, given the brutality of the transportation system, all six had survived and were brought home to Dorset in triumph.

While imprisoned, George Loveless had penned the words: 'We raise the watchword liberty. We will, we will, we will be free.' He was right, and his clarion call has inspired uncounted thousands ever since.

In Tolpuddle, the little Methodist chapel is still there, preserved as a Grade II listed building. It may well have been built by two of the martyrs – George Loveless and Thomas Standfield. A larger chapel was built in 1862, making the earlier building redundant. Afterwards it was used as a barn, but more recently the Tolpuddle Old Chapel Trust has formed to preserve it as 'a quiet place' in which people might sit and think.

Not far from the old chapel stands the sycamore tree. For long its connection to the Tolpuddle Martyrs was doubted. Many folk said it could not be old enough, was not big enough to have been the same tree where the men met. In 2005, however, a new technique developed by the Forestry Commission was used to find its true age, and science silenced the doubters. It most likely took root back in the 1680s and so would have been around 150 years old when the Martyrs were in need of its shelter. On account of their role in the history of the Labour Movement, the village green and the sycamore are in the care of the National Trust.

There in the shadow of the tree, or caught among its roots, are memories of a time when hardworking men and women sought only dignity and a fair day's work for a fair day's pay. That the rise of so simple and straightforward a thought is younger by far than a 300-year-old tree seems too much to believe.

75

Abbeystrewry Cemetery, Skibbereen, County Cork

An Gorta Mór – *the Great Hunger*

IN THE CEMETERY at Abbeystrewry by the town of Skibbereen there is a mass grave for 10,000 men, women and children. They died of starvation, or dysentery, cholera, typhus and other diseases that prey upon those made weak by hunger. The 10,000 were dead, but the living were too few or too debilitated to give them proper graves. So no coffins, no stones to mark their resting place.

A single mass grave containing what amounts to the population of a small town is bad enough. But they are only a few among the many – the million and more Irish people who died for want of food in the late 1840s. At least a million more fled the horror, emigrating to North America and Canada. At nearby Baltimore, where pirates had come and carried the inhabitants off into slavery two centuries before, around 2,500 people left while they still could, boarding ships for the New World. In the aftermath of those few years, the island's birth rate fell as well, so that within a generation of what the Irish call *An Gorta Mór* – the Great Hunger – the population had dropped from eight million to fewer than four and a half. Starvation, slavery – these are blights we associate with the story of Africa, but they are part of the story of the British Isles as well.

Plaques on stones are dotted around the cemetery at Skibbereen. On one it says:

Pause and you can almost hear the sound echo down the ages
The creak of the burial cart
The rattle of the hinged coffin door
The sigh of spade on earth
Now and again
All day long.

The tragedy is especially hard to imagine in such a place. When all else is so green and peaceful it seems it has always been that way there. Hardest of all is the realization the deaths were avoidable. Most of the history books and websites call it the Irish Potato Famine, but the modern use of the word 'famine' implies a scarcity of food. While those Irish were dying, vast quantities of food were being exported to England, much of it under armed guard in case the starving might try to grab any of it for themselves. Christine Kinealy, of Quinnipiac University in Connecticut, has detailed it all. Her research shows that during 1847 alone – arguably the worst year – some 4,000 ships departed the worst-hit parts of Ireland carrying all manner of food: oats, barley and wheat, calves and sheep, bacon and hams, beans, herrings, lard, honey, onions, oysters, rabbits, salmon. The list goes on. More than 800,000 gallons of butter left the country that year too, bound for the ports of Bristol and Liverpool rather than the bread of the Irish – not that they had any bread to scrape it on.

The starvation was the consequence of years of abuse and neglect of the Irish people by absentee British landlords who regarded Ireland as a place utterly foreign, even malign. Ireland was a conquered country and the land was owned by families who might visit their holdings there once or twice in a lifetime, if at all. Their estates and farms were managed for them by middlemen who leased the land and sublet it to the locals. Profit from rent was maximized by dividing the land into smaller and smaller plots. The mass of the native Irish population worked the farms as part of their rent, producing animals and crops for export. If they had any money at all, they might buy some of the land, but mostly they had not and did not. Those poor patches they had for growing their own food were so small, on account of all the subdividing, that they became dependent on a single crop – potatoes. Originally from the Americas, the potato was the only plant that produced enough food from such small plots to feed whole families. During the 1840s a potato disease originating in Mexico made its way to these islands in tainted cargoes aboard ships. It blighted harvests all over Europe, but in Ireland, where millions of people ate potatoes and little else, the failure of the crop in 1845, 1846 and 1847 was a disaster.

Some writers have accused the landlords and the British government of the day – a Whig administration led by Prime Minister Lord John Russell – of murderous intent. The word 'genocide' has been applied as though the failure of the potato crop was exploited as an opportunity to wipe out a people wholesale. Parallels have also been drawn with the 'Holodomor' – the Hunger Plague that afflicted the Russian Ukraine in the 1930s. There, the Communist dictator Joseph Stalin stood by while millions died – apparently because he regarded the region's population as mostly troublesome opponents of the Soviet cause.

Others have it that the Irish suffered only the consequences of ignorance and neglect, of a failure of the authorities either to see the tragedy coming or to respond in any useful way when it began to unfold. The starving were supposed to fall back upon workhouses and soup kitchens, but such facilities as were put in place were too few and too late.

Some of the responses to the starvation from the wider world sound almost surreal. The first donation of cash is said to have come from Calcutta – raised by Irish expats, soldiers and employees of the East India Company. The USS *Jamestown*, a repurposed warship from the United States, arrived in Cork harbour in 1847 with food paid for by donations from an American public horrified by what they were reading in their newspapers. There were private donations from the Pope, from Queen Victoria and from Tsar Nicholas I of Russia. None of it was enough, not nearly, to make a difference. *An Gorta Mór* soured relations between these islands ever after.

The desire of the Irish people for independence had started even before then. During the eighteenth century and the first decades of the nineteenth various popular and political groups had channelled Catholic unrest and called for change – the Society of United Irishmen, the Irish Patriot Party,

Young Ireland. The carnage of the famine, however, inspired armed struggle and a commitment to using bombs and bullets instead of any more peaceful protest. Those emigrants who fled to North America and elsewhere took the same feeling with them, leading to the establishment there of groups like the Fenian Brotherhood. The calls for a bloody end to British rule in Ireland had begun and would not be quieted.

76

Fastnet Rock, off County Cork

Ireland's Teardrop

I OFTEN LIE IN bed in the small hours and listen to the Shipping Forecast on Radio 4. I usually hear the broadcast that goes out sometime after midnight, and on nights when I can't sleep at all I will likely hear it again around the back of five. Sleepless but safe, I feel the familiar rhythm rising and falling like an ocean swell: '. . . Stornoway. South-east veering south-west 4 or 5, occasionally 6 later. Thundery showers. Moderate or good, occasionally poor . . .'

Even after years of listening, I do not understand the half of it. It should be a lullaby and yet as often as not I lie there and imagine being in some little boat, alone in the dark with a wind howling loud, rain lashing, and only a radio for comfort.

'. . . Biscay . . . Trafalgar . . . FitzRoy . . . Sole . . . Lundy . . . Fastnet . . . Irish Sea . . . Shannon . . . Rockall . . .'

On and on it goes, the lulling litany. Some locations I can picture, others not. It can be like half-remembered fragments of a dream. Of all of it, the name I always listen out for among the rest is Fastnet. Like the barb on a fishhook, it catches me. I have swallowed it deep and its hold is fast.

I sailed around Fastnet once, aboard a little boat of a sort called a towel-sail yawl. It was a hundred years old or more and had been restored with much love by its skipper. *Towel*-sail is a corruption of the Irish *teabhal*, pronounced the same way, and mine sat light upon the water like a resting gull. My trip aboard came at the end of the day I had spent learning the story of Skibbereen and *An Gorta Mór*, the Great Hunger.

Fastnet is a sharp little rock that thrusts up like a blackened fist 100 feet out of the sea about 8 miles off the coast of County Cork in the south of Ireland. The name might be from the Old Norse *Hvasstann-ey* (those Vikings got everywhere, and put a name to half of it), which means 'the Island Like a Sharp Tooth'. The Irish have called it Carraig Aonair in their own language – 'the Lonely Rock' – but since the second half of the nineteenth century it has been known to most as Ireland's Teardrop.

Seen from above, it has something of the shape of a tear right enough, but it earned its name for another reason. Since it was the last part of the old country that emigrants ever saw, a final glimpse of home, many viewed it with eyes wet with tears. The emigrants in question were those driven to depart their homeland to escape the hunger and the sicknesses that followed in its train.

The Fastnet rock was a threat to shipping and therefore the cause of heartbreak long before the famine came. The lighthouse that perches upon it now was completed in 1904 and has the familiar oak-tree-trunk silhouette pioneered in 1759 by engineer John Smeaton at Eddystone, 9 miles off England's Cornish coast. The keepers of Fastnet are said to have watched a German U-boat surface close by a fishing boat in May 1915. They saw the crew buy the catch and then the vessel disappeared once more. The British ocean liner RMS *Lusitania* was sunk with the loss of 1,200 lives soon after, off Ireland's south coast, and likely by a single torpedo from that same vessel. It was the first time a submarine had sunk an enemy ship without first surfacing to issue a warning. Germany had declared total war on all British shipping, and they meant it.

Fastnet also figures in many people's memories on account of the yacht race that bears its name. The route takes crews from Cowes on the Isle of Wight, around Fastnet and then back to Plymouth. In 1979 near-hurricane conditions beset more than 300 yachts taking part. A total of eighteen lives were lost.

The lonely rock – Ireland's Teardrop – Fastnet is wreathed in sadness as well as seaweed. It is a fitting memorial to lives lost and to lives driven off to be lived elsewhere.

77

Eyemouth, Berwickshire

The Black Friday fishing disaster

T HE PRICE PAID by these islands for the privilege of joining the Common Market, a precursor of the European Union, in 1973 was the surrender of our fishing grounds. That priceless asset, once the basis for a huge and thriving industry upon which thousands depended for both a livelihood and a way of living, had long been coveted by fishermen from France, Spain and elsewhere, and understandably so. The Conservative government of the day, led by Edward Heath, decided it was a sacrifice worth making.

Nearly a century before all that, the community of Eyemouth in Berwickshire in the Scottish Borders was made to satisfy the sea god with another kind of sacrifice – one made in blood and tears. At the end of the second week of October 1881 a hurricane swept across the North Sea while the fleet was at sea. A total of nineteen local ships went to the bottom and 189 fishermen lost their lives – 129 from Eyemouth itself.

It is likely not the part of Scotland that springs to mind for most folk when they think of bustling fishing ports. Places like Fraserburgh and Buckie are more familiar, yet for much of the nineteenth century the fishermen of Eyemouth were landing some of the richest catches of haddock and herring. But while the silver darlings flowed into the nets, and the port, the fishermen were made to haemorrhage coins into the coffers of the local church. In ages past it had been the norm all around Scotland to pay a tithe – a tenth – of all their incomes to the Kirk. By the middle of the century the practice had almost entirely died out – until only the Eyemouth fleet continued to suffer the leeching.

What is known as the Great Disruption of 1843 had seen hundreds of ministers break away from the established Church of Scotland. Anger at the close ties between Church and state had reached boiling point and those who left formed the Free Church of Scotland. Even then, despite so many fishermen following the rebel preachers and turning their backs on the old tradition, those in Eyemouth continued to pay their tithes. Finally, a local man – indeed a local hero – called William Spears led a peaceful rebellion that culminated in the ending of the hated 'teind'. They called him 'Kingfisher'.

Still the trouble and ill-feeling rumbled on in the town for another thirty years, until eventually the Lord Advocate intervened and brokered a compromise. Grudgingly the Church give up its claim to the tax in return for an annual payment of compensation from the town.

All the years of unrest had seen Eyemouth neglected by the wider community. Rather than attending to the fabric of the place, the townsfolk had seen the necessary funds go to the Church. One consequence was the poor state of the harbour itself. Elsewhere, government investment had seen large-scale improvements to sea walls and such, but troubled and troublesome Eyemouth had been avoided and overlooked. Entry to the harbour was difficult even in fair weather, and the protection afforded by the existing walls and piers was dangerously inadequate. The place had been in disrepair for so long, however, that the fishermen had grown used to taking risks, sometimes setting out against their better judgement.

The old salts knew there was a storm coming that October day. Their instinct was to stay in port, but the younger men wanted to take the chance and, as tradition dictated, when just one boat cast off and headed out, the rest felt duty-bound to follow. They were all in deep water and far from home when the hurricane hit them. They turned for home, but it was too late. Even those who came close enough to see their families waiting for them found the wind and waves so strong they could not make the turn into the meagre sanctuary promised by the harbour wall. Wives and children looked on in horror as one boat after another was overturned in the surf or pounded into matchwood on the Hurkar Rocks by the harbour's mouth.

Like every other fishing town, Eyemouth had swallowed its share of loss over the years. By the time the latest storm had blown itself out, however, by day's end on that 14 October, it was home to nearly a hundred new widows, almost 300 children newly fatherless.

While families mourned behind closed doors, a single ray of light lanced down out of a sky torn and bruised. Just one boat, the *Ariel Gazelle*, limped into harbour two days after the hurricane. Rather than run for home, her skipper had had the wisdom to stay at sea and ride it out. She was badly battered, her sails torn, but all her crew were safe.

It was a bitter irony that plans for the long-overdue improvements to the port had recently been circulated around the town but not yet started. It would take nearly a century until the population returned to anything like what it had been before the disaster. In Eyemouth, that day of days is still remembered as Black Friday. There is a statue to William Spears, who fought the good fight against the Church and won them their freedom from the hated tax. On the seafront another work, grey and sombre, depicts the women and children howling in despair as they look on helplessly at their drowning menfolk. Still today the fishing boats head out from the harbour and there is not a man among their crews that does not know the tale of what happened to those who went before.

The sea is the toughest mistress of all and her lessons are still being learned.

78

The Victorian Channel Tunnel, near Dover, Kent

Connecting with Europe

IT WAS THE Storegga Slide off the coast of Norway 8,000 years ago that formed this archipelago of ours when, with an awful jolt, a great slice of seabed slipped deeper into the dark and the tsunami that rushed across the North Sea in its wake severed our connection to mainland Europe.

All in an instant our fate was sealed, once and for all, and the resultant separateness has been the making of us. We are set apart and this has, quite evidently, made this place different, and us too. For one thing we have been protected. In order to get here, invaders and immigrants have had to find ways across the sea. Even the narrowest point between Dover and Calais is challenge enough. Rather than strolling across a land border, incomers have needed boats and a plan. People have come, of course – the farmers, metalworkers, Romans, Angles and Saxons, Vikings, Normans – but they had to be determined, committed. Those that made it were worth having, from the point of view of quality stock if nothing else. Our success ever since has been founded upon our mastery of the sea – our skill as sailors, navigators and adventurers. To go anywhere at all we had to get into boats, and that has made all the difference.

Our separation also meant most of those who managed to get here had to make do and get on with it. Here was the end of the line. For centuries, short of crossing the Atlantic, this archipelago off north-west Europe was as far as most folk could or would go in the world and it bred a kind of stoicism. After all the millennia of migration, the slow spread into the west, the British Isles were a terminus. Like finches on the Galapagos, or flightless birds in Australia, we grew as a species apart. The rest of Europe got on without us.

The idea of ending all that separateness came very late in the game. It was in the early part of the nineteenth century that the idea of a tunnel connecting Britain to our nearest neighbour, France, first bubbled to the surface. It was Frenchmen, not Britons, who sought to re-establish the connection. The first of them was Albert Mathieu-Favier, in 1802, with a proposal for a two-deck tunnel lit with lamps and through which horse-drawn carriages would come and go. Nothing came of it, but then in 1839 Louis-Joseph-Aimé Thomé de Gamond set himself the challenge. Utterly determined, he had his daughter Elizabeth row him out into the Channel. From the boat he dived into the water and down towards the seabed, wearing inflated pig bladders round his waist for buoyancy and sacks of pebbles for ballast so that he might go deep. He was a qualified doctor and reasoned that by keeping his mouth full of olive oil he might expel air without having water forced into his lungs. By such means he apparently reached depths of as much as 100 feet and was able to collect samples to confirm his belief that the two land masses were connected by chalk. In 1856 he submitted to Napoleon III plans for a tunnel that would have cost around £7 million. In spite of his Herculean efforts, his scheme was neglected. He died in obscurity in 1876, unfulfilled.

It was in that same year, however, that a joint Anglo-French agreement brought the dream closer to reality. Sir Edward Watkin, chairman of the South Eastern Railway, and Alexandre Lavalley, contractor of the Suez Canal, came together with a bid to link Britain and France with a railway tunnel. By 1880 they were at work with a fantastical burrowing machine invented by one Captain Thomas English. It was estimated that the 33-foot-long contraption could cut through half a mile of chalk every month.

Vertical tunnels were dropped near Dover on the English side and at Sangatte near Calais to enable the horizontal boring to commence. Steadily, two ends of a pilot tunnel 7 feet in diameter began nosing towards one another. If and when completed, the whole would have been enlarged to take a standard gauge railway line. By 1882, when the British government pulled the plug on it – fearing the link posed too much of a risk to national security – the English side had advanced by over 6,000 feet and the French by more than 5,000. When work began on the present-day tunnel, completed in 1994, care had to be taken to make sure the new workings did not intersect the old.

The Victorian tunnel is still there. At the foot of Shakespeare Cliff between Dover and Folkestone an anonymous grey steel door set into a red-brick hatchway opens upon a tunnel leading to the older workings. Water drips and the smell is of dank and damp stone. More than anything, however, the effort made by those engineering pioneers is surprisingly modern in appearance. Rather than roughly hewn, the tunnel is perfectly circular and smooth. The rifling marks left by the cutting edge of Captain English's machine twist away into the dark in perfect corkscrews. Around 100 yards in, on the left-hand side, a worker has left his mark, etched into the greying chalk. The words are slick and shining with wetness but as clear as the day they were made:

THIS TUNNEL WAS BEGUN IN 1880

He apparently struggled with the word 'begun' and it is a jumble of letters, false starts. He signed his name too – William Sharp.

The ambition and achievement of Victorian Britons is all around us. A great many of us live still in the houses they built. Their bridges span our valleys and divides, their sewers carry away our waste. They built cathedrals to everything from banking to commerce. When they used plate glass for the first time, they even invented window-shopping, revealing the goods within to potential customers passing by on the pavements.

Preserved beneath the grey water of the English Channel is evidence of yet more endeavour, and also caution. Although a tunnel to France may well have been within their grasp, some relic suspicion about the wisdom of such a connection had them stay their hands. Their reach was long enough, yet they chose to draw back and wait. Separateness had served them well, and within living memory: Napoleon I himself had been kept at bay by those few miles of water. The time had not yet come to undo what nature herself had done.

79

The Rutherford Building, Manchester University

Ernest Rutherford, the father of nuclear physics

GIVEN THE ETERNAL brightness of his contribution to our understanding of the texture of reality, it is fitting that a museum remembering physicist Ernest Rutherford, near the family home at Pungarehu on the Taranaki coast of New Zealand's North Island, is housed in a lighthouse. (Incidentally, it is Rutherford's face on the Kiwi 100-dollar bill, their note of highest value – another mark of his worth.)

Ernest was the fourth of a dozen children born to James and Martha Rutherford, and their second son. James had emigrated from Perth, in Scotland, with plans to 'raise a little flax and a lot of children'. Martha worked as a schoolteacher and saw to it her children had a thorough education. When the family lived at Brightwater, Nelson, on South Island, they often struggled financially. James's advice to his brood then was, 'We haven't the money, so we've got to think.' In 1888, when Ernest was seventeen, they moved to Pungarehu.

Ernest's academic ability was spotted early, along with an urge to experiment. When he was ten he built a cannon, which exploded on first firing, but his curiosity was left undamaged. He won a scholarship to a private school and then another to Canterbury College in Christchurch. By 1895 he was a research student in the famous Cavendish Laboratory in Cambridge, where he began his study of things radioactive. For five years he was professor of physics at McGill University in Montreal and found fame there for his experiments with the building blocks of the universe.

In 1907 Rutherford was back in England, at Manchester University, where he gathered around him a team regarded as one of the finest and most influential ever assembled. Hans Geiger was among them, inventor of the radiation counter that bears his name; philosopher Ludwig Wittgenstein; Lawrence Bragg, winner of the Nobel Prize in 1915 for his study of X-ray crystallography; and Niels Bohr, another legend in the field of physics.

In addition to everything else, Rutherford was apparently easy company, affable. Sir Isaac Newton was famously awkward in social situations, difficult to relate to and possibly autistic to some degree. It is a sad fact of human nature that we often demand too much from our brightest. It is not always enough to change and enhance our species' understanding of the world; such figures are required to be likeable and accessible as well. But in common with James Clerk Maxwell, the Edinburgh-born titan of the study of the electromagnetic field, Rutherford was both a genius and the sort of man to whom lesser mortals might relate.

He led the study of physics at Manchester University for eight years. Opened in 1901, the Physical Laboratories on Oxford Road were purpose-built for the job of studying Natural Science. At that time the building was one of the largest and best equipped of its kind anywhere in the world and its presence in what was regarded as a provincial university was a great source of pride for the city.

It was there that Rutherford and others conceived the experiments that, in 1911, would reveal for the first time the nature of the atom. The word is Greek and it was those ancient philosophers who first imagined the existence of a fundamental, infinitesimal grain of matter. Before Rutherford, most scientists accepted the notion that an atom was like a tiny pudding – mostly soft dough but with some raisins, representing the atom's mass, the hard stuff of it, scattered all through. Rutherford and his colleagues put together an experiment in which a stream of particles was fired at a sheet of thin gold foil. He and they had expected the dots would pass through – and some did. Others, however, rebounded. It was a result that flabbergasted all who witnessed it. Rutherford described it as like firing a naval shell at a sheet of tissue paper and having it bounce straight back. His physicist's mind enabled him to deduce that, rather than being evenly distributed like those raisins in the pudding, an atom's mass must all be concentrated at the centre – the nucleus. When that nucleus collided with the similarly hard centre of a particle of gold, it bounced away – much like what happens when the positive ends of two magnets are brought rapidly together.

Rutherford and his team had discovered the *nuclear* atom. In essence, they had shown that the atom was not the smallest particle in the universe. Instead it was itself composed of smaller constituents:

> *Big fleas have little fleas*
> *Upon their backs to bite 'em*
> *And little fleas have lesser fleas*
> *And so ad infinitum.*
>
> AUGUSTUS DE MORGAN, 1872

An atom – so tiny in itself that it would take more than five million, placed side by side, to cross a full stop on this page – has at its centre a nucleus that is a thousand times smaller again. Around it, spinning like tiny satellites, are a few particles called electrons. The rest of it is . . . nothing at all. The American physicist Nick Herbert said humankind exists in a Midas-like state – doomed never to experience the true texture of reality since everything we touch turns to matter. Rutherford had been among the first to reach out and sense what matter itself was actually made of.

He is regarded as the father of nuclear physics. For his effort and insight he was awarded the Nobel Prize for chemistry in 1908. During the First World War, he developed the means to detect enemy submarines using sonar. In 1917 he found a way to bombard the nuclei of nitrogen atoms with radioactive particles and so 'split the atom' – his most famous achievement of all. By 1919 he was back in Cambridge, where he served as professor of physics and director of the Cavendish Laboratory. He was made a life peer in 1931, taking the title Baron Rutherford of Nelson in honour of the city of his birth.

The Physics Laboratories in Manchester, built in 1900, were later renamed the Rutherford Building in his honour. A blue plaque between two bay windows on the ground floor to the right of the entrance bears his name and dates. Within the triangular pediment above the front doors is a relief carving of the university's motto, *Arduus ad solem* – 'striving towards the sun', which feels apt. The study of physics has moved to other premises now and the Rutherford Building has been largely given over to university administration.

When in 1937 the *New York Times* covered the news of Rutherford's untimely and unnecessary death, resulting from a strangulated hernia, it noted that:

> It is given to but few men to achieve immortality, still less to achieve Olympian rank, during their own lifetime. Lord Rutherford achieved both. In a generation that witnessed one of the greatest revolutions in the entire history of science he was universally acknowledged as the leading explorer of the vast, infinitely complex universe within the atom, a universe that he was first to penetrate.

Rutherford knew what he had done – the possible future he had ushered in. Above all, he understood the elemental power of his discovery and saw it could be weaponized. Despite his hope that his successors might resist the destructive potential of what he had revealed until mankind had learned to live in peace, experiments with nuclear fission were taken on by others. Hiroshima and Nagasaki lay ahead.

His ashes are buried in Westminster Abbey close to the graves of Newton and William Thomson, Lord Kelvin. Time has moved on, leaving the Rutherford Building behind, but it still has a formidable presence, its red-brick façade punctuated by windows shaped with mullions and transoms of pale stone. Leaded glass, in the art nouveau style, looks to the future too. Inside, in spaces now given over to other purposes, our entire view of the world was changed for ever and the future was born.

80

Berwick-upon-Tweed, Northumberland

A place apart

THE BRITISH ISLES are dotted with oddities, constitutional anomalies. The Channel Islands are a self-governing Crown dependency – so too the Isle of Man with its Tynwald and its own language and its determination to stand up, no matter how it's thrown. Even on the mainland of the long island there are places where folk feel an identity separate and distinct from the principal choices of British, English, Irish, Scottish or Welsh.

Berwick-upon-Tweed, cheek by jowl with the Anglo-Scottish border, is just such a place apart. While some of the town's inhabitants will claim either Scots or English identities, it usually feels as though most 'Berwickers' are just that – from Berwick first, the Borders second and Northumberland third.

It is a state of affairs that stems from a long, tortured history of being pulled like a child between warring parents. Berwick was founded before any of the modern nation states existed – by the Anglo-Saxons as part of their kingdom of Northumbria. There were Celtic Britons in residence thereabouts even before that. Thereafter it changed hands again and again. For a long time it was a busy Scottish port with trade to the east and the Baltic Sea. In the twelfth century King David I gave it burgh status.

The bloodiest rupture came in 1296 when John Balliol, King of Scots, invaded England in support of France. Edward I had been busy making war across the Channel and was outraged to find his northern neighbour honouring the terms of the so-called Auld Alliance – a treaty of mutual support and protection between the monarchs of Scotland and France. While Balliol was a bit of a house cat, Edward was like a lion with a broken incisor. At best he regarded the northern kingdom as a troublesome little brother, at worst like a disobedient woman he felt entitled to beat. He invaded Scotland, took Berwick and had his men set about putting the entire population, men, women and children, to the sword. Thousands died and the river ran red. Apparently it took desperate pleas from local churchmen to bring the slaughter to a halt. Edward built walls around his new acquisition and the survivors stumbled into a new world, one made suddenly English.

Still the argy-bargy went on. Edward's son and successor, Edward II, mustered his army at Berwick ready for the advance to Bannockburn in 1314. Four years later the town was once more in the hands of the Scots and for more than a century and a half after that it passed back and forth between the two. By the time Richard, Duke of Gloucester (the future Richard III) captured it for the last time for the English in 1482 it had changed hands more than a dozen times. Yet it was only in the eighteenth century that Berwick was formally and unequivocally made part of England. Even after that, the town was still mentioned separately in some official government paperwork – international treaties and the like. When Britain declared war on Russia in 1854, Berwick was listed as a distinct entity; Victoria signed the necessary paperwork as Queen of Britain, Ireland, Berwick-upon-Tweed and all British Dominions. Someone forgot to include the town in the subsequent peace treaty, however, which for many people meant Berwick remained at war, all on its own. In 1976 a Soviet envoy came to the town and the relevant document was completed, finally concluding the Crimean War 120 years after the fact. It was tongue-in-cheek, but still it reminded everyone that the town had evolved a different way of doing things.

Nowadays Berwick is a stunning little town, mostly built of red sandstone. The present town walls are Elizabethan and on their battlements it is easy enough to get that sense of how the town was held ready for war and strife for the longest time. The River Tweed is spanned by three elegant bridges and the view from them, over the silvered waters flowing towards a melding with the North Sea, is of the sort that gives a person pause to think of all the centuries of history that have flowed through there as well.

Berwick is England's most northerly town – just a couple of miles shy of the border with Scotland. Listen to the accents of the people in the shops and on the streets and that atmosphere of a place that is all its own, neither English nor Scottish, is palpable. Time and again around these British Isles it is local rather than national identities that have the deepest roots. We are hobbits right enough, and often our loyalties are first and foremost to our shires.

81
The Grand Hotel, Scarborough
The rise and fall of the British seaside

T HE QUEEN OF THE COAST has long since fallen off her throne. The sea-side town of Scarborough in North Yorkshire is mostly a monument to times past. Like Morecambe on the west, home of the sometimes lethal shifting sands, Scarborough once regarded itself in all seriousness as a 'Nice of the North'. In more recent times the locals have nicknamed it 'Scarbados', a darkly humorous concession to how much every British sea-side resort has lost over the last few decades.

In spite of the hardships and decline, there is still no doubting the beauty of the location. By any measure Scarborough sits in a splendid spot, with the North Sea ahead and the moors rising behind. The castle that looms on the cliffs today began life as an Iron Age fort. There was a Viking settlement in Scarborough too and the town's first heyday came not with Victoria but in the thirteenth century with Henry III, who spent considerable sums bolstering the defences of what was then a thriving port.

In the early seventeenth century a local woman called Mrs Farrow declared that the mineral waters rising in the town had curative properties. From then on, Scarborough was a spa town where folks came to take those waters, briny and brackish. Such was the popularity of the enlivening, salubrious atmosphere that Scarborough was soon able to lay claim to being England's first seaside town. The spa was made ever grander, with wrought-iron swirls and twirls, and acres of glass through which to appreciate the ever-changing sea. There were bathing machines on the beach and life was grand in every sense.

The Grand Hotel was completed in 1867. Designed by Hull architect Cuthbert Brodrick, it was the first purpose-built hotel in Europe and, for a time, the largest in these islands. Everything about the fading exterior still smacks of intense pride and Victorian ambition. Pale sandy bricks from the nearby village of Hunmanby, chased with red. The hotel's footprint is a V-shape, in honour of the queen herself. Like the Millennium Dome that would come 133 years later, its design was full of references to the notion of time. There are twelve storeys representing the months of the year and four domes atop four towers to symbolize the seasons. When it opened, there were 365 rooms, for the days of the year, and fifty-two chimneys for the weeks. The baths in the rooms had two sets of taps – one for fresh water and the other for that from the sea.

All was grandeur and the 'right sort' of people. Right up into the 1970s it had airs and graces. There was no access, none at all, to anyone wearing jeans. And then came the cheap package deal to Spain and the Med. Instead of spades and sandcastles and fish and chips and revelling in what, by then, were charms made more of brass than gold, the holidaymakers began staying away in droves.

The fortunes of the Grand Hotel went into an elegant, then an inelegant, decline. For a while it was owned by Butlins. Instead of the high and mighty it was a destination for bus tours and budget breaks. The spa and the rest of the town slid with it, slumping like a cliff eroded by the thoughtless sea. Wages fell until the average pay was the lowest in the land. Unemployment took its enervating toll.

I still find something grand in Scarborough, something that will not fade or rust or be carried away by the tide. The hotel has been refurbished. More to the point, it is still there, still dominating St Nicholas Cliff. The spa is still all glass and stubborn iron. The beach is as stunning as a long curve of pale sand can be. Long live the Queen.

The Cobb, Lyme Regis – revealing and comprehending the elegance of evolution.

Fastnet Rock, off County Cork, washed by the sea and by Ireland's tears.

The Grand Hotel, Scarborough – the faded grandeur and the 'Nice of the North'.

Somerled Square, Portree, Isle of Skye.
The Great War and a band of brothers,
not forgotten.

John Brown's Shipyard, Clydebank ... Seaward the great ships, and a breed of men gone over the hill into history.

Alderney, Channel Islands. An island idyll, stolen away into darkness and returned to the light.

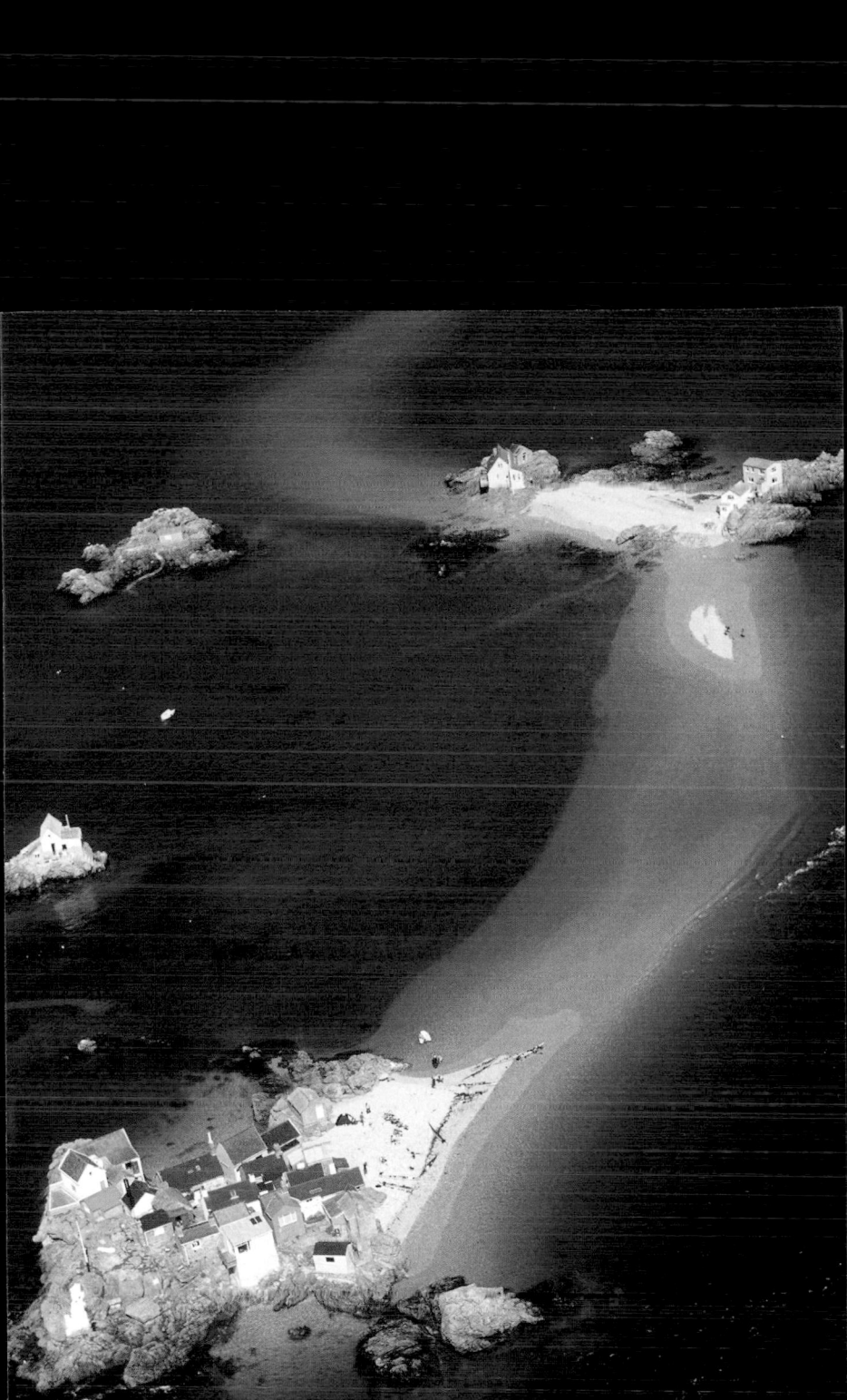

Glen Lyon, Perth and Kinross …
where the creator goddess of the
Celts waits and watches over all.

82

The Coal Exchange, Cardiff

Feeding a global hunger

SAY WHAT YOU will about the Stewarts of Scotland, but there is no denying they were a fabulously fecund lot.

While Tudors like Henry VIII and his offspring struggled to conjure successors into being, or failed altogether, their cousins north of the border were popping out legitimate heirs like there was no tomorrow, not to mention basket-loads of bastards for good measure. Genius – political or tactical – naked ambition, even ruthless cruelty and Machiavellian machinations, none of it could compensate in the end for what nature and genetics had left out. Kings and queens succeed only if they make more of their kind.

Given a few hundred years, the fertility of the Stewarts spread their progeny through the story of these islands like fat marbled through good beef. Their family name was a corruption of Steward, an Old English word meaning 'guardian of the hall'. The Latin alternative for the same responsibility at court was *dapifer*, the bearer of the meat. Fine beef or scrag-end, in the game of thrones it is all about being able to deliver the goods.

One Walter Fitzalan had been made Steward to King David I sometime around the middle of the twelfth century. After David, he performed the same duties for Malcolm IV and then William I. His descendants kept themselves close to the fire, simmering nicely. When David II died childless in 1371, he was succeeded by his uncle, Robert the Steward. This Robert was the son of Walter, 6th High Steward of Scotland, and Marjorie, daughter of Robert I – Robert Bruce – by his first wife, Isabella of Mar. Thus came the Stewards, later the Stewarts, into the kingship of the Scots.

Fertile like the rest of them, King Robert II fathered many children – almost more than anyone could be bothered to count. By his first wife, Elizabeth Mure, he had ten offspring who reached adulthood. His second wife was Euphemia de Ross and she gave him four more. As if those legitimate children were not enough, he sired as many bastards with any number of mistresses. One of those, Moira Leitch, bore him just one, born around 1399. This was John Stewart, later known as the Black Stewart on account of his dark hair and complexion.

King Robert must have struggled to find lands and titles for his brood, but somehow he managed. To Moira's John he granted the hereditary title of Sheriff of Bute, relating to an island in the Firth of Clyde. As well as Bute, this Black Stewart received the islands of Arran and Cumbrae. From him are descended all the marquesses of Bute.

The seventh in the line of descent from the Black Stewart was James Stuart, created 1st Baronet of Bute in 1627. During the lifetime of Mary, Queen of Scots (another helpfully fertile daughter of the line), the family had changed the spelling of their name. Since she had been raised in France and married to the king of France – and given that the French had no W in their alphabet – Stuart was the compromise. And so it remained. Mary Stuart's son was James, the king of Scots who sat upon the throne of England as well, after Elizabeth I – Good Queen Bess and barren.

Stewart, Stuart – a rose by any other name. Technically, the Royal House of Stuart died with Henry, brother of Charles Edward Stuart, the Bonnie Prince, in 1807. That said, there are still plenty of Stuarts around. The eighth largest landowner in these islands is Richard Scott, 10th Duke of Buccleuch, a descendant of James, Duke of Monmouth – he of the Monmouth Rebellion and the Battle of Sedgemoor and eldest illegitimate son of King Charles II.

While their preoccupation with the throne was over by the early years of the nineteenth century, some of the Stuart clan found power and prestige elsewhere – sometimes in unexpected places. Before the Industrial Revolution, Cardiff was just another small town in Wales. In the latter part of the eighteenth century just two ships moved all of Cardiff's trade. But with the turn of the nineteenth century Britain found a limitless appetite for iron, steel and the coal with which to make them. Since the Rhondda Valley of south Wales was Britain's richest source of the stuff, all hands turned to finding better and faster ways of getting it to where it was needed and wanted. Railways and canals were opened like arteries to let the coal flood south to the sea – and one man in particular saw the potential of Cardiff as the port for shipping it all to the wider world.

One of the main seats of John Crichton-Stuart, 2nd Marquess of Bute, was Cardiff Castle. He had estates in south Wales and spotted the opportunity presented by the burgeoning appetite for coal. From the early 1820s he was at work exploring the potential. At first his commitment to the venture was viewed by contemporaries as wild speculation. To finance his goals he had to mortgage possessions elsewhere and there were those around him who saw only ruin ahead. In the face of scepticism he opened the Bute West Dock in Cardiff in 1839 and after a slow start the coal started to flow out and the money poured back in.

He died in 1848 but his son – also John, the 3rd Marquess – continued to develop the port. Steam coal then was what oil is now: the black gold that powered the world. The Admiralty decreed that only coal from the Welsh valleys was good enough for the engines of the Royal Navy. During the second half of the nineteenth century, the port of Cardiff became Britain's busiest and most important, and even outstripped New York. At its height in 1913, the volume of coal it exported would have been enough to fill the Millennium Stadium to the brim a total of nineteen times.

By then the Coal Exchange in the city's Mount Stuart Square in Butetown – a model housing estate built by the 2nd Marquess in the early 1800s – was the centre of the entire industry. Opened in 1888, it was where the price of coal was determined for the entire world. As many as 10,000 people passed through its doors every day, making deals. In 1904 the world's first million-pound deal was struck there, the first million-pound cheque signed.

For a few bright decades Cardiff exerted what amounted to a gravitational pull, drawing hopeful souls from every corner of the globe. It put

Butetown on the map and the cosmopolitan community that developed there, with folk of at least fifty different nationalities, became known the world over as Tiger Bay. No one is sure why. One theory has it that the seamen feared the swirling tides at the entrance of the dock and said the patterns on the water looked like fighting tigers.

As long as the global hunger for coal continued, Cardiff thrived and grew. But all booms come to an end, of course, and after the First World War the market was flooded by cheap German coal. Cardiff never had it so good again and by the mid-1960s the port had grown quiet, the tigers an endangered species. The Coal Exchange closed its doors for the last time in 1958.

It is still there – most recently refurbished and repurposed as a luxury hotel.

83

Titanic Slipway, Belfast

A world sinks to its end

FOR ALL THE time she was afloat – seven weeks or so short of a year – the British passenger liner RMS *Titanic* was the largest man-made object that had ever moved across the face of the Earth. Just shy of 900 feet long, 92 feet wide and weighing in at 50,000 tons, she sounds big enough even today.

(Set beside the dimensions of *Prelude*, a gas-pumping vessel completed in 2017 and owned by Shell, however, *Titanic* is comprehensively dwarfed. The new girl on the block, the world's largest, *Prelude* measures 1,600 feet long – longer than the Empire State Building is tall – by 243 feet wide. She weighs 600,000 tons.)

Titanic was built for the White Star Line at the Harland and Wolff shipyard in Belfast. Her construction was a major challenge for the yard and for the thousands of men who laboured like ants around her vast bulk. Rather than an only child, *Titanic* was one of a set of near-identical triplets. One sister – *Olympic* – was built alongside her and the third – *Britannic* – was completed and launched just before the outbreak of the First World War.

White Star's great rival was the Cunard Line. Their record-holding liners *Lusitania* and *Mauretania* each had four engines and four funnels and therefore great power and speed. *Titanic* and her Olympic-class sisters had only three engines, so to distract from the fact that they were slower, a dummy fourth funnel was added to each. In the case of *Titanic* the empty space inside the folly was used for storing passengers' luggage. It was all about the show.

Harland and Wolff had purpose-built two new slipways, the largest in the world at that time and side by side on what was then Queen's Island in Belfast harbour. *Olympic*'s keel was laid down first, in December 1908. She launched in 1910. Work on *Titanic* began on 31 March 1909 and two years and two months later she thundered down her slipway, on a slick of soap and tallow, and into the River Lagan. She was longer than *Olympic* by just a foot.

A multi-million-pound development opened on the site in 2012, a hundred years after the loss of *Titanic*. Known now as 'Titanic Quarter', it is home to film studios, private apartments and businesses, as well as a glitzy visitor centre dedicated to the legend of the world's most famous lost ship. Shaped to suggest ships' hulls, it shines and glistens, not unlike an iceberg.

The twin slipways are still there and seem somehow too small ever to have cradled the makings of a story so grand and terrible. Elsewhere in the Quarter, *Titanic*'s outline is picked out in white stone so that you might walk around her and get a sense of her scale. It is especially striking to see just how narrow she was across the beam, her widest point. The power output available from her engines meant she had to be slim as a fish or her propellers would have been unable to push her great mass through the water at a satisfactory speed. As a rule of thumb, great ships built in *Titanic*'s day had to restrict their width to around one tenth of their length or even less.

Hardest to take is the thought of more than 2,200 souls, passengers and crew, contained within that space during her tragic maiden voyage in April 1912. She departed first from Southampton, then crossed the Channel to pick up more passengers at Cherbourg. From there she steamed to the port of Cobh in Queenstown, County Cork, where she collected the last of them before heading out into the wild Atlantic Ocean. More than 1,500 were lost in the end. With that in mind, her ghostly footprint back in Belfast takes on the look of one of those chalk outlines left as evidence at a crime scene after the corpse has been taken away.

The birthplace of *Titanic* is worth remembering, and seeing. Always visible, seemingly from every angle, are Harland and Wolff's two gigantic yellow cranes – nicknamed 'Samson' and 'Goliath' – looming like gallows.

By the time the broken hulk of the great ship was dropping to her resting place, over 2 miles down in the Atlantic, the First World War was just two years away. In 1912, the world of before – that world as yet untouched by all the horrors of the twentieth century – was steaming full tilt into the dark. Technology was moving fast. Machines were on the rise and outstripping humankind's ability to keep them under control, to see where such reckless advance might lead. Other modes of transport were making great strides – Daimler-Benz automobiles, the Wright brothers and Louis Blériot showing the potential of flight – but ships were still dominant and the 'unsinkable' *Titanic* was supposed to be the brightest and best of them. 'Dreadnought' was a new word, for the very latest marque of British battleship. An arms race was fully under way between Britain and Germany, so the British public wanted more and more of the new vessels and learned to chant, 'We want eight and we won't wait!' The European nations were bound in a web of alliances and ententes that set a destiny for all.

Aboard *Titanic* was the carefully crafted and scripted British world, but in miniature. Sixty years before, another ship, HMS *Birkenhead*, had struck a reef and sunk off the coast of South Africa. Aboard had been hundreds of British soldiers bound for the Cape Frontier War, together with their wives and children. There had not been enough lifeboats for all – there never were in those days – and for the first time the order was given that the spaces in those few available would be taken by 'women and children first'. This was what became known as 'the Birkenhead Drill'. Every woman and child survived, while hundreds of men went willingly into shark-infested water. In all, 430 were lost. Their sacrifice was soon legend. In Prussia, every soldier in every regiment was taught the story and left in no doubt they must seek to emulate such valour.

In 1912, on the slowly tipping deck of *Titanic*, men knew what was expected of them as well. Captain Edward Smith was heard quietly telling his officers, 'Be British, boys.'

Some rose to the challenge; others cowered and slunk off to the life-boats. J. Bruce Ismay, chairman of the White Star Line, was among them, safe in the company of the ladies. Most of the boats were still unfilled when they were rowed away.

As she sank, the ship's officers were greatly concerned that panic would break out among the third-class passengers. Just as governments across Europe feared the rise of organized labour movements, so the captain and crew of *Titanic* dreaded an uprising from the lower decks, the lower ranks.

Famously, the band played on. They were neither passengers nor crew but self-employed contractors, and it was up to them to decide their own fate. All chose to remain behind. Band-leader Wallace Hartley, from non-conformist stock in Lancashire, led them to the end. Legend has it that 'Nearer My God to Thee' was the last tune they played as the water rose about them.

It was a terrible portent of the years lying just ahead, out of sight. *Titanic* steamed hubristically towards the iceberg and Europe plunged heedlessly towards carnage. The middling-class men would take a heavy hit, drowning in droves, and it would be more of their kind – the Rupert Brookes, the Wilfred Owens and the like – who would be so disproportionately represented among the dead of the war to come.

Aboard *Titanic* a world was coming to an end. The British Isles her passengers knew, or thought they knew, were about to be changed for ever.

84

Somerled Square, Portree, Isle of Skye

The First World War – a terrible harrowing

PORTREE – *PORT RIGH* IN Gaelic, which means 'King's Port' – is the largest settlement on the island of Skye, off Scotland's west coast.

For the longest time, as Bonnie Prince Charlie would attest, Skye was accessible only by boat. Since 1995, however, the island has been connected to the mainland by a pale-grey bridge. Today's visitors merely continue their road journey along the A87 from the Kyle of Lochalsh on the mainland to the village of Kyleakin on Skye's east coast.

In my experience, Skye is an island washed in heaven's tears. The Cuillin – two mountain ranges that dominate the place – seem mostly wreathed in cloud, a grey shawl pulled tight around old and bony shoulders, and those clouds usually bring rain. For much of the time the sky feels low enough to touch, a grey ceiling held aloft only by the Cuillin's jagged peaks. On those occasions when the clouds surrender their hold and the light breaks through, it can feel as though someone has opened the sunroof and you are left blinking with surprise. Blue above and sun bright on ancient crags. Only then are hidden valleys cast briefly into sharp relief. Only then does the air feel clear, even thin, so that there is a brief illusion of being suddenly at altitude, closer to space. At such times, few and far between, a person might gasp at the rarefied majesty of it.

Most of my visits to Skye, too numerous to count now, have been rain-drenched. I often wonder if there isn't a sadness about the place, woven through the clouds. There may well be. Of all the regions and counties of

Britain, the Scottish Highlands were hurt worst of all by the First World War, losing more of their sons per head of population than any other.

Skye suffered a terrible harrowing. For all that the island often appears moody and maudlin, it is still an especially lovely place, in sunshine or in shadow. The true Cuillin – the Black Cuillin – is formed of gabbro, a dark, coarse-grained rock like basalt that forms when magma is trapped underground until it slowly cooks and then cools into a mass of infinitesimal crystals. The lesser, so-called Red Cuillin is made of a paler granite that has a reddish hue when the peaks are viewed from certain angles, in certain lights. Both ranges are the mere stumps of ancient, greater mountains thrown up by volcanic activity tens of millions of years ago and humbled since by time and glaciers. Their rocks seem freshly made or freshly shattered, though, so that their age-old agony is plain to see.

Portree is another 33 miles along that continuation of the A87 from Kyleakin and is a modestly pretty place. Down along the approach to the harbour and the pier, built by Thomas Telford, the houses are painted in soft pastels and are reminiscent of the fictional town of Balamory in the children's television show. Behind the harbour, on Bank Street, is the Royal Hotel. An earlier building on the same footprint housed MacNab's Inn, where in 1746 that ill-fated prince, Charles Edward Stuart, bade a final farewell to Flora MacDonald before fleeing to France in the aftermath of Culloden with his tail between his legs.

For anyone alive today, the First World War is surely too much to comprehend. Any summary of the events bookended by the years 1914 and 1918 is soon sunk in a no-man's-land morass of numbers – millions of dead soldiers, billions of spent bullets and shells, families without number damaged or destroyed. A visit to the most famous battlefields of the conflict, in France and Belgium, can be similarly overwhelming. Mostly it is a disorientating tour of peaceful farmland, punctuated only by stops at cemeteries filled with row upon row of white headstones. At the great charnel houses of the war – by Arras, Ypres, the Somme – the serried ranks of the dead beneath manicured lawns are too many to count, far less to make sense of.

And yet if we are to know the British Isles, then understand the Great

War we must. It is not just about history – rather it is necessary, vital even, to see that it was that conflict more than any other that changed everything here, and for ever. We are living in its aftermath. Decisions made during the fighting and in the stunned silence that followed remained hot beneath the feet like coal seams left smouldering after a pit fire. Flames reignite and blaze even now – far from the original conflagration but a consequence of its heat. Old wounds left rotten with corruption cause pain and suffering still. Countries flinch and writhe from time to time, tormented by the phantom agonies of limbs lost long ago. Bonds made between nations at that time – fused in the heat and strained to breaking point though they often are – still survive too.

Since both my grandfathers fought in and survived the First World War – my dad's dad in France, my mum's at Gallipoli – I have felt connected to it all for as long as I can remember. I am middle-aged in the second decade of the twenty-first century and yet I was raised by a man whose father came back from the Somme and then Passchendaele, and a woman whose father was shot through by friendly fire at Gallipoli. This is still astonishing to me, facts of my own existence that I struggle to assimilate.

The events of those four years have been described as a set of iron railings separating past from present. We can see through them to the world of before, but we can never reach the place those spars set aside, nor touch the blooms that flower untainted there.

Britain in the second decade of the twentieth century was still an Edwardian dreamland that had known no meaningful war since the threat of Napoleon and the immortal triumph of Waterloo more than a hundred years before, when fighting was waged on horseback by men clad in scarlet and wielding sabres, or by ranks of musketeers. The young men of those pre-war years were the sons of a Britain that had learned to take peace for granted. Even as conflict loomed, it seemed to promise nothing more than a grand adventure for clean-limbed, light-footed lads. All that happened between 1914 and 1918 obliterated every last shred of that former trusted and trusting existence as though it had never been.

In the spring of 2014, after many years spent struggling to make sense of the war, I followed the story of a company of Territorial soldiers who in 1915 set out from Portree for France and ultimately the Battle of Festubert. By the end of the telling of it, for a television documentary, I felt as close as I ever have to understanding what it meant to the people who lived through that war. They were natives of the world of before who passed through the fire, until they too could do no more than look back at their own callow past through those newly forged iron railings.

In the years before the war, the British government announced its intention to raise a new army reserve called the Territorials. Those part-time units, established the length and breadth of the country by most of the existing infantry regiments, were nicknamed 'Saturday Night Soldiers'. Originally planned only as home defence, they would soon volunteer to serve overseas as well.

In the west Highlands, the local Cameron Highland Regiment, swash-buckling and the stuff of legend, raised a battalion of Territorials too. One company was formed of men living in and around Portree. Life in the sur-rounding crofts was blighted by a squalid poverty most of us would struggle to imagine. Men and boys therefore signed up to the Territorials for the promise of a little bit of pay and the prospect of a two-week training break each year that was as good as a holiday.

Portree at that time was a community of no more than a thousand souls. Of the hundred or so men and boys who joined up, twenty-eight were neighbours living close by the town's harbour. To walk the streets and lanes of Portree now is to follow in their footsteps and the shortest of strolls passes home after home of those who marched away.

They were led by Captain Ronald MacDonald, a graduate of Glasgow University and the town's lawyer. Second in command was 45-year-old war-veteran Sergeant-Major Willie Ross, a champion of the island's high-land games. All the rest were young men or boys. William MacDonald was twenty-four and a clerk in the local estate office. From Mill Road came Sergeant Donald MacLeod, who worked in Captain MacDonald's law firm. Nearby was the Back Wentworth Street home of John Grant, twenty-two, a stableboy who lived with his mum. John Nicolson, twenty-four, was a fish-erman from Bayfield. Charles Sinclair, twenty-one, lived in a house on the harbour and worked for the ferry company MacBrayne's; it was said he could find his way across the black sea at night using only the chart in the sky above. William Turnbull, twenty-nine, was a plasterer from Bosville Terrace. From another house on the harbour came the stonemason's son, John MacFarlane. He was under-age when he joined up and would send many letters home to his mum from far away in France.

Soon after war was declared, those Portree men and the rest of the hundred or so making up their company marched along the harbour to meet the ship that would carry them off.

On 19 February 1915, after six months of training in Bedford in England, they departed for France. Young John MacFarlane's early letters home would reassure his mother that he and his comrades were 'enjoying the fun'. They fought the enemy first in the grounds of a farmhouse northeast of Neuve-Chapelle and then, on the night of 17 May, in fields by the village of Festubert. There, together with a company from Kingussie, close by their Skye home, and two more from Bedford, the Portree men were cut to pieces by the machine guns of a German Jäger – or hunter – battalion reinforced by two companies of Bavarian reservists. Soon after that awful night, thirteen telegrams arrived in Portree on the same morning, all of them bearing bad news.

Among the dead were William MacDonald; Donald MacLeod; William Turnbull; Company Sergeant-Major Willie Ross; John Grant; John Nicolson; John MacFarlane, the letter writer; Charles Sinclair, the celestial navigator. Their captain, Ronald MacDonald, had suffered a throat wound at Neuve-Chapelle and would die the following year, still in France.

Of the twenty-eight Portree neighbours who had marched away from hearth and home, ten died in a single night at Festubert. Only eight would survive the war. It is on those streets, and by that harbour, that the First World War seems closest to me.

At the heart of Portree is Somerled Square, lined now with shops and hotels. Somerled was a Viking – led by the summer, indeed, to Scotland a thousand years ago – and his descendants are the MacDonald clan. In pride of place in the square is the war memorial bearing the names of 104 Skye men who went to war and never came home. It is a neat hexagon of golden sandstone and rising from its centre is a thin white column of marble, topped with a lion. John MacFarlane's name is there among them all, of course – young Private John, who loved his mum and sent her as many letters as he could. His body was never found. It was his father, Thomas, the stonemason, who built the memorial, raising more stones towards the unflinching sky.

It was British government policy to bury the bodies of the dead wherever they fell, rather than bring them home. Too many carcasses, too much butchered meat. A necessity in view of the numbers, it did however add to the heartbreak, for now the grieving had no graves to visit. All over these islands memorials were raised, lightning rods for sadness or places for the laying of wreaths at least. If the bodies of the men and boys could not come home, then their names would be remembered in stone and bronze.

> For heroes have the whole earth for their tomb; and in lands far from their own, where the column with its epitaph declares it, there is enshrined in every breast a record unwritten with no other tablet to preserve it, except that of the heart.
>
> PERICLES, 431 BC

85

St John the Baptist Church, Great Rissington, Gloucestershire

The lost Souls

Down some cold field in a world uncharted
the young seek each other with questioning eyes.
They question each other, the young, the golden hearted,
of the world that they were robbed of in their quiet paradise.

HUMBERT WOLFE, 'Requiem: The Soldier', 1916

THE TOWNSFOLK OF Portree on Skye lost twenty men to the Great War. Just one family from the Cotswold village of Great Rissington lost five sons.

William Souls was a farm labourer. His wife was Annie and they lived with their six sons and three daughters in a tied house by the village green, across from the local school. The would-be soldiers were Frederick, the eldest boy, then identical twins Alfred and Arthur, born an hour apart, then Walter and finally Albert. The sixth son was Percy, who was too young to enlist. They all had jobs on the estate of the local manor house and in a different world would likely have lived out quiet lives. They could read and write, and there is a story that all the Souls boys carved their names into the beam of a barn thereabouts.

When Horatio Herbert Kitchener, the secretary of state for war, put out his call for volunteers for a new army – 'Your Country Needs You' – Albert and Walter were the first of the siblings to join up, in the 2nd Battalion,

Worcestershire Regiment. Albert, the youngest of the Souls to put on a uniform, was the first to die, on 14 March 1916.

Frederick and the twins, Alfred and Arthur, joined the 16th Cheshire Regiment. Fred was killed at the Somme in July 1916. His body was never found and he is listed among the missing of that battle, all seventy-odd thousand of them, on the towering memorial of stone and brick at Thiepval. Walter was wounded at the Somme the following month and died in a field hospital there.

Alfred was killed in April 1918, at Ploegsteert Wood. Arthur won the Military Medal during the desperate fight to hold the Villers-Bretonneux plateau, but died of wounds there in the same month as his twin.

Two centuries earlier, following the War of the Spanish Succession, John Churchill, 1st Duke of Marlborough, had been made a duke and given Blenheim Palace as the gift of a grateful nation. Annie Souls received a shilling a week for each of her dead boys. Tongues wagged about how well she must be doing on the extra income. Finally, the gossip was too much and the remnants of the family moved to nearby Great Barrington. It was there that Percy, the last and youngest of the Souls brothers, died of meningitis sometime after the war. Annie Souls never stood for 'God Save the King'.

Great Rissington is a lovely little village. At the time of the 2011 census it had a population of 367. There are houses of pale stone, roofed in mossy slate, behind neat hedges. There is a village green and a cricket ground. Some parts of the local pub, the Lamb Inn, are more than 300 years old. St John the Baptist Church was built in the twelfth century. It sits up high on a natural rise between, on one side, an avenue of trees leading to the manor house where the Souls boys worked before the war, and on the other a Georgian rectory. Inside the church, on the north wall opposite the main door, is the war memorial – a slab of grey stone bearing the names of the Souls brothers and seven other men and boys of Great Rissington who died in the war. Under the names is engraved a line from 1 Corinthians 15:54: 'Death is swallowed up in victory.'

Below the memorial are photographs, young men of long ago – the young, the golden-hearted. For the Souls family and for these islands, the toll of the Great War was too much to bear. A century later, a person might think we had moved on. A hundred years have passed right enough, but the scars are for all time.

86

The Cenotaph, Whitehall, London

Remembering the dead

FABIAN WARE TRIED to join the British Army at the outbreak of the First World War but at forty-five he was too old. Determined to do his bit, he kept harrying the authorities until he was eventually put in charge of a mobile ambulance unit in France. From the first he was not only appalled by the number of casualties but also troubled by the way no one was recording the graves of the dead. He began keeping note himself, and it was on account of his efforts that the organization now called the Commonwealth War Graves Commission came into existence. Today it looks after some 1.7 million graves in more than 150 countries.

When the war was over, Ware worked out that if all the soldiers who had died for Britain and her empire were somehow to rise from those graves and march four abreast past the Cenotaph in Whitehall, their procession would last three and a half days. It is impossible to know exactly how many men died in that war. Best guesses put the number of British and imperial dead at either just over or just under a million.

Alongside the unthinkable numbers, and impossible to bear, was the reality of the government's policy of burying men where they fell. Although logical, the absence of graves – places at which to mourn – made the dead seem even more lost.

A few weeks before the first anniversary of the Armistice with Germany, on 11 November 1919, it occurred to someone that perhaps there ought to be a focal point for the victory parade. The French had plans to build a memorial to march past, so surely Britain should have one too. The architect Edwin Lutyens was given two weeks to come up with a suitable design. The drawings he showed the prime minister, David Lloyd George, were for a Cenotaph – an empty tomb. Quickly accepted, his offering was rendered in wood and painted plaster on a site in Whitehall just around the corner from Downing Street. It was supposed to stand for just a few days, but Lutyens' creation proved impossible to surrender. Once the march-past had taken place, people stepped forward to lay flowers and wreaths around the base. It was unplanned, spontaneous. In the days that followed, more people came, more flowers. The government bowed to what they sensed was the public will, and the wood and plaster were replaced with Portland stone in time for the second anniversary in 1920. Just as the soldiers' graves in France and elsewhere had been marked with temporary crosses before being replaced with the familiar serried ranks of Portland stone, so that first iteration of the Cenotaph was transformed from something fleeting to something that would stay. By then the Unknown Warrior had been brought home and was en route to Westminster Abbey and his place among kings and queens. The gun carriage bearing his coffin was brought to a halt before the Cenotaph, still shrouded beneath Union flags and ready for its unveiling. King George V stepped out then and laid upon the coffin a wreath of red roses and bay leaves.

The need for places in the landscape where grief might be taken and laid down – places like the Cenotaph – inspired the greatest public art project in British history. It seemed every community that had known loss – and even those lucky few, called the Thankful Villages, that were giving thanks for the safe return of all their fathers and sons – commissioned the making of a war memorial. Since they could not have their men's bodies back, they would at least ensure their names were not forgotten. Now there are just shy of 40,000 memorials scattered across the land, remembering the dead of all wars.

The Cenotaph might seem a simple thing, little more than an outsize gravestone. It has no religious symbols, just one carved wreath at each end and a third on top of the sarcophagus. The only words on it are 'The Glorious Dead'. The subtleties of the design are therefore invisible to the eye.

The sides are not vertical but slightly tapered, so that if the lines were extended they would meet at a point a thousand feet in the air. Likewise the horizontal lines, which are arcs of a gigantic circle that would have its centre a thousand feet below ground. In this way the Cenotaph is reaching up into the sky and deep into the earth. In an article entitled 'The Secret of the Cenotaph', published in 1999, architect Andrew Crompton suggested the Cenotaph might have been designed to suggest the hilt of King Arthur's Excalibur, the invisible blade sheathed deep in the soil of England.

I have wondered if other inspirations are not detectable too, conscious or unconscious. In 1901 Lutyens was commissioned to restore Lindisfarne Castle for its owner, publisher Edward Hudson. To my eyes that finished shape upon its tapered thrust of rock seems like a glimpse, a premonition, of the outline of the Cenotaph to come. There is something too of the hulk of Glastonbury Tor with its terraced slopes rising and narrowing towards infinity. Folklore has it Glastonbury inspired the Neolithic builders of Silbury Hill, so it seems there is a shape that beguiles and recurs in these islands, again and again.

In Australia, the original inhabitants of the land have their songlines. By singing the right song, an Aboriginal person can find his or her way over tens or even hundreds of miles. Each song, older than old, lists all the landmarks in order – mountains, hills, rivers, valleys – so that the walker is never lost. In Kerala in India the locals perform a fire ritual. Holy men sing ancient songs that rise into the sky alongside the flames, songs they learned in childhood. Within the songs are sequences of sounds that cannot be translated into any known language and that are not even understood by the priests, who only learn them by rote. Linguists have suggested those parts, those cadences, are from a time before human language, when we communicated more like birds, and that their echoes have survived by being enfolded among great long screeds of other speech.

Surely we once had our own songlines here that led the way from hill to river and from river to valley and on and on. If the songs are lost and forgotten, then the land survives and the shapes still speak to our imaginations.

87

Scapa Flow, Orkney

A graveyard beneath the sea

SCAPA FLOW IS roughly cradled in calloused hands, between Orkney's Mainland and the South Isles of Graemsay, Hoy, South Walls, Flotta, South Ronaldsay and Burray. The Vikings found it a useful harbour and named it *Skalpafloi*, which means 'the Bay of the Isthmus'. It was first used by the British Admiralty during the Napoleonic Wars as a safe base for merchant ships bound for the Baltic ports, and then throughout the First World War as the home of the Grand Fleet. It was to the anchorage there, around 80 square miles of safe water, that the bulk of the surrendered German High Seas Fleet came as part of the Armistice in 1919. On 21 June that year, operating under the mistaken belief that the peace talks had broken down and that the British would surely seize the fleet, the German commander Ludwig von Reuter ordered his men to scuttle every ship. Of the seventy-four vessels anchored there, fifty-two went to the bottom, 20 fathoms down.

There is no denying Scapa Flow can be a bleak spot. Sheltered or not, a cold wind often blows, agitating the dull, grey water. At certain times of the year there is, too, a pervasive air of sadness or regret. A lovely face, but a broken heart.

Royal Navy sailors from home ports elsewhere found Scapa Flow a tough gig. Believe it or believe it not, but in those parts folk will tell you it was London boys who made the name, Scapa Flow, their own. So keen were they to get away somewhere else, anywhere else, they made a

rhyming slang of it – Scapa Flow . . . go. The more familiar 'scarper' therefore owes its coining to the blue lips and chattering teeth of disgruntled
cockney sailors of HM's Royal Navy.

It is a place associated with tragedy. Lord Kitchener sailed from there
aboard HMS *Hampshire* on 5 June 1916. He was bound for Russia on a
goodwill mission – or rather to put a bit of backbone into a people poised
for revolution – but never made it. The ship struck a mine and all but twelve
of her crew of more than 700 men were lost, Kitchener among them. HMS
Vanguard went down in Scapa Flow the following year when her muni-
tions exploded while she sat at anchor. Of over 840 men aboard, only two
survived.

Scapa Flow was still the Admiralty's preferred choice of safe harbour in
1939, at the outbreak of the Second World War. It was the appalling event
that unfolded there overnight between 13 and 14 October 1939 that had me
make my own first visit to the place in 2005.

Kenneth Toop and Arthur Smith were boy sailors in 1939, aged sixteen
and seventeen respectively, aboard the battleship HMS *Royal Oak*. A veteran of the First World War and the Battle of Jutland, she was one of just
two Royal Navy vessels in Scapa Flow that night, the rest of the fleet having
departed for ports elsewhere. The admiral of the home fleet, Charles
Forbes, had been unsettled by the sight of German reconnaissance aircraft
some days before and, fearing an airborne assault, had ordered most of the
ships to weigh anchor and move out. *Royal Oak* stayed behind to maintain
a defence of the anchorage and port.

Like a snake into a bird's nest, a lone German U-boat found its way in
on the night of the 13th and fired three torpedoes into *Royal Oak*'s hull.
She sank in a matter of minutes. Out of a crew of 1,400, 833 perished –
including around a hundred boy sailors under the age of eighteen.

I was with Arthur and Kenneth when they travelled to Scapa Flow for
the sixty-fifth anniversary of the loss. For Kenneth it was an annual pilgrimage, but Arthur had not been back to Orkney in all those years. I
watched him lay his wreath – leaning out from the deck of a ship that gently rose and fell above the site of the wreck. It was a deeply unsettling place
to be. Scapa Flow is relatively shallow and, while there was nothing to see

but grey water, we knew the wreck was not far below us, a great dead leviathan lying on her side just out of reach.

Afterwards I asked Arthur what thoughts had come to mind as he watched the poppies float away, and he said he had been remembering the lads he was with earlier on the evening of the 13th. As boy sailors, they were forbidden to smoke, but a handful of them had gathered in the dark on deck, hidden in the shadow of one of the ship's guns. Someone struck a match, but the flame blew out at once, stolen away by the wind. The same boy tried a second light, with the same result. When he struck a third match, the rest of them drew back. It was received wisdom, after all. Soldierly caution had it that a first light might catch a sniper's eye, a second would let him get a bead on the target, the third would put a head into the line of fire. It was just plain bad luck to accept the third light – and on Friday the 13th . . .

'But I took it,' said Arthur. 'I lit my cigarette on the third light. I survived, and all my friends there with me by the gun – they all died that night. So what does that tell you about luck?'

I had no answer.

Kenneth Toop died on 27 May 2015. Arthur Smith was the last of all, the last survivor of HMS *Royal Oak*. He died on 16 December 2016.

Every year Royal Navy divers replace the white ensign on the sunken stern of *Royal Oak*. One hangs there now, like an empty shroud, down in the cold, green water of Scapa Flow. In some people's minds that battleship is still on active service, still fighting the Second World War, and around the bay the memories of it all hang as still and forlorn as the ensign.

During that sixty-fifth service of remembrance, the local minister described how the loss of the ship and all those men and boys is ever present. 'The *Royal Oak* is never far from Orcadians' minds,' he said. 'There's not many days go by when we don't remember . . .'

Scapa Flow is a place of memory then. In some ways it is a tomb, where so many of the lost are cradled.

The steel, brass and other metals of the scuttled German fleet were a valuable source of scrap metal and during the 1920s and 1930s salvage teams came to Scapa Flow to reclaim the prize. Huge steel tubes with airlocks fitted inside were welded to the sunken hulls. Air was then pumped inside the wrecks, creating spaces where men could work. I have often imagined climbing down one of those umbilicals to crouch there in a bubble of breathable air on the seabed while the sea presses down and down.

Once the welders had made the hulls fully airtight, yet more air was pumped inside until the monsters rose from the deep like bad memories. Back on the surface they could be towed away and cut up. In all, nearly forty German ships were salvaged in this way. The rest, those that resisted recovery, remain where they have lain since the First World War, gradually being consumed and reclaimed by the sea herself. Only scuba divers visit them now.

The British Isles have been touched by so much, so many. A great deal of this book has been about how these lands have changed, and for the better, whatever has come here. In the case of Scapa Flow, it turns out the waters there have conspired to do quite the opposite, to put some things out of reach, making them untouchable, inviolable. This is part of our story too.

Ever since the United States of America began testing atomic bombs in the 1940s, the amount of background radiation in Earth's atmosphere has increased markedly. Whenever new steel is made, vast volumes of air are drawn into the blast furnaces. Since that air is contaminated by the radiation, so too is the steel those furnaces produce. Anyone wanting uncontaminated steel – for medical or scientific instruments perhaps, or for especially delicate pieces of kit required by those involved in the exploration of space – might turn to metal made before the A-bombs were dropped. As long as such steel is just sliced up and re-used as it is, and not made molten and therefore exposed to the inevitable contamination that happens in furnaces, then it stays clean.

For a while the world's richest source of such steel was that salvaged from the German High Seas Fleet in Scapa Flow. Among the many things NASA neither confirms nor denies is the suggestion that Scapa Flow steel has been to the moon, that yet more is aboard the *Voyager* twins hurtling now through the dark of interstellar space bearing messages for alien life, 13 billion miles from Orkney and from Earth.

Scapa Flow then, pilgrims . . . Scapa Flow . . . go . . .

88

John Brown's Shipyard, Clydebank, West Dunbartonshire

Clyde-built

THE SHIPBUILDERS OF Belfast did their best. Legend has it that when word of the loss of *Titanic* reached the men back at Harland and Wolff they said, 'Well, she was all right when she left us.' But everyone in the world knew the best ships in the world came out of one river and one river only – the Clyde, in Glasgow.

In a history lesson at school I learned the old line that 'Glasgow made the Clyde and the Clyde made Glasgow'. So it was. The river was wide and shallow at first, meaning ships had to moor downstream and put their cargoes aboard horse-drawn carts for onward passage. Once the tobacco trade was up and running, the tobacco lords demanded the river be made deep enough to allow their ships right up into the heart of the city. By the end of the eighteenth century, a succession of engineers, including John Smeaton and Thomas Telford, had succeeded in creating navigable channels that boosted Glasgow's circulation in the manner of stents introduced to a clogged artery.

Shipbuilding came next, and perhaps the most famous yard of the many that came to dominate the industry was John Brown's in Clydebank. Established in 1871 by J. and G. Thomson, it was taken over in 1897 by Sheffield steelmakers John Brown & Company. From the end of the nineteenth century and until the middle of the twentieth, the fitters, riveters and welders built and launched some of the most famous vessels that ever sailed the seas.

For all that the engineers had managed to make the Clyde deep enough for great ships to ply up and down, it was scarcely wide enough for launching them from its banks. John Brown's was able to take advantage of the presence, directly opposite their slipway, of a tributary of the Clyde called the Cart. Bigger, longer ships could nudge across the river, their bows entering the Cart and so giving them room to manoeuvre.

By 1907 the skyline at the yard was dominated by a massive crane they nicknamed 'Titan'. A landmark ever since, it enabled the lifting of the colossal engines and boilers required by ever larger and more powerful ships. It was John Brown's that built RMS *Lusitania*, flagship of the Cunard Line, and her sister ship RMS *Mauretania*. The looming First World War created an insatiable appetite for ships of another sort and, one after the other, down the slipway came legends like HMS *Hood*, HMS *Repulse* and scores more battlecruisers besides. Before the days of transatlantic flights, it was luxury liners that captured the imagination. Among the greatest of them all were RMS *Queen Mary* and RMS *Queen Elizabeth*, built during the 1930s. By the time the 1960s arrived, it was clear the world had changed, moved on, and that the shipyards of the Clyde were falling into irresistible decline. The last hurrah for John Brown's was the *Queen Elizabeth 2*, known to everyone as the *QE2*, launched in 1967.

The Clyde fell quieter and quieter after that. In 1968, John Brown's was merged with four others – Charles Connell and Co., Fairfield, Alexander Stephen and Sons, and Yarrow Shipbuilders – to create Upper Clyde Shipbuilders. It was well intentioned but a failure. Global market forces worked against the effort and in 1971 the consortium went into receivership. There was defiance from the unions and a legendary 'work-in' led by charismatic shop steward Jimmy Reid. It won publicity and public support, but it was not enough. There were further attempts to keep some blood flowing, but there was no fighting a future of bigger ships built elsewhere, in bigger yards for less money. John Brown's was sold to a company that refurbished oil rigs for the North Sea, but by 2001 that had closed too.

There was a time when a fifth of all ships in the world were built on the

River Clyde. It was commonplace, almost expected, that when a new ship was delivered to its owners it came with a Scottish engineer in its engine room. When Gene Roddenberry made the engineer aboard the Starship *Enterprise* a grumpy Scotsman called Montgomery 'Scotty' Scott (albeit played by Canadian actor James Doohan), he was paying homage to tradition and to a whole way of life.

I grew up hearing about 'Clyde-built men' – skilled, tough, hardworking. There is no such thing now, no such men. The river is mostly silent, passing unnoticed like time itself. The old yards are graveyards of rusting metal.

John Brown's, with Titan rearing up alongside the old slipway, is a tourist attraction now. Where men once worked, now the likes of us can only stand in its shadow and consider what once was but will not come again.

89

Blenheim Palace, Woodstock, Oxfordshire

The birthplace of Winston Churchill

THESE ISLANDS CANNOT care if we live or die. The rock is moved and shaped only by time, pressure and the rest of the elemental forces of nature. The British Isles are real, actually *there*, but the nations etched into maps of them do not exist in any absolute sense. The United Kingdom of Great Britain – England, Scotland, Wales – and Northern Ireland; and the Republic of Ireland and the rest of the smaller islands: like every other nation on the planet these are just figments of our collective imagination. They exist only in as much as millions, billions of people have agreed to believe they do. A city is only a collection of buildings, streets and open spaces unless the people living within its perceived boundaries accept the suggestion a Glasgow or a Manchester or a Dublin or an Aberystwyth or wherever is greater than the sum of the parts. In the same way, a nation is only a dream shared by its inhabitants.

Sometimes the dream, however old and long-running, faces an existential threat. During the 1930s there arose just such a threat in the form of the chancellor of the German Reich, Adolf Hitler, and the Nazis that followed in his train. Left unchallenged, Hitler and his ilk would have done away with the Britain that had existed till then. These British Isles would still have been there, but not the notions of identity that had been established by Britons in the preceding centuries. Hitler would have brushed all of that away like so much chalk dust off a blackboard.

In the end he was stopped and put away by millions of people from many different countries, all acting in concert and dreaming a dream in which he and others like him were gone. The first population to dream that dream were the British – and the Briton from whom the dream sprang, fully formed and quick with life, was Winston Churchill. He could hardly stop Hitler on his own. Neither could the population of Great Britain. But his was the first voice that said 'No', and it was his stubborn belief – and that of most of our predecessors – in the rightness of their thinking that inspired the dream that was eventually dreamed by the necessary millions.

Churchill, the son of Lord Randolph Churchill and Jennie Jerome, was born on 30 November 1874 in Blenheim Palace, the home of his paternal grandfather, John Spencer-Churchill, 7th Duke of Marlborough, in the market town of Woodstock in Oxfordshire. Given what he would become, what he would do, the palatial setting might seem an appropriate starting point. Blenheim Palace had been conceived as a gift of thanks from the nation to John Churchill, 1st Duke of Marlborough – the same that had so distinguished himself fighting for his king during the Monmouth Rebellion of 1685. It had been the victory he choreographed at the 1704 Battle of Blenheim, in Bavaria, the most decisive clash of the War of the Spanish Succession, that made him a legend.

King Charles II of Spain had died in 1700, leaving his vast demesne to his grand-nephew, Philip, Duke of Anjou. Since Philip was a grandson of King Louis XIV of France, his inheritance of Charles's empire raised the spectre of a world dominated by the House of Bourbon. Britain, Austria and others had been well aware of the imminent threat posed by the Spanish Succession and diplomatic efforts had been progressing for years with a view to breaking the feared monolith into smaller parts that might be shared out among other candidates. The roll of the dice Charles made from his deathbed took everyone by surprise and war, as is so often the case, was the result. Hostilities began in 1701 and would rumble and thunder on for thirteen years. Blenheim came early in the proceedings, but the combined military genius of Churchill, acting in concert with the similarly able Prince Eugene of Savoy, made a wound from which the French would never fully recover. It was in recognition of his success in humbling a French army that had hitherto regarded itself as invincible that Churchill was awarded his grand pile at Woodstock.

Blenheim Palace was built on the site of a former royal manor. Queen Anne had Parliament set aside nearly £250,000 for the construction job – a massive sum. Churchill's wife, Sarah, a close friend of the queen, was a fan of the distinguished architect Sir Christopher Wren, but her husband had struck up an acquaintanceship with one John Vanbrugh, an up-and-coming playwright who had lately also been dabbling in architecture. With his fellow architect Nicholas Hawksmoor, he had begun cooking up the grandiose wedding cake that would be Castle Howard in North Yorkshire. The new duke fancied something at least as good, but his choice of Vanbrugh put his wife in the huff. Happy wife, happy life, they say – but while Churchill was a master tactician on the battlefield, he was less able regarding some of the intricacies of being a husband. Vanbrugh embarked upon the task of creating the masterpiece expected of him, but for the newcomer Blenheim was a poisoned chalice. The extravagance of his concept was soon putting all sorts of noses out of joint. All too quickly he fell from favour and was eventually put off the job altogether. He hardly worked as an architect again.

Hawksmoor carried on alone, weathering storms of his own. Parliament baulked at the cost. Sarah Churchill fell out with the queen, so the project became a Cinderella. The house itself was finally completed only in the early 1730s and has divided architectural opinion ever since.

Vanbrugh planned the original gardens as well, but the present park is the work of Lancelot 'Capability' Brown, who was employed by the 4th Duke in the late 1700s to create the more natural look for which Blenheim is now so famous. The estate sprawls over 2,000 acres. The house alone covers 7. Within the 187 rooms are housed some of the most important collections of art assembled anywhere. The library shelves groan beneath the weight of 10,000 books, many of great historical significance in their own right.

Blenheim Palace is a vast Baroque confection that inspires awe, wonder, love, hate and every other response in between. It is the only accommodation not lived in by a blood royal or a bishop that is accurately described as a palace. Grander than any home ever inhabited by a British monarch – Buckingham Palace appears positively modest by comparison – it drew a gasp of astonishment from King George III when he visited in 1786. Turning to his wife, Queen Charlotte, he is said to have whispered, 'We have nothing to equal this.' Herr Hitler was so enamoured of the thought of making it his home after what he considered to be his inevitable victory that he apparently ordered the Luftwaffe not to bomb it.

Here, then, is where Winston Leonard Spencer-Churchill was born and spent his first years. His relationship with his parents was distant at best. He was unhappy at school and needed three attempts to pass the entrance examination for Sandhurst, though in later years his academic skills shone through. His disasters are well known. As First Lord of the Admiralty he took the blame for the disaster of Gallipoli in the First World War. He fell from favour within the Conservative Party in the early 1930s and endured what he called his 'wilderness years'. He was gradually rehabilitated and at the outbreak of the Second World War was reappointed to the post of First Lord of the Admiralty. It was when the prime minister, Neville Chamberlain, and so many others failed to understand the reality of Hitler and the Nazis that Churchill stood alone as a defiant voice. When Chamberlain resigned in May 1940, Churchill was eventually chosen to replace him.

He was the only man capable of saying and doing all that needed to be said and done. He was sixty-five years old when he was made prime minister, yet he seemed like a man half that age. Before and after the Battle of Britain he stood in the Commons to make the speeches that inspired the belief that victory, like happiness, was to be pursued. He said he had nothing to offer but blood, toil, tears and sweat. He vowed he and his fellow Britons would fight on the seas and oceans . . . on the beaches . . . in the streets. He looked up into the blue at darting Spitfires and Hurricanes and recognized the priceless endeavour of the few.

There are carefully laid-out walks through the grounds of Blenheim and some of them follow the footsteps of her most famous son. There are glimpses to be had of the man he was, before and after the legend his people made of him. The great love of his life was Clementine Hozier and it was in the Temple of Diana in the palace grounds that he proposed to her. Legend has it he almost blew his chance. He had overslept and it had been down to his cousin, the 9th Duke, to take her riding in order to delay her return to London. He got to her just in time and they were happily married until his death at the age of ninety.

Less than 2 miles from the palace is the village of Bladon and the graveyard of St Martin's Church, where he lies buried in the family plot. These two locations are the bookends of his life.

Whatever else you might think of it, Blenheim is undoubtedly grand, a leviathan. Churchill was grander yet. Vincent Mulchrone, the finest journalist of his generation, described him as having become a permanent, immovable part of these islands. After attending the great man's lying-in-state in January 1965 he wrote: 'Two rivers run silently through London tonight and one is made of people. Dark and quiet as the night-time Thames itself, it flows through Westminster Hall, eddying about the foot of the rock called Churchill.'

And so it goes.

90

Slapton Sands, Devon

Exercise Tiger – sacrifice on the road to victory

But I have dreamed a dreary dream
Beyond the Isle of Skye
I saw a dead man win a fight
And I think that man was I.

'The Battle of Otterburn', c.1550

As EARLY AS 1940, Winston Churchill made it plain that he and his fellow Britons would never surrender. These islands were to be defended, he said, at whatever cost. Beaches and landing grounds, fields and streets – wherever the fight, the nation would be made ready. Adrift in the North Sea, the British Isles became as a lone battleship under attack from the air, from the surface of the sea and from below.

Battleship Britain endured, weathered the storms and the bombs, and Nazi Germany was defied for long enough. Gradually the Allies began to prepare to turn the tide and push Hitler back the way he had come and into oblivion. By the end of 1943 plans were well under way for the invasion and liberation of Europe. The most important Allied offensive of the Second World War – Operation Overlord – was soon to be unleashed. It would begin with amphibious landings on a string of five beaches in Normandy, where a great wave of Allied troops would seek to gain a foothold on territory occupied for so long by the enemy. Hitler knew such an attack must come sooner or later. He had prepared every conceivable obstacle. For the

Allies there might be only one chance, so preparation and rehearsal were of vital importance.

The US Army planned to land thousands of men on a stretch of the Cotentin Peninsula they called Utah Beach. It would be the westernmost of the five D-Day beaches. The rest of the intended footholds, travelling eastwards, were Omaha (also to be taken by the Americans), Gold (by the British), Juno (by the Canadians) and Sword, last and most easterly in the line and also a British target.

The Allies knew the lie of the land they intended to assault. From the air and through covert operations by sea they had reconnoitred and surveyed. At Utah, the attacking soldiers would splash ashore on to a long, narrow curl of sand and shingle. Beyond the beach were dunes topped by a coastal road. Behind the dunes the Germans had flooded the low-lying land to create an obstacle for any would-be liberators heading inland. The first challenge for the War Office, then, was to identify somewhere in the British Isles that mimicked, as far as possible, the enemy-held terrain. Any simulation had to be as realistic as possible.

At Slapton Sands in Devon the topography was so similar to that of Utah Beach it might have been heaven-sent for the purpose. Behind the 2-mile stretch of beach lay a broad strip of grassy dunes topped by a road – and beyond that Slapton Ley, the largest freshwater lake in the south-west of England.

As the autumn of 1943 wore on, rumours spread through the nearby village of Slapton. No one knew for sure what might be afoot, but military types had been seen sniffing around the whole area. There on England's south coast they were on the front line, after all. Something was up. Sure enough, in the November of that year every household received a letter giving six weeks' notice to pack up and move out. Every home, business and farm was being requisitioned by the army – no exceptions. Some 46 square miles of territory, including 180 farms, were to be emptied of all human life and livestock. Many residents had never been away from home before, but now they were being told to grab their things and move on out, without any guarantee of when or even if they would be allowed to return.

By Christmas 1943 Slapton was a ghost town and the army moved in.

Around 23,000 Allied soldiers were soon to take part in a full-scale rehearsal for the invasion of Utah Beach.

During April 1944 the men practised their drills – forming up in their lines and boarding the vessels, called tank landing ships (known as LSTs), that would ferry them directly on to the Normandy beaches. On 27 April a drill with live ammunition was held, codenamed Exercise Tiger.

From within his tent close by Hampton Court Palace, home to kings and queens, General Dwight D. Eisenhower, the Supreme Allied Commander, had insisted the operation at Slapton Sands had to be as close as possible to the real thing in every way. Garbled messages and late changes of plan, however, meant thousands splashed ashore at the wrong time. Friendly fire claimed many lives.

In the early hours of the following morning yet more thousands boarded their LSTs ready to rehearse a full-scale landing. Each vessel carried hundreds of men. The Channel was known to be a hunting ground for German patrols operating out of the French port of Cherbourg and the whole exercise was supposed to have been covered and protected by vessels of the Royal Navy. Yet more mistakes and miscommunication, however, allowed a pod of German E-boats – fast moving and armed with torpedoes to sniff out the presence of so many vessels. The Germans were spotted right enough, and a covering vessel radioed a warning, but yet another mix-up meant the LSTs were using the wrong frequency and so heard nothing. The E-boats loosed their torpedoes, sinking two LSTs and the hundreds of men aboard them. At least one other was struck and set alight, and confused accounts in the aftermath suggested damage to more vessels besides. Men burned to death within blazing vessels. Other soldiers ended up in the dark water of the Channel, which in April was cold enough to kill. Weighed down with full kit, they found it impossible to stay afloat. Many of those wearing regulation life vests had put them on incorrectly. Hundreds drowned.

Hurried orders were issued, on the correct frequency at last, and the rest of the vessels returned to shore. The skipper of at least one chose instead to hunt for injured men and pulled as many as 140 souls from the water, saving them from hypothermia. Several high-ranking officers carrying top-secret details of the plans for D-Day itself had died with their men and in the immediate aftermath of the tragedy there were fears the Germans might recover a body and find the crucial information. The possibility of cancelling Operation Overlord was very real until miraculously every man who had been issued with the plans was accounted for, dead or alive.

Exercise Tiger was ill-starred from the outset, but with D-Day so close and so secret, details of all that unfolded on and near that beach in Devon were buried deep and left for other days. Even now there is controversy and debate about the number of casualties. Official figures on both sides of the Atlantic make the death toll 749, but there are those who say it was much higher; yet others say that we will never know for sure how many perished that night.

Men who survived, shaken and traumatized, still took part in D-Day itself on 6 June 1944. In a crushing irony, US losses on Utah Beach were fewer than 200, meaning far more men died in the rehearsal than in the real attack. But blighted or not, Exercise Tiger was necessary training. Without efforts of this sort at places like Slapton Sands, and the bitter lessons learned, who knows how many more might have died on D-Day.

In time, the people of Slapton were allowed back to their homes. All that had happened out there in the bay was quietly and deliberately forgotten. During the 1970s, however, word circulated about fishing boats having problems with snagged nets. Locals investigated and found the cause was a US Sherman tank, lost in Exercise Tiger and rusting on the seabed. One Slapton resident, Ken Small, found out what he could about the tragedy and set about bringing the story back into the light. It was largely due to his efforts that a team was put together to recover the tank and make a memorial of it. It sits now by the village of Torcross, at the south end of the beach.

The terrible wounds of the Second World War are all around these islands. It was only through sacrifices such as the one made at Slapton Sands that this country survived to cradle the generations that live here now.

91

Alderney, Channel Islands

Occupation

ALDERNEY SITS 60 miles off the south coast of England. Of all the Channel Islands it is the one closest to Britain. It is also the closest to France and when looked at on a map it does indeed seem strange that it and they belong to us and not to them. Nestled in the shadow of Normandy's Cotentin Peninsula, they certainly appear more French than English, in terms of their geography if nothing else.

That said, the Channel Islands have been jealously guarded by English kings and queens and British governments for hundreds of years. Only once in a thousand years have they been wrested away – by Adolf Hitler from 1940 to 1945.

The Führer had had bigger dreams. He had hoped to invade mainland Britain, but in spite of the pounding administered by the Luftwaffe, intended to soften us up and break our resolve, his enterprise had come to nought. As every schoolchild used to know, in September 1940 the Royal Air Force held the line, Hurricanes and Spitfires up in 'the burning blue', and Hitler's invasion was first postponed and then abandoned altogether.

Thwarted, he clung on to what fragments he already had. The Channel Islands had been invaded on 30 June 1940 and, having got himself a toe-hold on British territory, Hitler set about digging in like a tick into the flank of a sheep. Around a third of the population, some 30,000 people, had been evacuated from Jersey and Guernsey in the months before the Germans took control. The rest of these islands' populations remained, though, and faced four years under occupation. Some drew close to the invaders, even collaborated with them. It was war and a daily fight for survival, and there seems little point or justification in judging them now.

Little Alderney, 3½ miles long and 1½ wide, was a different story. As the Nazis bore down on the place, all but a handful of the 1,500 residents boarded ships and fled to Britain, where they lived out the duration of the war. Perhaps half a dozen, no more, remained behind, determined to try to get on with the lives they had always known.

The island, then, presented all but a blank canvas for the Germans and upon it they drew something ugly. Since Hitler was determined to hold on to the Channel Islands at all costs, he expended massive effort fortifying Alderney in particular. A 3,000-strong garrison arrived and work was quickly under way, building gun emplacements, forts, barracks, great walls and the rest of the defences needed to keep out any threat of liberation by the British. The hard work, however, was not done by German soldiers. Instead, thousands of Jews, Russian prisoners of war, political prisoners and others deemed undesirable to and expendable by the Reich were brought to Alderney to serve as slave labour. Their efforts were overseen by Organisation Todt, the Third Reich's own civil and military engineering unit. Driven on by beatings and fed a starvation diet, the slaves laboured to meet Hitler's demands that Alderney become part of the 'Atlantic Wall' of defences designed to protect his gains in the west while the bulk of his fighting forces took on the Soviets in the east. A bewilderingly complex array of armoured towers, bunkers and casements spread across the island like psoriasis. For a while it was the most heavily defended few square miles of territory in Hitler's hands. For uncounted numbers of slaves, it was a long, slow march to death.

The Channel Islands were liberated in 1945 and steadily the evacuees came back to pick up where they had left off. For the British government, the Nazi occupation of the islands had been an embarrassment. The less said the better. There was ill-feeling, to be sure, towards those who had collaborated, but it had to be smothered for the greater good. Women who had taken up with German soldiers and willingly borne their children were called 'Jerrybags' and shunned by many who returned; some were beaten, tarred and feathered. For the most part, though, it was deemed more important simply to move on, suppress as much as possible, pretend the worst of it had never happened.

Most unspeakable was what had happened to the slaves. For a long time it was acknowledged only that some few hundreds had died on Alderney on account of mistreatment by their captors. More recently, however, there have been convincing claims that the death toll may have run into the thousands, perhaps even the tens of thousands. The SS, Hitler's elite, were on Alderney and oversaw two concentration camps, at Sylt and Norderney. Records kept by MI19, transcripts of interviews with survivors, reveal details of at least two crucifixions, accounts of men hunted with dogs, finished off with knives and the butts of rifles, death made commonplace. There are known graves of nearly 400 who died, but rumours persist regarding many more whose bodies may have been disposed of at sea.

Whatever the truth, the thought of it all is chilling. Alderney is quiet now, and peaceful. The rightness that was there before has been returned. Seeds buried deep, which waited through Hitler's winter, were ready to put forth new life and have done so. Those who know the island best would live nowhere else. They talk about 'the Alderney feeling' and mean by that a unique character, a sense of safety and of home. The rightness lies in the reclaiming of that which was ours, briefly lost, and made ours again. The flowers are plentiful and lovely, so too the beaches. Tourists visit, by air and by sea. It is a safe place and kindly. There has been a mending. But it would be wrong if ever there was a forgetting.

The concrete is still there, the rusting steel breaking through from within like truth. It is hard to imagine a time when it might be gone. Maybe the marks made between 1940 and 1945 are indelible, like a number tattooed on a survivor's wrist. When the sun is lost in cloud, there is a feeling of a too-thin blanket stretched over something unbearably sad. Among the most sinister-looking of all the alien constructions is the observation tower they call 'the Odeon'. Like a gigantic version of Robocop's helmet, it looms on a cliff top in the north-east of the island, ever watchful. We must be watchful.

Alderney is a reminder of how close Hitler came. We try to pretend the horrors of his Reich were contained on mainland Europe, and for the most part they were. But just out of sight and on British territory men were starved, tortured and beaten to death, their bodies hung up for monuments.

What we have here in these British Isles is precious and fragile. We have come close to losing it and we must remain on guard.

92

Orford Ness, Suffolk

Operation Cobra Mist and the Cold War

SIR FRANCIS DRAKE's flagship the *Golden Hind*, built at Aldeburgh on the Suffolk coast, had reached out into the unknown, far beyond the horizon. Its bold and daring exploits are hard to relate to the quiet backwater left behind today. Further south lies the shingle spit of Orford Ness, more peaceful still. For the longest time the area was mostly given over to grazing cattle.

During the First World War it was that atmosphere of isolation, of a place tucked away from prying eyes, that attracted the attentions of the military. Their presence there was secretive from the start, and on that thin, outstretched finger known as 'the Island' the men in lab coats set about developing and testing all the new-fangled gadgetry of the day. The Royal Flying Corps practised thereabouts and one Everard Calthrop was an early visitor. A railway engineer and inventor, he had designed a prototype parachute he called the 'Guardian Angel'. It drew interest from pilots for obvious reasons, but the top brass decided such a contraption might take the spirit out of the chaps – make 'em more inclined to quit the fight and bail out early. (It was for this same reason that sailors had been discouraged from learning to swim – so they would pay more attention to the welfare of the ship.) Calthrop was sent on his way.

Sir Robert Watson-Watt conducted some of his early experiments with radar at Orford Ness in the 1930s, and during the 1950s the island saw tests on Britain's first atomic bomb, called Blue Danube.

All of it, all the secrecy and strange lights and noises, the comings and goings at every hour of the day and night, year after year, gave Orford Ness an unmistakable mystique. Soon enough local rumours included talk of the search for UFOs. When people were not discussing flying saucers, they speculated about death rays or invisible beams that could stop car engines. But arguably the most mysterious of all the projects hidden behind the veil of secrecy at Orford Ness was the one called Cobra Mist.

Folk are always most fascinated by what they cannot see and there is more than one way to peer into the invisible. Sir Francis Drake did it from the deck of a timber ship built just up the coast. Nearly four centuries later, from 1967, Europe's largest shingle spit was home to an ambitious plan hatched by US Army and Air Force boffins to reach out into the unknown once more. The Cold War was at its height and amid all the paranoia was genuine fear of imminent nuclear war. What the Americans wanted was the space to develop an experimental form of radar called Over-the-Horizon detection (OTH). For populations fearing the arrival from over that horizon of nuclear missiles fired by the Soviets, or planes carrying something similar, time was the crucial factor. The more advance warning of an attack that might be given, the better.

Lorries and landing craft transported thousands of railway sleepers on to Orford Ness, where they were laid down in the marshes to create long corduroy roads over which heavy lorries might be driven with the rest of the materials needed. Soon enough an installation of the sort that might have featured in a James Bond film had taken shape. At its heart was an anonymous building clad with corrugated metal as pale and grey as the sky and the North Sea beyond. Radiating out from the dull cubes and rect-angles of windowless structures was a vast array of radio masts, some as much as 180 feet tall and laid out in the shape of an open fan. Over all of it – a site covering some 700 acres – was a fine protective mesh.

Access was restricted to US military personnel. In darkened rooms, scientists and technicians watched screens and monitors, carefully analys-ing radio signals that had been sent out into the void, bouncing like invisible ping-pong balls across the atmosphere. The objective of Cobra Mist, of Over-the-Horizon detection, was to pinpoint the location of aircraft and ships many thousands of miles away. The hope was, quite literally, to see round corners.

Despite six years of work and a cost of more than $150 million, however, Cobra Mist was a failure. No matter how they adjusted and fine-tuned their instruments, the signals received by the scientists were always crowded out by background noise – some sort of interference that made them next to useless. On more than one occasion they were sure they spotted incoming missiles when there was none. Orford Ness had long been a place of rumours and soon the men of Cobra Mist were suspecting foul play. Was the interference coming from some Russian trawler, or a submarine maybe, sitting just out of sight and broadcasting the troublesome clutter? No one knew and no one ever found out. In June 1973 Cobra Mist was abandoned. More recently part of one of the buildings was used by the BBC for transmitting the World Service.

The site still has a queer air about it, a sense of something strange. Some of the radio masts are still there, like the desiccated bones of giant insects. In their shadow and in the vicinity of the buildings, the Cold War is easy to imagine.

93

Les Écréhous, by Jersey, Channel Islands

A place of magic

SOME PLACES MATTER to the human soul for reasons as subtly elusive as a dropping tide. Five or six miles north-east of the Channel Island of Jersey lie Les Écréhous. At high tide the place amounts to just three tiny islands – large rocks, really – upon which perch a clutch of brightly painted shacks and tiny buildings. The name might sound French but in fact it's made of two words of Old Norse – *sker*, meaning 'reef', and *holm*, meaning 'island'.

When the tide is in, the dry land is reduced to a patch just a few tens of yards on each side. There have been permanent residents from time to time – even one, a Jersey-born fisherman named Philippe Pinel, who built himself a cottage on the smallest islet, La Blanche, styled himself king and lived there for half a century. Legend has it he was visited by Queen Victoria and that the two monarchs exchanged gifts – a seaweed basket of fish for her and a coat of blue for him. Nowadays the little buildings and shacks are holiday homes for a lucky few. There is no fresh water and all supplies must come by boat. But the limitations are utterly – utterly – overwhelmed by the ethereal wonder of it all. Magic is hard to glimpse, but there on those tiny islets a person might catch the odd glimmer out of the corner of an eye.

When the tide falls away – and around Jersey the tidal range is as much as 40 feet – an expanse of sand and rocks two thirds of a mile wide is revealed to the light and air. The experience of stepping out on to dry white sand that was, only moments before, the bottom of the English Channel is enough to rejuvenate the weariest heart. Lobster and crabs, caught out by the change from wet to dry, seek hiding places among the rocks or by burrowing into the sand. In the rock pools, cuttlefish attempt the same trick with clouds of ink. Everywhere the water is as clear as tears, a tracery of a myriad channels and lagoons.

Since the place feels like somewhere imagined by Robert Louis Stevenson or J. M. Barrie, it is no surprise to find the isles were, from at least the seventeenth century, a hideaway for smugglers. Fires were lit when the coast was clear, a signal to co-conspirators on Jersey and on mainland France that precious items of contraband might be exchanged.

Given that France is only 8 miles away, it might seem strange to find Les Écréhous governed by Jersey, and therefore us, but the same constitutional oddness that makes the Channel Islands British also confers the honour upon those few specks of granite. It is all a leftover from the back and forth of the ownership of the Duchy of Normandy, the dealings of kings and queens of England and France, and on a place as filled with wonder as Les Écréhous the details hardly seem worth bothering with. That said, as recently as 1994 a bunch of militant French fishermen, Norman separatists mostly, and eccentrics seeking the restoration of the French monarchy attempted to reclaim the place. Police from Jersey were hastily dispatched and there was some argy-bargy concerning the right to raise a tricolor on the flagpole on Maitr'Ile, the largest of the rocks. It all came to nothing in the end – in fact, the matter was peacefully settled over a picnic in the afternoon sun.

I went there by yacht and kayak, and I suggest anyone else wishing to visit do something similar. There is a former Customs House on the middle-sized islet of Marmotière. There is even a paved courtyard, like half a badminton court, called 'the Royal Square'. If no one objects, that might be the best place to unroll a sleeping bag for an overnight stay.

If you can only choose one destination from this book, one place worth a visit, make it Les Écréhous. Your heart will thank you.

94

St Bride's Church, Fleet Street, London

Britain's obsession with news

You cannot hope to bribe or twist
(thank God!) the British journalist.
But, seeing what the man will do
unbribed, there's no occasion to.

HUMBERT WOLFE, 'The British Journalist', 1930

ALONG WITH MUCH else, most of London's rivers have been squeezed underground. Out of sight they run, tributaries of the Thames and the Lea made dark by the filth of the city above and pressed into one foul service after another. The Fleet is, or was, the largest of them. On its way to join the Old Father beyond Blackfriars Bridge it suffers all manner of indignities. By the time it passes beneath the east end of Fleet Street, at the road junction known as Ludgate Circus, it is just another sewer.

The ancient, busy thoroughfare that bears the river's name (from the Anglo-Saxon *fleot*, meaning 'a tidal inlet') was for long home to the most prominent of the nation's newspapers. *The Times, Telegraph, Sun, Daily Express*, Reuters News Agency and others besides all had their offices there. Even now, long after the last of them has abandoned the place to shops and sandwich bars, Fleet Street remains a byword for the British Press. More specifically, it recalls what the British Press was, for good or ill, before everything changed.

All that Fleet Street became in the nineteenth and twentieth centuries began in the first year of the sixteenth when German immigrant Wynkyn de Worde, an acolyte of William Caxton, set up a printing shop next to St Bride's Church. It was books that de Worde was about then, and among other places he had a stall in no lesser venue than the churchyard of Old St Paul's Cathedral. The newspapers came later, rags by any measure. By 1702 the capital's first, the *Daily Courant*, was publishing in Fleet Street. Next to take up residence, in 1769, was the *Morning Chronicle*. There were already coffee houses and pubs scattered along both sides of the street and the first of the papers traded mostly in the gossip and tittle-tattle picked up in those meeting places. Gossip or not, the so-called 'penny press' proved popular and they bred like rats.

Where water had flowed, powering mills and filling wells before joining the Thames at a wide-mouthed inlet, now it was words – a veritable torrent. The British people, as it turned out, were obsessed with news, couldn't get enough of it. Soon the inhabitants of these islands were mystifying visitors and commentators with their daily consumption. The British were, by an order of magnitude, the most voracious buyers and readers of newspapers in Europe. Our relations across the Atlantic have been hearty consumers too, but their home-grown press has never come close to offering the variety of coverage taken for granted here. We are a fascinated people – nosy neighbours. Other people's lives have been our oxygen and, while often we have meddled directly, we have always watched and wondered and known what's best.

The river of words flowed hard and fast. There was always partisanship – with papers serving and circulating the emergent ideologies of the left, right and centre. The *Daily Mail* was blatantly fascist in the 1930s, even if most Londoners laughed at Oswald Mosley and his followers. For a while the *Daily Mirror* offered up a left-wing bias, just as objectionable to many, as a counterweight, but its presence has diminished, as has that of all print media. The *Independent* wafted around the middle ground for a while, preachy and pious by turns, before waltzing off in a huff to digital irrelevance.

The Fleet Street that was died in the 1980s. The unions had knowingly extracted the Michael for too long, fouling their own nests. They had claimed countless sacks of pay for non-existent members, with names like D. Duck and M. Mouse; they had worked to rule and downed tools on a whim, often just because they could. It was shaming and a shame. A movement born of honesty and pride turned inside out. With the support of the prime minister, Margaret Thatcher, press baron Rupert Murdoch waged war on all of it. In no time, and in spite of the shop stewards' best menaces and the howls of their boo boys, Wapping and Canary Wharf in the city's East End replaced 'the Street' as the heart of the British newspaper business. There was more to it than industrial strife and bottle-throwing, of course. New technologies had arrived in the 1980s too, the first steps along a road that would soon lead to the behemoth of the world wide web.

In 1979 Paul Weller and the Jam had sung about the public wanting what the public gets. By the end of the next decade us proles were being served up celebrity gossip and diets, soap-star bad-hair-days and post-gym sweat-stains whether we wanted them or not. Anyone addicted to the red-tops was left punch-drunk.

But whatever else they would eventually stoop to, the 1990s Press, tabloid and broadsheet alike, would never hunt anyone as determinedly as they did Diana Spencer, the hapless soul who stepped into the cross-hairs of the Royal Family in 1980 and so into the sights of the media. With Diana – Lady Di, Princess Di, the People's Princess – a line was crossed and there was no going back. Much of the front end of the news has been dominated by obsessive scrutiny of the famous ever since. Back in the 1980s and 1990s, however, the paparazzi had a bona fide royal princess to hunt down. They would never again have it so good.

Diana and the Press brought out the worst in each other, as we well know. While the whole world of journalism was changed for ever by the coupling, hers ended altogether amid the flashes of some of the same cameras that had trailed her for most of her adult life. No lessons were learned in the aftermath, not really. The river made first of words and then of pictures had spilled its banks by then. Instead of a princess, in the years since then it has been the stars of the screen – particularly reality television – that are routinely swallowed whole and spat out by the leviathan that swims in its shallows. And in the end, the media has evolved into a different, lower animal that has its natural habitat in the unedited, unfiltered and indiscriminate world of online.

Although the journalists and the printing presses are long gone, it is still worth taking the mile-long walk along Fleet Street, from Temple Bar to Ludgate Circus. There are glimpses all around of the lost world. Here and there are pubs laying claim to the hacks of old – like El Vino at No. 47, Ye Olde Cheshire Cheese at No. 145 and the Punch Tavern at No. 99. Twin Mercuries run east and west above the door of what was the Daily Telegraph building, at Nos 135–41. The Reuters Building at No. 85 was designed by Edwin Lutyens, the same that shaped the Cenotaph and the fairytale castle on Lindisfarne. Upon a bronze globe, within a large round window, sits Fame, blowing her own trumpet as she should and would. Just across the road is the dark art-deco splendour of the Express Building, all black glass and chrome. Those who thought less of its styling called it the 'Black Lubyanka'.

The reporters of D. C. Thomson were the last to leave Fleet Street. Their mean sliver of a building at No. 185 still has on it, built in with the bricks, the names of their legendary titles – the *Sunday Post*, *People's Friend*, *People's Journal* and *Dundee Courier*. It looks, and they sound, too couthy and provincial for such worldly surroundings.

Down an anonymous lane by the Reuters Building is St Bride's Church, close to the spot where Wynkyn de Worde had his shop. In the absence of the industry that made Fleet Street Fleet Street, its stained white presence seems like the anaemic heart of something otherwise absent. St Bride's calls itself the spiritual home of journalists. Inside are boards and pamphlets declaring that the site has known Christian worship for 1,500 years or more. It is an unexpected union – journalists and Jesus.

Like St Paul's, the present iteration of St Bride's is the work of Christopher Wren, another of his commissions in the wake of the destruction wrought by the Great Fire of 1666. Lucky for some. The spire is tall, so tall indeed it's hard to appreciate its reach towards higher things from the extreme close-up vouchsafed by its cramped environs. They say the steeple's tiered shape became the inspiration for the now traditional wedding cake.

St Bride's was hit by incendiary bombs during the Blitz of 1940 and gutted. What visitors see now is largely the work of a renovation completed in 1957. The place seems full of journalists' ghosts, as real or imagined as the so-called celebrities that preoccupy their digital successors. Every pew bears the name of some or other legend of print, from the Lords Rothermere to Ross Benson.

There is no escaping the fact the journalists are long gone. It is a salutary lesson in impermanence. That the Press lived in Fleet Street seemed, well within my lifetime, as fixed as St Paul's. But then, today's St Paul's is only the latest replacement for something else long gone. The newspaper titles have fled for less seemly circumstances, and a future even more uncertain than any before. The public are as hungry for news as ever, although more and more read it not from finger-staining paper but from glowing screens they keep in their pockets. Once upon a time the news flowed between riverbanks, directed by paths determined by editors and others trained in setting a course. Now the news is a flood, wholly unconstrained. No one knows what's fresh water, or drinkable at least, and what's sewage best kept underground and out of sight.

95

Penlee Lifeboat Station, Penlee Point, Cornwall

Tragedy at sea

B Y ANY PEACETIME standards, 1981 was an eventful year.
Prince Charles married Lady Diana Spencer. Pope John Paul II was shot and wounded in St Peter's Square by escaped Turkish prisoner and would-be assassin Mehmet Ali Agca, and MPs Shirley Williams, Roy Jenkins, David Owen and Bill Rodgers broke away from the Labour Party to form the centrist Social Democratic Party. Bucks Fizz won the Eurovision Song Contest, technology entrepreneur Clive Sinclair launched the ZX81 home computer and Muhammad Ali fought his last fight. Shergar won the Derby and former actor Ronald Reagan was inaugurated as the 40th President of the United States of America. No one could believe it – a mere celebrity as leader of the free world. IRA man Bobby Sands died on hunger strike in HM Prison Maze, Yorkshire Ripper Peter Sutcliffe was put away for life, Andrew Lloyd Webber's *Cats* opened in London's West End and *Chariots of Fire* was on in the cinemas. There were riots in Brixton and Toxteth, and British police used tear gas for the first time. US uber-soap *Dynasty* launched on British TV, Tory employment secretary Norman Tebbit delivered his legendary line about how his father had 'got on his bike and looked for work' and Ian Botham inspired the English cricket team to retain the Ashes against the odds.

It was a pivotal year all round. The previous October the prime minister, Margaret Thatcher, had declared she was 'not for turning' and during the first weeks of 1981, in an echo of the rise of Jeremy Corbyn in 2017, the hard-left policies of Michael Foot, the Labour leader, saw his party ahead in the polls by twenty-four points.

I was fourteen years old in 1981 and what I see most clearly when I look back now is the loss of the Penlee Lifeboat with all her crew.

The boat in question was the *Solomon Browne*, a 47-foot Watson Class vessel. On the night of 19 December, she launched from her boathouse at Penlee Point on the outskirts of the village of Mousehole, 3 miles west of Penzance.

Most people know Mousehole now as a tourist destination. Like so many of the villages on the Cornish coast, it looks like somewhere that might have been designed and built for a perfect childhood holiday. Granite cottages painted white, winding cobbled lanes, golden sand and turquoise shallows. It takes its name from the conspicuously narrow entrance to its harbour – barely wide enough to let a ship pass, you would think – and it is this precaution that hints at another truth about this part of the world. For all that a place like Mousehole can appear idyllic on a fine day, the fisher folk of Cornwall have learned bitter lessons from the sea.

The loss of men and boys has always been a recurring feature of life. Like all fishing communities, the Cornish have understood that the sea gives life and takes life, almost on a whim. At Mousehole you hear the legend of Tom Bawcock, a brave fisherman of years past. During some long-ago December, the weather was so bad for days and weeks on end that no boats had been able to venture out of the harbour. By the week before Christmas, people were starving. Knowing what needed to be done, Tom took his boat out through the mousehole, found the fishing grounds despite the mountainous waves and came home again with a catch big enough for all. Every 23 December, Tom Bawcock's Eve, the locals make 'Stargazy pie' – the one with the fish heads poking through the crust – in memory of a brave man.

On 19 December 1981, the phone rang in the home of William Trevelyan Richards, coxswain of the Penlee Lifeboat. A 1,400-ton coaster called *Union Star*, on her maiden voyage and with eight souls aboard, was in terrible trouble. She had been 8 miles east of the Wolf Rock lighthouse in south-west Cornwall when her engine had failed. The weather was a horror show, a full-blown hurricane, and they were drifting helplessly.

A Dutch tug had come across the coaster and offered to throw them a line. Acceptance of the help would have rendered the *Union Star* 'salvage' and skipper Henry Morton could not bear the thought – the loss of the valuable, brand-new vessel into the hands of another. He turned down the offer and in doing so made the decision that would change everything.

Aboard his ship were four crew and also his pregnant wife, Dawn, and her two daughters, sixteen-year-old Sharon and fourteen-year-old Deanne. When further efforts to start the engine failed, Morton made a radio call to summon the rescue services.

A Sea King helicopter was scrambled first, but the weather conditions were so appalling, the wind so fierce, they could do nothing to help. Richards assembled his lifeboat crew – Stephen Madron, Nigel Brockman, John Blewett, Charlie Greenhaugh, Barrie Torrie, Kevin Smith and Gary Wallis – and they launched into the throat of the hurricane. Richards had taken care that night not to take any two men from the same family.

The helicopter crew could only watch what happened when the *Solomon Browne* came into view, dwarfed among waves 60 feet high.

Time and time again Richards sought to bring his vessel alongside the much larger coaster. More than once the *Solomon Browne* was tossed like a landed fish on to the deck of the *Union Star* and then off again. At one point Richards was able to maintain a position in its shadow long enough for four people to jump from the *Union Star* into the arms of the lifeboatmen. Richards radioed Falmouth Coastguard to say so, and that transmission was the last anyone heard from either vessel. Accident investigators would later suppose both had finally been driven too close to shore and that the exposed rocks of the seabed had inflicted damage that could not be withstood. All eight from the *Union Star* were lost, so too the eight men of the *Solomon Browne*. In total, only eight bodies were ever recovered, four from each.

I remember the news coverage of the aftermath, an upturned hull in grey water. Over the years I have read a lot about the loss of the Penlee

Lifeboat and her men. I have written about it all before as well. The lines I find hardest to think about were composed by Lieutenant Commander Russell Smith, pilot of the Sea King helicopter. He was a United States officer, on exchange with the Royal Navy, and his letter was read out to the accident inquiry:

> Throughout the entire rescue the Penlee crew never appeared to hesitate. After each time they were washed ... or blown away from the *Union Star*, the Penlee crew immediately commenced another run in. Their spirit and dedication were amazing. They were truly the greatest eight men I have ever seen.

Mousehole had known hurt before, but nothing so bad. Undaunted, defiant, more of her sons stepped forward. By the morning after the tragedy there were already more than enough volunteers poised to take the places of the lost men.

The lifeboat station they left behind, crouched above the sea, has been empty ever since – a memorial to them. The towering wooden doors are closed now against the sight of the steep slipway that sent them on their way for the last time. There is a little garden there too, carefully tended. On each anniversary of the tragedy, in the evening, Mousehole's Christmas lights are turned off for an hour of darkened remembrance.

The story of the bravery of the Penlee lifeboatmen affects me like no other. Perhaps it has to do with the fact that RNLI crews are all volunteers, people who put themselves in harm's way simply because they would rather do that than turn their backs on people in danger on the sea.

Truly the greatest eight men.

96

The Millennium Dome, Greenwich, London

A monument to a new age

Purists would say that, there having been no Year 0, the Christian clock started counting from AD 1 and so the third millennium really started on 1 January 2001. For most of the world's people, however, it began when the numbers on Planet Earth's odometer rolled over to read 2,000 years of flight into the dark since the birth of Jesus Christ. It was supposed to herald an era of peace. There had, however, been anxieties for many – not least the fear that the advent of the third millennium would bring down computer systems all around the world. Word was that twentieth-century computer programs mostly represented years by just their last two numbers – 99 instead of 1999 and so on. The so-called Millennium Bug was predicted to work its mischief when 1999 turned into 2000 – or rather 99 became 00. Since dumb computers might confuse 2000 with 1900, many foresaw chaos. Newspapers illustrated the point with apocalyptic images of planes falling from the sky. Others were convinced the year 2000 would witness the Second Coming and so the ending of the world.

When the dials finally turned and the nines mutated into zeros, nothing of the sort happened, nothing at all. Instead there were fireworks in one capital city after another. The people of the Chatham Islands, east of New Zealand in the South Pacific, were first to feel the momentous dawn. Those on America's west coast were among the last. In Bethlehem, 2,000 doves of peace were released into a sky that cared not a jot. In Rome, the Pope preached a special blessing from his balcony in the Vatican and called on the peoples of the world to set a course for a thousand years of harmony. Here in these islands the first four minutes of the new millennium saw 5 tons of fireworks explode in the sky above Edinburgh as uncountable hordes gathered on Princes Street for the biggest Hogmanay party the city had ever seen. It was a huge deal, and yet it was also just a number.

In London, there was a foretaste of the same old, same old, when thousands had to queue for hours in the cold, waiting to enter an outsize white tent. It was the Millennium Dome, conceived by John Major's Conservative government, taken on and massively aggrandized by Tony Blair's New Labour. In a speech in the Royal Festival Hall on 24 February 1998, Blair had declared, 'We will say to ourselves with pride: this is our Dome, Britain's Dome. And believe me, it will be the envy of the world.' And it had been bungled in almost every conceivable way.

The structure itself worked well enough, even if it was not, strictly speaking, a dome. Designed by architect Richard Rogers it was, and is, held aloft by cables attached to a dozen 300-foot-high towers. A true dome is a self-supporting work of masonry and so the structure still sitting on the up-thrust thumb of the Greenwich peninsula is really a tent. It is a clever creation just the same – the fabric of which it is made weighing less than the air encased within. The twelve towers represent the months of the year. The inside diameter was made exactly 365 metres, one for each day of the year. The whole respects the Prime Meridian, the imaginary line running from North Pole to South Pole, passing through Greenwich and marking 0 degrees of longitude.

It was all supposed to echo the triumph and triumphalism of the Great Exhibition of 1851 in the purpose-built Crystal Palace. The dream was to showcase all that was best about Britain and the British. In the event, twentieth-century man's reach quite exceeded his grasp and what was created was roundly ridiculed from the word go. The punters actually quite liked the thing in the end, but on that night of all nights, when the clocks clicked round and it opened for the first time, it was regarded almost instantly as a great white elephant. It had cost £800 million (or maybe more; no one ever seemed quite sure just how much had been spent). It would attract only a fraction of the visitors it was supposed to and just about every commentator and critic lined up to pour scorn on the entire concept and its execution. Inside were exhibits and displays intended to declare 'Who We Are', 'What We Do' and 'Where We Live'. There was more besides, scattered across the lone and level sands of the interior, and yet none of it seemed to live up to expectations that had been raised unreasonably high. Ozymandias was back, and he was a large white full stop.

Most inexcusable of all was the mishandling of the opening event itself. Her Majesty Queen Elizabeth II, Tony Blair and the rest of the Cabinet, plus a host of other VIPs, were whisked inside smoothly enough. But hundreds and then thousands of lesser mortals found themselves in logjams behind security checks that kept them waiting for four hours and more at the specially built and newly opened North Greenwich Station. It was a lesson in hubris and, instead of a crowning glory and a beacon to the world, the poor Dome spent its first days and weeks as a national embarrassment.

But there was no hiding it away and, slowly and in ways none had predicted, it evolved. Renamed the O2 in 2005 and taken over by American entertainment company Anschutz Entertainment Group (AEG), it has become a successful venue for all manner of music, sports and other events. Trains still deliver visitors, sightseers. The irony is that it was only when the interior was completely emptied of everything it had once contained, scraped clean of every supposedly British notion and then filled with ideas imported from the New World, that it finally shook off the shame resulting from its messy birth.

Perhaps, in the end, the Dome acquired the form it ought to have had all along. These isles had not changed, but the peoples living upon them apparently cared – and care – less about all the history that lies behind them and beneath their feet. The story we used to tell ourselves, that we had been telling ourselves and each other for hundreds and then thousands of years, was falling on deaf ears or being forgotten. The Dome had been intended as a beacon, to show a Britain that was still *Great*. It remains to be seen exactly what, if anything, is still great about that ancient edifice.

The Roman poet Juvenal saw the same decline of vision and ambition in his own nation in the first century AD, back when the clock had only just started ticking: 'The people that once bestowed commands, consulships, legions, and all else, now concerns itself no more, and longs eagerly for just two things – bread and circuses.'

97

The Scottish Parliament Building, Edinburgh

Devolution

CLOSE BY THE end of the Royal Mile and cheek by jowl with the Palace of Holyroodhouse sits the Scottish Parliament building. A wave of devolution had moved across the United Kingdom in 1997 and 1998, decentralizing government and giving independent powers to the peoples of Northern Ireland, Scotland and Wales. In the aftermath of public votes, assemblies were created in Belfast and Cardiff and a parliament was recreated in Edinburgh.

The reality of devolution has been different in each case. In Cardiff, the dockland that had flourished while a black river of coal flowed from the Rhondda had grown cold and sad after it all ran dry in the 1960s. It was there, overlooking the water and with hopes of a rejuvenated future, that the Senedd building was created. Built to be sustainable, it cost something like £70 million and is tipped to last a hundred years. The referendum there had been a close-run thing, with just a fraction over 50 per cent of the electorate choosing devolved powers. Referenda in Northern Ireland and the Republic of Ireland, on whether or not to go ahead with the Good Friday Agreement, returned results of 71 per cent and 94 per cent in favour. Devolved powers came to Northern Ireland as a result of the poll but have been suspended and reinstated by Westminster more than once in the years since.

In Scotland, the result was 74 per cent in favour of a new parliament, the first since 1707 when the bells of St Giles' Cathedral played 'Why Am I So Sad, On This My Wedding Day' as a national lament at the Treaty of Union. By the summer of 1998 a design for a new building, by Spanish architect Enric Miralles, had emerged as the popular choice. The site at the foot of the Royal Mile had been occupied by a Scottish and Newcastle brewery, but the closure of the building presented what was regarded as the ideal location for a place in which Scots might gather to organize their own affairs.

A long and agonizing process then ensued. Originally intended to open in 2001 at a total cost of around £40 million, it was finally completed and ready for business by 2004 after a final bill of over £400 million, ten times the original estimate. A great deal of public and political ill-will had arisen by then. Many baulked at the cost; others were critical of the look of the finished building. In the intervening years there have been all manner of news articles and television documentaries either praising or vilifying any and every conceivable aspect of the project.

Miralles, from the Catalonian region of Spain, did not live to see the completion of his work. He died of a brain tumour on 3 July 2000 at the age of forty-five. He had taken some of his inspiration for the design of the parliament – the roof in particular – from the look of the upturned herring boats Edwin Lutyens had used as storage sheds while he worked on Lindisfarne Castle nearly a hundred years earlier.

The building materials included oak and sycamore, stainless steel and Caithness stone. All manner of imagery is said to be there – both inside and out. There are hints of Saltires, nods to curtains pulled back to let someone within look out through the windows, glimpses of Charles Rennie Macintosh's love of flowers. Miralles was also apparently inspired by Henry Raeburn's painting of the Reverend Robert Walker skating on Duddingston Loch, although it is hard to say if, or how, that thought ever actually manifested itself in the structure. In 2005 it was awarded the Royal Institute of British Architects Stirling Prize and also shortlisted for demolition by viewers of a Channel 4 documentary series about the worst architecture in Britain.

Power was devolved (and the buildings in Scotland and Wales were built) in a different world. It and they were conceived before everything was changed by the terrorist attack on the Twin Towers of the World Trade Center in New York City on 11 September 2001. By the next month there was war in Afghanistan. We learned about Al-Qaeda, the Taliban and all the rest. The first two decades of the third millennium have been made of war as much as anything. 'Look upon my works ye mighty and despair.'

Before the planes flew and crashed, and the towers burned and fell, we were living in more optimistic times. In the West, the notion had been spreading that the whole world was ready to accept a limitless stability, an end to constant change and disruption. In his 1992 book *The End of History*, American writer Francis Fukuyama had considered the possibility that the liberal democracy of the West might prove indomitable and therefore permanent. It was a way of living and being that worked so well it might be adopted by everyone.

The ever-spinning wheel had more to do, however. The fires of war are still burning and in many different places. People finding their homelands intolerable for one reason or another are ceaselessly on the move. Out of Africa they come, out of the Middle East, following dreams of safer, richer lives in Europe and North America, in Australia and New Zealand. The world is warming up and cracks are forming on a surface made more brittle by the day. At the time of writing, Miralles' home patch of Catalonia is torn by calls for independence from Spain. The European Union is facing an existential crisis in the form of demands for separation by Czechs, Hungarians and Poles. Britain is in the throes of the 'Brexit' negotiations that will sever our own ties with that Union. In Scotland, the Scottish Nationalist Party calls endlessly for a second referendum on the matter of independence. Basques and Corsicans are shouting for the same.

Nationalism is on the rise and the consequences are anybody's guess. Here in these islands it has been pooling in the cracks between the nations. It remains to be seen if it will freeze and break the United Kingdom apart as well.

Whatever your politics, the Scottish Parliament building, open to visitors from Monday to Saturday, is well worth a look. If that look offends, you could turn your back on it and see if the frontage of the Palace of Holyroodhouse is more to your liking. Looming nearby are the Salisbury Crags, the heart of the burnt-out volcano that brought the rock of Edinburgh into being.

As the ink dried on the document that dissolved the old parliament in 1707, the Earl of Seafield, Chancellor of Scotland, is said to have declared, 'There's an end of an auld sang.' But the song goes on.

98

The Old Kirk, Parton,
Dumfries and Galloway

James Clerk Maxwell and the laws of the universe

SIR CHRISTOPHER WREN'S epitaph in St Paul's Cathedral reads: *Si monumentum requiris, circumspice* – 'If you seek his monument, look around'. Wren's creation of the new St Paul's, the replacement for that destroyed by the Great Fire of London in 1666, marked an ending and a beginning. The conflagration had seen to the death of the world of before and the birth of the new.

In the village of Parton in Dumfries and Galloway there is a more modest church, built in 1834. Stand with your back to its main door and the view takes in the kind of soft round hills, water and woodland that give the county its gentle character. The River Dee, which rises in the Galloway Hills, flows into Loch Ken within sight of the church. The Water of Ken, now wedded to the flow from the Dee, runs on to Kirkcudbright and there joins the Solway Firth and the Irish Sea. Parton is a corruption of the Gaelic word for 'top of the hill', and the village sits high, with a grand outlook, right enough.

Turn and walk around and past the church, on the left-hand side of the façade, and you will see the remains of an even more modest building, dedicated to St Ninian, who came from Ireland in the eighth century to convert the local Picts. This earlier place of worship was built near the start of the 1500s and was the heart of the village for three centuries and more.

It is only a rectangle of dark-grey masonry now, standing head high, but inside, in a place of raggedy grass and ivy and moss, there are a couple of gravestones. One has four names on it – John Clerk Maxwell, Frances Cay, Katherine Mary Dewar and James Clerk Maxwell. Open to the sky and therefore limitless, the space described by the walls of the Old Kirk seems a fine and fitting resting place.

James Clerk Maxwell was born in a house at 14 India Street in Edinburgh on 13 June 1831, son of advocate John Clerk Maxwell and his wife Frances Cay. From there the family moved to Glenlair House near the village of Corsock in Kirkcudbrightshire. They were well-to-do and the house had been specially built for them on land owned by John Maxwell's brother, Sir George Clerk of Pennycuick, the 6th Baronet.

As soon as little James could talk he began asking questions. Anything and everything caught his eye, so that for him the world was a source of profound fascination. 'Show me how it doos,' he would say, or, 'What's the go o' that?' Like most children, he was rarely satisfied with just one answer. If his curiosity remained unsated, he would likely follow up with another question, one his family grew familiar with: 'But what's the *particular* go o' that?'

His attention was especially drawn to colour – in the sky above, on the ground below; on fabrics, objects, light itself, anything at all. First, he might simply ask the colour of the thing. On hearing the answer, however, he would invariably follow up with, 'But how dae ye *know* it's red?' or 'How dae ye *know* it's blue?'

In some essential way he spent the rest of his life looking out at the world with questioning eyes, like a child. His aching curiosity, which made a plaything of infinity, was ever present. On all sides, above and below, there were wonders to be gazed upon and, better yet, understood. He would sit rapt in church, listening to the sermons as though the answers he sought might be found woven through the old, well-polished words. From an early age he memorized great tracts of Scripture and the Psalms.

Taught first at home by his mother and then by a tutor engaged by his father, he was eventually sent to Edinburgh Academy. He was a country mouse in town, in home-made clothes. To begin with he was awkward and unsure, often seeming to struggle to learn. The other boys teased him, called him 'Daftie', but soon enough he began to leave them all behind. He studied at Edinburgh University – logic, maths, metaphysics and the rest. A place at Cambridge University came next, then the Chair of Natural Philosophy at Marischal College in Aberdeen. He was making huge conceptual leaps all the while, observing and understanding Saturn's rings and marvelling at the effects of light, electricity, magnetism. His obsession with colour remained. He was the first to identify the scientific primacy of the three colours – red, blue and yellow – of which all others are made. While at King's College, London, in 1861 he took and developed the world's first colour photograph. He was among the founders of the Cavendish Laboratory that later played host to Sir Ernest Rutherford and the splitting of the atom.

Most famously of all, Maxwell showed that electricity, light and magnetism were all governed by the same fundamental and natural laws. The equations he wrote to explain how those three were also united with radio waves, flowing like invisible, intermingled vapours from an elemental fire, are regarded by many as the most beautiful lines ever written in maths, the language spoken by Mother Nature herself.

James Clerk Maxwell is regarded as the scientist who took the necessary steps beyond the reach of Newton. Albert Einstein, who stepped even further forward into the unknown, said his special theory of relativity 'owes its origins' to Maxwell's equations. 'This change in the conception of reality,' he wrote, 'is the most profound and the most fruitful that physics has experienced since the time of Newton.'

Einstein also said of him, 'One scientific epoch ended and another began with James Clerk Maxwell.' The theoretical physicist Richard Feynman – who won the Nobel Prize in Physics in 1965 and was among those leading the way beyond Einstein, through the looking glass and into the topsy-turvy world of quantum mechanics – wrote: 'From a long view of the history of mankind – seen from, say, ten thousand years from now – there can be little doubt that the most significant event of the nineteenth century will be judged as Maxwell's discovery of the laws of electrodynamics.'

Genius is often a troubled and troubling gift. And yet by all accounts Maxwell was also easy company, known for his warm sense of humour. He had many friends with whom he remained close for all of his life. He was forever writing letters home to his father and whenever the chance allowed he would go home to Glenlair to help with the harvest.

In that way of men of his time and class, in photographs he appears far older than his years. He might be Gandalf from *The Lord of the Rings*, or Old Father Time, and yet he was only forty-eight when he died. He has been revered by the cognoscenti ever since. Physicists place him at the centre of a holy trinity with Newton and Einstein either side. Since it was his understanding of radio waves, and therefore radar, that enabled us to witness the secrets of the solar system, the highest peak on Planet Venus is named Maxwell Montes in his honour. Back in Scotland his name is less familiar. There is a bronze statue of him at the St Andrew Square end of George Street in Edinburgh and his birthplace on India Street is a museum now, but his popular fame is nowhere near that of Newton or Einstein.

Without his imagination, his curiosity, we might live today in a world without radio, television, mobile phones – even the Global Positioning System (GPS) and the internet. What came before James Clerk Maxwell was yesterday and where he led was tomorrow. Beyond him lay our present and our uncertain future. Try to imagine now a world without the internet, a presence in our lives that feels at times like little less than collective consciousness. British scientist Tim Berners-Lee was at CERN (*Conseil Européen pour la Recherche Nucléaire*) in Switzerland when he invented the world wide web, but his contribution to all of that automatic information-sharing between computers, and other work to that end by fellow scientists like the Americans Jon Postel and Vinton Cerf, would not have been possible without Maxwell.

Perhaps his most fitting memorial is back in Parton, within the four walls of the Old Kirk – not the grey granite of the stone over his clay, but the limitless space above. In the crypt beneath the floor of St Wystan's Church in Repton, Sir John Betjeman had found 'holy air encased in stone'. For James Clerk Maxwell it seemed the whole Earth was sacred – encased, or rather set free, in infinity.

99

St Peter ad Vincula and the Tower of London

Shadows of a bloody past

In truth, there is no sadder spot on earth than this little cemetery.
Death is there associated, not, as in Westminster Abbey and
St Paul's, with genius and virtue, with public veneration and
with imperishable renown; not, as in our humblest churches and
churchyards, with everything that is most endearing in social and
domestic charities; but with whatever is darkest in human nature
and in human destiny, with the savage triumph of implacable
enemies, with inconstancy, the ingratitude, the cowardice of friends,
with all the miseries of fallen greatness and blighted fame.
Thither have been carried through successive ages, by the rude hands
of gaolers, without one mourner following, the bleeding relics of
men who had been the captains of armies, the leaders of parties, the
oracles of senates, and the ornaments of courts.

THOMAS BABINGTON MACAULAY,
The History of England, 1848

THE TOWER OF LONDON, nearly a thousand years old, is dwarfed by
the world of now, there is no denying it. The painstaking maintenance
that keeps it spick and span, and safe, only makes more blatant its existence
as an anachronism. The traffic and lights of the modern riverside leave
King William's work looking like some boy's toy, a plaything of cardboard

and ply – a toy much loved but set aside in a box of memories. The moat, once flooded by the Thames for defence, is a grassy gutter. The walls are only picturesque, not imposing at all. The fussy, fusty caps of lead upon the towers of the Keep are kitsch, or even cute, like bonnets.

All this is only the consequence of time, which nudges all things out of the way in the end. Read other books, however, and know that the Tower was, for centuries, a place that pricked hairs and shortened breath. You may well underestimate it, as it appears now below the blown-glass impermanence of the city all around, but remember too the part it has played in our story. In order to make the Tower matter – and it does – the visitor must bring to it a willing suspension of disbelief. It might be best in this twenty-first century to see it at night, when the dark of the looming city and closer shadows made of olden walls blot out the present and leave a person to fill the spaces with imagination and dread.

The Ceremony of the Keys is therefore a good thing to see, since it is the last that happens before the Tower of London is closed up for the night. It has happened every evening, without fail, for hundreds of years, for longer than anyone is sure. It is a tourist attraction and so you will find yourself among dozens of others gathered there, but it is the best glimpse to be had, after all this time, if it is a sense of ancient days that you are after.

The ceremony is all uniformed men and shouting. One, called the Chief Warder, bears the keys in question and, standing before the Main Guard, asks for 'The escort for the keys.'

After that come soldiers, one carrying a tallow lantern, and a great deal of urgent marching between gates and through the shadows of towers.

'Halt! Who comes there?'

'The keys.'

'Whose keys?'

'Queen Elizabeth's keys.'

'Advance, Queen Elizabeth's keys: all's well.'

'God preserve Queen Elizabeth.'

'Amen!'

If it feels theatrical now, it is only because what was once life and death has been left behind by a world moved on.

Back behind the locked gates and in the dark that remembers everything, the Tower still feels like a place of awful secrets swept beneath the
carpet. All through the daytime, with tourists milling about with their
smartphones and sunglasses, it is easy to forget this was the place where all
manner of people were brought to be hidden away or tortured into broken
pieces and got rid of altogether.

Within the Inner Ward, in the north-west corner by the Waterloo Barracks, is the Royal Chapel of St Peter ad Vincula – St Peter in Chains – named
in honour of the big fisherman's time as a prisoner of Herod Agrippa. The
building as it stands now was commissioned by Henry VIII, but a chapel of
some sort occupied the spot before the coming of the Normans and their
insolent masonry. By the time Queen Victoria ordered its renovation, the
church was reportedly in a poor state. The floor was uneven, collapsing
into hollows and hinting at the presence of buried secrets. The details of
the walls, and the roof beams of chestnut wood, were hidden behind plaster stained and crumbling. Lord Macaulay lamented 'the barbarous
stupidity which has transformed this interesting little church into the likeness of a meeting-house in a manufacturing town'.

Nowadays, though, it is as neat and tidy as the rest – all the better to
conceal the fact that St Peter ad Vincula is notorious as a shallow grave of
queens and lords and ladies and all manner of folk dispatched by butcher's
knives and hurriedly concealed. All in a plot measuring 6 yards by 4, right
in front of the altar, lie the remains of fifteen of the great and the good of
the land, brought low by so-called treason.

Queen Anne Boleyn, Henry's second wife, is there. She was put to
death on a scaffold erected for the purpose on the north side of the Keep. A
specialist swordsman had been brought from Calais, in her honour, and
Anne had knelt upright before him, in the French style. Imagine. This is
what we were like. As others still do now, we did then. We had young
women kneel, we covered their eyes so we did not have to look in them and
we cut off their heads with swords. Happily we learned not to, and have
done no such thing for the longest time.

Once Anne's head had been parted from her body with a single stroke
of the blade, to land heavy as a bowling ball amid straw spread thick to

catch the claret, her remains were gathered together by her weeping, horrified handmaidens and placed inside a chest of elm made for storing the red yew staves of longbows. In this repurposed box the mother of Queen Elizabeth I was set down into that space before the altar and dirt kicked in upon her.

Katherine Howard, Henry's fifth wife, is there too, a victim of the axe rather than the sword. Then there is Lady Jane Grey, queen for just nine days. Close by is her father-in-law, John Dudley, Duke of Northumberland, the man whose own designs on the throne may or may not have led the girl to her fate – and also her father, Henry Grey, 1st Duke of Suffolk, similarly dispatched. On and on the sad roll call goes – St Thomas More; handsome Robert Devereux, Earl of Essex and sometime favourite of Queen Elizabeth.

Scotsmen do get everywhere and there are a few in St Peter's, as is only right. Within those walls, tucked beneath some stones or other but unmarked now, are four Jacobite lords whose luck ran out. They are William Boyd, 4th Earl of Kilmarnock; George MacKenzie, 3rd Earl of Cromartie; Arthur Elphinstone, the Lord Balmerino; and the one they called 'the Fox', Simon Fraser, Lord Lovat, who in 1747 became the last man beheaded in Britain.

In a space alone, beneath the altar itself, is James Scott, 1st Duke of Monmouth, the eldest of the illegitimate sons of Charles II and leader of the rebellion against his uncle, James II, in 1685. After his capture at the Battle of Sedgemoor he was put to death on Tower Hill. The axe was wielded by Jack Ketch, already infamous for his cruelty or plain clumsiness. According to some accounts, his butchery needed five blows to get the job done.

The journalist Walter George Bell wrote several books about London. Among the most appealing of them is *The Tower of London*, published in 1921. Much of what Bell considered worthy of remembering, artefacts and buildings, no longer exists, destroyed either by the Blitz or the casual thoughtlessness of modern planners. The Tower has survived, of course, and Bell's words concerning St Peter's recall a style and an attitude long gone:

One stands silent before these dead, when thoughts run back and the mind is filled with the large part which they in their lives have played, filling out so many pages of our history, and the idea seems grotesque that this tiny plot should hold all . . . Where else in the world does so little space hold so much, telling so poignantly of the end of all human grandeur?

As Lord Macaulay wrote, St Peter ad Vincula is the antithesis of Westminster Abbey, where the dead are proudly cradled. Behind the walls of the Tower of London is hidden away a remnant of all the cruelty of old days. Stand outside St Peter's walls, or on the marble tiles before the altar if you have the stomach for it, and be reminded that savagery is part of our past. The rule of law, the right to live in peace and free from tyranny – these are not the natural states of mankind. If you doubt the truth of it, look around at a wider world still haunted by the ideologies of the nineteenth and twentieth centuries. We have arrived where we are in these islands at the end of a long and bloody road. Our predecessors smelled the iron tang of blood spilt by the butcher's axe. The path back to that chaos is quick and straight and easily taken. Like it or not, believe it or not, we live protected by a shelter made only of our old mistakes. For good or ill we have moved beyond the Christianity that shaped our culture and society for most of the last 2,000 years. We are secular now, blown in the wind of political cant. But the order we still enjoy and mostly take for granted is made of all the agonies of our past. As a wiser man than me has said, 'We are living inside the corpse of a whale. There is plenty to eat for now – but only because there was a whale.'

100

Dungeness Headland, Kent

At nature's mercy

Tʜᴇ ᴍᴏsᴛ ᴜɴғᴏʀɢᴇᴛᴛᴀʙʟᴇ locations in Britain are, to me, the most unforgettable in the whole world. No doubt many feel the same about the places they know as home. Archaeologists can tell, from enamel ground out of a skeleton's teeth, where its owner had his childhood and so it is true to say the land where we were young becomes part of us. Some of it, then, is a physical thing. Our hides are tanned by the sunshine, our hair bleached a paler shade. Other places soak into the soul later on until we are changed again.

Dungeness, a windblown, storm-washed headland of pale shingle thrust out like a nose into the sea off Kent, has left some permanent marks on me. It is not mine, has never been my home. But when I think of it and close my eyes, I see it clearly, an endless horizon squeezed flat beneath all the weight of the biggest, bluest sky. I can hear it too, the crunching of the pebbles slipping and sliding beneath my feet while the sea rolls.

Those who know it best – better than me – call it the Ness. It is one of the largest expanses of shingle in the whole of Europe and designated as a Site of Special Scientific Interest on account of both its geomorphology and its varied plant and animal life. More than 600 plant species grow there, a third of those found anywhere in the whole of Britain. Those on the look-out for bees, beetles, moths, spiders and such may spot a few that can be seen nowhere else.

Two roads take you there – one along the coast from New Romney and the other from Lydd. The Ness is also famously served by the Romney, Hythe & Dymchurch 15-inch-gauge light railway via the station at Hythe.

It is altogether another world, and people do come. Artists, photographers, dog-walkers, pop stars seeking backdrops for their publicity shots, birdwatchers, fishermen in search of peace and quiet as well as prey. There are permanent residents too, in little cottages and shacks, many made from abandoned railway carriages and with boats parked outside instead of cars. Filmmaker Derek Jarman made a home there from 1986 until his early death, at Prospect Cottage, a shiplap building painted black with buttercup-yellow window frames. On to one wall he put lines from 'The Sun Rising' by John Donne:

> *Busy old fool, unruly Sun,*
> *Why dost thou thus,*
> *Through windows, and through curtains, call on us . . .*
> *Thine age asks ease, and since thy duties be*
> *To warm the world, that's done in warming us.*
> *Shine here to us, and thou art everywhere;*
> *This bed thy centre is, these walls, thy sphere.*

More famous than his cottage is the garden Jarman created to surround it, flowers planted among the shingle, sculptures made of driftwood and scrap metal. It has become a tourist attraction in its own right. All across the Ness are more hints and splashes of colour – dock flowers, sea peas, purple sea kale and yellow horned poppies.

Dungeness is famous too, or infamous, for the brace of nuclear power stations at its end. The first, the oldest, has been decommissioned, but Dungeness B is still thrumming merrily away. It ought to be utterly incongruous, but the Ness accommodates it with good grace.

It is, as well, a fragile-feeling place. Telegraph poles and pylons pierce its edges like skelfs beneath the skin. The shingle is fought over moment by moment and from all about by the waves of the English Channel. In summer it is parched by enervating sun – so much so that some folk will tell you it is a desert (though the Met Office says not) – and in winter it becomes a playground for wild storms and biting, knife-edged winds.

At Dungeness you see how fragile Britain is. Famed for defiance and for standing up to all invaders, it is at nature's mercy most of all. We must look after her. She will be gone sooner or later, and I would rather it were later.

Love, all alike, no season knows nor clime
Nor hours, days, months, which are the rags of time.

Conclusion

These Islands

IN OCTOBER 2017 there was a demonstration in Barcelona by those who wished to see Catalonia remain part of Spain. They carried banners featuring a heart containing the Catalan, European and Spanish flags – all together. On T-shirts were the words 'A flag is just a piece of cloth'.

Identity – let alone national identity – is a complicated notion. Gathered here in the archipelago of the British Isles, finding shelter from the storm, are people from all over and of every sort. This place has been attracting incomers and blow-ins for thousands, hundreds of thousands, of years. By now the rock of these islands has been touched by at least one of every kind.

The footprints at Happisburgh on the Norfolk coast were made the best part of a million years ago by another version of humankind entirely. Ice has come and gone, over and over again, shaping the rock and wiping it clean of one sort of human inhabitant after another. At present we exist in an interstadial, a warm spell between ice ages. It remains to be seen how warm it will get and how long it will last. Hunters walked here from the European mainland 10,000 and more years ago. Some of them left footprints in the mud as well and their descendants are still here. The farmers came and built their tombs and circles. They were seafaring people – able to transport themselves, their crops and their animals in boats of wood and animal hide. They left one of them behind at Dover, scuttled in a shallow stream. The flow of new arrivals has never stopped.

Some of the travellers came in search of the sacred places they had heard of – the Ness of Brodgar in the north, Stonehenge in the south, Newgrange and Knowth in the west. Those places were man-made, but there were others shaped by different forces – sacred waterfalls, rivers, mountains. At Fortingall, near the centre of Scotland, stood a yew tree that had been growing for ever at one end of a glen so sacred it could not be profaned by the raising of stone circles, the digging of henges. It seems the people living nearby had always revered the place as home to something precious – from which nothing was taken and to which nothing was added.

That idea – old even then – is still alive in the world. The Mehinaku people of the Brazilian Amazon believe the world is populated by spirits they call *yeya*. These are the originals, the archetypes of everything that exists around us. Just as the Australian Aborigines believe everything in the world – land forms, animals, us – was made by ancestor deities, so the Mehinaku believe all the birds are made by the bird yeya, all the fish by the fish yeya, all the monkeys by the monkey yeya, and so on. The yeya are deep in the ground, in the water, in the forests – and go about their reproductive business until their parts of the world are destroyed, by us. Do too much damage to the world and there will be no more yeya and so no more anything.

The glen beyond Fortingall and the yew (the one beneath which Pontius Pilate might have sat as a boy) is Glen Lyon. Celtic folklore has it that the glen was home to the creator goddess. Not *a* creator goddess, but *the* creator goddess. They called her Cailleach, the Celtic word for an old woman. On Schiehallion – the Fairy Hill, the Hill of the Constant Storm, where Nevil Maskelyne first weighed the world – the Cailleach rode the winds of winter, her face grey blue and her lips thin and white as snow.

When St Adamnan found his way to Glen Lyon in the late seventh century to convert the locals to Christianity, he likely knew the place was already sacred, and for older reasons than his own. Below the hill called Creag nan Eildeag is a tall upright stone, twice the height of a man. It is split in two and has the look of hands brought together in an attitude of prayer. They call it 'the Praying Hands of Mary' but it is older by far than Christianity or any other religion we could name. Hidden away elsewhere is a little stone structure called Tigh na Cailleach, 'the old woman's home'. Inside it, between autumn and spring, are kept a set of stones worn and shaped by river water. These are representations of the Cailleach, the Bodach ('the Old Man') and their children. Every May they are taken out of their house and left in the open until November, around the time of *Samhain* – the first day of November, marking the beginning of the Celtic winter – when they are put back inside. This is the oldest pre-Christian ritual still performed anywhere in the world. Glen Lyon has mattered to people for the longest time.

Footprints, hunters, farmers, metalworkers – an endless procession of pioneers and pilgrims. Romans, King Arthur, *Y Gododdin* and a warrior called Gwawrddur, who was good, but not *that* good. Vikings and Brunan-burh AD 937. War and war and war again. Always the promise of Arthur's return – something or someone buried out of sight until needed. Kings and queens, gods and saints. The Temple of Orkney, Stirling Castle, Westminster Abbey – boxes of memory and memories.

After all the years I have spent travelling around this archipelago, the strangest thing has happened to me. While I have come to see the places more clearly, I am also aware that my view has blurred in one way, and one way only. Instead of any sense of different countries, I see only one place. It is a difficult feeling to express – not least because the available vocabulary is not quite right. The labels, names of nations, are hard to use without causing some or other offence: England, Ireland, Scotland, Wales, Northern Ireland, the Republic of Ireland, Eire, Great Britain, the United Kingdom. It is all a minefield and for this reason in this book I have fallen back, again and again, on 'these islands'.

My own experience of visiting place after place has made me see these islands, lying off the north-west coast of Europe, for what they are: just a few patches of dry land where life has been made pleasant by the presence of the warming water of the Gulf Stream and the North Atlantic Drift. The rock of which they are made was cooked and forged millions of years before any thoughts of nations, far less national identities. When the Romans splashed ashore on the south coast of the long island 2,000 years ago and asked the natives what their land was called, they were told

'Prytain' or perhaps 'Prydain' or maybe 'Prydein'. Whatever they heard, the Romans called their new province Britannia, and the people living here Britons. And so Britain is an old name, no one knows how old.

Whatever we call it, whatever name we give to whichever patch, our nations are just products of our shared imaginations. The Canadian anthropologist Wade Davis said that the world into which we are born does not exist, at least not in any absolute sense: 'rather it is a model of reality. Other cultures are not failed attempts at being you; they are unique manifestations of the human spirit.'

England, Ireland, Scotland, Wales – these exist only while people believe in them. Great Britain is another dream, dreamed by millions of people for hundreds of years. If, at any moment, we stop believing in its existence, it will be gone. These islands will remain, however, with us or without. They were here before. They will always be here.

This is my love letter to the British Isles. There is more I could write – much more – but this will do. I love this place. I think I always have. I love this place and know that when I was younger I took it all for granted. Over the years I have learned how wrong that was, learned to see my homeland differently. It is no accident that these islands are the way they are. This place is different because it has been made different – by nature and by our own hands.

With that in mind, I have begun to wonder if enough of us realize or bother to remember how special are the British Isles. Western civilization is in a parlous state. On the one hand more and more of the world's people are realizing there are fewer and fewer places worth living in. Much of the world has been made a God-awful mess by religion, corruption, internecine war and stubborn stupidity. Many folk, from lands so blighted, wish they could have what we have, that they could live as we live. And who could blame a single one of them?

On the other hand we, the custodians of this last redoubt of Western civilization, this Olympus, are failing to cherish what we have been gifted by our predecessors. It is a thin veneer, a fragile silk keeping us alive. If we are not careful, our tissue of civilization will lie crumpled upon us like a sheet thrown over a corpse.

The world needs the British Isles – even the *idea* of the British Isles. Our unique and civilized culture, formed during thousands of years of often painful history, is a light in the dark. But that light is guttering and failing. The last petals are trembling on the stem. Olympus is falling.

A first step towards restoring the brightness would be an acknowledgement of all that is at stake here, all that we have, all that we have had. The time for that acknowledgement is now.

Acknowledgements

I AM SO PLEASED with how this book has turned out. Let me assure you, though, the finished effect is down to the care and attention of others. Without their talent and professionalism, *100 Places* would have been quite different – and truly a lesser version of itself.

My greatest debt is to the wonderful team at Transworld – publishing directors Doug Young and Susanna Wadeson, who first appreciated the idea and then stayed with it until it was right, along with managing editorial director Katrina Whone. I cannot write appreciatively enough about copy editors Brenda Updegraff and Ailsa Bathgate, who saved me from myself in so many ways – likewise proofreaders Kathryn Wolfendale and Elizabeth Dobson. Picture researcher Jo Carlill discovered some wonderful photographs. The index is the work of Sarah Ereira and the elegant design is by Phil Lord. Production was by Catriona Hillerton, Patsy Irwin looked after publicity and Ella Horne took care of marketing . . . thank you, thank you, thank you. Huge praise also for the sales teams.

As always, I am indebted to Eugenie Furniss, my literary agent – this time for putting me together with the Transworld team. Huge thanks also to Sophie Laurimore, at Factual Management, for introducing me, long ago now, to Eugenie.

Deepest thanks of all to my wife Trudi, who lets me do these things, and to Evie, Archie and Teddy for being the point of it all.

Any and all mistakes, as they say, are mine and mine alone.

Picture Acknowledgements

The Ness of Brodgar, © Jim Richardson; Flint mace head, Knowth, reproduced with the kind permission of the National Museum of Ireland

Cantre'r Gwaelod, Rex Features; Lyn Fawr, © Mal Durbin; Dún Aengus Fort, © Jim Richardson / Getty Images; Head of Sulis Minerva, Alamy

Lullingstone Roman villa mosaic floor, Getty Images; Bamburgh Castle, Getty Images; Crypt at St Wystan's Church, Alamy; Alfred Jewel (gold, rock crystal and enamel, side view), Anglo-Saxon (9th century), Ashmolean Museum, University of Oxford, UK / Bridgeman Images

Durham Cathedral, Getty Images; St Nectan's Glen, Getty Images; Fortingall Yew, Alamy; Harlech Castle, Getty Images

Stirling Castle, © Holly Hodge; Map of Aldeburgh, Ananias Appleton, 1588 / British Library, London, UK © British Library Board. All rights reserved / Bridgeman Images

Lacada Point © Chris Ibbotson Photography; Globe Theatre (detail from an engraving, 1616, Cornelius de Visscher, c.1520–86), © British Library Board. All rights reserved / Bridgeman Images

Heart of Midlothian and St Giles' Cathedral, © Lee Sie Photography; Schiehallion, Getty Images; The Iron Bridge, photo from c.1890–1900, copyright and courtesy of the Ironbridge Gorge Museum Trust; Poster advertising auction of slaves to be sold and let, 18 May 1829, English School (19th century), Wilberforce House, Hull City Museums and Art Galleries, UK / Bridgeman Images

HMS *Victory*, Getty Images; Brontë Parsonage, Getty Images; Cobb at Lyme Regis, Alamy; Fastnet Rock, Getty Images

Grand Hotel, Scarborough, Alamy; Portree war memorial, Alamy; *QE2* leaving Clydebank, 1967, Getty Images; The Odeon, Alderney, © Steve Phelan

Les Écréhous, Alamy; The Praying Hands of Mary, Glen Lyon, Alamy

Index